ACKNOWLEDGEMENTS

- Cynthia Gerdes for the countless hours of editing, the creativity she brought to the process, her strong support of the project and her collaborative spirit.
- My husband Ken, and the rest of my family for their patience and understanding.
- Gina Hardin who championed this project from the moment she learned about it.
- Donna Wood for preserving, organizing, and contributing to Vince Panny's extensive photographic record.
- Tony Teske, Kast Design Company, for the creation of the prologue image.

INTRODUCTIONS BY ALICE CORDS AND CYNTHIA GERDES

This project was a long collaborative road, beginning with my father's research 1977-1987, his participation in the memoir writing class at Gresham Manor, to the extensive work with Cynthia Gerdes from 1991 to 1997, and finally Cynthia's work with me from 2012 until 2019. With my involvement, our initial goal was editing to produce a final full length version to be enjoyed by the family, with only minor changes to the original. The second time through, the document was pared down by 235 pages. Our guiding principle throughout was to remain as true to the original as possible, keeping voice, syntax and quirky constructions. It is a memoir, Vince Panny's perceptions of the events of his life. For me, it was an exciting process of discovery as Dad never spoke of his time in the war to us as children and would not share the chapter drafts during the writing process. I was able to read the memoir only after his death, and I was riveted. Of course I was also overwhelmed with questions I wanted to ask him, but could no longer do so. ~ Alice

Remembering Vince

Vincenz Panny walked over to the piano at the break, interrupting my urgent preparation before I sightread the next number. The regular accompanist hadn't shown up and I was covering for a rehearsal of

Carousel, the University of Oregon summer musical. Vince cracked some wry comment that made me laugh with an accent I couldn't place. British? Australian? And something else.

Having just graduated from a small town high school on the Oregon coast in 1956, I was beginning at the university as a freshman that summer, and was a bit overwhelmed. I was not an expert at anything, including accents. It was easy to assume Vince was a theater teacher working for required summer credits by overseeing props. But he was not. He was a thirty eight year old sophomore scholarship student in languages, doing yard work for housing. For other necessities he delivered photography materials across town by bicycle and drove a bus for the Crippled Children's Hospital School. It could not have been an easy time and those days there were few older students who were undergraduates. I admired him for it.

In the spring of 1957 it was a surprise to discover both of us had signed up for modern dance as the least offensive way to get the required PE credits. The teacher assigned various characters, moods or little dramas, and the way Vince expressed himself made it obvious he was not a beginner. By then I knew he was German, had been a former army officer, had learned English from the British, and was a talented actor. But how did he come by modern dance? His expertise was way beyond that of any American male I'd known of. Because of his encouragement and playful confidence, interacting with him was the most delightful part of the class.

That summer Vince generously offered to help with my beginning French struggles, so I was on hand when he heard of his father's death. He told me his father had been "an errand boy for the Nazi party" and that, along with his father's cruelty to him when a boy, made it so he didn't feel much like mourning him. Later Vince confided that his father had to find a way to support seven people, and as a requirement to hold any job he had to join the party. The situation seemed as complicated as were Vince's feelings.

In October Vince and I and his friend Emil Smith sat on the grass and watched Sputnik cross the dark skies. We wondered what this amazing event might mean for America and the future. As I remember this moment, I picture Vince's description of underfed, under-equipped and ill-educated Russian soldiers captured by his platoon during the war.

We slowly drifted in different directions, though we still followed each other's performances and occasionally touched bases. As an actor he had a unique sensitivity for character. As a stand-up-comic in the summer variety shows he used his struggles with American idioms, English spellings and the American bureaucracy as hilarious fodder for his routines. His material combined with his impeccable sense of timing had us laughing till it hurt.

In the mid 1960's while traveling through Portland, our young families visited together at Vince's home. He was teaching German Language Studies at Reed College and had created their language lab. It was good to see him happy with his young wife and family, their Alice was a charming toddler. Then, we lost touch again.

Living in Portland around 1980, I took a relative to meet Vince to talk about studying at Reed. At that time Vince mentioned that during the Vietnam draft several students asked his opinion what to do about it. He regretted that as a professor he could not offer any advice. Their quandary, however, motivated him to put together a slide show telling his own story. Growing up as a middle class youth in Hamburg, Vince considered a career as an actor or maybe a radio announcer. Instead he found himself caught up in a maze of survival decisions leading through a narrowing tunnel of choices into the German regular army. He told his Reed students he was still trying to sort out that WWII period and would always be dealing with the consequences. His slide show evolved into a presentation he gave several times in various northwest communities.

Vince retired from Reed College in 1984 and by the late 1980's he had started his memoir writing class. In between those events an extended trip to Germany led him to observe that the younger generation was not being educated about German atrocities in WWII. He felt this was wrong.

Partly hoping that I could finally learn Vince's whole story and partly just to enjoy his company, I offered to type his dictation on my laptop computer and provide a print-out for him to read to his class. After each class critique we would meet and revise, then move on to type up the next section from his notes. Often he would improvise on the fly. He used my reactions as an audience test — if I laughed, was shocked, teared over — all good. If I felt the story was concerned with logistics for too long, I'd ask questions — simple things, like: What did you eat? What did you make of that remark? It sometimes served the story, sometimes not. When I was confused, he tried to make it more clear. Occasionally I prompted him to share his personal feelings about a situation. It was not always emotionally easy for him, but he tried. We did this over a period of about six years.

There were many other people giving support for his project as well. My husband Robert was a WWII vet during the American occupation in Germany and enjoyed talking to Vince about military paraphernalia. American air force veterans in Vince's memoir class were especially interested in what he had to say and they all became friends.

Vince's concern deepened as he watched Americans after WWII continue with the Korean War 1950-1955, the Vietnam War 1961-1975, conflicts in Lebanon 1982-3, Grenada 1983 and Panama 1989-1990, the Persian Gulf War-Iraq 1990-1991, Afghanistan 2001, and then the attack on the US, 9/11 in 2001. Still American military actions went on without a declaration of war by the US Congress, as must happen according to our Constitution. Vince watched all this and shook his head.

On a local radio show here in Portland, an interviewer accused Vince to his face that he was a "Nazi" trying to whitewash his personal history. Knowing Vince, I knew this was unfair. The anti-Semitic stance of the Nazi's had never been his, nor did he have any love for the military. A number of Jewish friends had accepted him into their circle. As he often admitted, his favorite acting role was the Jewish father in the play "The Diary of Anne Frank", one he performed with the Eugene, Oregon Little Theater. He left Germany for Australia after the war largely because he didn't want to be drawn into any future military situations, and at that point the military was all he had been trained for. In the case of this particular radio show, Vince did not dignify the interviewer's prejudice with a defense. It was not the only time he had to endure such accusations. I like to think he got up and left the studio, but I don't remember.

Vince's home office was indeed unique. He had partitioned his kitchen with aisles of ceiling height shelves packed with reference books imitating library stacks. His desk was at the end of one row with his back to the sink. Little space was left over for meal prep or doing dishes. Most telling was a poster over his desk showing a cartoon of thousands of sheep heading over a cliff, with a black sheep stuck in the middle, trying to force his way against the tide to safety, loudly baaing, "Excuse me! Excuse me!"

Prior to his death in 2003 and before his hearing and eyesight failed, Vince left an audio interview with the Oregon Historical Society covering some of his war experiences. He regretted that he had not been able to finish writing his book, for he wanted to add his years in Australia which he felt were crucial to understanding his past. Personally, I think he already wrote plenty.

Not until 2012 were Alice and I able to begin a careful edit of his manuscript. In 2018 we finished and Alice took the project from there. Our determined labors together evolved into a friendship I highly value.

The story Vince tells is an amazing adventure of survival, and is likely a historical document. More than a war story, though, I see it as a cautionary tale told by this particular everyman caught up by a sweep of politics and leadership gone very wrong. Mere circumstances put Vince as a citizen/soldier along with his friends into the middle of a devastating war involving German atrocities Vince could not forgive. We met over sixty years ago and I am still continually grateful to have known him, to have learned from him, and to have contributed in some way to telling his story. ~ Cynthia

MEMOIR OF A

GERMAN

ARMY OFFICER

VINCENZ PANNY

1918 – 2003

PROLOGUE

Wir find geboren, um für Deutschland zu sterben

IN 1936, I LEFT THE LABOR SERVICE AND THE NEWLY ESTAB-lished conscription, which, of course, again violated the conditions of the Versailles Treaty. And then two years later, when I was about age twenty, I stood in front of an oval-shaped poster under glass in a Hitler Youth Hostel. I saw myself in my uniform reflected in the dusty surface. The silver eagle on my chest showed a swastika in its claws. It was then autumn 1938, a few weeks before "Munich", which was the abandon-ment of Czechoslovakia by her sponsors and allies to the invading German Army. A few months later, again on November 9, 1938, all over Germany, Jewish synagogues had been put to the torch. World War II was about to break out and I was a second lieutenant in the German Army. As I continued to contemplate the poster, I read through my reflection, "We were born in order to die for Germany!"

CHAPTER I

"The means that wins the easiest victory over reason:
Terror and force."

Adolf Hitler: *Mein Kampf* (1933), vol. I ch. 2.

JANUARY 1923 WAS COLD AND WET IN HAMBURG. BELOW
on the street, last night's snow had turned into slush mixed with dirt
and bits of horse manure. I would have loved to be down there to build
wonderful dams along the curbs by pushing the slush ahead with the
inside edges of my boots and thereby obstructing the run-off to form
sizable puddles. Then slowly, at my whim, I might allow some of the
water to proceed on down the drain, or else to the next basin. I had not
been allowed to go outside that day and was annoyed about it.

Suddenly I heard a "whew" sound and something sped outside like
a fast seagull flying by. I looked up to my mother who said, "That was
one of those dangerous ricocheting bullets."

"Why are they shooting bullets, Mother?"

"Vinci, the bad Communists want to take the weapons from the police station at Mundsburg."

I tried to see more of these bullets, but my father had just installed wooden grates on the windows, which did not allow a full view anymore. The only comforting thought was that since I couldn't go down to play in the street, I would avoid a hiding for coming home a stinking wet mess. A net gain.

* ◆ • • ◆ • • ◆ •

My thoughts were interrupted by a loud "No!" from my father, who was on the telephone in his study next door. Everybody - Mother, Auntie and my sister, Carola, rushed to my father's office. By the time I got there, Father was roaring with an angry, reddish face, "Tonight's dinner party is canceled. The French have occupied the Ruhr district. They have all our heavy industry!" Mother started to cry and, as usual, I grabbed her apron and cried too. Crying seemed like a daily occurrence. Each morning there seemed to be bad news about money matters. "What is the dollar doing?" someone would ask. "One dollar equals 20,000 German marks and rising, more savings wiped out," I heard in reply.

I did not understand, but cried with them. What was so awful about the French occupying the Ruhr, whatever that was? Were they all crying because there would be no dinner party that evening at the German East Asia Club? Mother was crying, that was enough for me to join in too.

When Father had calmed down a little he became aware of me and yanked me out of the room into a dark corner of the hallway. "A German boy does not cry!" he yelled, over and over. "After all, you are five years old!" I stared at the bare wall facing me, afraid I would get another hiding for my unmanly behavior.

I heard Father moving up and down the long, narrow hallway, shouting and mumbling in turn, bewailing his lot saddled with such a wet rag of a son, who would likely never become anything like a real man. What hope was there for Germany to regain its proper place among the world powers if her boys were such cry-babies? I stood there, still sobbing, not daring to turn around.

Father continued his lament, mostly about the war. "Our army has not lost the war - not at all! The traitors in Berlin have stabbed Germany in the back! How could they have signed such a document as the Versailles Treaty and accepted the lie that Germany by itself was solely responsible for starting the war!

"And those reparations! We Germans will never be able to repay that much money. Look at us now. Look at the inflation! Germany is close to collapse! We believed in the Fourteen Points President Wilson promised including the myth of 'Self-Determination of Peoples.' What kind of self-determination do we have!

"And then the red menace! Those Bolsheviks will take over the country any time they want to! They are beginning to push at us outside our own apartment!" I stood there listening, not understanding any of it.

From those playroom windows, during the next few years, I often watched young men and women marching past our apartment building, the policemen waiting at the intersection below. Each time the police broke up the columns before they could reach the bridge over the canal. I thought I heard a faint thud every time one of the rubber truncheons hit one of those unarmed young people. The sight and the sound of their screams made me cringe, yet I went back to the window each time I heard those sounds. My father said the demonstrators were coming from Barmbek, one of the poorer districts in Hamburg, and they were just troublemakers. I never received much of an explanation from any of the grown-ups as to what it was all about. I didn't know whether they were communists or other militant radicals.

"Those kids are asking for it," my aunt would say as if that summed it all up.

* ◆ • • ◆ • • ◆ • •

After the January 1923 event, physical punishment was my father's primary method of parenting, "We have only your best interest in mind," was his standing explanation. Mother did not use the stick, but boxing my ears, the friction of her right knuckle rubbing through my fine blond hair on the side of my head, was just as unwelcome.

There never seemed to be a week without corporal punishment. At times, after a beating, I and my older sister found ourselves locked up in adjoining rooms; she in the water closet (w.c.) and me in the dark utility. We could communicate by whispering through a glass window as long as the air was clear. With footsteps approaching in the hallway we would re-start crying as if on command. That was as far as solidarity between us went. It was only now that I was age five that I could more or less defend myself with her.

* ◆ • • ◆ • • ◆ •

Sunday morning was the only time we children shared breakfast with our father. It was often the lowest point of the week as far as I was concerned. With some joviality my muscular stocky father would beckon me to come to his chair and look him straight in the eye. He then proceeded to hit me on the upper arm, just below the shoulder joint where there was little muscular protection. He hit me with a chop of his big hand or with the central knuckle of his fist. Whichever way it hurt, and I howled with pain. This fatherly routine demanded that I keep eyeing my tormentor and say, "*Feul ick gornich!*" which means in north German dialect, "I didn't feel a thing."

That ruined my Sunday every time it happened. I cried the minute I felt the blow and kept crying for being humiliated in front of my sister, who never failed to show her enjoyment of this spectacle. Only Mimi, Mother's sister, tried to intercede expressing her dislike for this method of education.

After the porridge, the big moment arrived when Mother lifted the cotton egg warmer cover sewn in the shape of a cross-eyed hen and handed out the soft-boiled eggs; the one egg of the week they could afford for each member of the family. I stopped crying in order to savor every bit of the event.

The genuine ivory spoons from China always seemed to distract me, stimulating visions of a faraway paradise I had heard so much about. I could imagine my parents being happy there in the wonderful myste-rious place where I was born. Their forced repatriation from China in 1919 was the worst thing that could have happened to me, I thought.

My eyes lit up in potential revenge when I saw the cautious expres-sion on my father's face as he prepared to crack his egg. More often than not, his egg would be either too soft or too hard or smell rotten, and each time Father would blame the poor hapless cook, mostly Mother. He was usually so rude about it that she was reduced to tears.

◆ ◆ ·· ◆ ·· ◆ ◆

My mother's diary, 1923 Christmas and 1924, uses those family nicknames or endearments I have always found distasteful and embar-rassing from the time I can remember. Mother always referred to herself as "Mami", the way she was addressed in the house. Carola was called Mausi, Jutta was just called Juttel, and Rolf was called Rolfi. I was called Vinci, which I hated because the German adjective *winzig* means diminutive or dwarf-like. I took quite a ribbing on account of this all through childhood. My father's name was Ignaz Alois. His nickname "Nazi" originated from parts of Germany where the Roman Catholic families give their children names of Saints, in this case Ignatius. Thus, my father grew up in Hamburg around the turn of the century being called Nazi, way before Hitler arrived on the scene.

Mother's diary recounts a few details of the 1923-1924 holiday season, at least enough to jog my memory about that wonderful Christmas.

The parlor had been locked up. We children could not see much of what was going on in there. The key-holes allowed only a limited vision. Then at 4:30 p.m. on the December 24, we all congregated in the adjoining room and with 'Silent Night' from the gramophone in the background, the double doors slid slowly open and there was that wonderful tree. The branches were laden heavily with burning candles and symbolic decorations. I was more interested in the round chocolates with holes in the center, decorated with colorful icing hanging from wires all over the tree. It was overwhelming.

This year we had a real Father Christmas with a huge bag over his shoulder and a large birch rod in his hand, a frightening specter to us children. There was no jollity about that one. Mausi (Carola) and I stammered our Christmas poems. My poem was simple:

> "Dear Father Christmas,
> Don't look at me with this angry expression.
> Please put away your birch rod.
> I promise to be a good boy."

Once we said our bit of poetry, he did become more friendly, emptied his big sack on the floor and then stomped out of the apartment on to the next family.

Each person had his or her own table with gifts. Not all gifts were wrapped and I remember feeling totally lost in the variety of toys that this particular Christmas had provided. After dinner, we were allowed to play some more and the next day I was told that I fell asleep on the floor with a wooden horse in my hand.

⁕◆⁕⁕◆⁕⁕◆⁕

Translation of the daily journal of Luise Panny Damsch:

Tuesday, January 1, 1924:

We got up late. The children played all through the forenoon. Uncle Herbert came by and had lunch with Mami and Papi and John Helmers. We went to Auntie Rola to offer our New Year's wishes. From there we went to the Family Berg, old friends from China. In the evening, we all played the new horse race game, which Vinci had received for Christmas. He didn't believe when we told him it was from Father Christmas. Little Jutta joined us at the game table but she just watched and kept playing with her animals very nicely.

Wednesday, January 2, 1924:

The big dining room, the Christmas room, was opened to the children for the last time. Vinci extended his railway across the precious parquet floor. Carola rearranged her doll house and Jutta sold candy in her grocery store. There was hot chocolate cooked in the little toy oven, which had served for all these decades since Mami played with it when she was a little girl in Berlin.

Thursday, January 3, 1924:

The Christmas tree was robbed of all its ornaments and what was left of its candles. All the toys went to the playroom, where they belonged, and the Christmas room was cleaned.

At 12:30 p.m., we heard the terrible news from the Kunath family that Hans had come home to his mother dripping wet and shivering from the cold. He and his brother, Richard, had gone walking on the ice of the Alster River and had broken through near Raben Strasse. There was no trace of his brother. Hans kept insisting that he had pulled Richard out of the water and that he had seen Richard running toward home ahead of him. But he disappeared from view. Until 3:00 p.m. Aunt Rola and Mami went through hours of agony.

We went down to the water, but found nobody and we kept telephoning. When we came home at 3:30 p.m. to question Hans again, Richard had just been delivered by car. He was in good shape. He had just knocked at a house, and the people had invited him in, and had taken care of him. They had warmed him, given him a hot bath and fed him. The family claimed there was no way to reach anyone at Auntie Rola's because the telephone there was constantly busy.

◆ ◆ ◆ ◆ ◆ ◆ ◆

Reading mother's diary brings vividly to my mind the events that followed. In the evening Auntie Rola came over to thank us. After a while she was more relaxed than I had ever seen her. They offered her tea and rum.

Later we played Black Peter, one of the new games, for the first time. I did not like it much because the loser gets his nose blackened with a bottle cork that had been held over a burning candle.

I do remember sitting down in the big dining room and looking around feeling sorry that this whole Christmas season was over. This Christmas of 1923-24 was a fantastic experience. I didn't remember any wrong notes, no problems, nothing but love and harmony. Even my father's sister, Auntie Rola, who had previously taken him into her business and was extremely critical of any move he made, did not chide him for anything.

After the new year, it was business as usual. Auntie Rola once again meddled, criticized and nagged everybody, children and grown-ups alike. She also let it be known that she thought that Father should not have spent that much money on Christmas. It's a good thing that we did not see her on a daily basis.

● ◆ ● ● ◆ ● ● ◆ ●

After two or three days of bliss, the thought of the coming Sunday kept bothering me. I wondered if Father would again use this opportunity to toughen me up and hit me in the established place, to begin again his regular routine of torment. It turned out I was lucky. Father stayed in bed with a capital hangover or something. I was secretly delighted, but, of course, I openly expressed best wishes for his speedy recovery.

I spent Sunday afternoon shoveling snow - great fun! But every time I took a fresh run to eke out another ten inches, the experience of the previous afternoon invaded my mind. Hans and Richard had been at the door around 4 p.m. looking somewhat sheepish, ignoring us little kids. When Papi came home he took first Hans and then Richard into the w.c. and without much ado beat them with a switch. I could not stand the noise of the cold-blooded flogging and their howls of pain. I saw myself in the same room suffering the same humiliation. It was awful. I hid and cried with them, as I listened. When it was all over, I watched through the slightly open door as both boys left with sullen expressions on their reddish faces; Hans still had tears in his eyes.

I hung onto the snow shovel and kept repeating to myself that those were big boys. Hans, for that matter, was even taller than my father. Without a doubt I now knew that this kind of parental treatment was not just for little boys, it was going to go on forever.

1924 must have been the beginning of my alienation. Jutta, who was much too small to understand, and Auntie Mimi became my confidants.

My mother seemed to lose hope in general. From snatches of conversations overheard from the grown-ups I began to see that anything my father touched in his business went awry.

•◆••◆••◆•

Carola and I were still sharing a bedroom and had a nightly routine game before falling asleep. It had to be done very quietly. We both had been careless once or twice and had received a few whacks as a good night beating because we had disobeyed father's orders. In this game or fantasy, Carola was the head nurse in some kind of medical institution. She insisted on being the head nurse and I was quite happy to leave that privilege to her. As she saw it, the life of a head nurse was a constant case of insubordination or dereliction of duties on the part of one or more of her underlings. She came to me, the chief surgeon, and gave me her reports complete with her judgmental commentary on the case. Then it was my duty to arrive at some kind of verdict and carry out the punishment - without witnesses, without confronting the accuser, without a statement by the accused - just sheer corporal punishment exactly as it was done in our family and with the very rod I was familiar with. The nature of the transgressions was mostly trivial, clumsiness was the most frequent complaint, dropping the knife or scalpel, minor matters.

I don't know how we arrived at the name for this never-ending saga of hospital crime and punishment. We called it *Uschalarzt*.

After a while this constant repetition of crime and punishment in the medical profession became boring to me. While I was playing lip service I developed my own fantasies, I kept the game going by giving the right answers and performing my duties, but secretly followed my own train of thoughts. Once I had done my bit flogging the poor nurse, she and I, as if by magic, were able to move out of the room through an invisible door in the paneling of the wall. I invented a sizable space separating the walls of the two adjoining rooms where this nurse and a number of her co-workers were living. It was modestly furnished and very comfortable and warm. Nobody was wearing nurses' uniforms. Come to think of it, they were dressed rather scantily, if at all.

This nurse and I were greeted by the others and it was a wonderful scene of fraternization, of kissing and making up, and everybody was trying to make me feel better about my role in their daily hospital routine. There was a lot of hugging and kissing, the kind of slobbery kisses I had to endure as a five-year-old, mostly from Aunties and friends of my parents. I still can't explain how we were able to get through the wooden part of the floor board. We were floating. And the older I became and the more often I got into trouble, the more frequently I had dreams where I was able to float away into safety whenever I got into a sticky situation.

❖ •• ❖ •• ❖ •

Come to think of it, I can associate this floating sensation to when I was taught horseback riding in the army, as crudely and insensitively as only the army could teach it. Instead of creating a relationship between man and horse, they managed to create in me a kind of phobia. As a result, the only time I felt comfortable on horseback was in gallop when I felt synchronized with the movement of the horse. To initiate this state, I remember tilting my head slightly to the left, shifting my weight and the position of my legs. This series of movements invariably brought a recognition of the sensation of that earlier floating into safety.

◆ ◦ ◦ ◆ ◦ ◦ ◆ ◦

Father went to England on the boat Orbita R.M.S.C. His letter to me, here translated, is dated June 27, 1924:

"My dear little chubby one,

Those few days before your birthday have passed quickly and I'll have a chance to write you this spectacular letter to congratulate you and wish you happy returns for your birthday, health and luck for the coming year.

This is the last birthday you'll be able to enjoy as a free man. Next time around you'll be a school boy who is serious about learning and does not cry anymore. Remember: *Fühl ich garnicht!* our little game? It is a very good device to keep away those wet tears.

Last night I was dreaming and, come to think of it, I saw your gifts on your birthday table. I can't recall in detail what I saw, but I think there was some beautiful toy.

We won't reach England this morning, maybe not before noon. Last night around 11:30 p.m. our ship started to blow fog warnings every three minutes. This lasted until dawn. We had struck thick fog in the canal as this waterway is called. We moved with only one quarter steam in order to avoid collisions. You could hear all the other horns and sirens around us, but your father, of course, got a good sleep anyway. Now the sun is up and we sail at full speed to make up for lost time.

Imagine, this is the same canal where you, Mausi, Papi, and Mami traveled five years ago, when we all came back from China. How old were you then? That ship was just about as big as this one of which I had sent you a picture postcard.

When you are a man and have learned a lot, you will make a long sea voyage too so you can see the world, other races and cultures, and make a lot of money. Then you will invite Mausi and Jutta to take a trip and you will all come back and tell your parents what it was like and where you think it is more beautiful, at home or far away in the world.

I hope everybody is okay at home and you'll make sure that Mami has nothing but joy with you children, that baby doesn't get hurt, and Mausi gets to school on time and that Hilda does not boil potatoes with their skins on. I hope the weather stays nice and you will all get some fresh air. If you have visitors give them my best regards and you, as we agreed, take my place in my absence. If these chores become too much for you, get yourself a little brother to help you. Talk to Mami about that. She may have something to say about that matter. But she will do that only if you are all nice children.

Okay, my dear boy, again 1,000 heartfelt wishes for your birthday. Enjoy your birthday and give everybody many kisses for me. I will be back with you soon and you will have to tell me what happened. Best wishes and heartfelt greetings to all of you from your Papi."

Mother read this letter to me before we went into the room where a table of birthday gifts was waiting for me. We knew father had to go to London on business at this time so nobody made a fuss about his being absent for this occasion. I found many wonderful gifts, mostly practical things, and some toys which pleased me enormously. I held father's letter in my hand as something valuable and unique, my first piece of personal mail. The stamps made me feel important, two pink one-penny and one green half-penny with a British king in the center. The King's profile and his beard reminded me of Pastor Remé, whose face I much preferred to the mostly either too fierce or much too benign looking characters in the many religious textbooks I was shown. But the more often I heard the passage about Father's toughening up procedure, the more clearly I remembered the pain of Sunday mornings. I saw this as a threatening gesture and, in my mind, it began to get mixed up with his best wishes for my birthday.

Mimi had to read this letter to me at least half a dozen times. With all the congratulations and best wishes he just had to refer to "our" Sunday morning toughening up routine. He had to refer to the fact that it didn't take much to make me cry in those days. My father wanted to teach me to behave like a man, as he called it. The more he and my mother nagged, the more they punished me for crying, the more I cried. From the time I could remember, the age of three or so, everybody around me had reasons for crying; if it wasn't the lost war, it was the loss of two brothers killed in World War I (WW I), or it was the still raging starvation all around them, or it could have been the inflation in 1923 where everybody lost their savings and the whole middle class ceased to exist. At the time I didn't understand what it was all about, just that my family was crying all the time. So I cried for many reasons: I cried when I lost a game. I cried when I was tired or sick. Then I cried when I won a game in the U.T.G., our gymnastics club, and then when I had won a race and received a big piece of chocolate. Above all, I could not stand watching Mami, Mimi or Jutta cry. I just couldn't and had to cry also.

●◆●●◆●●◆●

In September 1924, a baby brother arrived! Mother had to stay in the hospital for months to recover. We were never told about her depressions. Her sister Mimi and a housemaid tried to keep the family going. Carola was doing fine because she had spent her first two years in China under normal dietary conditions. We three younger ones were not doing too well. This new baby boy had the worst of it. He was severely ill two or three times his first year. At one time they kept him alive with only bananas since he could not keep down anything else. Of us three children, his was the most dramatic case of *rachitis* (rickets) then prevalent in Germany, as it was explained to us. His protruding chest was referred to as a "chicken breast."

Many children we knew suffered in this way. It was a combination of their mother's war-time malnutrition during pregnancy and their children growing up under sub-normal dietary conditions. A lack of fresh air and sunshine also contributed. Everyone had become leery of exposing their children to the outdoors with all the street-fighting and political unrest.

✦ •• ✦ •• ✦ •

The only walks that our family ever took began at the end of 1924, weather permitting. It was a routine walk around the huge pond across from our apartment. On one of those walks in the fall of this year, I noted a little boy in the colorful toy uniform of a pre-war Prussian soldier who kept playacting as a sniper behind trees aiming his toy pistol at us. Having ignored him on two or three occasions, my aunt who was pushing Jutta's pram finally stopped and talked to this boy. It turned out that he was Jürgen Remé, the son of the Lutheran pastor I admired so much, and they lived on the same street in the vicarage on the other side of the church.

So began a friendship with "JR" which was definitely instrumental in shaping my future. It opened up an entirely new world to me and provided all the answers to those questions that had puzzled me since my first encounter with politics in 1923. Whatever my father had been mumbling and yelling then in the hallway of our flat, now in the parsonage it was repeated as a thorough indoctrination into the nationalistic mood of the time. Revision of the so-called peace treaty ending World War I was uppermost in people's minds and could be found in the party platforms of the political center and right. I was certainly not old enough to understand history, but I soon found out who Lloyd George was, what Clemenceau had done, and what role Poincaré played during and after World War I. Even my father was impressed to see the education I was getting at the Pastor's house.

While there were some signs of returning to economic normalcy - the inflation was over - my father's situation still was tenuous. I was now in first grade in the Bertram private school for boys, which he really could not afford. My father was so reluctant to put aside the colonial lifestyle he had lived in China and he still fancied himself a member of the Hamburg elite. He even had a hairdresser come to the apartment every second Sunday to look after the tonsorial needs of the males in the family. I overheard the odd remark made by relatives and friends whenever family matters were discussed, that this was an absolute luxury and just as irresponsible as sending me and my older sister to private schools. I soon found out in school exactly what our family position was. Many of my classmates had their own horse, sailboat or at least a dinghy to play around with on the water of the Alster. In contrast, I experienced my own family's financial limitations.

◆ • • ◆ • • ◆ •

Every day JR and I spent all our free time together and we went to the same private school. From him and his father, I learned about military history, of which I had known very little. In turn, I tried to impress JR with a make-believe sports activity, a mystical relay race around the big pond, something he knew nothing about. The year before I had watched my uncle Herbert being part of the victorious relay team in a race around the Alster, which was an annual event in Hamburg.

From two-inch lead soldiers we changed to one inch tin soldiers, little figures on foot or horseback very elaborately painted. JR collected the Seven Years' War, Prussia under Frederick the Great against the rest of Europe, and I found under the Christmas tree 1925 hundreds of soldiers representing the 1870-71 war between France and Germany. We sank every bit of our modest allowance money into this hobby.

The routine never varied. While I was building some kind of fortress, JR was dramatically acting out an intrigue among the officers of a given side. Often these dramas were taken from historical disagreements among military leaders, however most of the time they were fantasies of his fertile militaristic mind. In summer we even dug an actual World War I trench in the back yard and had all the kids in the neighborhood join our war games.

His room under the attic of the parsonage was huge with a large rectangular table in the center. On this large table we were allowed buckets of sand and we molded battlefields, roads, built forests, villages, and arranged our hundreds of tin soldiers according to a given battle situation, mostly imaginary ones.

One neighbor, a rich banker, was so impressed by what we had started that he promised to buy whatever was needed, tin soldier manpower or whatever, if we would create a true to nature model of an actual landscape in a given battle. It was an offer we couldn't refuse. In JR's case, it was the Seven Years' War, Empress Maria Teresa versus Frederick the Great of Prussia. In my case, it was the War of 1871, which led to the downfall of Emperor Napoleon III. The bank director kept his word. We even set little toy houses on fire to perfect the illusion. We should have charged people for the viewing of our handiwork.

◆ ● ● ◆ ● ● ◆ ●

JR's father became so impressed that he quite openly expressed a certain relief to see his little boy suddenly provided with a constant companion. JR was a latecomer and was growing up without his real mother, who had died during his birth. The pastor claimed that I had some beneficial influence on him. Even though we had our disagreements, we were inseparable. We even were sent together to a vicarage in central Germany for two successive summer vacations with the pastor paying the lion's share of the expenses.

JR's father was an elderly Huguenot gentleman. He looked splendid in his pastoral robes and sported the most handsome beard I had ever seen. Every Sunday we went to the children's service, which lasted from 11:00 a.m. to 12:30 p.m. The sermons were way above our heads and they were so dramatic and so stimulating that I was never really sorry for having agreed to be there.

I thought that JR's stepmother wasn't much of a cook, but the alternative was far worse. A few houses down at my own family's lunch table I knew there was my father, most often smelling of liquor and most likely in a foul mood, having spent Sunday morning in his pub discussing politics. Invariably, the gentlemen there replayed World War I and concluded by condemning the Weimar Republic. This and the liquor didn't produce a cheerful father at the table. We children were told to eat quietly and so we did, except when something happened which we considered to be funny. From a knowing wink to a suppressed giggle to an explosion into the soup bowl, it always ended up in some kind of confrontation. I was told to leave the room more frequently than my siblings, often without having finished my lunch.

The conversations were controlled almost entirely by the grown-ups, I found it boring. Then sometime during the lunch, the old man invariably reminisced about the great times they had in China. I often thought, "If it was that great, why don't you go back." Of course, I would never have dared to say that out loud.

My poor mother was mostly moaning about her inability to make ends meet or speaking up about her fundamentalist church after the fourth child was born. She had to defend her newly discovered religious beliefs against the sneers of her husband and the heckling of her sister. It was never pleasant.

Sunday lunch at JR's, on the other hand, was something to look forward to. The old gentleman took both of us boys seriously and listened respectfully whenever we joined a given conversation. When needed, he gently corrected our youthful exaggerations or inaccuracies. Each of these lunches represented a history lesson for me, a revisionist German perception of history. The Peace Treaty in 1919 was referred to as a study in infamy and the need for its revision was constantly stressed.

◦ ◈ ◦ ◦ ◈ ◦ ◦ ◈ ◦

We entered first grade Easter 1925, as planned, at a private school for boys - Gustav Bertram. JR and I were not in the same class because the pastor felt that we would distract each other. Already we were known to make fun of authoritarian grown-ups. Any pompous remark provoked ridicule. We didn't always have to say anything, we just looked at each other and tried not always successfully to control our sniggering. We respected only a few grown-ups, JR's father among them, of course. JR had seen the bruises from beatings I had received, so he did not think too highly of my father.

JR's teacher, Miss Stephan, was a very attractive woman in her thirties, a tall sporting type with Polynesian facial features. I would have loved to have been in her class. There were, by way of exception, five girls in the class too. My own teacher, Miss Ottens, was a very handsome lady with dark brown eyes. She captured our imagination and loyalty once she started reading stories and fairy tales to us. We were spellbound by her animated delivery. I spent two beautiful years in her class and never regretted having been separated from JR.

It was just as well that I liked my teacher because already a certain alienation against my family had set in. The continual beatings at home had left me feeling as an outsider, not really belonging. In many cases, I knew I had done something wrong or stupid, and if this was the only way my parents could react, I would accept that. I promised under tears that I would never do again whatever it was I was punished for. I became very cunning in hiding my true feelings and in covering up or controlling the damage once I had misbehaved again. I found myself becoming negative about everything and contemptuous of the life in my father's house.

The classroom was a haven of peace compared to life at home. The school was a beautiful old building with tall windows facing the Alster. The classroom was at floor level and I was lucky to be able to see out of the window. Very often I caught myself watching the sailboats or follow-ing the busy steamers that were bringing people from the suburbs to downtown. Occasionally there were canoes and the row-boats from one of the many rowing clubs. Miss Ottens, more than once, threatened to move me away from the window, but never followed through. I was not too bad a student and had a certain amount of credibility with her.

●◆●●◆●●◆●

At this time I started reading fairy tales to my younger sister and brother in the dramatic way Miss Ottens had presented them in class. I discovered that there was a bond that had been established between us. I was pleased with myself for being able to keep their attention and the fact that they kept asking for more. Very often, fairy tales being what they are, both of them were crying and even I was caught up in tears over Hansel and Gretel's fate.

◆ ◆ ◆ ◆ ◆ ◆ ◆

Grade three and four meant a big change, not exactly for the better. From the classroom with a view and a gently spoken Miss Ottens, we were thrown into a rather dingy dark third floor classroom facing north and found ourselves at the mercy of a six-foot woman, age about 50 to 55, with a one-and-a-half foot ruler as an always handy weapon at her side. To be honest, she did not hit people constantly, but when she thought she had reasons it was a painful experience for the respective culprit or victim. The flat side impact right on the central knuckle of a firmly grasped hand was excruciating.

How Mr. Bertram was able to run the upper classes in this architectural museum still baffles me. Situated on one of Hamburg's most prestigious streets called Esplanade, it was developed around 1830 when the city fortifications at last were razed. In their place was a thoroughfare consisting of four lanes, two lanes in each direction separated in the center by a fifty meter wide park with majestic trees and tram tracks. Gorgeous slender buildings of uniform height, none of them much wider than fifty feet across the front, represented either the Biedermeier or the Neoclassical architecture.

Mrs. Barge taught nearly all subjects, even religion. She taught my class consisting mostly of Lutherans, which also included some Jewish boys whose parents had converted to Protestantism. This being Hamburg, a liberal and democratic city, there was separate religion class for the three Roman Catholics and for the five Jews held at the same time. Religious instruction was part of the curriculum at most German schools at the time. Since I was well primed through those regular Sunday School services at St. Gertrude, I made religion one of my areas of special interest.

I was mostly motivated by the intensity of Mrs. Barge's religious fervor. She was apparently a staunch sectarian who wanted to give us insight into the Old Testament. She worshipped on Saturday, she told us. Whenever I mentioned excerpts from her fire and brimstone perception of Christianity, either at St. Gertrude or at home, I was given plenty of material from which to ask questions in class. I kept reporting the latest from Mrs. Barge and started to feel like a snitch.

"There is no such thing as a devil." I mumbled, not being quite sure of myself.

"When I tell you there is a devil, then there is a devil!" she would yell.

The class was highly amused. The continuing dispute on religious matters between Barge and myself earned me some kind of standing in the class. Most of them were from rich family backgrounds, spoiled milk sobs who even had a maid to make their bed in the morning. I became an avid reader in the Old Testament and was surprised to notice that I could use my knowledge as a weapon with the grown-ups. I recall that sometimes when I had been bad or when I had expressed that I was bored, either my mother or some other grown-up would say, "Study the Bible." And I would answer, "I don't know. Too much begetting, begetting, begetting. By the way, what does it mean, begetting?" I would ask meekly. And more than once I was told to ignore what I don't understand.

Yes, sex also became a weapon too, I enjoyed seeing the grown-ups squirm in order to get out of a given situation. Alas, sometimes I made the mistake of throwing bits out of the big city gutter into the conversation. Gerd, the youngest son from downstairs, was my never-ending source for seamy talk or gesture, repeating his language or emulating his gestures more than once earned me a right hook with the open palm leaving the red imprint of huge fingers on my cheek.

Along with my studies of the Old Testament, the lovely face of Ingrid Jörgenson sitting in the first row of the choir loft, and the graphic boy's talk I was hearing, a certain tension was building. In the daily papers and the weekly or monthly magazines the female body was demanding more and more notice.

◆ • • ◆ • • ◆ •

School in Mrs. Barge's class became a boring routine. She made us memorize reams of bombastic ballads, all in the stilted flowery language of the nineteenth century. They mostly dealt with a largely mythological Teutonic past. Happy or sad, most had some wholesome morale in the end. I didn't like what I was doing, however I suppose even rote memorization was a useful skill to acquire.

JR, on the other hand, had a wonderful time in Miss Stephan's class. They even put on an enjoyable performance of a humorous work by Wilhelm Busch, *Max and Moritz*. The class wrote the dramatized version and the performance during a big school festival was absolutely wonderful. I was green with envy. I would have given a lot for a small part in that show.

My grades fell below B- as my interest in learning diminished somewhat. Indolence took over, a certain arrogant refusal to get involved. The natural curiosity of myself as a child disappeared during those two years. As a consequence, my performance was not good enough to automatically qualify for grade five, the lowest high school grade with eight more grades to follow. Most of my classmates at Bertram enjoyed this privilege, whereas I had to face a week of do-or-die qualifying examinations. I cursed myself for having squandered what would have been the reward of having gone to private school. In those days only an elite of school children made it to high school and relatively few, no more than five or ten percent of all school children went on to university. All the others went to trade schools or started apprenticeships in some blue-collar positions. Yes, I cursed myself, but I was quick to rationalize this blow to my self-image. Between family stress and Mrs. Barge's rigidity, I thought it was a miracle that I had not run away or done something irreparably rude or silly. I felt unloved and that no one understood me or even tried to.

For a whole week I had to travel across to the other side of the Alster and sit through four to six hours of exams, which were given to a crowd of promising youngsters from public schools. When the roll was called and my name and school was mentioned there was an audible gasp in the group. From then on they showed their disdain for me as the rich kid who didn't quite make it. As much as anything, this increased my anxiety. It was a hell week and then some.

• ◆ • • ◆ • • ◆ •

Having passed this hurdle, I was still suffering the aftereffects of this stress week when I was enrolled around Easter 1929 in the 400-year-old *Johanneum, Gelehrtenschule des Johanneums* (School of Scholars). There were other high schools around our neighborhood, the *Real-Gymnasium* (no Greek, but Latin and modern languages and natural sciences) or the *Oberreal Schule*, (no Greek or Latin, just modern languages and natural sciences); but my father who never graduated from high school insisted on the 400-year-old school for scholars for me (Latin in grade five, English in grade seven, Greek in grade eight along with math, German literature, natural sciences, etc.) It was a prestigious gymnasium for parents who wanted their sons to go into the clergy, pursue a university career, or become doctors, or other professionals.

The first day I was impressed by the massive brick building shaped like an upside-down U with an open front guarded by heavy wrought iron gates under a portico. The inner court where upperclassmen spent their recess time was dominated by the statue of a naked boy standing on a block of black marble. In the classroom, I found about thirty kids of rich and famous families, about one-third of them Jewish.

• ◆ • • ◆ • • ◆ • •

Mr. Simon called the roll and told us to wear our blue peaked cap with the red and white ribbon around the base for the convocation ceremony. These caps looked ridiculous to me. We looked like a room full of stationmaster apprentices and I remember discarding mine pretty soon afterwards. Besides, by not wearing it to school I saved myself occasional harassment on the forty-five-minute walk to and from school. Boys from "lesser" schools or trade schools enjoyed bashing high school kids at times. This was the beginning of the big depression in Germany which, of course, accentuated the latent lower class resentment of any display of elitist symbols.

The incoming students were solemnly inducted in the big chapel. Professor Doctor Stelter, the white-haired director, intoned a thunderous oratory welcoming us and opened the 400th anniversary festivities at the same time. My first year was long on parties and shows and concerts and short on substance. I almost flunked out Easter 1930.

The teachers were mostly returned soldiers from World War I, some of them severely handicapped. The war and the Treaty of Versailles were constantly discussed there as much as they were in the rest of the country in press and radio. I was pleased that some of my teachers took notice of my interest in history including military history.

The notion of toughening up the younger generation for future hardships was another daily topic. This was nothing new to me. I felt thoroughly brainwashed through my long relationship with JR and the grown-ups in my family. By now I was reading novels and history books on the subject which were, with few exceptions, a glorification of war, country, duty, honor. *A Day in the Life of a Bengal Lancer* - this movie classic JR and I saw at least three or four times. JR began to act and sound like Franchot Tone in his every day conversations, that is to say, sound like his German voice-over. He even used that voice and manner when he played a British school teacher in our performance of *Journey's End* by Sherriff in 1935!

The combination of schoolhouse and museum of art provided any amount of stimulation for people like myself who needed a challenge. The long passage on the third floor was filled with gods and goddesses, complete or with some limbs or parts missing, but most of them stark naked and larger than life. There was not a week in my short tenure in this classical gymnasium without one of these statues having acquired some outrageously funny physical adornment or some editorial remark written in bold black letters commenting on student life, on teachers or the world in general.

JR left for Silesia to study in a boarding school run by some pietist sect. As much as I had been critical of his temperament and his total lack of patience, now that he was gone I missed him a lot. I withdrew, started playing in my own world of fantasy, reading a lot, collecting soccer cards, playing imaginary championships. From reading Karl May I stepped up to Rilke, Hesse, Jünger, Dwinger or Remarque.

• ◆ • • ◆ • • ◆ •

A few years later, I was old enough to be able to get a better idea of what was going on in Germany during this time. Since that intense scene in 1923 and my father's history lessons, I became curious about history and politics. I had observed in the street below some of the communists who were trying their hand at an armed uprising in Hamburg. The same sort of unrest had occurred in Central Germany and in a few other places, which I found out later. I continued to listen to the constant venting about World War I, Versailles, "The Dictated Peace" as they called it, the German Revolution of 1918, the inflation, and all the other aspects of German suffering.

With my father's complaints from January in mind, I started asking questions, received unsatisfactory answers and understood very little. To me it looked as though my country must have been encircled and attacked by powerful inhumane neighbors just out of sheer envy. Our soldiers, according to the grown-ups, had resisted the onslaught of the whole world for four years. Only Austria, Hungary, Bulgaria and Turkey had been on Germany's side. I learned that the German soldiers were far superior to any forces the Allies could muster. At the end, in 1918, they were still defending their country and their loved ones with heroic resolve against all odds. But then came the betrayal. The socialists, the Jews and the intellectuals stabbed the army in the back. "They" signed the armistice in 1918, which was a vile deception by President Wilson, who in his Fourteen Points had promised self-determination for the minorities in the new Europe. The armistice, once signed, made it impossible for the German Army to continue the war. The subsequent Peace Treaty, the harshest ever in history, according to the grown-ups, again was signed by the same group of people henceforth known as the "November Criminals."

The most forceful speaker protesting what had occurred at Versailles was a certain Adolf Hitler, who this very year of 1923 on November 9 had tried to lead an armed uprising in Munich, which had failed dismally. In the following years, we heard some of his speeches, once he was released from prison, and he always started by running down the "November Criminals." I learned later that a number of the people who had signed the armistice and/or the Peace Treaty or had exposed themselves in trying to make the new German Republic a viable democracy had been killed, sometimes in broad daylight by nationalistic death squads.

For fifteen years the German politicians, it seemed, were devoting all their time and effort to a revision of the Versailles Treaty and negotiations to reschedule the payment of reparations. By 1929 the world depression hit the Germans by far the hardest, because when Wall Street collapsed the Americans had to call in their short-term loans, I was told. By that time my friend JR and I had played nothing but war games with little tin figurines and neighborhood war games with the World War I trench warfare in the backyard. He and I were sure we would have to be in the forefront once grown up to revise the treaty and restore Germany to respectability.

All this time the voice in Southern Germany, Hitler's harsh guttural speeches in huge halls and in the open air, had turned the Nazi party into the most powerful political movement in Central Europe. He became Chancellor, this time legally, and as always started all his harangues with 1918 and the "November Criminals." Everybody had read or heard this so many times that I got the idea the whole nation was quite sure that World War I was not really lost, the army was truly unvanquished. It had been stabbed in the back by the "November Criminals."

* ◆ • • ◆ • • ◆ •

I didn't begin to think critically until 1933 when I was fifteen years old and found myself in a co-educational avant-garde high school and at the same time a *Jungenschaft,* part of the German Youth Movement, which had existed since the turn of the century. There I had teachers willing to discuss and answer questions. They opened my eyes to a different set of values and introduced me to literature, art, the humanities. Practically overnight I found that I had a dramatic flair for reading out loud and was asked to take part in mostly amateur theater productions and professional radio plays.

Before that change, however, the seventh-grade class was the worst. A second language was added, English, which was taught by a real professor, Professor Doctor Häpke. We called him "Nucky," I don't know why. He was hard of hearing and always on the defense. After a few cases, where he accused and reported some of us unjustly, we began to react. It was mayhem. The nastier the professor behaved, the more stinging became the reprisals.

After Christmas, "Nucky" was sent on vacation and later given a job as an archivist. When we found out he had been buried alive in World War I most of us felt bad about our cruel behavior. However, before we developed some kind of sensitivity to this poor man and what we had done, we were being tyrannized by his replacement, a hefty, healthy teacher we called "Bacon Roll" (*Speckroller*) referring to the layers of fat around his chin and who hit students indiscriminately.[1]

We had to get especially resourceful. Except for Mr. Simon, who was our class or homeroom teacher (math, physics, chemistry), Zindler (religion) and Stork (Latin), we boys were mostly engaged in fighting back instead of learning.

The next language, classical Greek, was my undoing, 1933-1934. The professor was a gross, brutal authoritarian. With my weak sciences and barely passing Latin, I knew I would flunk and began to prepare my family and friends. On the positive side - and there were some those years at the Johanneum - there was a real friend, a bachelor teacher called KB (Krumbhaar). He had heard about my family problems and so once a week he helped me with my school work after a delicious dinner his mother cooked for us. We had long discussions in which he kept encouraging me to change my attitude towards this awful school. Later,

---

1. Mr. Mausch, "Bacon Roll," was fittingly immortalized as the worst of all the teachers in the Johanneum by Ralph Giordano who in his book *Die Bertinis* ‾ published in 1982 described his experiences as a half-Jew in the school.

we went on bicycle trips on the countryside surrounding Hamburg. His English was authentic, and so was his Anglo-Saxon sense of humor and his easy self-effacing musings about himself and his classes. He administered the school books and saved less fortunate students like myself by finding used copies for us.

Another remarkable teacher was Helmbrecht, who had our parallel class. Once my class went on an outing by bicycle, I had to go with Helmbrecht, because at that time I didn't have a bike. He turned an ordinary hike through some villages north of the city into a very interesting study of the social conditions of the peasantry.

On the return trip by train somebody started an orgy of vandalism. All accessible metal signs with instructions like "Don't spit on the floor, thank you," were removed. One idiot showed his loot to his neighbor, a retired admiral, who must have picked up his telephone immediately. The next morning, we had the big inquisition to ascertain who had done what and some of them must have pointed at me and hinted that I was the initiator of this escapade. Most of them got away with a warning. I was given the *consilium abeundi* (the advice to find some other school). Although I did take home one sign from the loo of the train, I certainly was not interested to the point of planning or participating, and certainly was not the one to bring the necessary screwdriver. I ignored the Latin advice and flunked out of school Easter 1934. Since this coincided with my confirmation at the local Lutheran Church, I enjoyed the distinction of being the only confirmand without gifts from the family.

Helmbrecht was in charge of both classes Easter 1934. He had just been fired, ousted by the Nazi dominated senator of education as a suspected socialist. He was in a very giving mood and said, "Well, I'll just read something to you," and commenced to read *The Death Ship* by Traven, one of the books on the index list, that is to say, not suitable for German readers, possibly one of the books burned by the

Nazi students early on. He talked to me afterwards and wished me well. He said he appreciated my discretion during the student interviews regarding the vandalism. Having carried out his own research, he handed in a written report to the school explaining I could not possibly have been the ringleader, but like everything else, the school ignored his recommendations.

KB did not think much of my role as a guest traveler on that fateful day when the vandalism had occurred. He had an almost sneering laugh at my *consilium abeundi* and my new image as a trouble maker. "You see," he said, "without ever having been a soldier, on account of my eye problem, I have been interested in reading up on group brutality. Whenever there are people bunched together, male or female, for that matter, be it in school, the military or a club, there often is a tendency on somebody's part to think of ways to out-do the others, to become dominant - first by showing off and later by taking initiatives in the direction of the reckless, the lawless or violent. I hope you keep away from that from now on, no matter what peer pressure you encounter. By the way, my grade eleven is reading Rilke. Would you come and read *The Coronet* next week?"

"You want me to -----?"

"Yes, exactly. The *consilium abeundi* doesn't mean you are an outlaw. Just act as though nothing significant has happened."

I couldn't believe it. "Well, thank you. Let me know when and where." I was flushed with this unexpected bit of encouragement. There were two students in my class, Edwin Roth and I, who were known to be stage-struck. Unfortunately, Ed sometimes had problems with his having to wear thick glasses, so he turned down public appearances rather frequently.[2] The reading at KB's class went very well.

---

2. Too bad really. He later became a celebrity as an actor, his unforgettable role being one of the returning POW (Borchert - *Draussen vor der Tür*) 1947.

My second experience with show business came about in KB's English class. We were reading Dickens' *A Christmas Carol*, and KB wanted me to read Scrooge. The teacher's lectern became Scrooge's office desk. A three-by-six portable piece of blackboard leaned against the lectern representing the wall of Scrooge's office. When the Christmas carolers appeared in the door I was supposed to chase them away and stress my "Bah, humbug," by throwing a wooden ruler at the pesky nuisances. I followed the script to the letter, but somehow lost my balance on my high stool and fell face first into this portable blackboard piece, which raised a big laugh in the class. They stopped laughing when I came up the color of the whitewashed wall, blood on my face and the broken remnant of one front tooth between my fingers. Once I could establish that my stool got hooked up in a deep gash in the wall behind me, the city of Hamburg agreed to pay for a jacket crown put in by the city's foremost dentist, Professor Doctor Pflüger. It lasted me until 1937 when the military introduced me to boxing.

All this was happening in the early days of the Third Reich. The rightwing veterans from World War I were cautiously optimistic that Hitler would succeed. The Nazis like "Old Bacon Roll" were throwing their weight around. Only Zindler kept his usual cool and encouraged discussion and dissent. I hated this school and I hated my inability to abstract myself from the raunchy insensitivity of many of my classmates. Now that Latin and English were more or less okay, Greek was indeed my undoing.

The summer vacation was spent in Bendesdorf where my poor mother had to cook upstairs on a makeshift basis. Nobody could expect her to cook downstairs in the kitchen where the flies had taken full control. The peasant was an unfortunate, unmarried weakling who was dominated by his unfortunate evil smelling mother and one sister. He had only one helper, an ex-con, who went through one STD after another, maybe purposely contracted, with my mother having to put up with two fighting teenagers in this mess. It was my idea of hell. Father came out some weekends; he could not come regularly, his business was falling apart. The State had monopolized all import and export.

Coming home from this ordeal, I was seething with rage. That very day a rosy cheeked boy hopped off his bike and started talking to me. He said his name was Hans and they had a boy's group called *Jungenschaft* which might interest me. "Or are you already organized somewhere?"

I had sampled the Free Corps of Young Nation, a very nationalistic bunch, and I had given up the Euthymia, a men and boys choir. My father had sent me to join this latter group, which was rehearsing downtown in a building which at some time served as city hall, at least 350 years old and was now in the hands of The Patriotic Society. This choir had a century old reputation; it even had performed for His Majesty, Kaiser Wilhelm II.

* ◆ • • ◆ • • ◆ •

With the help of KB, my academic fortunes improved; I passed into the next grade Easter 1933. The country under Hitler had changed almost overnight. There was law and order. No wonder. There was no more opposition and the propaganda over the radio and through the papers sounded optimistic. Most of the leftist politicians had disappeared across the border if they had a chance, otherwise they were now re-educated in concentration camps. Most of our Jewish classmates were gone. Speckroller must have had a special assignment to discipline our class. He was hitting hard with or without cause, frequently using collective punishment and draconian reprisals.

At home my poor mother was trying to keep the family running. Since we couldn't afford the seven-and-a-half room apartment, we had to move into a five room apartment on Mühlendamm about 1,000 yards away from our beloved canal. It was a humiliating experience. The entire move was carried out by volunteers from my mother's fundamentalist sect.

In the evening, Aunties Martha, Hannah and Frieda came all the way from their place down the river to start cleaning up and giving us a hand. I had never met them before, liked their spontaneous decision to become part of our family and disliked their loud laughter at anything or nothing. Martha came every night for quite some time to help my mother. All three of them worked at the telephone office and certainly represented a bit of fresh air in the atmosphere of my father's artificial elitism.

Late that evening I withdrew to our garrison. It was cold and wet and they were huddled around a very nice fire in the fireplace. I was greeted with warmth and sincerity, Hänschen (Hans) had told them apparently about my problems at home and at school. Two or three of them just nodded, smiling, while tuning their guitars, the others introduced themselves with mostly self-deprecating remarks to show their solidarity. The youngest one, twelve years old, and said he had heard about me, "So you have confirmation class with my sister? And your sister? Watch out for that gluttonous minister, he'll eat you into bankruptcy."

He was referring to my pastor Speckmann in the most disrespectful terms possible. This man belonged to those Lutheran pastors who had joined the "German Christians" soon after Hitler came to power. Hitler's lackeys, they were called by the other Protestant ministers because this had driven the church apart into two viciously warring factions. Most of us in the Wi-ju (Viking Youth) were disgusted with those thousands of Johnny-come-lately party members who had flocked into the Nazi party since early 1933, my own father included. Hypocrites and opportunists they were called when one used more civilized terms referring to them. Pretty soon the party had to stop accepting applications.

I was just as outspoken, I'm afraid, as the others. Father now had joined the party, his function being the dissemination of notices for the next meeting. These meetings took place every two weeks. They were merely alcoholic workshops in my opinion. Stuffing mailboxes with these notices up and down four or five story apartment buildings got to him; guess who ended up stuffing this garbage. I saw the various agendas in passing and kept wondering how one could spend the whole evening with a topic that one could easily exhaust in fifteen minutes. It wasn't until years later that I realized how important Father's political opportunism had been. His menial job in the bank adding sums of money from morning till night had one pre-condition, membership in the party.

My parents knew quite well that I had been accepted as JR's older brother since 1924 and influenced in a positive way by his father Pastor Remé, but they forced me to register with the Hitler's German Christians for confirmation classes just the same. I obeyed, firstly since I didn't have much choice and secondly I was sure there was no need to add insult to injury in light of my impending flunk. JR took his father's section; he was through with his Christian boarding school and intended to enroll in my Johanneum. My oldest sister took the same class, much to my chagrin. She wasn't doing too well in school either and was about to go into training as an assistant to a pediatric nurse.

I met Howard Beinhoff there, Lichtwarkschule student and St. George Boy Scout. His mother was a British half-Jewess and his dad was a well-known bookseller. Helga took the same class. We picked up where we had left off when I had seen her hobnobbing around at night with a party big-wig. So, with Howard and Helga, I had a good time after all. Howard made his school more and more interesting for me, since I certainly had no wish to stay where I was. I despised the two classes below us; their teachers were "Steel-helmet" chauvinists, members of the return soldier's league who helped Hitler gain power and still had dreams of the monarchy coming back to Germany.

By direct decree from Berlin all youth groups had to join up with the Hitler Youth, including even the YMCA and the Catholic Youth. This was now called the *Staatsjugend.* Saturday was from now on reserved for the activities of this immense organization. Only a very few young boys and girls managed to stay out of this first step into affiliation with the Nazi party. Rudi, our leader, was now in charge of a *Fähnlein,* about 120 boys in three platoons, and I was willy-nilly in charge of a *Jungenschaft,* twelve little boys between the age of nine and thirteen. We had weekly meetings in front of a fire, singing and planning the weekend activities. Most of the time we went northwest of Hamburg to an old peasant hut, which we had leased. If there wasn't room enough, we slept inside our Kote, a fold-up teepee with a comfortable fireplace in the center, a good place to sleep in summer or winter. The little boys had to take two-hour turns keeping an eye on the fire, which was a responsibility they found exciting.

The new uniform was a copy of our old youth group uniform; the Hitler Youth had copied our style. We had to wear a belt now with a shoulder strap and a little ceremonial dagger. It must have set German rearmament back to provide millions of these useless decorations for every boy between nine and eighteen years of age. There was one advantage, I had to wear this uniform for the confirmation. That was a relief, it was not our style to dress like a grown-up. I would have hated to wear one of those dark suits, never having worn long slacks in my life. The boys who did wear them looked as though mommy had bought the suit two sizes too big, something to eventually grow into.

Carola and I were not the only sister and brother act in our group, and my family was not the only one suddenly remembering that some of the younger children still had not been christened. Jutta and Rolf enjoyed becoming Christians in a mass christening along with a number of babies.

JR's confirmation must have been much more meaningful than ours. People talked in glowing terms about his father who seemed to be thriving on the controversy within the church.

JR himself was still giving his impressions of a school trip to Bayreuth where they were introduced to Hitler at the 1933 festival. I knew we would never hear the last of that one. Did I envy JR for having shaken Hitler's hand? I'm not sure. I was noticing a kind of aimlessness was showing up around me. Many people appeared to feel some uneasiness about the leadership. The behavior of the stormtroopers had become a nuisance at times, particularly when in some cities they were armed auxiliaries to the police. Reportedly, they were throwing their weight around, drinking too much and creating all kinds of embarrassments.

◆ • • ◆ • • ◆ •

Rudi invited the group to a camp around Pentacost. We camped not too far from our weekend hut in St. Dionys. We decided on our summer trek, how to finance it and plan the details. From June 15 to August 10, 1934, we proposed to live and travel 1,000 kilometers away from home, all the way down to Lake Constance and back. The plan was typed up and presented to the parents who, by and large, were rather impressed, though most may have had misgivings.

When the time came, saying goodbye to my parents was no easy matter. My mother was not at all convinced that we could sustain ourselves for seven weeks on our own, let alone travel. Father put a ten mark note in my backpack and I was astonished to see my stern tormentor showing tears in his eyes. It was like going off to the wars, or something equally dramatic when eventual return is much in doubt.

After a night at St. Dionys, we took the slow train to Marburg where we stayed in a student hostel. The next day we camped at Eder Lake, an artificial lake behind a newly constructed power dam in a very austere barren setting. The weather was so beautiful we decided to stay a few days swimming, sunbathing, cooking, eating, singing and sleeping. We made nice contacts with the local peasantry.

The next day we arrived at Frankfurt am Main. It was a short hop by train. We wore white shirts and our short black pants and created quite a stir wherever we went. This began on the main railway station where a portly matron exclaimed, "*Ach, ihr lieben Hitler bubbes.* Don't move. I'll get some ice cream." She did and hugged each one of us again with those unavoidable slobbery kisses.

Tickets for the open air performance of Schiller's *Wallenstein's Camp* were unavailable. We cruised around the city square looking for a break, because we really wanted to see this world famous show. These open air spectacles were a tremendous attraction for tourists. The most well-known in northern Germany was the Carl May Festival at Segeberg where Winnitou, the noble Apache chief, enjoyed a lifetime friendship with old Shatterhand. Open air spectacles sprang up all over the world. Even the Jewish refugees were putting them on in Los Angeles at the time directed by Max Reinhard, the most famous German director.

It was late in the afternoon and we still hadn't found tickets. All business on the city square ceased. The popular apple wine bars closed their doors. So, we finally decided to look for a private home and we found one in a central location and it allowed a perfect proscenium type view of the whole show. We found the lady of the house dressed up in an evening gown with more makeup than I had ever seen on a woman. She welcomed us with open arms and so did the other female members of her household. Slobbery kisses again, and quite a number of chocolate and ice cream treats.

We were allotted one window each for four or five of us in the second floor and had a perfect view of the show. During the intermission, I visited the room next door and talked to our leader Rudi. I found it interesting that this room had exactly the same furniture as ours: a bed, a couch, a washstand, etc., yet I had no awareness that this was a hotel. I went one room down the hall, which aroused my curiosity even more. When I pointed this out to Rudi, he took me aside and said, "Shut up, man. You are watching a classic German tragedy from the window of a house of ill repute." We both collapsed laughing. Later after the show we thanked our hostesses with a studied enthusiasm, which netted us some more slobbery kisses.

Out on the Römerberg all lights went up again, the apple wine bars reopened and so did all the other "businesses." On our way to the train station we were stopped by a heavily armed SS patrol. They asked for our IDs and told us to follow them, it was a matter of our own protection. At first we felt guilty because we did not wear the proper brown shirt, neither could we show any papers explaining our presence in Frankfurt. They marched us without explanation to a primary school and locked us into the gym where we were given some straw to sleep on, some SS rations and "coffee." The gym had a shower and rest rooms and we were told to stay there pending verification of our ID's from Hamburg. Around noon next day we were released, given huge amounts of rice and beans and dried peas to take with us.

Once we reached the main railway station we saw the headlines of the newspapers. It appeared that the government had in the last minute prevented a *Putsch* (insurrection) of Hitler's Storm Troopers led by Röhm. Hitler and the SS had arrested the SA leadership in Bavaria, brought them to Munich where they were summarily executed. There were lengthy descriptions purporting to give proof for the urgency of

Hitler's actions and repeated references to the fact that many of these leaders had been arrested in bed with a male companion.

Our hike to Heidelberg was unusually silent. Everybody was trying to digest the news. As a matter of fact, we had never had a discussion on homosexuality or on the very severe punishment the courts were meting out for that offense, and particularly involving a minor. At that moment, we did not know much about this phenomenon apart from having heard graphic language used by rough talking schoolmates. We could not make any connection between the almost military leadership of the stormtroopers and the sexual allegations that were inferred in the papers. In fact, the country was kept in the dark for weeks before Hitler made a long speech about it in July.

After a few days, our mood improved. We read the congratulatory telegrams and letters thanking Hitler for having saved the country all over again, including a wire from the President. That's all we had to go by at the time. Everybody seemed to be saying Hitler's timing was perfect.

We touched down Stuttgart and hiked to Badenweiler in the Black Forest where we enjoyed swimming in the thermal spa. It was only a few days after that when we were hiking through Freudenstadt that President Hindenburg died. Rudi said, "Oh no, not another election." But there weren't any elections. Hitler made himself Supreme Leader and Commander in Chief of the Army. We learned that the loyalty oath was not directed towards the constitution any more, but on the person of Adolph Hitler. Another fundamental change in so short a time without explanation or public participation. As young as we were, we were aware that this was just another logical step towards *Gleichschaltung* (absolute control).

So much for our summer trek. It had been upstaged by the Röhm affair and the death of President von Hindenburg. We did not see each other for a number of days afterwards, but the following weekend one of the boys called a meeting and charged Rudi, our leader, with some sex abuse during our journey. We, the full membership of the group including the platoon leaders, about nineteen all told, had a hearing in the garrison which lasted until way past midnight in front of a roaring fire. The alleged honor-violator, Rudi, displayed such a callousness in admitting even more well planned attempts to seduce youngsters, I felt like throwing up just listening to him.

I did not say much at all during the hearing, half the time I did not have a clue what this was all about. Even after Hänschen and I had had this go-around with the legal aspects of Paragraph 175 of the Penal Code, which pertains to homosexuality. Some of Rudi's victims were visibly agonized by the shamefulness and the humiliation of this procedure. Only "Uncouth" Willy put up a defiant stance, even aggravating the suffering of the younger ones. Willy had set this inquiry into motion by openly bragging about his relationship with Rudi. He and Rudi were ejected from the group by unanimous vote. Hänschen and I went home in a mood of utter dejection because we realized that this would never be the same group again. It seemed as though all friendship had lost its innocence and the new leaders, Kurt and Hank, just wouldn't have what it might take to repair the damage done.

Since the youth group time in Worpswede was such a bust, I resigned myself to take a look at the architecture of Bremen's Bötcherstrasse. We were allowed to spend some time with friends or relatives while we were there, so Karlchen and I took the tram to Bremen-Horn. My sister Carola and friends were there visiting her friend Putti's "villa," which turned out to be a stately mansion.

Putti and I met that evening and had supper near the ancient city hall. I was not the only one given the permission to go out by myself, many of us had friends or relatives in Bremen. Putti sat down across the table and thanked me over and over for my gallant bicycle ride to JR's father just to bail her out. She said that my sacrifice was really for naught, her mother's illness was nothing to be alarmed about. Her mother had been livid with anger because the local party boss was after her religious cult and the prophet, a certain Mr. White. I heard to my amazement that Mr. White cured people with the famous North German white cheese called *quark*. Apparently, Putti's mother was drummed out of the Nazi Women's League in spite of her fierce anti-Semitic zeal. Anything her husband had ever done to her was now qualified by her as typically Jewish and criminal. Putti thought it was rather a mouthful, considering her father was only a half-Jew.

My guest returned some of the money to me over my protestations. "A wasted journey," she said, "But I feel very close to you now so that is a gain for me." I don't know whether I blushed or not, but I suddenly became conscious she was dressed like a lady and I was looking down on my bare dirty suntanned hairy legs, my dirty Youth Movement shorts, my dirty hiking boots and my dirty fingernails as well. At that moment I wanted so much to be a man of the world, but here I was an overgrown boy. Putti took both of my hands into hers and we just looked at each other for a few seconds. I became so uncomfortable that I suddenly remembered that it was time to say goodbye. "The rules of Youth Hostels are very strict, you know," I said. She nodded her awareness of the time and we walked together to the tram stop. We had a somewhat awkward goodbye hug as her tram approached and I went home feeling wonderful.

The next day we had one more hike, which ended up in Cuxhaven, a town on the mouth of the Elbe River. Karlchen and I were allowed to make a detour through Sahlenburg to see the Hitler Youth summer camp under construction. We ran into Clüver who was rather taken aback by the sight of us, our long hair and the free-youth uniform. We exchanged a few words about the camp and his parting shot to me was, "Just you get here. We'll straighten you out, you bum." I was sure he wasn't joking, he was really shocked by our *wandervogel* appearance and Karlchen's guitar didn't help much either.

The class went home by train. I had to get ready for camp almost immediately. The first transport of our juvenile charges left the following Saturday. Hundreds of kids, total strangers, saying goodbye to anxious parents who had brought their little ones to the ship and waved to them with tears in their eyes.

At camp we were given a tent number, some hardtack and water. I was in charge of twelve boys in a brand-new round tent and the floor was covered with straw almost a foot deep. The next morning, I noticed a faint but distinctly unpleasant smell. There wasn't time to look into this because the loudspeaker was blaring, "Fall in." Somebody made a big speech, which was not audible in our corner. The camp flag was hoisted and we had earned our breakfast, which consisted of lumpy porridge and milk offered in steel bowls. Then we had to fall in again for some opening ceremony and listen to more speeches by visiting dignitaries. The way our platoon had to line up, we had the sun right in our eyes, and by lunch time I had some beastly cases of sunburn on my hands.

On the following night, one of my charges woke me up to whisper that he had just had an accident. That was all I needed after this dreadful first day. The little tyke volunteered the information that this happened to him rather often, a problem which was driving his parents to distraction. It appeared he had been whipped if he did not report the accident immediately. He must have thought that he would diminish the consequences if he immediately told me, even to wake me up in the middle of night for it. We took out the damp straw guided more by feel than by sight, my issued flashlight wasn't worth much anyway. We found some fresh straw a few yards away and he tried to get back to sleep.

I went outside and wiped my hands in the damp grass and for the first time noticed that it actually was the moment the sun was getting ready to come up. There it was behind Cuxhaven, it very slowly rose over the horizon. Masses of fog were creeping up to our camp from the ocean and now below the slowly rising sun there was a morning mist of sorts. Only the shakes of the windmills were visible above it, and this mist turned crimson, and then before my very eyes changed from crimson to reddish gold, and behind that the sun appeared translucent. I was just standing there overwhelmed by this pageantry of color in a place which is commonly referred to as the "boring flat low country." I'd forgotten I was out there to get rid of the smell from my hands and during this short moment I had lost sight of the drudgery I was in for the next five weeks as a glorified babysitter with these "toddlers."

Thank goodness Clüver, during the subsequent weeks, mellowed down considerably and discarded his plans for a paramilitary summer camp. We slipped to physical education and games. I don't think I could take credit for this change, but once I grasped what an assortment of little boys we had to accommodate I certainly used my personal stand-ing with him to make him see what we were up against. The boot camp went out except for a few exercises in marching which possibly was not a waste of time. Many youngsters never had learned any kind of coordination and had no feeling for rhythm. We had them try to guess distances. I didn't think that was entirely useless either, but any attempt to turn the camp to a parade ground would have been bound to fail.

The overkill and chicanery and humiliations of that previous camp at Malente were still fresh on my mind.

In the meantime, my tent smelled awful. My young bedwetting friend apparently was not the only one. I asked for fresh straw so frequently during the first and second class of boys that Clüver, having heard about this, half-seriously blamed the bladder problems of my kids on my liberal fine arts, Free Youth Movement background. He ordered a refresher course for the camp personnel, again run by frustrated ex-army sergeants in Hitler Youth uniform.

When the camp was over we were rewarded, the personnel that is, with a barge trip to Helgoland, the island which gave this bay of the North Sea its name. We spent our hard-earned money to buy duty-free chocolates and sweets. Some even bought alcohol for their parents. The day we were there, the island had received two boatloads of retired World War I sailors. We met them everywhere, they were mostly in various stages of inebriation. I admit we made fun of their monarchistic speeches and songs and their parading on the main promenade. Thirty-five or forty of us parodied these old sailors whenever we had an audience by our goose-stepping with the song *Wir wollen unseren guten alten Kaiser wiederhaben* (We would like to have our good old emperor back).

* ◆ • • ◆ • • ◆ •

The remainder of the year 1935 was spent in almost perfect isolation as far as my family was concerned. Father was busy with his digestive problems, he left me alone except maybe for the odd errand for the Nazi party. He had trouble moving his weight up and down those staircases to slip notification messages into mail boxes. I hated this chore, but turned it into a physical workout, taking double steps on the way up and jumping two or three on my way down.

Mother very slowly regained strength after her ordeal in the psych ward. She was still quite sure that Hitler would turn out to be the messiah of the German people. These "second coming" religious fantasies alienated her fellow believers and diminished the support that the membership in this fundamentalist cult had been for her. She could not do a thing with my sudden interest in the humanities. A high school with such a strong orientation towards fine arts puzzled her; however, she was very impressed with the three weekly meetings I had with Ilka and Anne to do homework together. We met in turn at each other's apartments and even had some refreshments and some tea together. My mother had never seen me so studious.

My old man, on the other side, still suspected foul play, so whenever he happened to be at home he just put his big head into the door every once in a while checking on us. The girls and I wondered what he might be afraid to find. A juvenile *ménage à trois*? Since neither Ilka's nor Anne's father showed this kind of interest, the two girls found this situation amusing.

My relationship with Jutta and Rolf was fine, now that Carola was out of the house. Nothing was left of our *Jungenschaft*, they had a fantastic hike along the Baltic Sea while I was sweating it out with my bedwetting mama's boys at summer camp. Since my friends had taken the trip to the Baltic Sea without authorization and left their Hitler Youth charges in Hamburg, they were drummed out of the Hitler Youth.

We all met at the Hitler Youth Players in Uhlenhorst. The leader was the son of our neighbors; his nick-name was Taa and it became an amalgamation of the *Jungenschaft* and Taa's group, which abounded with talent for show business.

There was a boy in acting school called Bux,[3] who proposed to do *Journey's End*, the pacifistic play by R. C. Sherriff. We had seen the

---

3. Bux died in Russia. Steffan has retired as one of the leading actors of the Hamburg scene.

German version at Thalia d'Arte and enjoyed the movie with Conrad Veidt. We thought this was the most articulate dramatic testimonial regarding the futility and barbarism of war by showing how the best young men are killed first. The message and development of character, we found overwhelming.

How could eighteen-year-old boys play World War I Tommies? Simple. Those men in the trenches in Flanders by and large were not too much older. Only three characters could be considered mature in this play. We were lucky, we found a somewhat beefy postal clerk for the part of Potter. It was almost type casting. We found a pompous elitist high school senior for the part of the colonel and the biggest surprise, JR, of all people, became Osborne. He was sounding like the German dub for Franchot Tone from the first rehearsal all through the production. Bux played the lead Captain Stanhope, and he persuaded Manfred Steffan to play Lt. Hibbard, the officer who tries to weasel out. The scene between Bux and Steffan was one of the high points of the show.

They asked me to do two parts: the captain to be relieved by Stanhope's company at the outset of the play and the Cockney sergeant major later on. The rehearsals were hard work. Bux was an excellent director and I was looking forward night after night, whether I was personally involved or not, to these meetings.

JR and I met privately every day in his big room in the attic and went through his part all through the play, but concentrating mainly on scene one. Even when we met at school, we fell into our dialogue week after week. No wonder he was never able to shed the name "Osborne." Nobody, not even Tutta, his wife-to-be, called him anything else to this very day.

We staged the show in the Congregational Hall of the Eppendorf Church. It was a red brick building in the style of the twenties situated across the street from the church proper. The Eppendorf Church is one of the oldest in Northern Germany built in 1600. The rent was low; we were, after all, Hitler Youth Players, but we could get the hall only for two nights. That meant we were still constructing the set during our one and only full dress rehearsal on our stage. The set was a masterpiece of improvisation in mostly dim lights. This was believable since the action took place in a British dugout in Flanders. Daylight was only visible through a small crack showing the edge of the parapet, barbed wire and the sky.

JR and I had the task of introducing the place, the situation and the leading man, Captain Stanhope, and this disposition of the play had to be done with a dialogue of about twelve pages of the script, hence we had rehearsed it with so much concentration, both neglecting school work in the process. Neither he nor I had ever been in a full length play before, let alone opened a play.

It was a cold and wet December when our work of love was shown. Everything was primitive - the sound effects, the lighting and the set. But when the curtain came down on the empty stage at the end, empty except for the body of the young Lt. Raleigh, the audience just sat there silently as if devoid of sensation or feeling and then silently they went out deep in thought. We were hugging each other triumphantly behind the curtain, celebrating this unexpected reaction of the audience, as something to be treasured for life. For days afterwards, we received letters and phone calls expressing how moving an experience this had been, improvisation and imperfection and all.

The Nazi party newspaper had a short paragraph two days later on page sixteen describing this show as not quite suitable for the Hitler Youth.[4]

---

4. When I translated the play in 1947 in the POW camp in Egypt, I still knew almost all the lines. We did not do the show, however, in spite of the urging of our British director because my fellow officers wanted to glorify heroism and ignore the message of the author.

CHAPTER II

"9TH COMPANY, 3RD BATTALION, (RANGER BATTALION) Infantry Regiment 6" was printed on my draft papers, which I took out once I detrained Saturday, October 10, 1936. Ratzeburg was so out of the way that there was not a direct train connection from Hamburg. I had to change in Büchen or go all the way north to Lübeck on the Baltic Sea to get there. What in the world possessed me to volunteer to this dreamy little town on the border between two northern German states? I could have had any number of army units right in or close to my home town had I tried.

Carrying my cheap suitcase half-filled with books and toiletries, I walked three-and-a-half kilometers across town to get to the barracks. They were on a hill overlooking the town and the lake. Every two or three hundred meters I had to stop and change hands. I felt sure that the length of my arms gained considerably, or maybe I was shrinking. It was hot. Why had I not joined one of those motorized companies around Hamburg? They would have picked me up at the subway station. What a fool I was!

I ignored the medieval city and its quaint little side streets while I was walking and contemplating my situation, thinking back on the last six months in the Labor Service (R.A.D.). The other young men I would be with would be the second group to be called up to do their half year in the Labor Service. My situation was different from theirs, in as much as I had applied for a leadership career in the R.A.D. and a training program for the cultural section attached to the headquarter of the service. These trainees were supposed to prepare to be instructors in speech chorus, acting, writing, and radio activities at the labor camp level. A great extent of it would be devoted to propaganda. I had found out about this when a Labor Service man had visited our Hamburg radio station and had reacted favorably to a radio play which, in the framework of the Hitler Youth, we had written and produced ourselves.

At this point on this muggy Saturday, I wasn't sure I had made the right decision to go back to the R.A.D. because my half year in Silesia from April to September 1936 had been a disillusioning beastly experience. The R.A.D., like everything else in this Third Reich, had to mushroom out of nothing, as it were. Since July 1935, every young man had to work for six months in this labor service organization, after that he had to serve one year in the army.

The propaganda of the party waxed idealistically that every boy in Germany should work with his hands and thus learn respect for the working man. It was a kind of voluntary Job Corps as now in the United States. The logistics problems were immense. It had to provide organization, shelter and leadership for between three and four hundred thousand boys with very little time to train adequate instructors.

The noncoms we had in Silesia were mostly people who had been unemployed for some time, some of them were ex-soldiers from World War I, with or without actual war experience. The group leaders I experienced were rather uneducated men between 25 and 30 years of age who knew almost as little as we did in technical respects and certainly had only a rough idea of what it meant to run a squad of fifteen workers. Most of the officers were inexperienced in handling young men and not articulate enough to reach them. It was my first experience with group activities in a limited environment, crammed living quarters, bad food and a group of boys three or four years older than I was. I certainly had not expected to end up in this dingy little camp with nothing more constructive to do than to improve a potential field of fire by pulling grass and weeds and leveling or raising the ground. We also added soil and sod to camouflage the structure of some shoddily built bunkers along the River Oder facing Poland.

Did we gain respect for the working man's labors? Maybe some of us did, but mostly we learned how to get around working hard by cheating or faking in many ways. When the supervisor was absent, so was the hard work. I was younger than most of my buddies. To some of them, I was suspect since I was a volunteer. They could not understand how someone would want to make this tedium a career. My goal to learn a different kind of trade in the cultural section under a certain Dr. Decker did not impress those men either.

I wasn't sure, particularly after our trip to the Party Rally at Nuremberg where the shortcomings of the R.A.D. leadership were most glaringly exposed. The long hike from the camp to the field where we paraded for Hitler was made bearable by the friendly reception from the populace of the town and the show in the vast arena certainly was impressive. When those 30,000 glistening spades came down on the grass in the stadium, the ground shook. Later eyewitnesses from the stands talked to us and expressed their enthusiasm for the powerful spectacle of the organized, sun-tanned healthy young people they had just seen.

The celebration after this show in our camp deteriorated very fast into a bawdy alcoholic orgy, where many of our noncoms and some people in commanding positions showed themselves to be disrespectful of the personal dignity of the boys. Many of these returned veterans were now in leading positions in the R.A.D. Some bragged about their life as gauchos in Argentina repeating themselves over and over in their drunken stupor. Others tried to proposition some of the boys and were badly bloodied by the intended partner. We found some of them the next morning in the gutter. We were all disgusted.

● ◆ ● ● ◆ ● ● ◆ ●

Later, I had a visit from my father who came from a neighboring camp where the party functionaries were housed and we had a short opportunity to talk. It was then I decided to volunteer to do my one year stint in Ratzeburg, my father's former garrison. He was surprised and pleased. For one short minute, I had the feeling I had done the right thing by him. After my commissioning in the fall of 1938, when I discovered a letter to my father from the Company Commander, I was furious.

> Ratzeburg, May 1, 1936
> R. U. Rodust
> Captain and Company Commander
> 9th Company, Infantry Regiment 6
>
> Dear Mr. Panny:
> The news that your son has been accepted as an officer candidate has pleased me very much.
> I'm glad, furthermore, that your son has found his true vocation, for he is a born soldier. The ethical strength of his character which renders him incapable of wrong doing and at the same time does not allow him to tolerate baseness or evil. His intellectual and psychological alertness and his

physical control will surely lead him through a successful career as an officer.

I (had to) remind him that as in any profession there sometimes would be stressful periods when one has to summon all of one's strength to persevere.

This letter confirmed my worst suspicions. When I had seen Captain Rodust the last time before leaving for 5th company at Lübeck, the Company Commander jovially had mentioned the fact that there had been communication by letter between himself and my father ever since fall of 1936. I must have had trouble hiding my surprise and indignation at that moment for he blushed and was quite ill at ease for the remainder of our conversation. He wished me well for my new assignment.

Afterwards I wondered why he seemed embarrassed. Did he expect me to be overjoyed at his indiscretion? Had he by chance communicated with any other parents for a reason other than in the case of accident or human loss? Come to think of it, my father had hardly ever bothered to talk to my teachers at school. I thought he was way out of line addressing my company commander behind my back, as it were. I was eighteen, for chrissakes, old enough to be a soldier, to risk my neck in the line of duty. I had picked Ratzeburg as boot camp to please him, certainly not to encourage him to meddle. In retrospect, it was a good thing I did not see Rodust's sanctimonious epistle until 1938. I would have been even madder.

◆ • • ◆ • • ◆ •

Learning to be a soldier is a humiliating, exhausting experience particularly in the German army of the time where there was a tremendous shortage of experienced instructors. Having had quite a foretaste of what was to come in the Hitler Youth Summer Camp and in the

Labor Service, I did not suffer quite as much as most of my peers. It was bad, though, even considering the hectic pace of expansion, from 100,000 in 1935 to 1,400,000 in 1939. We only had a limited number of noncoms in our company and not even one officer, outside of the Company Commander who, of course, had been reactivated of late and looked and acted like a high school teacher.

For anyone who had seen six months in the Labor Service, on the other hand, the army was a haven with a smoothly running organization with much better nutrition and health care. However, there was the usual bureaucratic bungling that goes with any army. Just after they had completed the building of a four-story ordinance silo, they discovered it was meant for Rendsburg not Ratzeburg.

Our building was brand-new too. It even had central heating and a parquet floor. Flooring like that may be pleasing to look at, but when it is trampled by wet and muddy hobnailed boots all week it was hard work to make it like new for Saturday when the whole house was readied for inspection. We were given pieces of metal webbing to scrape the dirt and last week's wax off. How long this parquet floor would last under these conditions was a question I didn't have to consider. All I had to do was scrape the hell out of it.

Our second story room was big and had four windows facing west, but it wasn't big enough for half our squad, eight men. There were double bunks and a huge locker for each recruit. The corporal in charge had a single bed in the corner. The table was barely big enough to allow all of us to eat breakfast and dinner.

Only the hot mid-day meal was served in the mess hall. It invariably consisted of some kind of soup served in a big metal bowl including split peas, lentils, vegetables, lots of potatoes and, of course, cabbage along with some meat of one kind or another and stretched with grains of all kinds. The breakfast and evening rations were handed out every afternoon and we stored this food stuff in our locker - cut meats and fish and whatever, all without refrigeration. Every night there was room and locker inspection and each of us had to develop some way of storing food stuff as neatly as possible. Some people played it safe and ate the stuff right away. On the table, where we had been cleaning our guns in the morning, each ration was cut in so and so many parts by the soldier on duty.

Our room was lucky in having the corporal Eilers, a student of divinity. At least he never pulled rank or did anything to increase the pressure of boot camp life. There were two chaps like myself who had finished nine years of schooling, Rolf from Lübeck and Jupp from Cologne. The others had left school at the age of fourteen and entered the trade school of their choosing.

Kosmalla, third-generation son of a Polish miner, quickly became the center of attention. I still find it difficult to describe him. He was at least six-feet-five-inches tall, practically no shoulders, very long arms, huge hands, two left thumbs and two left feet. He could read, but had trouble writing and was immediately singled out by all the noncoms. Bott, who grew up in a big peasant family close to Ratzeburg, was very shy and non-communicative. Schang came from the Belgian border from probably Walloonish parents - dark complexion, black hair, black eyes. We could hardly communicate with him because he could not speak high German. Bart came from the Rheinland as well. When the two of them talked it was like hearing a foreign language. If it hadn't been for Jupp from Cologne, we would have had to have an interpreter.

I'm afraid everyone was smoking except Kosmalla. Everyone was right handed except Kosmalla. Everyone could write, swim, march in step and have a family photo in their locker, except Kosmalla. From the beginning, this youth aroused my interest. After the first locker inspection when he was insulted by the noncom on duty concerning his sexual preference, meaning the lack of a female photo, he came to me.

"This is terrible. Panny, you don't have a spare photo do you? I don't want to go through this again."

It was immediately clear to me that all his life he had been made the butt of ridicule and I was happy to oblige him. This did not start a friendship since we had very little to talk about, but I certainly felt protective about him from the beginning.

The more unskilled and uneducated the noncoms were, the more often they pounced on Kosmalla. It became immediately clear that collective punishment was the accepted procedure. Whenever somebody did not function as expected, the whole squad or platoon had to pay for it. As in any other army, *Hinlegen!* (Hit the ground!), initiated the next round of punishing exercises. When we were chased across the parade ground for short sprints and another *Hinlegen!* or even crawling for variety's sake more often than not Kosmalla's inadequacy had been the cause. This, of course, led to peer pressure and worse, recrimination by some of the recruits.

Watching Kosmalla trying to be a smart recruit drove the noncoms to despair. Quite involuntarily his whole performance may have looked like a clever satire of anything our instructors were trying to achieve. We all lost two weeks of weekend passes because Kosmalla broke up the audience when we were supposed to learn proper saluting while passing a noncom or an officer. We could not suppress our laughter, and people watching from a distance couldn't either, which infuriated the noncom even more. When called upon the carpet Kosmalla tried to look and be apologetic, but I could see this obsequious frozen grin on his face of sheer embarrassment which was often interpreted as sheer bullheadedness and even contempt. We were punished for his sake time and time again; there was bad blood in the group, even in the platoon.

After two months of this, I had reasons to talk to some of his tormentors and explain that Kosmalla was now becoming a nervous wreck. There were threats of "the holy ghost" which, as we were told, was a physical attack at night with beating and then tarring the victim with black shoe polish. Allegedly, this was an old army routine of self-help support by the group. Most boys in our room agreed that we should try to protect him, but when Eilers was in the hospital and I was on guard duty they came, all right, and in the ensuing fight made a terrible mess of our room.

After a long discussion between Eilers and myself about this situation somebody leaked my concerns to the platoon sergeant who gave me hell. I ended up on report at the company commander's office and Captain Rodust didn't exactly mince words in dressing me down. While he was at it, he asked who I thought I was with my constant questions about inefficiencies and wastefulness and my inquiry as to the practicality of wearing hobnailed jackboots for military purposes. He said somebody had reported me for emptying the dirt out of these buckets in much too conspicuous a manner during an exercise. He ended up saying he was satisfied I was doing my duty and congratulated me on becoming the M-1, that is to say the soldier who is carrying the machine gun of the squad.

◆ ◆ • • ◆ • • ◆ •

Schütze Eins, machine-gunner! You could say this new job description was my first advancement in the army. Unfortunately, I had paid for it with a rosy red scar on my nose -- angry red when I had been drinking or been out in cold weather. It was difficult to ignore in either case. In fact, so was my "hook" nose, scar or no scar. It was fitting that the description of my nose from then on became the identifying feature for my military ID in 1936 until my last German passport in 1984. To be exact, this was the first time I shed blood for the Fatherland, no easy feat in peacetime. I still find it difficult to describe how it happened. It was that silly.

In each squad there was a competition for this job. Everybody was going through a series of exercises, which were supposed to determine the most qualified man to handle the machine gun. Some of these had to do with handling the heavy weapon on an obstacle course. As the crowning effort the candidate had to run toward the imaginary enemy and throw the gun from his shoulder to the ground about six feet ahead of himself. He then had to fling himself after it, brace the butt against his right shoulder, and steady the frontal support firmly on the ground, all in one motion, as it were. He was now ready to fire, provided that gunner number two was around to feed the necessary ammunition from his ammo bandolier. Needless to say, without number two being there, opening his trusty ammo box and feeding the ammo into the machine gun, the whole exercise is futile.

The all-important step is the cocking of the hammer by pulling a metal knob with a triangular blade on top. I have never found out what the function of this blade was. Nevertheless, it was sticking up sharply when my turn came. In my enthusiasm, I must have fallen into this useless piece of decoration face first. The blade neatly divided the tip of my nose into two halves. It was not a very deep cut, though a rather bloody one. It took six stitches to make my nose one again. For ten days I was not allowed outside and had to sit holding my "snorkle" over the central heating radiator near the window. I could watch my buddies being chased around up and down the parade ground. The enjoyment of this spectacle was dimmed by my concern for my permanent appearance. I had resigned myself early on to become a character actor but a character actor with a cauliflower nose was another matter.

This machine gun 08-XYZ became the curse of my life. It was another leftover from World War I. It played a role in combat training only, never on the parade ground. After each use I had to clean it, oil it and put it away. Number two gunner and I had to practice taking it apart and reassembling it over and over. At all hours, in all kinds of weather and even blindfolded. The trick was to put it back together without having some surplus nuts or bolts in your hand.

For the almost daily war games the platoon was chased up and down the very hilly countryside and, more often than not, the weight and the bulkiness of the gun became unbearable even when number two and I would take turns carrying it. Schroeder and I hit the proverbial wall many times in any given week. The moment when you have reached the end of your tether and are ready to give up and collapse, when every fiber of your being is stretched to the physical limit, the army maintained that this was the moment of weakness to be overcome. We had to defeat this. They called it *Der Innere Schweinehund*, the inner "pigsdog." What an insult to pigs and/or dogs, I always thought; but then *Schweinehund* was a derogatory term as readily used as s.o.b. in English. It was a constant testing of our human tenacity, driving us to the edge of our physical and psychological limits.

I still shudder remembering the bulky weight of this monster, particularly when the cooling chamber was filled with water. Many times I felt like tossing it into the ditch and giving up. On the plus side, when moving without enemy contact the MG was loaded on our horse drawn battle wagon, another museum piece from World War I. In this situation neither Schroeder nor I had to carry a rifle, just the standard OA pistol on our belt. Those were rare exercises. Most often our training situations assumed possible enemy contact. I remember only a few marches when the ordinary riflemen envied Schroeder and myself.

◆ ◦ ◦ ◆ ◦ ◦ ◆ ◦

I did not see much of Ratzeburg. On occasional walks I might have a cup of coffee and some pastry at the coffee house on the lake. The cashier was an attractive girl who smiled back now and again in a manner I took to be inviting; but then, I told myself that, surely, such a good-looking girl would have a steady relationship. Furthermore, she wouldn't want to bother with a one year recruit. I was proven right the first time I was on guard duty. At 1:00 a.m., I stood at the entrance of the military compound. Out of the fog I saw her approaching on the arm of a uniformed male. I grabbed my gun and yelled the German equivalent of "Who goes there?" By the time I had finished my inquiry I realized it was an officer.

"*Leutnant Schreiner, Sie Arschloch!*" (Lieutenant Schreiner, You asshole!)

Then they continued past me to his apartment. This was my first contact with a German officer outside of my company commander, the portly and fatherly Captain Rodust. I didn't particularly enjoy this exchange; however, my male vanity was still intact because I was sure she didn't recognize me. I was wearing a woolen frost-protecting mask over my face and, of course, I didn't report the incident. Schreiner and I had a good laugh remembering this incident when we were sharing a room in the military hospital later in the war, when he had been wounded in the Polish campaign and I had been bitten in the thumb by a lap dog.

◆ • • ◆ • • ◆ •

I much preferred those weekend passes to Hamburg and yet the ill-fitting smelly uniform of an army recruit did not make me think of pride as many of my comrades did. In Hamburg, I wore civilian garb, particularly when I went dancing with my sister or some friends. This was strictly forbidden and I almost got caught once by Petersen, the most obnoxious staff corporal in the battalion. We walked past each other on the Reeperbahn, in St. Pauli, renowned the world over for its "night life." If he did see me, he never reported it because at the point where we met he wasn't supposed to be either. He was in full uniform coming out of one of "those streets" strictly off limits to soldiers and sailors.

Come to think of it, Captain Rodust would have had to eat his sanctimonious pronouncements about my "flawless" character and my inability to be part of anything base. Had Corporal Petersen reported me, I would have been in big trouble. I was a recruit in civilian garb coming out of the narrow-offset opening, which separates the street from the normal traffic and obstructs the view from the outside. It still does. My date and I were just coming out of that brothel street from visiting Putti Winter, the former friend of my elder sister who had been a frequent weekend guest when they were on leave from their beekeeping apprenticeship in Bremen. Putti worked there on and off as a stand-in for a colleague. She called herself *Schwarze Katja* (Black Katya) and was making good money at the world's oldest profession. As a *mischling*, a half Jewess, she had given up her planned studies at the University and was hoping to make enough money to emigrate to relatives in France. Putti and I became very close friends until I was posted to Munich. Then we lost contact.

Apropo, my mother must have gone through my pockets while I was "advancing my sex education in St. Pauli," so to speak. She called JR for help and told him that I had condoms in my possession. She had reasons to believe I was seeing bad company. Could he please have a talk with her wayward son? When JR approached me, he was just as concerned in tone and manner as his father had been in dealing with delicate and grave matters of this kind. I was able to set him straight and have a good laugh on top of it. No German soldier was allowed to go on furlough without showing this "package" to the guard on duty. JR had to promise me that he would explain this to my mother. I did not have the heart to tell her myself and embarrass her further. She and my old man were going through a severe crisis at the time, from what I could gather. Besides JR needed this comeuppance. I had no idea he was still such a priggish ignoramus.

◆ ● ● ◆ ● ● ◆ ●

The exceptionally cold winter of 1936-37, the battalion did some war games in some freshly plowed fields southeast of Ratzeburg. It was the first time I was allowed to use the machine gun with dummy ammunition. Schroeder and I found out what it was like to operate this monster in temperatures below freezing. If we touched parts of the gun, which were made of steel our skin became stuck. It was an exhausting experience, particularly because it took hours of us having to wait lying flat on the ground, unable to increase our circulation by motion of any kind. We did all right, at least we were not singled out for having done anything foolish afterwards.

During this post-exercise critique, which lasted for hours or so it felt, Captain von Salviati of our machine gun company drew me into a conversation. I was flattered because I knew he was revered by his soldiers as an officer with a tremendous sense of humor who on occasion would generously overlook a given regulation when there were no serious consequences involved. It was said that he was related to the royal house of Hohenzollern as the brother-in-law of the former crown prince. Stories about him elevated the man to something larger than life, highly decorated in World War I and still wearing the huge steel helmet worn by the German army in those days. Some claimed he had detonated hand grenades by pulling the trigger then balancing the weapon on top of this helmet on his head to demonstrate that the hand grenade was nothing to be afraid of when handled with "discretion."

After introducing himself he asked me, "You're the man who split his nose, aren't you?"

"Yes, sir," I replied.

"Keep it warm, man, keep it warm."

"I will, sir."

"Had your first guard duty the other day, didn't you?"

"Yes, sir." I looked him straight in the eye while my mind was on a quick fishing expedition. How on earth would he have known about something so routine and to him trivial. I may have looked down and have seen his slightly bowed legs which distinguish horsemen from ordinary mortals, to my mind, the same legs I had noticed on Lt. Schreiner whenever I had seen him. Machine gun company had lots of horses so these chaps always wore the most fashionable riding boots and spurs. I immediately concluded it must have been Schreiner who had reported our early morning confrontation. I may have blushed, but then looked Salviati straight in the face and was glad to see that he nodded, then changed the subject.

"Tried out your little machine gun today, did you?"

"Yes, sir."

Was I to understand that he knew and that he did not find fault with my not reporting the incident? I was still uneasy when he suddenly launched into a far more serious discussion, namely the impending expansion of the army, the sudden switch from one year to two year service requirement and the dire need of noncoms and officers.

"I understand you plan to go back to the Labor Service?"

"Yes, sir. I was hoping to get accepted in Dr. Decker's Culture and Propaganda Section, which would include voice and stagecraft training."

"Did you ever consider becoming a regular officer?"

"Yes, sir, but I left school early and don't have the necessary qualifications."

"That's all right, Panny. The army would make exceptions in cases such as yours. I understand you have been in the Youth Movement and in the Hitler Youth."

"I have, sir."

"I'm just bringing this up because you might want to think about staying in the army as an alternative. I know for a fact that Germany is in for a rough going as you can imagine and I think people like you would be much better off with us. Think about it."

"Yes, sir. Thank you, sir."

I was momentarily so overcome by this unexpected suggestion that I forgot why I was trembling. Was it because it was cold or the emotional impact of having been singled out with this flattering attention? Salviati had hinted at some personal knowledge of serious developments. He didn't specify what he knew, but there were rumors German soldiers were involved in the civil war in Spain at that time and it was well-known that Mussolini had sent some Italian volunteers as well. Hitler had made a solemn declaration of breaking with the Treaty of Versailles and announced a speed-up of rearming Germany in light of the French-Russian liaison, which, according to Hitler, was a grave threat to Germany.

•◆••◆••◆•

I spent all weekend ruminating. The half-year in the Labor Service had left me disillusioned. There was no guarantee that I would be accepted when my stint in the army, which was now two years instead of one, would be over. All I had was an oral commitment by some higher-up official in the Labor Service offered during the party rally in Nuremberg and given in a slightly alcoholic state. I had his name and his address, but he didn't know me at all.

How serious was I in my conviction that the stage should be my vocation in life? I had switched two years ago at age sixteen from the childhood militaristic preoccupation with JR to the free and easy ways of the Youth Movement. Could someone like myself having gone through the last two years of the liberal arts almost *avant garde* pacifist experiment of my high school, now change back to JR's world of the military?

Was I about to do exactly what I had objected to in my father choices all these years? Had I become an opportunist just like him? My father had joined the Nazi party because he had to figure out some way to support his family. He had lost his viability in business since the Third Reich took over all import and exports to become a state monopoly. He had never espoused the Nazi doctrine since he had a moderately conservative outlook connected with his business orientation. I felt he had compromised himself by joining the party in March 1933, and he didn't even believe in what they were saying. I had been particularly incensed when he gave me from time to time bundles of notes, which he was to carry to the party members he was responsible for. By chance I had found out he was accepted at the German State Bank under the condition that he joined the party. At the time huge numbers of people had applied to join the Nazis. The public at large made fun of them by calling them *Märzgefallenen* (The people who succumbed in March). In January Hitler had come to power, by March such people were trying to get on the bandwagon. After my father and I had our little talk during the Party Rally in Nuremberg, when I had decided to please him by going to Ratzeburg, I had meant this to be a gesture of my remorse over my being so judgmental at his opportunism, without knowing exactly why he had joined. These thoughts were with me during the train ride to Hamburg.

❖ •• ❖ •• ❖ •

I did not talk to my parents. I went straight to my former teacher Alice Pollitz. We drank Madeira until 2:30 a.m. and she encouraged me to drop my qualms and consider this option seriously. She was concerned about the political situation in the world, but like anybody else in Germany had come to respect Hitler by his resolving a number of crises in Germany without resorting to violence. She told me how impressed her friends in America had been with the new Germany when they were interviewed upon returning from the Olympic Games. The thought pleased her very much that I might have a chance of a responsible steady position, even though I had left her class prematurely and had no qualifications whatsoever. She couldn't refrain from teasing me saying that she was sure the army would see to it that I would come down from my high horse, figuratively speaking.

The following Monday I was summoned to Captain Rodust. As usual I kept asking myself what have I done now, but I was mildly confident he would bring up the proposal that Salviati had mentioned. I didn't ask for time to think it over. I just said, "Yes, thank you, sir."

The barracks at Lübeck, at least the ones of the 2nd Battalion, 5th Company, IR 6th, had seen better days under Emperor Wilhelm 1st and Wilhelm 2nd. In other words, they should have been under the protection of historic monuments, particularly as far as plumbing and electricity was concerned. Here in 1937, we were crammed twelve men in one room. It was nauseatingly tight. Coming into this squad as a potential officer candidate was an awkward position to be in. It was like joining the Ku Klux Klan while you were a card-carrying member of the ACLU. My roommates had still not quite adjusted to the fact that they had to spend an additional second year of service in these crummy conditions. I felt just as welcome in this role as I had felt as a volunteer in the Labor Service.

My bunk buddy (he had the upper bed) fortunately took me off the hook and started to shield me. He was a huge steel worker from Sudetenland, formerly a Czechoslovakian citizen. He was so glad to have someone close who could identify with his predicament. Zepp had to flee the Czech authorities under indictment as a "Nazi rabble-rouser." He was longing to go back to his people across the border, even to his bone-crushing job. My limited knowledge of the historical and political situation in Bohemia (northwestern Czechoslovakia) must have touched him. The other men in the squad had not taken much interest in him because the word refugee meant very little to them. With him I found myself blessed with a bodyguard of sorts, a bodyguard with a language problem. He had never been allowed to properly learn his German mother tongue and had been the butt of some jokes among the platoon.

I had a second surprise, my advisor, Lt. Becker. He was in charge of the officer candidates, class of '37. He just happened to be born in the same hamlet in China as myself and had returned with the same troop ship named Antilochus as my family did. He encouraged me to phone Fabers, another family from Kuling and friends of my parents. The daughters Alice and Hertha were born over there, Beate and her brother Alfred in Hamburg; they too were repatriated on the Antilochus. Becker, a balding intellectual with very expensive taste in art and cuisine, took me under his wing. He even claimed to have met me in my pram in Kuling. His mother had taken him to a tea arranged by the ladies auxiliary where the knitting of warm woolen socks for the German prisoners of war from Tsing Tao was organized. He was six at the time, he continued, and he remembered how my older sister Carola had constantly tried to cover the baby's face, my face, with an unfolded diaper, a clean one, mind you. He himself had not had much contact with the Fabers. Mr. Faber was too chauvinistic, too patriotic for him, too boorish in his display of an anti-Semitic Nazi follower. This, Becker considered, was a high wire act in light of the fact that Mr. Faber was half-Jewish himself.

The company was run by Captain von Wangenheim who was drunk or close to it, rather frequently, by afternoon. His specialty was coming back into the garrison by 1 or 2 a.m. and staging company roll calls with highly unpleasant field exercises to follow; or, as unwelcome, phony roll calls, "standing to" for endless minutes in full battle dress and then being chased back to bed. That first week he just loved to do marching drills with the whole company in the hot mid-day sun, yelling at us from horseback. This was one of my first impressions I registered as a sample of man's inhumanity to man.

Suddenly, I was told we were to have a big parade of all the military units in the whole Lübeck garrison in honor of Hitler's birthday. Our captain tormented us, including our two lieutenants, by rehearsing a march-past at company level, all three platoons in line, only to find out that the parade on April 20 was done on the platoon level, that is, the platoons following one another rather than trying to keep three straight lines of 150 men. We survived it, but I have a photo that shows glaring deficiencies. We never saw Von Wangenheim on his horse again, thank god! He saw himself ahead of his company in nineteenth century fashion and he had to be disappointed.

The eleven officer candidates did not represent a homogeneous selection. Lanky von Blomberg couldn't even ride a bicycle, he had to compete with Sergeant Steuer, ten years our senior, a former candidate of jurisprudence with many scars on his face to show for his membership in one of those dueling fraternities. By now he denounced that elitist leftover from the nineteenth century having made the switch to the Nazi student group, which was instrumental in the burning of perfectly good books early on. Some choice! Becker told me to ignore my educational handicap, but to hit the books whenever I could find a chance.

Röhrssen and I became friends. He was from a patrician family from the city of Lübeck. His wrists were just about as thin as a girl's and his derriere was not exactly of the male proportions. "Signs of decadence," he used to say. "Do you remember *Buddenbrooks* by Lübeck's Thomas Mann?" His physical attributes did not concern me at all, well, maybe I did notice the rather feminine shape of his pasty white thighs in the shower, but he was a good sport, an excellent horseman and very sharp in his dry North German sense of humor. Hertha and I took Röhrssen with us to Hamburg and introduced him to my parents and afterwards we went slumming in St. Pauli dancing to Teddy Stauffer's band until the wee small hours.

After April 20, the company went down to Döberitz by train to be used as guinea pigs - a new rectangular foxhole was to be tried out with actual tanks which would come and cross our line. The ground was still damp enough. We were confident we would be able to come out of it all right. German soldiers are not known for being efficient about digging foxholes, but this night since we didn't know when the tanks would come, everyone was shoveling like crazy. As per usual we spent hours and hours sitting in our damp mini-graves until the clatter of tank treads woke us up around 2:30 a.m.. By that time we had a full moon and could figure out way ahead of time whether one of these beasts was heading for us. No casualties, nothing to report.

The active lieutenant who was leading the second platoon took the company out into the hills. He had two reserve officers assisting him. Von Wangenheim apparently was busy somewhere else, I did not miss him. The lieutenant assigned reconnaissance patrol under very realistic conditions. He gave out a printed battle situation with some enemy forces possibly dug in on top or below the crest of the hill facing us. The company moved into our jump off area under densely growing shrubs and trees, settled down and watched the reconnaissance take place. I had to pick two other grunts and move out towards the objective to reconnoiter that hill. I had Zepp and his friend join me. We covered our faces with wet brown mud until we looked like the US entertainer Al Jolsen, the whites of our eyes flashing for quite a distance. I told them to pull their pants out of their hobnailed boots and let them down on the heel. Hobnailed boots, the bane of my existence. We gave quite a number of time consuming moves utilizing every bit of knolls and vegetation for cover. This took hours, or so it felt, but once over the crest we could finally flash the signal that the top was free of enemy.

Coming back to the garrison, we were called out and had to face the company to receive a short commendation for a job well done, followed by a stinging rebuke. "And just what was the idea of looking like Chinese coolies. Kindly correct your unsoldierly appearances."

• ◆ • • ◆ • • ◆ •

Our assignment ended, we went by rail to Büchen and marched from there to Hamburg-Wandsbeck. Here we had a rest day and a maneuver ball, or dance. I did not stay in Wandsbeck, but took the tram to Mühlendamm to freshen up in my parents' flat. I called Alice Pollitz and we talked for quite a while. About fifteen minutes after I had put down the receiver, Alice called back.

She said, "It's thoughtful of you to give me the reasons why you can't come and visit me, but I just talked to Miss Stahl, remember, the teacher of your parallel class." She went on to say she wouldn't mind if I reeked of dust, manure, sweat and the indefinable stink that goes with an infantry unit on a march. She understood I was going from here to Lübeck and she would have an urgent message to go to Lübeck from the family K. to a former Lichtwarkschule (my liberal arts high school) woman about to emigrate. Would I be willing to drop this letter off in Lübeck? I did not have to think this one over. The K. family had one girl in my parallel class. There were three classes of tenth grade students. I agreed to meet Miss Stahl immediately.

She was at her usual energetic best. She had a cup of mocha for me and we talked in her study. I learned the whole family K. was about to or already had emigrated to Sweden. Anneliese was with her cousin in Lübeck waiting for a few more formalities to be taken care of. She needed these documents. Would I be so kind as to deliver them in person. Stahl was sure she could meet me somewhere; it would not do to go to her apartment or mail it. She might be under surveillance. All perspective emigrants were under observation to prevent smuggling of *devisen* (foreign exchange) out of the country.

This was quite a handful, I thought, but I found nothing wrong with it and I refrained from trying to find out which of the daughters we were talking about. It might have been the one who had left shortly before I did. She was our athletic idol, the most amazing Amazon of her age group. The blond, blue-eyed, six-foot all-around athlete who had won all competitions she had entered at the yearly track and field at the high school sports fest. She was so strong she could have beaten most of the boys in my class in discus, shot-put, and javelin. It was the level of age where boys are usually way behind girls in their physical development. I had heard stories how she had "whupped" some boys when they had attacked a girlfriend of hers. Yes, I remembered her as a sun-tanned Brunhilde. Karlchen, having some fun with the current political rhetoric, used to call her a "Nordic disappointment" (*Nordische Enttäuschung*), since there was some hint she might have had a Jewish grandmother or something.

We were supposed to be back in Lübeck by Friday, May 14, 1937, so I told Stahl that everything being equal we would have Saturday and Sunday off after the long march, which would be enough time to reach this person. "Phone her Saturday," Stahl said. "I think her boat is due to leave on Sunday, and thanks very much. I always thought you were on the other side, the way you appeared in 1934, the way you behaved. I really appreciate your doing this," and she hugged me goodbye with some emotion.

Saturday I called the number I was given and we agreed we would meet at Niedereggers, a well-known Café. I knew immediately that this was my athletic idol, and if I had been in doubt the handshake would have sufficed to confirm it. We had a wonderful time reminiscing and comparing notes on who else had left Germany and who was about to. Now I could not help falling all over myself praising her contribution to the tenth-grade classes and what an outstanding talent she had been on the school stage, such as it was.

Anneliese said that, admittedly, she didn't think much of me when I entered in 1934, now already in Hitler Youth uniform, and she couldn't understand why anyone would follow Zindler, at that. The latter had moved from the Johanneum to the Lichtwarkschule to install the new spirit in that "pinko" morass. It had become known rather quickly that I defended the man no matter how foolish he might have behaved early on. I nodded and explained that Zindler had been the only teacher I had encountered over there with whom one could discuss freely. I was aware that he had been a soldier in World War I and fiercely nationalistic. Anneliese must have granted me mitigating circumstances, because she knew all about our trip with the *Jungenschaft* in 1934 and how I had managed to con the adults in question to allow Karlchen and Osborne (JR) to come to the Lichtwarkschule.

We took a long walk, we even went sailing, that is to say she sailed the boat and I was occasionally allowed to steer or to grab a piece of very important rope. Saturday evening we had some food and found ourselves sitting on a bench overlooking the River Trave. I registered similar couples on most of the other benches. Well, it was spring and we found ourselves kissing each other. After a while I remarked that many of the men around us were in uniform, as I was, mostly with very young women, au pair types or domestic servants. She said, "If it disturbs you to share this lovely evening with ordinary bourgeois, you elitist bastard, we can go to my place. It is not far from here." So we did.

I have no clear recollections of the happy moments and the despair. All I can recall is the uncanny intensity of our encounter. I was close to tears at times thinking about the absurdity of our situation. Here was this perfect young woman, strong and immensely bright and gifted, having to leave her home, her childhood, all she had been cherishing, to face an entirely different situation in a foreign country, either in Scandinavia or somewhere in the Anglo-Saxon orbit. She had to leave because of her Jewish ancestry and because her mother took the new regime in Germany seriously, unlike her father and many others who thought they were only German and had nothing to fear, for varied reasons. The mother insisted that they become refugees, the World War I decorations on her father's coat did not mean anything safe to her. She did not want her children and their offspring staying in a society where this kind of bigotry existed.

Whenever I became emotional she said, "No, that's taboo," and closed my lips with her hand. She repeated that these hours would be it. No farewell, no phone-calls, no letters, and she would go down to her cabin on the boat on Sunday.

◆ • ◆ • • ◆ • • ◆ •

Some days later, it could have been weeks, I was not paying much attention to anything, certainly not the calendar, I felt frequent discomfort. I had some discharge and other urology problems. I told Sepp about the symptoms. He gave me a lengthy description about a first aid course in his steel mill in Czechoslovakia where early signs of infection as a result of intercourse had been discussed briefly. As I was sure nothing that disgusting could ever happen to me I dismissed his advice, but when the symptoms intensified I followed his urging and reported sick.

The doctor took some specimen and asked me to come back in twenty-four hours. I concentrated on my daily routine as if by sleep-walking. Anneliese was with me all the way. All the more, I was dumb-founded the next day when the company clerk told me that I was reported in writing as suspected gonorrhea. Of course, I told myself this was out of the question, this was all some ghastly misinterpretation by some technician at the lab. I told the doctor what I had told Sepp, denying this possibility. The doctor must have heard that before. He solemnly heard what I said and accepted my statement at face value and I thought I detected a sneer. This "well, we are all men of the world," I detested. He took another sample and would call me back in two days.

Now, I was at the end of my tether, completely exhausted. Sepp did his best to steer me through the day's chores except for a class by Lt. Becker where Sepp could not attend. The lieutenant looked up at me more than once during the lecture and called me back to his desk afterwards. He asked me point blank what was the matter with me, that I looked unhealthy and had lost some weight. I told him what was happening to me and he was very upset.

"Man, you're doing very well, extremely well, better than most, and now this. How could you do this to me?" After a pause, "Let me talk to this doctor and keep the whole story under your hat, do you hear?"

"Yes, sir, but it may be a bit late for that. It's in the company sickbay report."

"It's what?" Becker fairly jumped at me.

"I saw it, sir, I'm suspected of G.O." Another pause.

"Well, I'll see that doctor right away. Will you pull yourself together?"

"Yes, sir. Thank you, sir."

The doctor still wasn't sure. To get more of the discharge I had to drink one glass of Port per day, walking downtown and back to the recommended restaurant, a Lübeck historical site. I even had its old name, Schabbelhaus.

It wasn't a very long hike from Marli barracks to the restaurant, but for someone in my situation it was endless, a veritable *via dolorosa*, a drag. Near the bridge over the canal I saw a mother pushing her crippled son about age five or six along the footpath. Well, yes, I thought, he may have an incurable condition, but he sure doesn't have what I have.

At a tram stop downtown there was a group of people staring at a man down on the ground. He was twitching convulsively. Someone was opening his tie. Yes, he will have this all his life, but he does not have what I have, and on and on. My self-pity was sickening, even to me. The restaurant was rather empty in the forenoon, nobody took any interest in a lonely soldier. I kept watching the traffic through the big windows, slowly rotating the glass of wine between my fingers.

On the whole, drinking Port in the late morning is not a very useful approach to mental stock-taking, but here in the Schabbelhaus this moment I was so filled with anxiety that the Port did not have its usual calming effect. On the contrary, my head was swimming with a multitude of intense images. The few hours of happiness with Anneliese and then my first sobering encounter with tanks at Döberitz, the miles and miles of marching in scorching sun, Lt. Becker's disappointment in me, which really hurt. When I thought about that uncaring, smug military doctor, I clenched my teeth in rage.

What if I really did have G.O.? I knew it was impossible. My sex education had been spotty, admittedly, but this much I knew, you can't get this kind of affliction through picking daisies or by touching some piece of plumbing in the loo. Anneliese could not have given it to me, that was out of the question. She just was not the type! But what if I had now infected her? Oh my god. My mind raced around in a vicious circle and I always ended up saying, "No, out of the question! I do not have it, so she will be okay."

What if I did have it after all? My "career" would be over as fast as it had started. I would be a corporal at the end of my two-year service and then what? Was it the Port that made this latter possibility sound desirable, or was this wishful thinking? No more soldiery, no more loyalty oath. I would be free from any further obligation. Everything being equal, that is, that there wouldn't be a war all of a sudden and they would call me back.

By this time we had been promised peace and prosperity so often, I think everybody trusted Hitler. So far he had done very well without causing a military confrontation. What about Austria? Well, the Austrian uprising in '34 was a disaster, of course, but was Hitler directly responsible?

This was the time when world opinion seemed to ignore the plight of the German opposition, the concentration camps and especially the fate of the Jews. Since the Olympic Games of 1936, numerous dignitaries, politicians, members of royal families et al., had come all the way to Germany to meet and shake hands with Hitler. He, in turn, kept assuring the world over and over that he, as a front-line soldier in World War I, had only peace in mind and would not try any solution of a given problem by force of arms. Goebbels had a field day with the photos of these visiting celebrities from Charles Lindbergh in 1928 to the San Francisco Men's Choir in 1937. Early on Hitler had withdrawn Germany from the League of Nations, a drastic step, to be sure. This year, in April 1937, Belgium had canceled all her alliances and declared herself strictly neutral. This was another shock for France and Britain and a gain in prestige for Hitler.

What would I do once I was released from the army? Would I try to get abroad? As what? I had not accumulated the necessary academic credential for university studies anywhere. Would I starve my way through apprenticeship in the theater? Acting schools were very expensive. This was hopeless.

Did I really trust Hitler's peaceful protestations? Somehow, I did, as I always had, identify with survivors of World War I who now spoke up against war as he had done. On the other hand, I vaguely remembered his remarks in *Mein Kampf* about the necessary expansion in the East. These remarks were so simplistic, I just stopped reading the few times I had attempted to read this book.

I learned from the radio and other media reports, all directed by Goebbels, of course, that Stalin this very year had started to purge the Russian leadership including his generals. Was this the first step to the total breakdown Hitler was predicting? We heard about show trials in which Stalin's old cronies confessed their guilt, and then were sentenced to death. Had this to do with the fact that the Rome, Berlin, Tokyo axis clearly anti-Communist in its intention was signed this year? I read about the tension in East Asia and open clashes between Russian and Japanese troops in Manchuria. Occasionally, I snatched bits and pieces of broadcasts from radio Moscow confirming rumors in Germany that Hitler's volunteers were fighting with General Franco in Spain, Russia being the only country openly assisting the loyalists.

What about the German Jews? Would they all have to leave the country? How many Jews did we have? Goebbels' propaganda constantly was at loggerheads with one or more Jewish writers in, let's say, New York, Los Angeles, Chicago or London. The minister labeled them "The Jewish World Conspiracy," which was out to spread lies to defame the "New German Order." Occasionally he quoted these foreign sources to show how those journalists were going about this and how they tried to conspire against our country and to foment hostility against Germany. We could never check on the veracity of these claims, but sometimes Goebbels did win a point. I wondered how many Jews in Germany had German citizenship? How long? Years? Decades? If they leave, what about their property? Anneliese said that her family had lost a lot to "friendly, helpful" buyers when they were forced to sell. What about the law regarding copyright or patents? The Jews were very much in entertainment, the arts, research, business - all the professions. I admired the strength of Anneliese's mother at this moment. What must she have been through - what she had to give up- her country, her family and her friends in order get her immediate family out of Germany.

Anyway, my glass was empty. I slowly, cautiously navigated through rows of tables and chairs, took great care not to stumble on the steps between levels and finally found myself in the open in the mid-day glare of a sunny spring day. I was hoping against all odds that nobody would notice I had been drinking, even if it were doctor's orders. I'd have given anything for a taxi, but I couldn't afford that.

On the way back to Marli, I followed a man who made some strange sounds every fourth or fifth step, his body lifting itself simultaneously. I saw people crossing over to the other side of the street once he had come into their view. I figured they probably did not want to be too close, they didn't want to get involved in case something happened to this poor man. I hesitated to overtake him, but I didn't want to cross over to the other side of the street just to avoid him. Coming closer I saw what a powerful jerk went through his body each time he let go of his rasping hoarse bark. Well, I said to myself, he probably was shell-shocked or buried alive in the war. I had read about such cases. He will do this for the rest of his life, but - I could not finish my idiotic wallowing in self-pity. I suddenly felt woozy and had to sit down on a bench nearby. It was one of those benches along the river where Anneliese and I had stayed briefly. I covered my face and cried.

●◈●●◈●●◈●

When I got back to the barracks Sergeant Steuer was waiting for me and took me to Lt. Becker. The lieutenant gave Steuer strict orders to stay with me day and night to make sure I would not get any suicidal ideas. He then turned to me and apologized for the scandalous handling of my case and added the doctor would face a disciplinary hearing, I could be sure of that. Meanwhile, I was to write down in detail all the activities I had been engaged in during the last two months that might have been the source of my difficulty. So Steuer and I went to my room. He spent the day reading some instruction book and I spent the day writing the prescribed account, which, of course, took quite a bit of doing. Anneliese K. did not appear in this "novel."

Then Becker came to my room, shook my hand. "A deplorable snafu - you have an ordinary inflammation, possibly through sitting all night in that confounded damp foxhole at Döberitz you told me about. You will spend tomorrow at the officers' mess on the river helping with the inventory. They should get the cobwebs off your brain. The doctor had a short hearing and has been transferred."

"Thanks very much, sir," I said.

◆ ● ● ◆ ● ● ◆ ●

He left, and in my mind I was immediately back with Anneliese. She would now be free of any possible harm from our being together. She was in the room saying again, "Come on in."

"This is a charming apartment," I remarked, admiring the wooden paneling. I felt like touching the mythological carvings that glowed with years of painstaking care.

She nodded with a certain resignation in her eyes. "Right, they had been renting this flat since the turn of the century. The landlord will have little trouble finding a new renter. By the way, he offered to buy their furniture too, 1000 marks in all, take it or leave it."

I protested, "A fraction of what it's worth!"

"Yes, he is a good Samaritan, all right, just trying to be helpful. Since he joined the party in 1934 the good will and respect established in two generations between the two families went out the window. His mother came by, she was crying and urged me to phone her if I thought she might be of help. She said her grandfather had installed all the wooden paneling from one of his ships. She used to be proud of this flat, but not anymore."

"Shit," I said.

She turned around and put her hands on my shoulders, "Could we agree not to talk about this situation anymore, could we? Time's wasting."

When I wanted to say something she placed two fingers across my lips, "*D'accord*?" (Okay?)

◆ ◆ ◆ ◆ ◆

I was reliving the many vignettes and dialogues which made up my weekend in Lübeck with Anneliese. I thought about her while hiking through the countryside north of the city of Kiel as a corporal, thirty to thirty-five kilometers per day in step with the other soldiers of the platoon. The divisional maneuver went by without my being actively engaged. I was savoring the images and conversations as I recalled our short encounter. Sometimes Sepp had to give me a slap with his big right hand to alert me whenever some action was called for, be it only the shout, "Incoming!" or "Fighter planes!" whereupon we found ourselves in the next available ditch or furrow, sometimes on our backs firing at imaginary planes with exercise ammunition. Without Sepp my absence of mind might have come to the attention of my superiors, something I wanted to avoid at all cost.

On the third day we had a "Maneuver Ball," a dance organized by local peasantry to show their patriotic identification with our boys in field gray. This part of Germany had voted 100 percent for Hitler. Sepp, Röhrssen and I did not dance those polkas, waltzes and tangos or any of those country folk dances. We just sat there and had some beer and schnapps. The two played chess at times, on and off, Röhrssen had a very expensive wallet-sized chess game. I was again free to be back with Anneliese in Lübeck.

• ◆ • • ◆ • • ◆ •

"Since we were talking about *The Coronet* as the Rilke part of your repertoire..." She was bringing this up for the second time.

I said, "No, we just liked it so much somebody was always reading it whenever we met and were sitting around the campfire or the fireplace in our garrison. Later the Hitler Youth made use of it, overuse, abuse. As in World War I, quotes from *The Coronet* became part of patriotic rituals with brass bands and military tattoo in the background to heighten the emotional impact to glorify the death of soldiers. I have read somewhere that Rilke watched this misplaced use of his writing with great concern and became defensive about it, would not personally read *The Coronet* in public anymore and he tried to prevent performances of this work. In our capacity as the performing group of the Hitler Youth we refused the Nazi party leaders requests to perform it for their militaristic purposes at their party meetings."

Quite artlessly and directly she asked, "Would you read it now to me just for old time's sake?"

She handed me the Insel edition when I did not object. I had never read it to a single listener before, it felt rather odd.

> "Riding, riding, riding, through the day, through the night, through the day.
>
> Riding, riding, riding.
>
> And courage is grown so weary, and longing so great.
>
> There are no hills any more, hardly a tree. Nothing dares stand up.

Alien huts crouch thirstily by mired springs."

Here I faltered for the first time.

I had read the introduction more or less mechanically. How many times have I celebrated this with the *Jungenschaft* or in private circles. Here I am to go through this with a young woman, all at once very close to me, a beautiful human being who is about to leave this country, leave her home, her childhood, her friends, her relatives, just because her father had a Jewish mother. I'm reading Rilke to someone who obviously loves his poetry as much as we all did. She will be in a foreign country with her family in much reduced circumstances, trying to rebuild her world, to learn a foreign tongue and to get adjusted to a different way of life. How many years will it be until she can share this kind of enjoyment of literature and discussion in her new language? I had to stop reading. Anneliese touched my hand. She was avoiding my eyes when she asked, "Would you like a cup of tea?"

"I am sorry." My tears were welling up. I had trouble holding on to myself. I gazed out the window into the night above the city. Clouds were now racing by the moon. When she was gone I let go, inwardly raving, swearing. My shoulders were moving convulsively. Then I caught myself, calmed myself, took a few steps, and stretched, supporting myself on the window sill. "Why us?" was the thought. This generation, what have we done to deserve this madness?

I was still snarling under my breath when she came back in with the tray. She had changed into a black and gold kimono, not quite her size. She smiled and gave me a glance of acknowledgment. "Cream? Sugar?"

"No thanks."

The paper-thin china allowed the golden glow of the tea to shine through against the desk lamp behind it. The North German tea ceremony. What a pleasure to relive it here. I enjoyed watching her strong beautiful hands pouring the tea and helping herself to two lumps of sugar. We both took a few sips in silence.

"Are you okay? Don't go on if you don't feel like it."

"I'll try." She nestled down next to me. Her kimono was too small and she sensed my noticing it.

"It belongs to my cousin. He wants me to go to him once I get to Sweden."

So I went on. I was fine for about fifteen pages or so.

"And von Langenau grows sad. He thinks of a blond girl with whom he played wild games. And he would like to go home, for an instant only, only for so long as it takes to say the words ...."

Then I stopped.

◆ • • ◆ • • ◆ • - -

Early in 1937 I had to go back to Ratzeburg and help with the packing and checking of my huge chest. It was a joy to see the little town of Ratzeburg and to visit with my former buddies and the former noncoms. Captain Rodust was away on business. Staff Corporal Petersen made his very own contribution to a round of "do you remember" parties. He kept mumbling that he had seen me in civilian garb, against regulation, in the arms of a lady of easy virtue on the Reeperbahn in Hamburg. He just wasn't quite sure, he said. He could not even remember the date or the time, so I denied everything, knowing that he was right. Putti Winter had buried my face in a long embrace. I remembered it very well.

Would this next hurdle be the last preventing me from becoming a regular army officer? I wasn't sure. It did not appear that way once I reported at Munich, Kadetten Str. 15, a forbidding looking nineteenth century structure opposite a huge brewery, Spaten Beer, if memory serves me.

The pompous strutting inspection adjutant immediately singled me out for not wearing my cap according to regulations, as he understood them. I looked like a "Swing Heini," he said. (What did he know?) Luckily, von der Chevallerie, my class advisor, came by wearing his cap even more lopsided and smiling at the irate Bavarian lieutenant until the latter turned away looking uncomfortable.

"If I make a suggestion, Panny, I tilt the cap to the other side, once you are commissioned." I knew I was in good hands, I had a *bon vivant* from the cavalry as an advisor - 'I shall not want.' In retrospect, if only I had remembered this first advice he had given me regarding the tilt, that is, but that is another story.

I had three roommates. Each of us had a locker and a study table. To accommodate all this, we had to sleep in double bunk beds. I was lucky to get the upper one next to a window. The washing facilities were separate from the rest rooms, thank god, and we had hot showers at will, I was very happy to find out. On the lower bunk was Rexroth, a signal man from Saxony. Oswald, an infantry soldier from Stuttgart, and little Dessau, called "Fipps" shared the other double bunk.

After ten days, Gerd Franke was appointed spokesman and platoon leader by Major Geissler. The major was our "home room teacher," as it were, and tried to teach us tactical principles at the battalion level. Once a week he took us horseback riding. With Franke he had made a popular choice. We saw Gerd as a decent human being and a competent soldier in spite of several strikes against him: he was older than the rest of us, he had studied law as a member of a dueling fraternity and to top it off he spoke the dreadful Saxon dialect.

Courses: We had tactics three times a week, most other courses only once or twice. There were communications (signals), ballistics, engineering, military history, social life, current topics, cartography, hygiene and logistics. Physical education was apparatus, boxing, horsemanship, basic skills in the field and swimming.

All in all, it was a depressing range of how to instruction - tactics and ballistics being the only exceptions. The former was comparable to a bonehead language course. We were supposed to learn to express ourselves clearly once we had made a judgment and come to a decision, rightly or wrongly; we hardly ever came to the same decision as our instructor with a given set of circumstances. I found it helpful because my German was certainly in need of improvement. The major's hobby was punctuation and word order. Sport was limited to jogging in the morning, boxing twice a week, swimming and diving once a week, horseback riding once a week. Most, if not all other courses, were taught by experts in their field who were knowledgeable, but not very articulate.

The general tendency of many of these instructors was to overstate the importance of their branch of the armed forces and to glorify their achievements in past wars. The engineer out-bragged the lot of them. He personified the type of spectacle these instructors offered. We always featured his latest hype in our class paper, which I began to turn out the beginning of the fourth week. The engineer instructor was supposed to have signed a guest book at the Munich Army Headquarters with the manly quote, "To be a *Sapper* (engineer) means to attack!" Some major from a different army branch supposedly had countered, "To be a barber means to develop a lot of foam."

The weapons instructor was his very opposite. He was always denigrating the importance of himself and of his branch, the artillery, "Don't believe all this bragging about new and improved weapons. For every new weapon a countermeasure is quickly developed making the new, top-secret wonder weapon obsolete before it is even mass produced."

None of our instructors had anything good to say about the developing new branch of the army, the mechanized Panzer Division. Most of them made light of tank warfare. They taught and planned in terms of World War I as the be-all, end-all of wisdom in such matters.

Soon my only problem was staying awake in these endless lectures. The starchy Bavarian food and the long evenings of R and R with Bavarian beer took their toll. I devised some outlandish methods like self-inflicted pain, or leg exercises under the table to keep my eyes open, not always successfully. Most of my buddies didn't do much better. It must have been a discouraging sight for the instructors to see their audience drop off one by one. Memories of my first high school came to mind, what a dreadful association. My friends and I turned this into a never-ending topic in the class paper.

Boxing was the most senseless of all physical activities. The teacher seemed to be badly in need of finding weaker candidates he could humiliate and make fun of. Unfortunately he took over swimming as well, so I knew I needed help. Michael, our best swimmer, very patiently taught me how to dive and thus avoid the stinging sarcasm of that jock in charge of the class. I was beginning to enjoy myself until my eyes became bloodshot and some discharge developed. The doctor said that was the end of swimming. What a relief. No diving from five and ten meter boards, no jumping into the murky water in combat fatigues and undressing in the water without losing anything. I started jogging to use the free hour and spent more time on the class paper, listening to "Alexander's Ragtime Band" in the background. My roommates thought I had it made.

The third week we were graded in boxing, three times - three minutes, sparring partners paired by size. Birnheim and I knew he would pair us again so we rehearsed nine minutes of pugilistic brilliance designed to not hurt one another.

It was the afternoon before the weekly ballroom dancing. I had a date with one of the young women who were our captive partners. A busload of young ladies came from a boarding school at Miesbach near Munich. These socialite girls learned everything the wife of an industry captain was supposed to perform gracefully. We called their school

"Cooking School-Miesbach" (KSM, which were the identical letters of our Kriegsschule München). Birnheim likewise had a reason to come out of our match unscathed, he wanted to go to a concert.

Sure enough, the teacher paired us again. During the first round we must have overacted a bit. He told us we were faking. Round two started at safe levels of exchange, but my buddy slipped and inadvertently punched me in the nose. I was furious when I saw blood trickle down my T-shirt so I whopped him right in his left eye which closed immediately. When round three was over we were limp with exhaustion, my precious jacket crown had been bashed out of its mooring and was making dreadful sounds when it hit the remaining teeth. He and I both were smeared with blood.

No more boxing. I do not think my date that evening had a good time. With my front tooth missing, my not impressive sex appeal at any time was apparent. Come to think of it, I avoided talking altogether, considering my newly acquired speech defect. In hindsight, I can't imagine why it never occurred to the school to provide the students with mouth protectors, since this sparring for grades frequently turned into a free-for-all. Anyway, I had even more time for my beloved class paper and had to go to a distinguished dentist to get a new jacket crown at taxpayer expense.

◆ • • ◆ • • ◆ • • ◆ •

Munich was everything I had expected. On the one hand it still was a small country town. You could see peasants in their colorful garb and leather pants crossing the busy streets downtown at will, just as if this was their little hamlet in the foothills of the Alps. Most of the men carried a big staff called a *Knotenstock* and fully expected cars to let them pass unscathed. They had a cloth bundle with some food so they wouldn't have to waste money at a restaurant. You saw them sitting in the beer gardens polishing off a fried chicken with their beer. On the other hand Munich had grown into a cosmopolitan center, a tourist attraction of the first order. The opera, the theaters and concert halls featured well-known performers. I spent whatever money I had on theater and concert tickets.

I received an invitation at the end of October to come to a party at Hildegard's place in one of the suburbs. I was immediately made comfortable and enjoyed meeting the three little girls who were born in the same village in China as I was, the youngest one in the same year, 1918. Hildegard's husband Walter was working for the government. I never found out how high up in the party he was placed. The middle girl was Ingeborg, Gerda was the youngest, there was an architect called Stein and his wife.

The more often I talked to Walter, the more mysterious his position in the party became. I didn't want to ask outright, but we had long discussions and he expressed many of the doubts that my friends and I had ever since 1934 when the SA leadership was killed. He too had reservations about racist notions and the treatment of the Jewish citizens. According to his wife, he was a pure idealist and at odds with much of what was going on, including the condemnation of modern art which struck directly at her focus as a young painter.

Ingeborg was not as gifted as her sister, but she had an uncanny ability to sketch with a few strokes of her pen the essence of what she saw in a person or in a situation. She took me to watch professional matches and came home with stunning reproductions of given expressions or emotions. She had a collection of sketches showing the overdressed, overly made-up women who were sitting in the most expensive seats.

It was Ingeborg who had the guts to take me skiing. Alice Pollitz sent me her skis and her cat-skins which arrived by rail just in time for my first ski weekend. Lacking lifts, everybody had to walk up the mountain on their skis aided by closely sheared cat-skins mounted on the undersides of the skis, which gave enough resistance in the snow to keep from sliding back. At the foot of the mountain a long chain of skiers were slowly zigzagging uphill. Nobody struck out on his own, it was so much easier to stick to the already packed snow on the path. This took three or four hours. We arrived at a little hut at twelve-hundred-meters above sea level, drenched in perspiration and close to fatigue. We all had a drink, a mixture of orange juice and soda and then we got ready for the descent.

I received plenty of advice how to go about skiing downhill, thanked everyone, and hurled myself down the mountain. There is no other way I could describe my skiing. When the *schuss* became too fast, I just pulled the emergency brake, meaning falling on my behind, fervently hoping not to get entangled in my skis. It must have been quite a sight for Ingeborg and by miracle I did not get hurt. The mountain rescue team came by to tell Ingeborg that it was irresponsible to take a Prussian neophyte up that slope. This was my only ski experience until spring '38 when our whole class spent ten days in a ski hut near the Austrian border. There we did have some instruction on the beginners' hill during which I lost my "innocence," the feeling that nothing can ever happen to me when I fall down. They had a saying in Bavaria that rank beginners, children and drunkards don't get hurt.

April '37 then, began with a number of developments which, for all practical purposes took care of my most immediate problems. My main anxiety, the dive from the ten-meter board had been eliminated by the doctor's orders. As in high school swimming, at the time, I gained valuable hours which I used for running middle and long distances. Just for myself, I had to acknowledge the fact that I was just as much of a coward as anybody else and that I would not have made a very favorable impression stepping off that suicidal height to bomb feet first into the murky water. The weekly boxing also fell by the wayside. Again I gained time to write my silly satirical stuff which made me achieve a certain position among my peers, a position which I would not have had without this. It gave me a certain amount of *Narrenfreiheit*, the leeway given a court jester, if you like, with the establishment, the officers in charge of our class.

The most positive aspect of my stay in Munich was the friendship with the three diminutive Tochtermann women. They were born in the same village in China as I was and yet I had never heard about them until now. Their brother Siegfried was a friend of my sister Jutta in Hamburg and gave Jutta the address to pass on to me. Walter, the husband of Hildegard, was constantly gone on business for the Nazi party and the government. With or without him we had many wonderful parties. Their dog, Ivan, singled me out and Hildegard was pleased each time I offered to take the dog on long walks so she could get on with her work. The evenings at their place were so enjoyable and comfortable that I had difficulty in leaving on time. I will never know why my late-night window-sneak-ins did not land me in disciplinary actions or dismissal from the school. More often than not I came home past tattoo in civvies or in uniform. The "homecoming window," as we called it, had to be slightly ajar all year round.

My correspondence with Hamburg was limited to Jutta and Putti. The latter was facing mounting difficulties in her quest for getting permission to study at university level because of the limitations set out for half-Jewish candidates. She must have played her cards wrong initially, she admitted ruefully, there was no end to complications. I did not have a chance to get a furlough, but then what help could I possibly have given her, me being a lousy officer candidate noncom with no connections to influential authorities.

What else was there to enjoy in Munich? Mainly performing arts, the theaters were offering splendid shows and standing room tickets were affordable. American movies were still predominant, dubbed with great care in German studios. Dancing swing was not permitted in public places, but all the movies like *Broadway Melody* came into the *Kinos* (the movie theaters) before 1933, which is before jazz was banned. However, abstract art was taboo, all modern art was withdrawn from showings including my beloved Barlach, Nolde, and Kollwitz. Only in those two years in the Lichtwarkschule had my eyes been open to expressionism, which was now called "Cultural Bolshevism."

The Octoberfest, Munich's big tourist attraction, I ignored entirely. If one really likes these fantastic rides one has to have money, which I didn't have, and I wasn't into studying the Bavarian mentality, as such.

They did take us, the whole school, to watch *Olympic 1936*, meant as a propaganda film by Goebbels, but superbly produced and directed by Lene Riefenstahl with Jesse Owens as the central figure. The film cleverly counteracted the allegedly Jewish propaganda using the racism of the Nazis as a vehicle. Jesse Owens was immensely popular as the athlete of the century in Germany.

Another film became required viewing, *Triumph of the Will*, the 1934 party rally at Nuremberg. It had been done a few weeks after the SA leadership had been liquidated on June 30, 1934, and now, discussing this movie with my friends, I found out some more gory details regarding the Night of the Long Knives, as it was called. This new information put the official version of "a quick strike at the last possible minute to prevent the SA mutiny" into grave doubt. Walter Moessel, the husband of Hildegard, was unusually restrained in his answers and did not favor me with his interpretation of the killings. None of my military superiors was willing to take a stand, which was disturbing since two generals were among those slain, one of them together with his wife at their breakfast table. My uneasiness about our leadership increased when both generals, von Blomberg and von Fritsch, were fired, the CNC Commander-in-Chief of the armed forces and the CNC of the Army. Some of my friends from military families dropped guarded hints as to the reasons of their dismissal, there was no one I could trust to set me straight on the facts.

My relationship with Walter cooled off considerably when all the decadent art was brought out from their storage places and displayed with gross defamatory comments in the "Haus der Kunst" in summer, 1938. This exhibition was to be shipped and put on display in many showrooms all over the country to demonstrate examples of degenerate art, that is to say, "Jewish Bolshevistic" art, as they called it. I stopped asking questions when I saw Walter and Hildegard exchanging pained glances. She certainly had not joined Hitler's photographic larger than life portrayals of Nordic supermen and women. It made me feel good to find out that international interest in the works of German expressionists was still considerable, particularly in the works of my hero Nolde. I heard Nolde acknowledged in a commentary on the BBC during that summer.

The chasm at school between out and out ideologists and those of us who had reservation about Germany's new stance widened within the group, as it had in the labor group and my last high school class. I faced a special dilemma of imagining I would soon be in charge of a platoon consisting of one hundred percent Hitler Youth Nazis. This would occur on December 1, 1938, the date of my commissioning. How could I handle myself without losing my self-respect? Was I supposed to pay lip service to that racial twaddle? And on and on.

The school work became another headache. Had there been assigned textbooks, had there been a library, had there been comparative studies of modern military thinking from other countries, it might have been a different story. All we had was this valiant apostle, Major Geissler, who spent endless discussion time on punctuation and word order. I was grateful for his criticism, my prose needed help; however, along with my buddies I too was growing increasingly anxious about finding the right way of expressing myself in order to please Major Geissler.

This same young man who could write satirical verses and adapt German classics for the same purpose would find his "appraisal of situation and decision" characterized as "childlike" and "stilted" by the teacher.

•◆••◆••◆•

Around the end of 1938, I felt pretty low. I went through the daily routine pretending to be interested in what I was doing. I didn't talk much, tried to be overly polite, cringing to avoid any kind of attention. Ingeborg took me to the Circus Krone to watch professional wrestling. She was the only one who had noticed something was amiss. I tried to find out under what rules this free style wrestling was performed, free style not to be confused with the American style of catch-as-catch-can, although we did have some Afro-American on the local wrestling roster. She made one sketch after another of the wrestlers or the mostly female fans in the more expensive seats. She had an uncanny talent to tell a whole story with a few strokes of her pencil, and I had a great time observing the progress of each satirical study.

We had a drink afterward in a corner restaurant. That's when she mentioned in passing, "I'm going skiing for two weeks. Would you like my studio apartment for a break? Care to have a change of scenery?" I knew she had a boyfriend, but that didn't stop me from hugging and kissing her. I was so touched by her sensitivity and her trust.

No Christmas at home in Hamburg, not even at Alice Pollitz's flat. I had privacy for a few days. She even offered me her gramophone and her records, to boot. She showed me the place that night: bedroom, studio, kitchen, shower, all in one room. It was meant to be an artist's flat. There was a big skylight, which could be opened and raised all the way to let a sun-worshipper out on the roof. Paradise.

The news from Hamburg was not so good. Putti had disappeared again. Neither one of my sisters nor her other friends could give me a hint as to her whereabouts. Her mother was just as clueless. I walked all the way downtown to the main post office, the only place I could do a long-distance telephone call.

"Hello, Mrs. Winter. I hope you're well. I'm curious where I could find your daughter?"

Her answer, "You're not the only one," she grumbled and hung up. I stood there with the receiver in my hand. I remember Putti telling me that she had frequently put her mother into difficult situations. Anyway, it was a wasted journey and I was a bit miffed.

My stay in Ingeborg's apartment, charming as it was, took an unexpected turn. After an informal and cozy Christmas at Hildegard's, I left at 8:00 p.m., December 24. My Christmas gift to the Moessels had been a success, a glass cylinder on a wooden base housing a candle which could be protected from the wind so they could use it outside on the back porch where they loved to sit in the summer.

I walked all the way across Munich, picked up my mail at the school and continued on to Red Cross Square. It was snowing lightly, there was music here and there from corner pubs and the occasionally open windows of the lower flats. I could see the decorated Christmas trees in all their colorful splendor and live candles. This Christmas I felt reasonably warm about our German way of celebrating, whereas the last four or five Christmases in Hamburg had been personal disasters.

Once in the apartment, I sat down on Ingeborg's couch and put on a record by Marlene Dietrich, "Alone" and immediately my mood changed. I started pacing up and down the small room, switched off the gramophone and went downstairs to buy a bottle of cheap Christmas cheer, whatever it was. It didn't help.

"Alone in a big city..."

Across town there was little Gerda on leave from the Labor Service for women. She had become restive; the occasional kiss would not do anymore or so she hinted. I was very fond of her in more than a brotherly fashion, but I feared very much to take on a certain responsibility and the inherent commitment. Her wonderful mother treated me as a son and a gentleman. I could not even finish thinking along this line. Marlene had finished. I wound up the gramophone.

"One lives in a big city, yet one is so alone ...."

At that time, Marlene Dietrich had not come out against the new Germany and against Hitler. She was working in Hollywood and must have had her own thoughts about her "Fatherland."

I tried to write a letter to Gerda, while listening to Marlene sing her plaintive song over and over. I tried, I didn't get anywhere. How could I explain to this lovely naive young woman how much I valued her friendship and the hospitality her whole family was showering on me? How adorable a young woman I thought her to be and how attracted I was to her unspoiled love and zest for life. How could I find words to express that? Having said this much, quite bluntly sexual desire had played a very minor part in our short relationship, as far as I was concerned. I could see looking after her, enjoying outings with her, enjoying her company, but I was just not in a position to go beyond that. Sex would come cropping up and I would be unable to handle it responsibly. Would she please not blame herself; I am in a hell of a fix at this very moment in my career, I can't even be sure I can pass the final exam and, what is worse, I am very doubtful of my vocation, my place in the army and in this kind of increasingly regimented German society. How could I tell her that I needed her, her strength and her unspoiled spontaneity? I was very upset to see that someone of such value had come along and I could not hang on to her.

Would I have the guts to talk to her about my self-doubt and my reservations about the direction we were all being dragged into? I knew she believed in the new Germany. She had not seen what I had and she worshipped her brother-in-law who was an idealist of the purest type, or so it seemed. I fell asleep in my chair.

I woke up and had to bury myself in Ingeborg's huge goose-down bedding, fully dressed and still shivering for a while. I found myself comfortably warm under the covers in the morning. The sun came in brightly through the skylight, promising a tanning session on the roof around noon. Would I ever be able to afford a place of my own with a skylight? That brought me back to my self-pity. How could I get out of this mess, I wondered; I had sworn the soldier's oath of allegiance and total subordination to Hitler.

I had wild daydreams, crossing the border to Austria. No, there were too many followers of Hitler over there. How about Switzerland? No chance - unless I had a million dollars in my pocket, they would send me back. How about France, via Alsace or Lorraine? They are supposed to speak German there at least some of them. Where would I find them? The ones who spoke German lived in the South. There would be a river to cross, the Rhine at that, very fast and dangerous. At this point in history you could not just walk across the border to France, or any other European country for that matter. Those few bridges were constantly guarded. After listening to the record one more time, the gramophone wound itself down to its final stop with Marlene singing, "*Jetzt ist alles aus, eine Welt stürzt ein*" (It's all over now, a world collapses).

After the two weeks, Ingeborg came back sun-tanned and very happy. She suggested that we go to the Munich Fasching together, since her friend as well as her sister Gerda were unavailable - both on duty for the Fatherland, as it were.

The remaining weeks of the winter became sheer drudgery. My grades deteriorated further and particularly the *Tanzinstitut* Wellenberg became a weekly bother. We were faced with a different class of socialites from Miesbach, on the whole somewhat overweight. We had to push them around the huge dancing studio, the mirrored walls reflecting our clumsy efforts.

The teaching staff began stressing the waltz, which to me was just a leftover from happy imperial Germany. The constant gyrations made me dizzy. I knew I would never excel at it so I said to myself, what's the good of trying. The teacher thought differently. I even had to come ahead of class time together with my sparring partner in boxing and two or three others. They had us doing the waltz by ourselves with an imaginary partner. I thought it was a humiliating and fruitless exercise.

The same week all candidates were tested for our fitness as possible placement with the Air Force. We were put into all kinds of machines, tied up in various safety belts and then whirled around in the air simulating flight conditions. I called stop as soon as each experiment evolved. If the oscillation didn't nauseate me fast enough, all I had to do was reinforce my dizziness by recalling the confounded experience with our Viennese waltz in our mirrored cage. The young female interviewer, probably a student of medicine, obliged and stopped the machine each time, and said in the end, "Your tendency toward the Air Force seems rather low, am I right?" I nodded, she said okay and wrote "not suitable." As far as I know, she did not report me for faking.

January 1938 brought all kinds of drastic changes in the hierarchy of the army. Von Blomberg, the war minister, got married, with Hitler and Göring as best men and then suddenly retired. The public was not informed as to the reasons of this surprising change. My usual sources, that is to say, sons and relatives of generals in my class merely hinted that Blomberg's spouse was not acceptable. Hitler took over the army himself with von Keitel as his executive.

General von Fritsch retired on February 4. No comment. No official announcement. My sources whispered something about a sex scandal. Fritsch was being replaced by General Brauchitsch. Göring became field marshal at the same time. Munich was awash with rumors as to the meaning of all these changes. Since I knew very little about the gentlemen in question, I did not insist on finding out the details. Besides, quite a number of elderly generals were retired at the same time. Newspaper and radio commentaries began again concentrating on political developments in Austria.

We spent ten days R and R living in a ski hut at the 2,000-meter level, absorbing the sunshine and learning how to ski. It was supposed to give us a respite before the final exam. We were in the snow all day and had a party every night. I was very busy writing or redoing satirical material for my captive audience.

The news from Austria became more ominous. Up to this point the German public had ignored Austria ever since 1934, when some Nazi hotheads had staged an abortive coup and had murdered Chancellor Dollfuss in the process. Since then Austria had been ruled by a quasi-fascist dictatorship, guarantied and protected by England, France and Italy. A great number of left as well as right-wing extremists lost their lives in those years.

Since 1936, however, when Mussolini invaded Ethiopia and the League of Nations imposed strict sanctions on Italy, Hitler and Mussolini had become partners. Germany delighted in supporting Italy with war materials, food and medical supplies, so much so that the embargo against Italy had become ineffective.

We followed the steadily growing propaganda from Berlin on the radio towards the end of our ski vacation. I hurled myself down the slopes of the Wetterstein and landed in the hospital with a rather nasty shoulder contusion. The hospital in Munich blared the news from Austria creating a mounting tension. My physical therapist, a huge masseur, was from Austria and taught me the Austrian dialect while he was inflicting a tremendous amount of pain on my arm. He was quite sure he would join Germany in a few days, talked himself into great enthusiasm, which he punctuated with his massive hands on my lame shoulder.

I almost forgot about the final examinations over all this when suddenly the door opened and our commanding general, the school director, came to my bed and handed me my diploma, "Too bad you couldn't take it, my son. I hope you're better. We have decided that your past performance has been adequate enough to warrant this."

What amazing good fortune! I knew full well that my performance as an officer candidate was nothing to write home about, but this could only be proof that my classmates weren't exactly geniuses either; and possibly the army was hard up for lieutenants.

❖ • • ❖ • • ❖ •

The Austrian news did not appear to be an attempt to sidetrack public attention from all the juicy army and Nazi party scandals. The Austrian invasion, as it was called in the "hostile" foreign press, really was a stupendous political coup. Since the end of World War I the Austrian people had been specifically prevented from achieving a union with Germany by the peace treaties dictated by the Allies and signed by both Germany and Austria, part of the tragic legacy from World War I. The self-determination of peoples, as quoted in President Wilson's "Fourteen Points," had been denied to this small country which, without its former hinterland, was economically and politically handicapped. An Austrian democratic plebiscite had been brutally ignored.

At the time we did not know how the Nazis had used threats and terror to achieve the *Anschluss*. We did not hear that many Austrians and Jews had to flee their country to escape the German Gestapo. The world saw the Austrian's wild enthusiasm in the newsreels and heard their cheering as background to the radio reports. The subsequent ballot in both countries most certainly showed that the overwhelming majority supported this development. Only after the war, we realized how many people had to suffer for political reasons when they were unable to flee the country in time.

A few weeks later, our Austrian opposite numbers, i.e., officer candidates-to-be commissioned in the fall of 1938, came to join us. They were mostly enthusiastic by this sudden change in their fortunes and enjoyed their new comrades-in-arms in Munich. We traveled together with them all the way to East Prussia for the grand opening of the Tannenberg Memorial where President Hindenburg's remains were laid to rest. We all enjoyed East Prussia, which most of us saw for the first time. The military pomp and circumstance did not impress me much, but the hospitality was overwhelming. The return trip was done first by ship from Königsberg to Stettin and then by rail 1,000-kilometers to Munich, an exhausting journey sitting on wooden benches.

●━◆━●●━◆━●●━◆━●

Back in Munich springtime had broken out and we had a dry warm wind, the *Föhn*, which was blowing from the south. I experienced this phenomenon for the first time and I immediately found out that all the attributes given to this warm wind that comes down from the mountains to the south were not exaggerated. There was a general tension in the group, some were depressed and irritable. I remember I even

thought that the facial features of my roommates had changed somewhat, Oswald in particular. He snarled at me more than once and it was
rather frightening. I didn't think that it had much effect on me, but then
I was still riding high on having achieved graduation without the final
exam. On top of that the hospitality of my friends brought me into the
company of many young artists so I felt pleasantly distracted.

As luck would have it, the same week we had a sports festival, a
five-discipline competition between all the classes of the school. There
was a swimming relay, without me, my arm was still in a sling and I
was forbidden to enter the water. There was hand grenade throwing,
without me, I couldn't throw with my left hand. The same thing applied
to shooting.

Franke had us train for the 3,000-meter run, which was a mistake
because we were still sore on the day of the competition. I was so sore
I had trouble climbing into the window at 2:00 a.m. and my roommate Ossie blew the whistle on me. At 3:00 a.m. a group of my buddies
attempted to punish me for my irresponsibility by bringing the age-old
"Holy Ghost." In this case it was harmless, all they had in mind was to
apply some black shoe polish at certain parts of the body. Luckily, I
was awake and had a relatively easy time defending myself from the
upper bunk. They finally gave up in frustration, but we all looked
well decorated.

The next day we appeared at our scheduled starting time, 10:00 a.m.,
and were instructed to pace ourselves since it would harm the team
aggregate if any runner would not make it to his finish line. All through
the race I was in third position very close to the two leading runners
and a whole minute ahead of the boy following me, while Franke, struggling manly through this distance kept yelling, "Slow Panny down, for
chrissakes. He's going to collapse any minute!"

None of us had to give up and the class did very well in the place-ment. My nocturnal attackers grudgingly apologized and a few days later we all parted as friends.

In May, the school went for a final bus trip along the Neckar River. There, we inspected dreary primitive defensive arrangements pointing west. According to our guide, some mysterious agency had constructed them clandestinely some time ago in contravention of the Treaty of Versailles. We saw small concrete bunkers arranged with various cute ideas to conceal them. Sometimes mysterious sheds were constructed on top of them. We were not impressed because we had just seen some photos of the French "Maginot Line." If the enemy had been fooled by these secret constructions, they certainly had to know by now with busload after busload of sergeants traipsing through the weed patches around them.

We then turned south to Stuttgart. Our major obviously had a penchant for inspecting the ornate medieval wood carvings in choir stalls, and so we made frequent stops at one monastery after another on the way. Around Lake Constance we enjoyed a few days of subtrop-ical climate and marveled at the variety of colorful flowers and shrubs.

Back in Munich, I found a letter from Auntie Lotte, my mother's older sister. I recalled my frequent stays with her in Berlin as a child in 1927 and 1928, and her return visits in Hamburg at just about every Christmas time until 1933. During her last visit she received word that her longtime boss had shot himself and I remembered she admitted to us tearfully that she had some kind of special relationship with him. She broke off her visit with us and never came back.

In this letter she said she was *kneipping*, meaning taking the waters at the sanitarium Bad WörisHofen. She invited me to join her as her guest for one weekend. I could not very well weasel out of it. I was fond enough of her, besides, a terse family postcard from Hamburg helped me to make up my mind to accept her invitation, albeit grudgingly. My weekends in Munich had become very precious to me. A plan to get even with her and this family pressure began to form in my mind. I would arrive in gray flannel pants and a blue sports jacket and would not pack my uniform. I knew she wanted to use me to show off my "military manliness" to her single women friends and it turned out I was right.

I arrived on a Saturday afternoon and she was very upset to see me in civilian garb. She even had prepaid for a session with a professional photographer. Had I been in uniform I could imagine her writing across the bottom of the subsequent photo: "Me and my nephew, on duty for Germany," or some such damn thing. As it was, she gritted her teeth and went through the motions anyway.

Later she introduced me to all the people with whom she was sharing this experience. She had a hotel reservation for me and I learned she expected me to follow her around while I was her guest, take all my meals with her and her company. It was obvious I was to have little time to myself, but then what would have I done by myself on a weekend in Bad Wörishofen?

Auntie Lotte told me that the rigorous approach to the health regime used here at the Kneipp Sanitorium had become renowned all over Europe since its discovery in the second half of the nineteenth century by its namesake, a clergyman. I learned that every morning at 6 the patient was greeted by a cold water hosedown. After a frugal breakfast, which I shared with them, I could watch them doing their "*Tautreten*," traipsing around the meadows in the ice-cold dew, barefooted, of course, for a certain prescribed period of time. I tried it Sunday morning. After fifteen minutes my legs had lost all sensitivity, they felt numb. Even after a hot shower followed, you guessed it, by another cold shower, my legs still felt as if they didn't belong to me.

Auntie paraded me around like a piece of newly acquired property, albeit without uniform, in front of the middle-aged patients. She had me make small talk with them. Predictably, there was no other topic, but their ravaged bodies and their being born again the cold-water way. They all proudly announced that they had signed a pledge to strictly adhere to the diet while they were staying there. When Auntie had her beauty nap in the afternoon I looked around the town and found a number of Kneipp's disciples eating and drinking merrily in expensive restaurants. I couldn't blame them. The prescribed diet consisted of raw vegetables and grains and presented another shock to their systems.

To make up for not coming in uniform, I had to promise to join her on a trip around Lake Starnberg on the next weekend, her last! Two weekends shot! Well, she had been nice to me during my miserable childhood. She had even defended me by assuring my parents that I had been a perfect gentleman during my stays with her in 1927 and 1928. Her status as a well-to-do relative, i.e., inheritance, did not impress me. We kids thought she was a frump, boring to have around and always successful in fishing the largest and choicest bits of whatever food was offered.

When asked about her, I always had to think of anything positive to say until I remembered her music. She certainly banged our piano with gusto, a welcome change after listening to the Czerny etudes my sister was fumbling through. With her swooping alto, she had us all enthralled until we outgrew this kind of sentimentality.

The trip to Starnberg was atonement for my sins, all right. It was sultry and hot on the deck of the excursion boat; the sun beat mercilessly down on us. There was no escape. She insisted we not miss any of the view, which, in this case, meant we had to stay out in the sun. It wasn't that spectacular anyway, just ordinary foothills of the Alps, there was so much haze you could not even see the Alps proper. I could not even open the much-too-tight collar of my uniform or even take off my cap, since there were some other officers on board. Posing for endless snapshots, perspiring heavily in my ill-fitting uniform and having to salute every time someone in field gray sauntered past on their way to the restaurant, it was a certain kind of hell.

Since we had very little in common we had difficulty talking until she started prying more negative news of my folks in Hamburg out of me. I couldn't offer anything, she switched to the Czechoslovakia crisis and gravely predicted that war was imminent. She said she would be glad to get home to Berlin before it broke out. She repeated the same story later in the Munich railway station, thanked me for my patience, and waved goodbye until the train disappeared in the haze.

◆ ◆ • • ◆ • • ◆ •

I came to my room disheveled and tired, one ear and my face badly sunburned the color of lobster. My roommates enjoyed the sight when I took off my confounded cap revealing my contrasting white fore-head. I was doubly repulsed as I saw my face in the mirror. The next day Hildegard had scheduled a goodbye party and here I was not exactly in my best form.

Hildegard's party took place without Walter, her husband. This time I was careful not to ask questions. During the prelude to Austria's *Anschluss* I had done so, merely asking for information, when just about everybody turned around to me as if to say that it was the most understood thing for Walter to be absent whenever there were political stress situations.

Gerda could not be there, she was still doing her labor service on some farm. Ingeborg came without her partner, he was still doing his stint in the army. Stein and his wife came and two other women with two SS men, one a Bavarian body builder and the other rather effeminate, I thought, and henpecked by his overwhelming girlfriend who constantly fussed about his tie or his collar as a mother would treat a little boy.

Ivan, the dog, must have had some notion of something unusual about to happen. He never left my side. Hildegarde was touched and she said, "If I ever have to give up this monster of a dog, for instance to have a baby, I know to whom I would like to give Ivan. I must warn you, though, it's of a dubious value. Ivan has mauled a number of male dogs, no matter what their size. We had to pay for the veterinarian's bills."

Meanwhile the political situation in Europe created a tremendous anxiety and brought uneasiness into everything including my send-off party. The two SS chaps, whatever their ranks were, after a few drinks started throwing their weight around, claiming knowledge of big military surprises. Their comments about the Czechoslovakian nation became graphic in a very repulsive way. I had heard this kind of talk before over the telephone talking to my distant uncle in Vienna, formerly a dignitary in the Austro-Hungarian monarchy. He definitely considered them to be second class people. Knowing how many relatives I had in Vienna, I wondered how many more I would have had had I gone through Czechoslovakia.

The week after the party I looked at the map, the new map of Europe. With Austria now part of Germany I could well imagine the concern the government in Prague must have felt as they looked at this map. It even made it understandable why the Czechs had been so adamant in 1919 to deny the Austrians to become part of Germany. Bohemia, Czechoslovakia, was now flanked by Germany in the north, west and south and of course the German minority groups were populating the border regions which had much industry and vital commerce for the Czechoslovakian nation. To quote the German propaganda, "Bohemia presents a dagger thrusting itself into the German heartland," whereas for the Czechs it was the other way around, they felt encircled. Tensions had mounted ever since April, and by May 20 the Czechs ordered a partial mobilization claiming German military preparations outside of their borders. Hitler succeeded to convince the world, London and Paris in particular, that there were no German troop movements, but obviously Hitler must have been furious at this humiliating development.

My sources, sons of high ranking officers in the class, reported that Hitler was beside himself and wanted revenge for this accusation. At that time I didn't understand. On the one hand, my instinct told me that the German propaganda was up to something. On the other hand, I was glad to hear that the British and French had accepted Hitler's explanation. It was most interesting to see how active the British became in trying to find out about the facts in this confrontation. They even sent a fact-finding team without getting permission from either the Czechs or Hitler. Mr. Chamberlain was quoted as saying, "This is a quarrel in a faraway country between people about whom we know nothing."

My classmates hinted that there was generally a tremendous resistance of the German Army against any kind of military involvement, since in their professional opinion, apart from any other aspect, the army was in no way ready to become embroiled in a war. The radio and press campaign continued. I detected a certain similarity in the German claims in the case of the Austrian crisis, sometimes they even used the same phrases.

In a Swiss paper, I found an article detailing the ethnic problems involved. There were one million Hungarians in Czechoslovakia mostly settled along the Slovakian border, likewise half a million Ruthenians. There were three-and-a-quarter million Germans, mostly in the border area towards Germany and along the former Austrian border.

There were two-and-a-half million Slovacs and seven-and-a-half million Czechs.

The paper said that Czech immigrants had met in Pittsburgh in May 1918, and had worked out a paper based on President Wilson's "Fourteen Points," which would have given each ethnic group limited autonomy. Prague had not felt bound by this and the Czechs began to suppress cultural and political activities of the minority groups. It was fair to say that the ethnic minorities had not been treated fairly and Wilson's "Fourteen Points," "The Self-Determination of Peoples," had been abandoned. While I felt ready to identify with the Sudeten-German cause, the steadily mounting horror propaganda in our media disgusted me.

Hitler started fortifying the German border versus France during this month of June. A special organization was created for this purpose; this, too, did not serve to put people's minds at ease.

◆ ● ● ◆ ● ● ◆ ●

On July 2, I arrived at Döberitz near Berlin. This was the second time I had to live in this military training camp. This time around I had my own room in a hut occupied during the 1936 Olympic Games by athletes from all over the world. All the Olympic facilities were now turned over to the people except this village, our quarters. We enjoyed the concerts in the famous open-air theater and went downtown whenever we found a chance. I still was furious for not having been able to attend the Olympic Games at the time, but I was generously compensated by being able to enjoy the new Berlin and the many shows and concerts that were running through the summer season. I stayed away from my relatives; the Starnberg Lake experience still rankled.

The schooling was perfunctory, very relaxed. Even the field exercises were no problem for this former Machine Gunner No. 1. Here the new lightweight MG 34 handled like a toy, although it gave us some problems whenever dirt got in it. Arguably, it was an improved weapon.

Once a week I went to Berger and Co., Potsdam, for taking measurements or enduring the final fittings of my required military uniforms. It was a mind-boggling inventory I accumulated in a few weeks, to wit, two dress uniforms (one for parade and one for social occasions), three tunics for everyday use, two pairs of riding breeches, two pairs of long pants, one greatcoat, two pairs of riding boots and one pair of shoes for social purposes.

When I saw the bill I couldn't believe the expense. At the time my father had promised the army, he would provide the funds. He refused to tell me how he had managed to handle this. He had mumbled something to the effect that I should leave this to him and Captain Rodust. I did not find out from whom he had borrowed this money until Uncle John wrote me a letter in 1942. In it he said he was still waiting for the first installment.

The school was run by a Colonel Hube, a World War I invalid of tremendous energy and drive. The loss of one arm did not affect his performance in the least. I admired his skill on horseback in particular and his presence of mind in two situations, which could have ended in accidental loss of life. Where others would have started to scream and dish out punishment, he merely watched the bullets whiz past him and said, "Eh, potentially, this could have started a court-martial and created a lot of 'paper war.'" We knew how he hated the bureaucracy of the army. He deplored how little we were offered by way of tank warfare and defense against mechanized forces.

* * * * * * * *

August brought the long-awaited postings. To my extreme surprise and joy, they sent me to Berlin Spandau, IR 67, 5th Co. Most people in my class expressed envy, some said I must have connections high up. While I was sorry to be through with Lübeck and Ratzeburg, I saw the list of towns and hamlets where some of my comrades had ended up. The army was sprawling, mushrooming all over the country, in its much too fast build up.

Infantry Regiment 67. August 8, 1938, I arrived with all my luggage and went straight to Berlin Spandau by taxi. It was a hot sultry day and a Monday with the usual colossal hangover. My uniform was suffocating me, particularly around the neck, but no relief was permissible if I wanted to make a good impression. Why did I have to go to the reunion last night with seven of my former roommates in the Labor Service? I really did not have that much in common with them, never had. After a no host meal we had gone to St. Pauli, Hamburg's red light district, to celebrate. I wasn't sure what there was to celebrate. I had tried to convince my former buddies that this was a "joy" district for tourists, notably rich Scandinavians, which came by the trainload. Denmark even lost a king who had a heart attack in one of those brothels, I had been told. The local citizenry did not waste much money in this honky-tonk area. I had pleaded in vain. Hamburg had numerous restaurants to offer providing quiet tables where one could talk and reminisce. They did not listen to me, never had. After all, I was the youngest, the volunteer, the career man.

They all had finished their two-year stints in the army and they pitied me as someone who had to go fight his way into Czechoslovakia ahead of his platoon, poor bastard. We all drank a lot and tried to talk politics, "I told you so," was the recurring phrase. Riemasch, a sworn pacifist who had been introducing me to the works of Bertoldt Brecht during the time we roomed together - he predicted war to break out this fall. "Remember the 'Guns of August of 1914,'" he would repeat as he got increasingly inebriated. The meeting broke up in the early morning hours when Riemasch suddenly had another one of his epileptic fits and two people who lived close to him had to take him home in a taxi. I admit some relief at the relatively early breakup of this group, who knows what crazy situations might have resulted had we gone on. We were all sorry to see that he was still having these attacks, yet someone quite bluntly expressed the thought that, "After all, it had kept him out of the army."

The buildings in Spandau looked exactly like the ones in Ratzeburg. I had one room to myself with a wash stand, a couch, a cot, a table and two chairs, all army issue, bloody awful.

A pleasant young corporal reported for duty and explained he had to look after me as my "Batman." Now I had a manservant! What next? Someone would always be there to shine my boots, take care of my errands, organize my laundry, clean my weapons, bring food, and on and on. He would remind me of appointments, wake me in the morning and bring hot water, etc. This called for a big adjustment, one that I was slow to make. I had no experience with "help" ever, hired or otherwise. I certainly was lucky with this one, he was from Berlin and knew his way around. He claimed to be an apprentice cook with good references from restaurants. We got along well from the start. He was not the ingratiating type one found so easily in this type of business. As a Berliner, he had the quick repartee and the refreshing wit to boot I had always liked when I had contact with them.

My single window looked down on the yard. I opened it and watched my company going through various types of drills. I was immediately struck by some of the NCO's circling around their charges like ill-mannered sheepdogs. The air was filled with their graphic language, a constant din from at least a dozen voices. It was Monday all right. That's exactly the way it was in Ratzeburg on Monday morning, the proverbial "day after" when the sergeants let us have it to compensate for their weekend frustrations and other mishaps, many of them still reeking of alcohol. What I saw here was no different, maybe worse.

"*Hinlegen*" (Hit the dirt). The men collapsed in the dirt with their full backpack and their rifle. "*Sprung!*" (Prepare to advance), "*Auf marsch, marsch!*" (Advance at the double), "*Hinlegen*," "*Achtung!*" (Attention). There they stood, panting with half open mouths trying to get their steel helmets out of their sweaty faces, a disgusting sight for me. I'd been there.

Even without being able to follow spoken words I could detect collective punishment procedures. The instructor in question finding fault with one hapless grenadier, abusing him verbally, and then tearing into the whole group to punish them for having this dunce in their midst. One sergeant even let all of them go down on their haunches and then jump like little rabbits with their outstretched arms. It's traditional military behavior, but it always made me sick. I resolved to take this matter up with my company commander at the earliest opportunity. The nineteenth century style of subjecting men to bloody-minded bullying and humiliation was still fresh in my memory from boot camp in 1936.

I closed the window and changed for my appointment with my company commander, Captain Lutze. Entering his office, I smelled Schnapps. For a second I thought it could possibly be my own hangover. I saluted and then coughed into my cupped hand to see if I was the source of this odor. Soon he gave me a full dose of Schnapps breath as we shook hands. He smelled awful and talked with a rather loud voice, bragged about his company, the battalion, and his regiment and then put me in charge of the Third Platoon. He assured me he would always be available if I needed information or help. With that he burped and dismissed me.

Rodust, my Captain in Ratzeburg, may have been rather pompous, this one in Spandau did not even speak like an educated person. I knew immediately I was in for a rough going, for I could see that my diction startled him, although I did not say more than a few words.

I met the other officers. There was Lt. Lochner, class of '37, a likable alcoholic. I liked his self-deprecating sense of irony. No role-model, but a good buddy. Lt. Zimmermann, East Prussia, a career conscious yes-man, devout ex-Hitler Youth leader, former Roman Catholic Scout, full of pharisian righteousness. At the first handshake we recognized each other as being at fundamentally opposing viewpoints. I decided right then to watch my tongue and be on guard in his presence.

The sergeant major was well-oiled effectiveness personified. His servility towards the captain was different from the almost sneering contempt with which he accepted us youngsters. He was always quoting rules and regulations, always glad to show that he knew the Army "good book" better than those upstart young officers. Towards NCO's and the men, he was uncaring and handled them with unnecessary roughness, I thought.

My three noncoms, all younger than me, none of them taller than five-foot-six-inches, turned out to be the loudest among their peers, compensating for tough bullying what they lacked in height and insight. In short, given my own ambivalence versus my new situation, I was sadly aware I could expect many difficulties here. There was no one to talk to. I could not even trust Lochner, I found out he was often indiscreet when under the influence. He, the battalion doctor and I went out in civvies a couple of weekends, but I soon gave that up. It was too much alcohol and no fun. I suppose "painting the town" for its own sake was not my favorite relaxation. Besides there was much too much alcohol in the officers' mess anyway. Sometimes Lochner and the battalion doctor tried to make me pay for the drinks, since I was the rookie. I didn't need that.

The company took part in divisional war games north of Berlin, while the political crisis between Hitler and the Czechoslovakian government mounted. September 12, some Sudeten Germans rioted and were beaten down.September 15, the British prime minister approached Hitler and visited him in Berchtesgaden, Hitler's retreat. Mr. Chamberlain's deviation from normal diplomatic channels shocked the whole world. September 18, France and England agreed that the Czechs had to let go of the German minority groups. The German newspapers howled with glee, but we were given very little information about what had taken place in these discussions. Hitler and Chamberlain met again on September 22, and negotiated until September 24 at Bad Godesberg. We were again given very little information, except that Czechoslovakia had refused to budge. On September 26, Hitler made a speech in Berlin announcing, "This is my last territorial demand." There was talk about an ultimatum around the end of the month.

The tension became unbearable. In the middle of our war games, we turned in our practice ammunition in exchange for live bullets. On September 28, Mussolini was reported to have gotten involved and on September 29, Mussolini, Daladier, Chamberlain and Hitler met at Munich and sealed the dismemberment of the unfortunate country. Poland and Hungary received a substantial share of the booty. The Czech representatives were not even invited to come to the Munich conference. "Peace in our time." All four politicians were celebrated in their own countries, the population of Munich gave them a heartfelt send-off. The German people certainly were in no mood to go to war.

On September 28, we were ordered to move back to Spandau. I made a bet with Lochner that I could get permission to leave early to "discharge some family business in Berlin." I would meet him with a newly acquired radio, record player and some additional His Master's Voice records, and we would have a celebration of this peaceful outcome after half a year of building political tension.

I was granted special permission to leave the battalion prematurely. I hitchhiked to Berlin, took the light rail for the last ten miles and from overhearing conversations I had a good opportunity to see how concerned and depressed the people had been. After all, most of them had put all their trust in Hitler's promises to keep peace.

In my sweaty field togs, I bought the electronic equipment and the records, and took a taxi back to Spandau. The taxi was hopelessly stuck in a traffic jam. Unbeknownst to the sweaty swearing driver, a military unit, motorized division was crossing our westerly thoroughfare. It moved by without ever stopping to let cross-traffic pass through. The driver claimed it was a total surprise to him. Had he known about it, he would not have accepted a job of going from downtown to Spandau, would I please believe him. The trucks, motorbikes and guns rolled by. The soldiers in full battle dress sitting in rows staring solemnly above the throngs of bystanders were just as trapped as we were and looked on this military display in a leaden silence. Their faces again, just as in the S-Bahn earlier this day, were not showing one bit of enthusiasm or patriotic fervor. The oppressive ominous listlessness of the public response must have registered with whosoever ordered this demonstration. For such it was, because nobody routes a troop movement straight through the center of a huge capital city unless there is some very urgent reason to do so. It was a weird scene. Later eyewitnesses told me that the same thing was observed under Hitler's window. There were many people as usual, but they did not break out in cheers or yelling *Sieg Heil*. According to this story, Hitler disappeared from the window, the curtains were drawn and the lights switched off.

When Lochner arrived the next day, caked with sweat and dust, I received him, draped across my couch smoking a British Woodbine cigarette and humming along with a Benny Goodman record, whatever the tune was. The bubbly was cold and now he had to pay for it. The turntable kept spinning and spinning quite a while that afternoon of September 28. While the population of Munich gave the French and British diplomats a rousing send-off, bubbly was flowing and we were celebrating. The apparent diplomatic breakthrough, of course, enhanced Hitler's image again, and when the radio news included Chamberlain's statement, "Peace in our time," our party really got off the ground, much to the disgust of some of our senior members who thought it was bad style to celebrate a bloodless victory. Teddy Stauffer's band was heard loud and clear in the Spandau barracks that evening.

The next day, we had another shock coming. Our captain had been posted somewhere else right at the end of the war games and we were not told why. We were just relieved to see that he was gone because during the games his behavior had become repulsive. He made a number of mistakes, in some cases the company had to pay for it, being subjected to additional moves and dislocations. He had tried to mask his inadequacies behind a lot of noise, while following Lt. Lochner's suggestions. His speech at a dance with the local populace outdid Goebbels' rantings. He kept repeating, "Germany's borders are on fire," whenever he got stuck. It was most embarrassing.

I found only one woman partner who liked to dance the way I liked to dance. She claimed to have a job in Berlin. The captain sneered that it was typical for me to pick such a person instead of asking one of the local women to dance who were dressed in a more wholesome way.

The new company commander was a kindly reserve officer, World War I vintage, who mostly left us to do our own thing. He put me in charge of physical fitness, "sport," as he put it. The day he came, he had watched me doing some rifle drills and I agreed that I liked that better than being in charge of teaching the new recruits the goose-step. I worked out a plan to stress endurance in various disciplines, and I became known for doing a respectable job. That was a good idea because my reputation was in need of repair. So, we introduced cross-country running in the morning with ever increasing length and level of difficulty, and gymnastics with and without rifles, which we used in lieu of weights. My simple trick in all these endurance exercises was that I did exactly what they had to do, but I knew when I came close to the limit of my endurance - they did not. The whole group was struggling along with me, expecting to collapse or just give up. Sure, I was sore afterwards, as were they, but we did get into shape somehow. I didn't mind paying my share of the price, secretly blessing the daily exposure to sport at my high school when somebody showed appreciation for my efforts.

My reputation as an outsider was quickly established and the consequences for doing things "my way" were quick to manifest themselves and were well-deserved. I asked for it. As per usual, I had taken great care to "sit down between two chairs," to translate a German adage. Zimmerman kept saluting and saying, "Yes, sir," and I saluted and kept asking questions. I was fighting windmills, or better the treadmills of a shaky bureaucracy. Our regiment was a very self-conscious army unit saturated with police officers who were *subsonös*, as we called it. In other words, most of them had a chip on their shoulders.

During the political crisis that was gaining momentum, I made quite sure I would have my own exigence neatly developed. Well-meaning people observing my antics would ask: "What is this mad man doing?" The not so well inclined disciplinarian types began collecting a file on my deportment. Apart from my haircut, which was a constant irritation to my superiors, (twice I was officially censured for it), I just could not do very much right and proper. My penchant for questioning age-old traditions of Prussian militarism landed me in the proverbial doghouse more often than I care to be reminded of. Nobody likes a "wise guy." Practical or ethical considerations in question, I just could not keep my mouth shut.

I coined disrespectful names for each of the World War I bits of equipment or any of the World War I hassles that made our lives more "interesting." There was some positive reaction to my irreverent mumblings: I found some kindred souls, a small group of "young Turks," mostly lieutenants, always ending up in a cluster standing in a corner of the officer's mess exchanging serious and more often than not hilarious approaches to reforms. Ever since the Ottoman empire bottomed out around the turn of the century, young people with revolutionary ideas were labeled "young Turks." The Turkish reformer Kemal Ataturk considered the term to be an honor.

Lt. Mügge, son of a Berlin industrialist, was the leading light of the group. He and I promptly found ourselves transferred as of November 10, 1938, to a Fourth Battalion, training reservists and older recruits for twelve weeks. We had large numbers of reserve officer candidates thrown in for good measure. Thus, I could boast having "graduated" two university professors, a number of graduate assistants, and Henner Henkel, the doubles partner of Germany's world famous tennis star, Baron von Cramm. For these career people a lot depended on their finishing the twelve-week stint with a creditable standing to be advanced in rank. This was not a foregone conclusion. We did not give them any special consideration.

One Sunday night, I had to be the officer on duty checking each room as was the prescribed routine. The professor who was doing the cleaning chores that day, a very unpopular rotated assignment, had yelled, "Room 107, all accounted for." I did not check each bed as I was supposed to do. On my way back to my quarters, fifteen minutes later, I saw a grenadier from 107 just turning the corner of a building and facing me. His hand was wrapped in a bloody handkerchief. I ignored him, but sent my batman to invite the whole squad to my room at 11:30 p.m. in battle fatigues. I figured this would give them a chance to talk things over among themselves while getting dressed again.

I invited them in and had all six of them sit down as best they could on one chair and a couch. After a long silence, the professor got up and apologized for lying to me. He said he was aware of the consequences and had to take full responsibility. Then the culprit got up and tried to defend the professor whose action he described as altruistic, but foolish beyond reason. He asked to be made accountable for the whole mess, if that was possible, and kindly regarded the professor's oversight as a regrettable mistake. Nobody started finger pointing, although everybody knew exactly what was going on at the time, and they were all hoping against hope that they would get away with it. They all knew their advance to reserve officer status had been seriously jeopardized, I didn't have to say anything. They kept up their stiff-upper-lip loyalty to each other. They could not have done better, I was really impressed.

I did not care to sound like a bombastic King Solomon with some kind of verdict or something. I just asked the culprit to relate how he got into the compound undetected. He said he was quite sure that nobody had seen him. I left the whole mess to their discretion and told them to be back the following night at 9:00 p.m. As luck would have it, the culprit was right. There were no charges, no reports, no repercussions. Security had failed to notice him.

The next day, one of them, a candidate in medicine, who said he was a neighbor of the delinquent soldier in Dahlem claimed the story checked out. The doctor who had treated his friend had confirmed this over the telephone to him. Would I allow him to leave it at that?

The problem causing the tardiness had been the result of a problem of extremely delicate nature and he would prefer not going into details, unless I or other authorities insisted. He would hate to drag a number of other people into this affair including a certain young lady. He was sure I would have an idea what kind of physical mishap that this was all about between two people of the opposite sex requiring a doctor's services. Of course, I hadn't the foggiest notion, but I just vaguely nodded as affirmative as I could muster, covering up my lack of experience in these matters.

For the remainder of their twelve-week stint, I had six overeager grenadiers on my hands falling all over one another to please their superiors. With some of them I kept contact until 1939. The professor, I forgot what his rank or academic situation was, age-wise could have been my father. He had come with a distinct beer-belly and lost at least twenty-eight pounds in those twelve weeks.

CHAPTER III

JANUARY 25, 1939. HITLER ORDERED A COMMAND PERFOR-
mance for the second lieutenants from the class of 1938; the newly
commissioned officers of the air force, army and navy had to report that
evening 6:00 p.m. at the chancellery. We came from all over Germany,
which for some of us meant traveling up to twenty-four hours. My good
friend Mügge and I were still serving at the Replacement Battalion
Grenadier Regiment 67 in Berlin-Spandau. Our battalion took in a new
class of recruits every twelve weeks and these were an odd mixture of
people. Some were reserve officer candidates, some were born before
World War I and had never worn a uniform, and some were Austrians
or Germans from the western borders of the Reich.

Göring made his usual theatrical entrance. He was wearing a fantasy
uniform, which to me made him look like a footman outside a garish
Berlin hotel. He introduced Adolf Hitler saying, "Class 1938 reports to
you, Mcin Führer."

While Hitler was speaking I looked around. I secretly envied the air
force officers next to me. Their tunics were not closed tightly around

the neck as ours were and they wore a shirt and a tie. Our collars were patterned on the World War I design, which were closed tightly with hooks and eyes. At times, I feared for my blood circulation, particularly in hot weather. I hated our general appearance of ramrod stiffness and the resulting goose-like posture. That was the only aspect of life in the air force that I envied. When we were all tested for flight aptitude, I had continued to excuse myself saying I was going to be sick any minute and would she please turn off the centrifugal contraption that was shaking me up. The young female doctor was smiling all the way through my ordeal and waved me off in the end with the words, "Your tendency towards the air force cannot be very strong." I felt the urge to hug her, although I had no idea whether she had flunked me as I had hoped or had reported me as a cheat.

Hitler was giving his usual routine review of the last twenty years. He was speaking in a relaxed fashion and seemed to be in good shape. Only a few months ago he had experienced his momentous triumph in having the German minority of Czechoslovakia and their border region ceded to the Reich as he had demanded. This Sudeten crisis almost brought Europe to the brink of war. In the end, England and France gave in and left Czechoslovakia in the lurch. "Peace in our time," the British prime minister had said arriving in London from Munich. We had all rejoiced along with the general population. So as far as we could tell Hitler again had achieved a solution without bloodshed. The German prestige certainly had been increased.

Of course, there was Kristallnacht, November 9, 1938, when a German diplomat had been killed by a Jewish student and all over Germany an allegedly spontaneous pogrom took place. Hitler was kept out of it in all reports and commentaries just as if he had nothing to do with it. There were even hints in the press that he and Göring who felt responsible for law and order were furious about the tremendous waste caused by the looting of Jewish property and the burning of the synagogues. Allegedly, Hitler ordered the Jews who had been taken into "protective custody" in concentration camps to be released at the earliest convenient time.

Mügge and I each had our own comeuppance on November 9, 1938. He got into an argument with a police officer who just stood watching the looting of a shop. The officer gave his name and number, but refused to act so Mügge reported him. That afternoon a noncom came back from a christening downtown and reported to me what he had seen. I took him with me to the company commander and had him repeat his story. A number of eleven to fourteen-year-old boys had been busy looting a Jewish owned jewelry store in broad daylight. I respectfully suggested to the captain that we should take some action since obviously the police were overtaxed and didn't have enough manpower to keep order. The captain sharply rebuked me and told me to stay in my flat together with my Austrian roommate Lieutenant Heider, whom he expressly ordered to feel responsible for my staying there. "If Panny goes out and does anything stupid, I'll hold you personally responsible." Repeatedly he told us it was not the army's business.

I was devastated and felt helpless. All night we could see the glow of the burning synagogues against the clouds as we listened to the reports on the radio. The riots were declared to be the spontaneous outburst of rage and indignation by the populace. *Gesundes Volksempfinden*, (healthy instinct of the masses), the party propaganda machine described it.

Both the triumph in Munich and the barbaric pogrom of November 9 were on everybody's minds as we were listening to Hitler. Watching him and listening to him speak, I remember being tempted to accept the usual explanation given by many people I knew and heard. Whenever something unsavory happened, it was said that Hitler didn't know about this. They blamed the SA, Goebbels, Himmler or Streicher or somebody else, but not Hitler.

The dolorous drone of a male voice had always made me sleepy during a lecture. Suddenly I asked myself, "Am I hearing this right?" If I can recall the gist of what brought me out of my reverie, I thought I heard Hitler say that, "only lately in so-called 'modern times' we have managed to discover conflicting distinctions made between war and politics, which, objectively speaking, in reality cannot exist," or words to that effect.

The speech continued, "At those high points of history-making significance, that is to say, when new nations, new political entities are formed, politics becomes the art of the doable (*des Machbaren*). That means the attainment of a goal by whatever means necessary or imaginable". I remember this verbatim, "Persuasion, duty, wisdom, tenacity, kindness, cleverness and, yes, brutality, that is to say, violent means when all others fail."

Mügge and I exchanged glances. I certainly was dumbfounded and I knew something must have bothered him as well. Hitler ended at long last. Somebody gave a ringing appeal to the group, "A lieutenant always must set an example for his men in every field of endeavor. Dying in an exemplary fashion is only part of that." (*Vorleben-Vorsterben ist nur ein Teil davon.*)

We gathered in loose groups of conversation along the seemingly endless hallway, which we had seen so often in newsreels and photos. Hitler went slowly up and down the hall stopping here and there to address one of the young officers. Mostly, he chose to speak to some mountain ranger or a lieutenant from the former Austrian army. The latter were conspicuous by their new ill-fitting German style uniforms, which were apparently improvised by their Austrian tailors right after the takeover in early 1938.

Mügge and I kept talking. He stood with his back to the huge tapestry filled with battle scenes from Teutonic mythology. They were done in the new larger than life photographic Nazi style depicting idealized heroic figures triumphantly defeating dark sinister forces. My impression that Mügge and I always reacted in tandem was proven wrong in this case. He just found the odd sequence of quasi-oxymorons remarkable. "Persuasion, duty," for instance. "What was duty doing in this context?" he asked. "Wisdom, tenacity, kindness, etc." It just didn't make sense to him and I agreed.

"That wasn't so much my concern," I said. "The man just threatened war only a few days after he had solemnly declared that Germany would have no further territorial demands. He gave this promise to the British prime minister, Mr. Chamberlain, in writing."

We both had argued with some energy until I noticed that Mügge's attention was drifting away from our conversation. He gave me a slight kick to my shin bone and made a slight motion with his head to me to turn around. I did with some irritation about being interrupted and found myself facing the Führer. Thank god he was shaking the hand of Ortner, a former friend from my Munich days, and didn't notice anybody else. Again, this man was from an alpine regiment. Just as well it was Ortner. I had totally forgotten where I was, so to speak, and I wasn't keen on being overheard.

When the Commander-in-Chief had retired, SS orderlies came with large silver platters laden with sandwiches and poured champagne, to be sure it was the German kind, a sparkling white wine called *Sekt*. We called it *Rülpswasser*, the drink that makes you burp, unlike the French product of this kind. It was a good thing the press photographers had left. The SS men barely made it into the crowd when their platters were pounced upon in the most unseemly fashion.

Some of us sauntered into the basement attracted by guitar music and singing. The so-called "Tearoom" where Hitler usually held court surrounded by female admirers, if one could believe the papers and newsreels, was now filled with a lively group of young celebrating officers. The music was that of the Free Youth Movement, the songs we had been singing in the early thirties and later about the time we had been taken over by the Hitler Youth. God knows where somebody found this guitar. In a few minutes a large number of us were sitting on the floor, our tunics wide open, our glasses of bubbly in hand, singing, "It's a Long Way to Tipperary," "Oh, Susannah," "Platoff, Our Cossack Hero, We Praise," "Men of Cornwall," etc. Not exactly German *Volkslieder*. We were singing and drinking until 1:30 a.m.. I am sure this was the most disrespectful crowd ever in this tearoom, which normally tolerated only one voice, that of the Führer.

In between songs Mügge and I kept discussing Hitler's speech with others. There was a consensus that this evening's speech was more than just an induction. When the singing ended most of us went home deep in thought. I think this was the beginning of my awareness of what might be in store for us. To be sure, I had read bits and pieces from *Mein Kampf*, but had never taken it seriously. In it all this talk of expansion towards the East was one thing, surely nobody would actually plan such a move. But what about the Poles? Hitler came to a friendship treaty with them in 1934. This was his first successful diplomatic move. In fact, if there was any danger of war in the East in the minds of the Germans after World War I, it had to do with the Poles who wanted to expand more and more into some German territory.

From this day on I became much more alert and followed political developments more closely. I made it my business to ask questions whenever I ran into someone who had previously made a critical comment or had shown that he was thinking about political matters. Even Auntie Else now had to explain some of her cryptic remarks to me. All the crises in recent history came up again for discussion, the Röhm Affair, General and Mrs. von Schleichers' death, the disappearances of von Fritsch, von Blomberg, and Beck.

Not knowing any details, I did not dare to draw definite conclusions, not even in Mügge's presence. I knew I now was in the same boat with everybody else. The submarine mentality had caught up with me. "Honor, Duty, Country" - the soldier's solemn oath of obedience! I, like everybody else had sworn to carry out orders promptly and without questioning. I started rereading the regulations. There was a clause regarding orders implying illegal acts, orders that involved murder or were of a criminal nature in some way. Those the soldier could refuse, but then who would decide? A court martial? My C.O.? Who else?

I went through a lengthy period of doubt and depression just as painful as the kind of experience I had been through in Munich, 1937. At that time, I was quite sure that this was not the right vocation for me, I did my duty adequately, almost automatically.

Major Günther continued to pressure me. During the time when our battalion had to train twelve hundred Austrians, mostly from Vienna, he singled me out with his attention. Many of these Austrians had been convinced Social Democrats at least two years earlier and had taken their "liberation" by their German neighbors rather hard. They talked about Hitler with some sarcasm and endured the twelve weeks in Berlin with a typical Austrian gallows humor. We survived the twelve weeks without unrest or disciplinary crisis and considered ourselves to be rather fortunate at that.

I had the dubious honor to be in charge of the train-load of Austrians on their way back to Vienna all by myself. No noncoms, not even a medic. It looked like a suicide assignment to me. Maybe it was another "well meant" measure by Major Günther who claimed to have been assigned to either make or break me. Surprisingly, the trip went off without a hitch. All the way through I had the company of these homesick boys. Some came into my compartment to show their appreciation for my not having talked down to them the way Captain Linde had been doing. Some wanted to discuss politics quite openly.

In the outskirts of Vienna, the train stopped at a signal. The sign there read "Hütteldorf" and most of my charges took off at this premature destination, suitcases in hand, waving goodbye to me. I could do nothing to stop them. They were stumbling across the numerous tracks, which was, of course, strictly forbidden and very dangerous. What was I supposed to do? I just stood in the window waved back and kept my fingers crossed that nothing untoward would happen to them. Only a few of them were left to detrain with me at the Vienna station. My naive conviction that nothing would ever go wrong when I was responsible had survived this last challenge. Admittedly, I had never included the possibility that almost the whole bunch risked their lives by crossing the huge shunting yard just to get home more quickly.

The twelve-week turnover routine in our battalion did not leave much time for personal reflection. I kept trying to discipline myself to make daily lists of desiderata. Top of the list was usually, "Where the hell am I going?" Those were fast changing times in Berlin. At the height of the Sudeten crisis, I went to my uncle, Dr. Schöler, and asked him to lend me some money so I could pay off my radio and turntable. In case of war I would be more comfortable in owing the money to a relative. He thought it was a good idea. Having received three installments from me, he forgave the balance saying that he had never experienced a lieutenant paying anything on time.

In reality the political tension in early 1939 did very little to draw my attention away from my miserable situation in Berlin-Spandau. "Getting along" with these ex-police types in army uniform, I found extremely difficult. They were everywhere and mostly in commanding positions. Only a small number of my fellow officers came from Potsdam, from the famous IR9, a regiment which was well-known and often sneered at for its high percentage of noblemen in its service. Here in my battalion, there were three reactivated captains, leftovers from World War I, who had never been free to settle down in civilian life. After twenty years in the police barracks, they had large chips on their shoulders and many of them could not at all be classified as gentlemen.

I abhorred the weekly dinner in the officers' mess. Very little was to be gained by allowing myself to be slowly filled up with cheap liquor in that company and the understood protocol was ridiculous. Whenever one of these gents with a rank above yours raised his glass in your direction you were supposed to get up, raise your glass up to your fourth button of your tunic (or was it your third) and click your heels to show your respect for the old boy. Clicking your heels without having spurs attached to your shoes made some awkward noise. Along with this clicking went a concurrent stiff nod from your hips suggesting a bow of sorts. Within fifteen or twenty minutes you had to approach the same officer with your glass in hand and request permission to drink to his health, glass at fourth button, etc., etc. What a bore it all was, what a waste of time and energy. The topics of conversation were a shallow mixture of puns, jokes and smutty male humor.

●◆●●◆●●◆●

Mügge and I volunteered to take lessons in Russian in downtown Berlin to get off the treadmill as much as we could. It so happened the language lessons were scheduled for Thursdays, our night in the officers' mess. Young officers were encouraged to acquire language skills. In fact, anyone interested in a career in the general staff was required to have a reasonable command of a foreign language. Neither Mügge nor I considered ourselves general staff material, but found it convenient to try out our new language in the bars, which in those days were hopping with Russian immigrants.

The colonel evaluated me and my file and pointed out to me that I would have to get over my tendency to interpret rules, regulations and orders with a certain selective liberality. This was not a report I would be inclined to show my father. I do not know what they had found wanting in the case of Mügge. Whenever I asked him, he just grinned and changed the subject. There we were in this god-awful battalion, every twelve-weeks new faces. It felt like we were turning out sausages in some huge meat grinder for mass consumption. I made no secret of my discomfort. When my little brother Rolf came visiting, I did not bother to pretend I was a happy soldier. I left it up to him what he wanted to report back home to Hamburg.

On the other hand, according to my friends with whom I had been sharing the training experience from Munich, I was to be envied for having landed a Berlin assignment. Berlin, even after most of the Jews had left or had lost their jobs, was still a culturally well renowned center. The performing arts attracted audiences from all over the world who chose to ignore the plight of the Jewish citizens, who since 1935 had been systematically excluded and disenfranchised.

At the first dinner dance at the officers' mess I met Irmgard von Keudell, a vivacious, very bright student of law who told me that she had been a guest in this establishment for years, but had never been able to dance swing because there wasn't anybody who knew how.

"Aren't you a bit reckless?" She said after I had inquired if she wanted to dance swing with me. "This dance is strictly forbidden," and she pointed to the sign on the wall the like of which was in every public dancing establishment. "*Swing tanzen polizeilich verboten*" (Dancing swing forbidden).

"I'm the black sheep around here anyway," I replied as we began to dance to the music. "One more bad mark on my record won't make much difference. Besides, this is the first time I ever enjoyed dancing in this place and you are as light as a feather."

I thought she was even a better dancer than my sister and we spent the whole enjoyable evening together. I don't have to mention that it was expected that every lieutenant was supposed to ask as many different partners to dance as possible and my captain let me know about my transgression in no uncertain terms the next morning. Anyway, this event started a beautiful friendship and she became my mentor in many respects, including simple matters of hygiene, table manners, knowledge of wines and wine drinking, social etiquette, do's and don'ts in letter writing and she raised my sensitivity towards women. She gave me a lot of help by tactfully filtering down whatever people were saying about me, mostly of a critical nature, in the hopes it might be helpful to me.

She also invited me to her flat on Budapester Street right in the center of town where she introduced me to her mother and to a pair of patent leather tap dancing shoes. I couldn't believe my eyes. She put a record on and tap danced in the European fashion, that is to say, only the tip of the shoe has a metal tap. She asked me to go and buy my own pair and report back for my first tap dancing lesson in a week's time when her next academic exam would be over. I had seen Buddy Epson in *Broadway Melody* and other US musical films. My idol was Eleanor Powell, the tap dancer who reigned supreme at the time. I kept telling Irmel that the American system was so much more enjoyable and shouldn't we both start that from scratch. Well, she was busy at the university and she convinced me that for the time this would have to do.

I don't know what the tenant below her room was thinking about this. We were two very hard working tap dancers making a hell of a racket. After an hour or so we would collapse on that huge queen sized bed panting with exhaustion and dabbing our faces with *eau de cologne* wipes. By this time, we had become swing partners not only in the officers' mess, but whenever we found a chance, whether in her flat, or in one of the many dance cafes around downtown.

She did tell me that she was engaged, yet there was a tremendous physical attraction at work between us. There was the odd kiss, but in such a moment she would immediately change the subject and say, "I think we are both very tired." That was my signal to leave, but our goodbyes would invariably be interrupted with a second thought, a new story, another goodbye etc., until I was finally somehow much later out the door.

Her mother was an enjoyable, highly articulate person who enriched my cultural awareness many ways, especially by suggesting new books or essays to read. At first, I was a bit afraid of her, particularly right after that first dinner we had together. There was a lull in the conversation and to fill it I rather recklessly picked my parody of the Saxon dialect to serve as a source of our entertainment. Mrs. V. K. seemed highly amused and was chuckling in response to my routine when suddenly I felt Irmel's pointed shoe tip tapping on my shin bone under the table. I quickly got the hint to change the subject to some other dialect.

As I was leaving that night Irmel continued her useful tutoring in deportment. She advised me that it was not good style to praise the quality of the food, because, obviously, her mother had not been cooking it. She also explained that the reason of her assault on my shinbone while I was making fun of the Saxon dialect was that, obviously, I had been in potentially sensitive territory. Her mother had been one of the ladies in waiting at the Royal Court of Saxony.

•◆••◆••◆•

A second cultural counterweight to the drab military existence of drilling new recruits in our twelve-week pressure cooker opened itself the minute I phoned my great aunt Else. She welcomed me to Berlin and to her family and she insisted on my visiting their flat at the first convenient opportunity. Following the correct protocol instructions I received from my parents, I first made a short formal call on Great Great Aunt Anna Rohde, Great Aunt Else's mother, with the obligatory bunch of flowers of the season.

The next day, I rang the downstairs bell at Alt Moabit 113, again with flowers, and was welcomed by a beastly jarring sound of the automatic door opener. There was a vestibule to cross, a swinging door to push, and then I heard what must be *Tante* Else's voice way above me from the fifth floor.

"Wait down there. We'll send the lift."

After a few seconds, I enjoyed my first hug and the slobbery kisses of Great Auntie Else, who would become another very important person in my new life in the big city. Uncle Fritz, a renowned eye surgeon, lavished his Baltic hospitality on me with a big glass of vodka with a slice of liverwurst resting on the rim of the glass.

His first words were, "I bet this is nothing new for you. To your health, my boy." Another hug and kiss on either cheek. Finally, I had time to look at my Aunt Gisela, five years my junior. She had grown considerably since 1927, but she wasn't exactly a tall girl. It felt wonderful to be welcomed with open arms and we sat down to a sumptuous dinner. The doctor kept filling my glass and because they asked me so many questions, I'm afraid I did more drinking and talking than eating. It was a wonderful first evening and at around 10:30 p.m. Gisela was commissioned to guide me down in the elevator and open the outside door for me. When I was about to ask whatever happened to the door mechanism, they said, "This is Moabit, not Uhlenhorst in Hamburg where your father used to live. We have to bring you down and be sure to lock the door personally."

Auntie Else quickly established a weekly routine. She would say that if I had nothing better to do on a given day she would have two tickets to *Othello* or two tickets to a given opera or the tennis tournament at the Red and White Tennis Club, one of the most exclusive clubs in Berlin. Gisela and I were left to enjoy whatever Berlin had to offer after a wonderful family meal each time. Her mother or her father discreetly put some money up my sleeve and wished us a good time.

They even sent us to the Presse Ball, the dinner dance arranged by the newspaper guild, and invited two of my fellow officers and myself to an afternoon dance on the roof garden of Hotel Eden. The host couple sat comfortably with a glass of wine while my friends and I were dancing with Gisela and two of her friends from her senior class in high school.

My relationship with Aunt Else became intimate. At least to the point that we had several long conversations in front of her big three-piece mirror, which was so ornate it could have fit in a palace. As we talked she arranged various hair pieces or put on her make-up. It didn't take her long to find out to what extent I had painted myself into a corner and she kept encouraging me to rethink my goals. She suggested that if the stage had been my first inclination, wouldn't it still be possible to switch? She didn't think that I was fed properly or eating sensibly. Each week from her I received a parcel with precooked food in cans from the gourmet section of big department stores. She kept saying what a wonderful break my presence was for her daughter and how much they enjoyed arranging afternoon dances.

I knew I was putting more effort and concentration into my social life than I did on my military obligations and this continued until the big parade in Berlin in honor of the fiftieth birthday of Adolf Hitler. For this, the doctor had the brilliant idea to utilize the temporary presence of my regiment in the barracks across the street. The Spandau regiment routinely had a free rest period in the Moabit barracks while the units were being fed before the short march to the inner city. The doctor wanted me to bring upstairs the same two boys who regularly joined us for those afternoon tea dances and join him and his friends for a breakfast *auf breiter Basis* (a breakfast of tremendous scope).

It worked out perfectly. We were wined and dined by a wonderful group of mostly professionals, nearly all of them from the Baltics. Tables and tables filled with the choicest appetizers: seafood, cheeses, omelets, meats, and caviar. It was a sight to behold. When my friends and I had to leave at the appointed hour, we were well-fed and reasonably high. On that day, I had to be the lieutenant on the right side of the three battalion colors to goose-step past the stands. There was a vicious wind, but I blamed my somewhat shaky performance on the vodka.

●◆●●◆●●◆●

It is part of the officer's procedure concerned with social customs within a given battalion that the incoming lieutenant pays a formal visit with all the fellow officers who are married and live outside the barracks. They are told a certain week will find these fellow officers "at home," or whatever, that a telephone announcement of the impending visit is required. Then the young man puts on his best uniform including that ceremonial saber and equipped with the necessary number of printed calling cards, he starts making the rounds. If you have the money, you do it by taxi, but people like myself walked.

You ring the doorbell. The servant will answer the door and receive your calling card while you stand there like an idiot in the half open door and wait for either the husband or the wife to greet you and ask you to come in. You keep your cap in hand and with the same hand you control your clumsy saber and you sit down facing the husband and the wife and make polite conversation. You should not stay longer than fifteen or twenty painful minutes. Then you should manly arise and announce that you have many more obligations. There is a shaking of hands and best wishes for your future. You will then be guided to the door by the husband to set out to your next formal visit.

I remember being relieved that it hadn't rained and I survived the first battalion visiting day more or less intact. However, in the twelve-week battalion a middle-aged woman with an apron opened the first door I was to approach. I handed her my card asking, "Would you please give this to the lady of the house?"

"Oh, that's me," she replied.

There was a confused long pause. I mumbled an apology and managed to sustain a frozen grin throughout this formal visit. I had been totally insensitive to the plight of this reactivated officer who obviously had not been in a position so far to hire a maid. The lady in question turned out to be equipped with a sense of humor and at the door as I left we had a good laugh at my bumbling first attempt. I wasn't so sure her husband ever forgave me, his male vanity being what it seemed in relation to his spouse.

◆ ◦ ◦ ◆ ◦ ◦ ◆ ◦

By August 1939, the active regiment 67 to which Mügge and I belonged was preparing for some kind of military display in East Prussia. We had been told that there was supposed to be a big national festivity in connection with the dedication of the Hindenburg Monument. Mügge and I were not involved. We had to stay with our replacement battalion and train reservists. Their ages varied from twenty through forty odd years, some of them had seen short service in World War I. This assignment was not a reward for excellence in performing our duty. Both of us had been reprimanded once or twice for not sticking to the prescribed procedure and it was obvious that we were not looked upon as A-1 material in the regimental establishment. Sometimes we met on the parade ground in Spandau and Mügge always finished the conversation saying, "Vincenz, only a war could save you and me." This gallows humor described our despair along with our conviction that if called upon we would do our duty quite well. On August 23, 1939, reality caught up with us.

We had been in downtown Berlin at a concert of the world-famous Don Cossack Mens' Chorus, which we had enjoyed so many times before while in the youth movement. We were standing near a loud speaker early in the morning, after a night of carousing with the Russian singers and dancers. The loud speaker suddenly blared, "Attention! Attention!" And then it was announced that Hitler and Stalin had signed a pack of friendship combined with extensive import and export arrangements. We looked at each other, mouths wide open. We were unable to speak. This was the end of the line. Hitler was ready to attack Poland and we both knew it.

The tension between Germany and Poland, which had been dormant most of the spring and summer, now flared up in summer and fall. There were border incidents and there were massacres and the German propaganda played exactly the same films that were seen during the Czechoslovakian crisis in 1938. Mügge commented dryly that all that remained was the pregnant ethnic German mother, due any day, pushing a pram across the Polish/German border into Germany whilst dragging another half dozen children with her. And sure enough there she was in the latest Newsweek newsreel and in the newspaper. Of course, there were real incidents and massacres perpetrated by mobs in some Polish towns. The German minorities in Poland were being pushed around for sure. But the propaganda was carefully orchestrated and utterly repugnant to us. This morning we two boys took a taxi back to Spandau hardly speaking to each other, each of us busy with our own thoughts about the impending war. A few days later the active regiment did move out and a step by step mobilization began.

Mügge and I ended up in the same regiment. We felt good about that, but that was all we could enjoy. This new Regiment 203, Division 76, was a unit of the "third wave," which meant that it was largely consisting of reservists with a sprinkling of active soldiers and officers. Now as I examined the platoon I was put in charge of, I fervently wished I could have been with the active regiment. My platoon consisted of mostly men who were the age of my father, some of them had seen service at the end of World War I and were now totally out of shape. The worst part was that Major Günther who had been the bane of our existence for the last year in Spandau, this former policeman who had vowed to either make us or break us, was now commanding our battalion, perish the thought.

As one of the few officers who knew Berlin, I was sent on a "sexy" side-car BMW motorbike to collect equipment and spare parts that were needed for this new outfit. I was impressed to see that every noncom I visited to ask for a given piece of equipment had the corresponding list in his hand and knew exactly what the "Battalion of the Third Wave" was entitled to receive. Meantime, the war had started and I found ways of finding out how my buddies from the active regiment were doing. This was, of course, the source of part of my on-going nostalgia.

The noncoms I visited were always glad to hear the latest news of the active division because they too had friends and relatives among those units. I used this opportunity to get these quartermaster sergeants into a cooperative mood. Some of them were even willing to go out of their way to provide our unit with items other units failed to get. Corruption and the black market were not the way things got done in the early days of World War II and I felt pretty good each time I landed a coup merely by my being aware. It was amazing how Major Günther suddenly became quite personable and even the new commander of the regiment expressed his satisfaction. I was not used to praise at all, and I enjoyed the comment of the colonel, "Of course, we did not expect anything else," future implication deleted.

Meantime, the "regiment of the second wave," which had taken up residence in the Spandau barracks, was ready to leave and Grenadier Regiment 203 became the lone inhabitant of the compound. I met Lieutenant Friedrich von Kirchbach, the adjutant to Major Günther. Friedrich's father worked in the general staff and provided the information on the whereabouts of the Division 76. The young man had been commissioned a few days before. I had always liked him, even as a recruit. We became friends very quickly, both having reservations about Germany's sudden turn with the use of force and the blatant superiority complex towards Eastern peoples, which manifested itself in official documents, the radio and newspaper propaganda of the Nazi party. He played the accordion beautifully, was interested in jazz as well as in all those songs dear to those of us who had been in the Youth Movement.

Wives and girlfriends walked their men back to the gate every night whenever passes were issued. I was almost glad my girl was in Hamburg. I observed some heartbreaking scenes. I also heard of some, which were on the lighter side. A couple got caught making love through the wrought-iron fence. Major Günther's reaction was to issue Battalion Order XYZ September 3, 1939: "Exchanges of an intimate nature through the barrack fence are forbidden."

It was probably the first time anyone had ever tried to move a whole division on trucks across the whole of the country. The strategic potential of Hitler's Autobahn had always been clear, but to move an ordinary infantry division – 15,000 men, thousands of horses, dozens of artillery pieces and miscellaneous lorries and carts – straight across the country surely was another first.

As one of the few regulars in the battalion, I was increasingly singled out for the more interesting chores. A noncom looked after my platoon and I, again on a sidecar motor bike NSU, dashed ahead of the regiment on the Autobahn in a westerly direction. I was quite excited about this assignment, to rush ahead of the convoy and find a suitable loop off the Autobahn with plenty of housing and trees lining the road where the regiment could bivouac overnight. There needed to be enough trees to conceal from the air the big overland trucks and their trailers. I had to measure the length of this loop carefully to make sure there was enough room to accommodate those big monsters and I had to make sure that the local population did not leave any implements or carts in those narrow country roads. That part of it was hair-raising. Those big vehicles were much too large to do anything but go in one direction on those roads.

On the way out, I was glad that I didn't have to be involved in pushing those poor unsuspecting horses up those steep ramps into the trucks. I thought of the company cook standing in the open truck braving the gusty cold autumn wind preparing the warm evening meal for 150 soldiers. Little did I know what a herculean task was ahead of me arranging the parking of these six axle trucks. I didn't finish my job before midnight.

The owner of the local estate had invited me to spend the night there. She was the widow of a German officer who had reported missing in action in Spain in 1936. The servant dished up a marvelous meal, which of course at that late hour had lost some of its appeal. I didn't meet the lady until next morning at breakfast. Her oldest son was fighting in Poland, she said, a lieutenant like me of the same class of 1938. It was obvious how heavy a burden she was facing. The two younger sons were almost at call-up age. She gave me a goodbye hug and tried to hide her tears.

The final leg of the trip was uneventful, no challenge from the air. They unloaded everything at Dillenburg in the Westerwald, a few miles east of the Rhine River. To put the battalion into any kind of shape near their billets in Westerburg was a farcical undertaking. There was no room for military training of any kind, at least not for units above the platoon level. It was impossible to train with weapons, you couldn't even dig foxholes because all the land was used agriculturally. The one attempt to use an obsolete quarry for target practice had to be scrapped because the neighbors complained about ricocheting bullets. There were soldiers all around with flags to ensure the local population wouldn't get too close, but a woman with a pram came to one of the flag men with a bullet in her hand saying that it had come down right next to her pram. I had only one hope and that was a swift end to this war before anyone might suggest this bunch of "heroes" would see any real action.

By this time, the war in Poland was almost over. I had to impress on my men at regular intervals to by no means reveal in their letters home where they were located. This is, of course, a universal rule with the military in any country at any time. Secrecy, conventional wisdom says, borders on hysteria in the early parts of a given war. All the more amusing was the fact that quite a number of the men very soon had established their loved ones in the surrounding countryside. They all told the truth when they said that they never wrote anything that might have infringed on their respective orders, but of course, the public telephone was functioning beautifully. It was a lower middle-class idyll, the whole scene. The Berliners were fraternizing with the local population who had never in their lives talked to someone from the big city. I remembered the Prussian Army before Napoleon crushed it in 1806. The soldiers had all their relatives with them and were not very keen on risking their lives. When the division was suddenly moved closer to the front line near Kaiserslautern a certain number of soldiers were not available and had to hitchhike after their units. I was amazed that the punishment of the culprits for being AWOL was surprisingly mild and no great harm was done.

The new billets were less comfortable. The Berliners had a hard time to understand the thick dialect of the local population. At least there was some stretch of wasteland where I could train my men in the handling of hand grenades, but that is another story:

Disciplinary action re: Vincenz P. On October 7, 1939, he was severely admonished by his commanding officer because he injured himself through willful neglect of all safety regulations in throwing live hand-grenades. He was prevented from doing his duty because of a lengthy convalescence in a military hospital.

For me, as a responsible leader of a platoon, the state of readiness of the men was a steady concern. How was I expected to lead these men when I had no way of preparing them for all eventualities in war? The throwing of live hand-grenades revealed the total inadequacy of my men as soldiers. Again and again a frightened grenadier would throw away the pin on a strap, which he had just pulled and stand there staring at the viciously hissing grenade. I barely had time to grab the grenade, hit the man down, throw the grenade over the parapet, all in one motion as it were. I was utterly frustrated.

Finally, I let the responsible noncom do the honors and I remained standing a few paces back watching the explosion through his field glasses. This idiotic gesture was meant to show the soldiers that all was not fatal in this procedure. I had seen other officers do it in Spandau in a similar situation, but I didn't consider the fact that in Spandau each grenade was bound to end up in some kind of crater from previous explosions, whereas here the surface was flat. It was a stupid thing to do. I realized this the moment a piece of hot metal had entered the base of my right hand fifth finger, which was helping to hold the field glasses. My first reaction was that it could have been the eye, it could have been the brain, it could have been anything. The sense of relief was drowned out by cold fury against myself. This was an outrageous act of folly and I knew I was in for trouble. The pain was excruciating. Since I was unable to pull the steel fragment out of the bone, I waved the medic and asked him to do it. The good man took one look and fainted. Luckily, his orderly stood close. He held the hand while the driver of his motor-bike pulled it out. It was the size of German mark.

"What a goddamn idiot I am," I swore.

"You were lucky, sir," Glauke said trying to quiet me.

"Lucky, my foot! I'm the biggest asshole between Cairo and Capetown. Isn't that clear?"

"No, sir."

"Only in Central Africa are there bigger assholes than I am."

"If you say so, sir. Can we go?"

He loaded me in the sidecar of his motor-bike and drove to the next military hospital at Bad Oeynhausen. On the way, I became more depressed as I sized up my situation and the driver's mention of tetanus didn't help any either.

CHAPTER IV

THE WINTER OF THE PHONY WAR 1939-1940 WE SPENT ON
the Moselle River billeted around Beuren and Kreuzweiler. Regardless
of weather conditions, all German units had an almost weekly routine of
first being put on alert, then loading up all gear, handing out ammunition to everybody and subsequently marching for miles in the middle of
the night to a given crossroad. Here, our battalion each time had to wait
until the other two battalions had moved past that crossing. The soldiers
were just as sick of this routine as I was. Finally, I took it upon myself to
instruct the men to leave all burdensome and heavy equipment at home
and enjoy these nightly trips into nowhere with less encumbrance. The
soldiers appreciated that and kept our secret. The other two platoons in
the company never found out about this fraud. In retrospect, it never
occurred to me in light of the icy roads and the low cloud ceiling that
in some of these cases Hitler meant business.

Two years later, my boss at the German general staff explained to
me that Hitler meant to attack France more than once between October
1939 and April 1940, but that the bad weather together with the expert

advice from his generals convinced him each time that without the use of the German air force any offensive in the West would be a very risky undertaking. The generals were correctly convinced that the combined strength of the French forces and the British Expeditionary Corps was formidable and in some respects even superior to the German Army, for instance in their supply of heavy tanks; but at the time I considered these exercises a stupid and expensive waste of energy. I would have looked foolish and probably court-martialed as well, if The Phony War had suddenly given way to our invasion of France.

Our preparation for the attack on France meant getting ready to storm Stromberg, a hill two or three hundred meters high towering over the three-country triangle of Luxembourg, France and Germany. To get there the regiment had to be loaded on Moselle pleasure boats, which were supposed to be beached on the Luxembourg side on the day of the attack. None of the bridges from Germany to Luxembourg could be used for a surprise attack because they were heavily blocked and prepared for demolition by the Luxembourg defensive forces.

On May 1, Major Günther and his men practiced boarding one of these steamers and we went down the river to the beautiful city of Trier. Now everybody knew what was in store for them. The commanding officers of each of the companies played through the attack on Stromberg with the help of a sandbox model. Everybody was solemnly standing around this table to find out exactly where to assemble and what to do. The sector for each platoon was carefully indicated in the sand by strips of colored ribbons. I had made a detailed drawing from this model outlining my platoon's assignment.

All my careful preparation was in vain. The commanding officer of the First Company had to go on emergency leave. I had to take over this company where I barely knew anybody a few days before the invasion of France. Before I had time to familiarize myself with their assignment, all units were put on alert and at dawn on May 9, 1940, this totally confused lieutenant embarked with a company of men who must have felt as insecure as I did.

In the preceding fall, while I was in the hospital, the division had seen two short stints on the Siegfried Line near Zweibrücken. These soldiers could say that they had some kind of baptism of fire, figuratively speaking. Basically, nothing ever happened between the Maginot Line and the Siegfried Line. A few patrols were launched on either side and most often came back without having seen the enemy. Both lines were so thoroughly mined that nobody felt like taking big chances.

Here I was faced with an overwhelming number of handicaps. The only information they gave me was that I had to lead First Company and take the left half of Stromberg. I did not even realize First Company once in motion would represent the outer left wing of the German attack, which would be hinged in with our taking the Stromberg.

It was pitch dark when we boarded the same quaint little pleasure boat which we had used on May 1. We disembarked at dawn on the Luxembourg side with about one-hundred-and-twenty men and moved a few kilometers in the direction of the border with France. At the edge of a mixed forest, we came to a stop and I recited from my written order our plan of attack. I pointed out the visual markings on the hill to establish the targets for the various units, but it didn't mean anything to me or to them because it was still foggy and we couldn't see much.

The noncoms kept nodding because they knew the thing by heart. There was no point in any detailed instructions. I felt like such an absolute rank beginner in the face of this foggy mess. I finally decided to roughly divide the borderline between the sections of the two forward platoons. I took a dozen lightly armed soldiers with me, mostly runners and wireless operators. The skeptical expressions on the faces of the sergeants did not bolster my confidence. So far there had been no resistance from any Luxembourg forces so this would be the first contact with the enemy. I had barely finished when the German artillery started to shell the Stromberg and the surrounding area. It was time to move out.

It was the most improvised attack any company ever staged, I was sure of that. We started traipsing through the knee-high wet grass. I was in a state of heightened awareness as we started moving up the hill, but there was no resistance. I began to have an eerie feeling of exhilaration and at the same time I felt resentment for having been placed in this predicament without the careful preparation that all the other officers had received in the weeks prior to the attack. I remembered Major Günther's resolve, which he frequently had expressed to other people that he was assigned up high to make or break me. I did not have time to enjoy the beautiful unseasonably warm morning. The steep climb and the tremendous emotional stress could easily have contributed to the amount of perspiration that everybody experienced. Sweat was running down our faces into our eyes and very soon I and two of the runners were on our own, the others dropping back one by one. We cut our way through two barbed wire fences and kept moving. Still there was no sign of French soldiers.

When we came to the edge of the crest of the hill we found out that the surface was a huge round flat top, which had been cut into an elaborate system of trenches. A couple of steps further we finally encountered the first French soldier who immediately took himself around the next bend of the trench. I remember his horrified expression. I fired my Mauser much too late for no reason whatsoever. Maybe I just wanted to keep him moving. The same Frenchman showed up two more times each time turning around the next bend.

This game was interrupted when all of a sudden, we were hit by a tremendous explosion from some kind of heavy artillery shells. The shelling hit us from the back and we were very glad we happened to be in those French trenches. I realized it came from our own German artillery. Considering it was the first time ever that I was exposed to shelling it was a tremendous shock. I was furious, but then I realized that nobody back there would have expected us to be on the top of Stromberg so fast. We used all our green signal lights to indicate our position which produced immediate relief from this predicament, or so we thought.

When we began to move three or four shells were right on top of us and one of my men was killed instantly. I was raving mad and sent the surviving two runners to find the radio man to send an urgent message. We stopped moving for the moment and one by one the more heavily armed men caught up with us and we cautiously continued to move.

There was still no response from the French. We kept moving within the trenches because we still didn't know if the support artillery had received our signals and wires. This went on until we reached the other end of the flat top and were able to look down into the Moselle Valley on the French side. In a matter of fifty minutes we were in possession of the left half of Stromberg. We looked down into the beautiful Moselle River Valley and were surprised to see that on the French side all was peaceful. No fighting anywhere.

Now it became clear to me that we were the southernmost company in the German invasion of France May 10, 1940. Here I was sitting on top of this pivotal hill in charge of an inexperienced company of men whom I hardly knew. The realization how critically important my assignment was left me shaky and vulnerable. All the more was I pleased to find that after the few short hours of our combined successful effort there were signs of acceptance, trust and a kind of bond between the noncoms, the men and this temporary commander. This was just as well because the French artillery from the Maginot Line around Diedenhofen began a furious shelling of Stromberg once they realized that there were none of their own left on the hill. The barrage lasted for four or five hours and I was extremely grateful for the foresight of the French, who had arranged for this marvelous system of trenches. We would have had serious losses without it.

The last time I raised my head over the parapet I saw the commander of Second Company who had just arrived on my right and who waved to me. I waved back while registering that this was the first time this man had treated me with any kind of friendly gesture. We never could stand each other back in Spandau. G. was everything that I disliked about the stereotypical arrogant Prussian officer.

A number of my men were wounded and had to be carried back, but it could be said that Stromberg was taken and I arranged the details to switch from attack to defense. The French kept shelling on and off day and night for about fifty hours and then gave up. We received a message from higher-up, which ended with the words, "Well done."

In the evening, we had warm food at last and a bottle of French champagne. I did my last round through the perimeter and fell asleep. When I woke up the next morning my sergeants presented me with about thirty French prisoners. In a predawn checkup, on the left side of the hill, they had found a whole French platoon waiting to surrender to somebody. This left side of the hill was under constant observation from the French side of the Moselle and could not be traversed in daylight.

On May 15, finally, the company commander came back and I could go back to my platoon in the Third Company. I felt relieved and couldn't help imagining that I must have aged ten years in this messy military undertaking. All the company commanders received the Iron Cross Second Class for valor on the battlefield. I, for one, could not hide a sheepish grin when I heard the news. I felt I had barely gotten away from a potentially disastrous situation by the skin of my teeth. I remember promising myself from now on to insist on adequate reconnaissance and cool professional judgment, rather than intuitive dash.

It was only a few days later that my platoon was picked to move over to the other side of the Moselle River, occupy a commanding hill and begin reconnaissance in the direction of the little hamlet Königsmacher. I was pleased at having been given this assignment and we found no resistance in setting up our perimeter around the top of that hill. There were even some sheds and bunkers that the French had been using that we took over. We spent two days reconnoitering the surrounding area. In the evening the company would send food, mail and, if necessary, ammunition. The French must have observed our presence and started arbitrarily shelling our hill and some of the approaches.

On the third day, the battalion encouraged us to move closer to the village. We moved out at 4:30 a.m. to probe possible French strong points. The map showed two entrances, so, I sent the machine gun crew and three riflemen to the left entrance and I took my runners and a medic to the approach on the right. I kept two men at the entrance to the village to give us cover and Friedrich, the half Jewish corporal, and I went through the barbed wire obstacle. He was excited because this was the first time I was able to give him the chance he had requested, to show his true mettle as a soldier and earn the required credit to study medicine.

We crossed one more barbed wire obstacle and suddenly stood face to face with a totally unnerved French soldier on guard duty. He jumped into the house and closed the door. I fired my Mauser and followed it up with a hand grenade into the entrance yelling, "*Prisonnier! Prisonnier! Kommt raus, Ihr Aschlöcher!*"

I still have no way of explaining what made me yell this rude invitation to come out with hands up. I was totally surprised to see that the French still were behaving as though The Phony War had never stopped. For them to have allowed us to arrive at their headquarters unmolested had given me this lack of respect, I guess. I only hope that those French who heard what I said and who survived the war kept mum about my embarrassing lack of professionalism.

The ensuing seconds were spent in a harried gunfight in which both Friedrich and I survived untouched as if by miracle. We heard a powerful alarm siren and noticed that the other half of our reconnaissance was engaged in an exchange of fire as well. There were so many muzzles flashing at us that we beat a speedy retreat straight back the way we had come in. The other two runners had already decided that we were outnumbered and had left for "home."

In the distance a number of heavy motor bikes were approaching the French position from the rear, however we were able to get back to our position without anyone following us. The other half of our squad arrived panting and covered with sweat and dirt. None of them were wounded, one soldier was missing and they had abandoned their machine gun. The same evening a telephone line all the way from Stromberg was installed and I was able to make a verbal report about Königsmacher and our reconnaissance. Words of praise for the report were largely overshadowed by criticism and a verbal dressing down over the loss of the one soldier and the machine gun.

We stayed on our hill until the beginning of June when we were relieved by a unit from another division. We then marched through Luxembourg City into the southern tip of Belgium and from there into France to begin the second phase of the attack. From there we marched for miles in the direction of Verdun.

The country around the fortress Verdun still showed destruction from World War I. We all were aware that hundreds of thousands of French and German soldiers had died fighting for this area. The dreadful thing about it was that the German headquarters had decided to attack this key fortress, not so much for its strategic value, but to have a suitable theater for a war of attrition. Now, when our company approached the assigned fortress, the French raised a white flag and were very happy to see that as far as they were concerned World War II was over.

Fleckner, the company commander, and I drank a bottle of French champagne that evening, but not in a boisterous celebration. We were totally overwhelmed emotionally by what we had seen and achieved that day. Fleckner was close to crying. The "killing fields" were still in the same shape as they were left in 1916: Crater next to crater, grass growing in a moon landscape still strewn with pieces of metal, ammunition and bones. We saw one spot where the rain had cut a gully exposing white bones of a human hand. It was overwhelming to think that we were able to walk into Verdun where our fathers and their contemporaries of both countries had paid such a price.

On June 15, 1940, from Verdun it was just a matter of marching in a south-easterly direction. We were hiking about twenty or thirty kilometers per day on the open French roads. Napoleon is supposed to have designed these highways flanked by huge trees, and the pavement was mostly in good condition. The heat and the mixed stench of gasoline and horse manure was with us for days, though. Except for that smell, it felt like a practice hike. There was very little contact with the retreating French. Just the same, I insisted on keeping about twenty-five meters between each platoon just in case there might be interference from the air.

Most villages were almost devoid of life. The peasants had left elderly people to look after their animals and property when they took flight in the general panic of early June. Around the villages, the air was filled with the desperate mooing of cows, which had not been relieved of their milk for some time. Whenever we came to a halt, the soldiers helped themselves and the cows. A sweaty, dirty steel helmet full of rich warm milk was considered a treat.

When we reached Commercy we heard the news that General Guderian had arrived at the Swiss border with his tanks. That could only mean that all remaining French forces in Alsace and Lorraine were trapped. A few moments later, the colonel brought the order that Fleckner's company was chosen to spearhead a daring raid of a mixed light mobile force, which was supposed to crash through the retreating French and take Nancy. I was to lead the way and ride on a sidecar motor bike as point man "heavily" armed with my one and only machine pistol. Two of my squads followed likewise on motor bikes to provide more fire power if needed.

Fleckner was supposed to lead the balance of the company on light, road-bound trucks. There was much excitement and the preparations had to be started this very evening. On second thought, we both agreed that it would take only one felled poplar tree across the road to stop this daredevil scheme in its tracks. But then one doesn't have the honor of riding point every day, so we opened a bottle of Veuve Cliquot, wrote our last wills and prepared for an early start. We both felt this was a flattering assignment.

We drank our champagne pensively, going through all possible scenarios with the help of a tourist road map, the only available information on the matter at hand. For the first time, we expressed our feelings of friendship toward each other.

"If we have to be in this tight situation, I'm glad it is under your command," I said as I looked into my champagne glass to hide my awkwardness.

Fleckner echoed, "If I have to be with this fly-by-night outfit, it is just as well to be able to rely on you."

We even shook hands and from then on, we addressed each other by our Christian names, a German custom representing the beginning of a friendship. We always had gotten along well and so did our dogs. Fleckner's medium Schnauzer was the only male dog that Ivan accepted as a friend and playmate. All other male dogs, he attacked straight away. He hated them and the only thing he hated more was cats.

By 10 the next morning, the "light mobile force" (which was a joke) was assembled and waiting. At 11:00 a.m., we started moving. Around noon, we came to a canal near Domgermain when we were apprised of the fact that the trip to Nancy was canceled. We weren't told any reasons. Rumors had it that someone had blown up a bridge between Commercy and Nancy.

My platoon became foot soldiers again and moved down the wooded hill approaching a canal. Ahead of us was another hill covered with dense forest. The platoon crossed the canal only to find out a few hundred yards ahead that they would have to get wet again. The damn thing was winding around the hollow. As I could see now, we could have stayed along the foot of the hill around this U-shaped valley and remained dry. We were wet up to our waists and not in very good humor. I heard the men swearing; I couldn't tell whether it was that they were relieved or disappointed over the cancellation of the raid to Nancy or just annoyed at their discomfort.

The moment we jumped over the last embankment, a hail of fire greeted us. I just had time to give out the cue for the agreed upon procedure and off we went, all guns blazing, in a left right alternation of fire and movement. One squad would cover the other with machine gun fire as the second squad would move ahead firing. Then they in turn would fire while the first squad moved forward.

The defenders along the edge of the forest obviously had expected a different effect from their badly aimed fusillade. The French withdrew leaving their guns and some equipment behind them. We took their position and set a perimeter defending in all directions, a perimeter not much larger than fifty-by-fifty meters. No one was missing and none were hurt, as if by a miracle.

We had barely time to think what to do next when we ourselves came under friendly fire from all kinds of guns from our rear, presumably from A and B Companies who were now trapped on the slowly descending terrain on the other side of the canal. They were firing blindly at the suspected French positions.

My boys and I were sweating blood and water. There is nothing worse than lying flat on the ground and having friendly fire directed at your back. Bullets were ricocheting every which way cutting big gashes in the bark of the trees around us. My boys, normally no masters in the art of digging while hugging the dirt, this time were quick and effective about it.

I crawled to either edge of the back of the perimeter fired signal lights and rammed a square colored, not yellow, signal poster into the ground to indicate the position of my platoon to no avail. The firing continued and this went on for hours. The platoon was stuck. Each attempt to widen the bridge-head resulted in French fire and brought in turn more friendly fire. Around 3:00 p.m., we were out of water and had to smoke the cigarettes the French had left us when they had left in a hurry.

Suddenly I heard my name. I could not see the caller, but I recognized the voice of Friedrich immediately. I was not about to raise my head in all this mayhem, so shouted from my prone position, "What the hell are you doing here?"

"Am I glad to hear your voice," Friedrich yelled back. "They've given you up for dead at the battalion. Are you guys okay?"

"Yes, of course. So far no damage. It's a miracle, believe me. We're flat on the ground hiding from our own German bullets. Do you have your radio man with you?"

Friedrich's face appeared over the embankment at a spot where a tree stump gave him some cover. "The radio man is forty meters behind me. I'll take care of it. I better hurry. Hang in there, man." The boys and I let out a sigh of relief. It took jolly well another hour until we really could feel that this part of the forest was in our hands.

Friedrich left me in a rather touched and elated state. I was overwhelmed to have found out what a friend I had in Friedrich. He had literally risked his life to ascertain our condition.

At dusk, the regiment finally attacked across the open ground on the left. At last, they had support of the artillery. The French stragglers either gave themselves up or ran further into the forest. It was all over within fifteen minutes. No *Blitzkrieg* here, I thought. The battalion had not exactly covered itself with glory on this last day of warfare on French soil.

Two days later, on June 30, the regiment buried its dead, and following the burial Friedrich and I received the Iron Cross First Class. I was given an advancement in rank and received a written commendation from the Supreme Commander of the army. Neither Friedrich nor I could believe what was happening to us.

At a reception that evening, Major Günther claimed all the credit, of course. He kept saying in his drunken stupor, "You see, I was to make you or break you." I was stunned. I didn't see what was so heroic about this whole terrible experience, and I resented that I was supposed to owe all this to Günther's hyperbole. We had buried about a dozen grenadiers, who had died on that day, when we were not allowed to take Nancy by coup-de-main. Instead, we had been had by a group of stragglers who were disoriented and who would have loved to turn themselves in to us. Friedrich and I agreed that this battalion was not battle ready and was lucky to have survived almost unscathed until this terrible day before the armistice took effect.

Maybe I was naive when I had accepted the Iron Cross Second Class on the Stromberg attack on May 10. It seemed to mean something to me then. Now I knew that in this army valor on the battle field was vastly overstated by the reporting commanding officer. If a given unit merited numerous decorations then the battalion commander who is reporting all this must be a hero himself.

As coincidence wanted it, this was all made clear to my mind when I received this very day the press releases on the Stromberg affair together with my birthday mail. As I read these clippings I was at first amused, but soon became infuriated as I read these glowing reports describing the "heroic storming of Stromberg by the Grenadiers from Berlin and Brandenburg." It had Major Günther's imagination all over it. To cross the river in a tourist steamer wasn't good enough for him, so he had them "cross the river in inflatable rafts." When they reached the Luxembourg side "they were sure of victory and full of pride because being from Spandau and Potsdam, they were carrying on the tradition of the old Royal Guard Regiments."

The article pointed out that the First Battalion had the most difficult assignment as the pivotal unit on the left wing of the German invasion. He described the artillery shelling as a "moving wall of fire, which the companies are following closely." "The battalion commander was shoulder to shoulder with his leading men in the front lines." The grenadiers "smoked out machine gun nests, hand-grenades are exploding all over the place." In short, it gave all the ingredients that Hollywood might dream up for one of its war movies. The report tried to convey a picture of planned perfection that rolled off mechanically. He compared it to the workings of a clock.

For me, this experience had been a good lesson not to expect any kind of orderly development of a given plan when it comes to the actual battlefield. Once the action started everything was chaos and at no time did anyone feel in control of the development. We were just lucky that the French had decided it wasn't their day and left. It was unthinkable what might have happened if any French soldier had decided to put up a resistance. The combined fire power of my advance group could have lasted only minutes. I resolved not to ever again just blindly move and put my trust only to luck.

The report continued, "Some soldiers are wounded, but without complaining and in a very manly fashion wait for the medic to tend to their wounds." Having had to jump all over Stromberg whenever I heard the cry for a medic in order just to make sure that a wounded man received help immediately, I deeply resented these sanctimonious lines. The wounded I talked to were in deep distress if not in shock and some of them not above crying or screaming with pain. The report mentioned some soldiers "who died for the greater Germany." I saw only the one who was killed by friendly fire and I was already trying to find the right words for the letter I would have to send to the family.

The report ends with the solemn pronouncement, "Stromberg is and always will be firmly in German hands." Pompous piffle.

We "heroes" hiked all the way to Saarbrücken and were sent east by rail. In downtown Hamburg, the train stopped over at Dammtor station. I phoned JR, by now a lieutenant himself, and we visited a while on the platform. JR wanted to know where we were going.

"East Prussia, you dummy. Isn't it obvious?" I replied. "I just took a detour through Hamburg, stopped the train at Dammtor station just to show you my Iron Cross First Class, you shit-head." I grinned.

This broke the strain of the moment. We had not been in very close contact lately after a disagreement on some family matters. JR had made some nasty judgmental remarks about my brother who had been a preacher in training, but had turned Anthroposophist, this was after our father had sacrificed a lot to get him into a Lutheran vicarage. I felt it was not any of JR's business what choices my brother made.

We detrained in East Prussia then marched into north-east Poland for another 200 kilometers. This hike was interspersed with war games and culminated in a midnight tattoo in some open field. While the regimental band of regimental glory prescribed by the Prussian military tradition played on, our whole regiment stood at attention surrounded by blazing torches. The band had just started a chorale when somebody yelled, "*Helm ab zum Gebet!*" meaning take your helmet off for prayers. The chorale, "I adore the power of love," was something totally out of place, in my opinion.

Suddenly the company cobbler tugged at my elbow and reported that Ivan had been lost during the afternoon. Someone had inadvertently opened the door of the wagon. I told Friedrich and Fleckner what I needed to do and excused myself from further ceremonies. I asked the young half Jewish corporal (also named Friedrich) would he come with me to look for the dog. So, the two of us with two automatic pistols and one flashlight began retracing the battalion's movement.

It was pitch dark until about 2:00 a.m. when the cloud cover thinned somewhat. We discussed the future and the study program he had in mind. We had common ground in discussing German literature and he tried to describe to me what it was like to be a half Jewish male in the Third Reich. It was a lively conversation, but in the back of my mind I cursed myself for being irresponsible again in risking the bones of a grenadier to retrieve a pet.

As it happened there was very little resistance in the open Polish countryside. The peasants were too frightened. We talked only to one old man who opened the door to his hut to find out why all the dogs were barking. He spoke some German and assured me that he had not seen any dog that didn't belong in the hamlet. On we went. I was about to give up when around 2:30 a.m. a very excited black shape dashed into my stride almost tripping me. Ivan had found us. We had the usual tearful, howling reunion all around.

By the time we had returned to the bivouac the sun had come up and the battalion was ready to move on to Ostrolenka on the Narew River. Fleckner let me ride his horse for a while so I could get some rest. Of course, that was a joke.

● ◆ ● ● ◆ ● ● ◆ ●

1941 Barbarossa. No matter how many kilometers we had covered, whenever we approached a Bulgarian village or town, I dutifully followed our explicit orders for formal marching. That meant we were to button the tunics up to our necks, carry our rifle on our right shoulder and, no matter how tired we were, we were to sing. I got weary of giving all those orders, so I got to the point where I just turned around on my horse and yelled, "*Klein Siegfried*," and the company would invariably yell back, "*Scheisse*!!" (Shit). Sure enough, in that little town invariably there would be a colonel, or a general, or worse - German newspaper reporters, generally referred to as P.K., propaganda unit.

I remember particularly in the city of Sophia a number of German diplomats and dignitaries standing in groups along the street, champagne glasses in hand. We were not allowed to stop inside the city except for a ten-minute break along the colorfully decorated tables where we were served hard boiled Easter eggs and some dark rye bread. It felt like we were some kind of side show and I was annoyed.

The hamlet where our company was staying was stretched out at the foot of a beautiful valley. We used that time to clean and repair as much as possible and enjoy some of the local color. Every two weeks the young Bulgarian peasants would come together in the center of town to dance on the village green. We noticed that the dancers touched each other only by holding on to some sort of belt attached around the waists of both the men and the women. The dancers would move in a large circle to the music of a half blind and somewhat intoxicated Gypsy. The soldiers thought the Gypsy was a remarkable musician and tried to tell him so. I was taken aside by the village elder who hinted that the Gypsies were pariahs and should be ignored. I had earlier noticed in Romania that the Gypsies were kept entirely out of the village life. My friends and I wanted to find out more about the local customs regarding the Gypsies, but only occasionally did we find a Jewish villager or a veteran of World War I who still remembered enough German words to communicate with us. Even those explanations were not satisfactory. I recalled Gypsies being reasonably tolerated in Hamburg during my childhood; they were not treated like untouchables as here.

Taking a walk together with Friedrich we discovered that the Gypsies were living near a swamp on the lower side of the hamlet. We watched a Gypsy pot mender going about his work. Both in Romania and here, the Gypsy walked in the middle of the road announcing himself by hitting a metal pot with a spoon. He only approached a given property when he was waved to come closer by someone who needed his services. I saw a peasant woman place her frying pan in the dirt with some coins in it and then wave the Gypsy tradesman to help himself. Neither spoke. It was obvious she wanted nothing to do with him personally and he accepted that. The Gypsies were ostracized by the local population here just as they were in Romania.

◆ ◦ ◦ ◆ ◦ ◦ ◆ ◦

Some of the officers and I took a trip by car to the Rozhen Monastery in southern Bulgaria to experience some of the ancient religious culture. Young initiates of the Greek Orthodox faith guided us through the 400-year-old monastery and explained in a general way the differences between their approach to religious philosophy and that of the Roman Catholic Church. Later, we witnessed young monks rehearsing an intricate medieval chorale for the upcoming post-Easter celebration. We observed the shoulder length hair and the full beards of the monks, their ornate gowns and the large ceremonial headgear. Their gaunt ascetic appearances together with the powerful Slavic male voices made a tremendous impression on both Friedrich and me. We recalled the days before the war when we had been fans of the Don Cossack Choir touring the European concert scene. Here was another example of the extraordinary vocal musicality of the Slavic people.

Friedrich was very religious in the Silesian tradition, but that didn't stop us from discussing some religious aspects of politics. We both found it unfortunate that the two main German churches to all extent and purpose had become handmaidens of the state. Unless a German specifically renounced his faith, he paid church tax every month. Thus the German guns, soldiers and ships were blessed with just as much Christian fervor as they were in the West. The old adage, "Render unto

Caesar,..." did not seem to lead to the conclusion that church and state should be separated.

Both of us were critical of the mindless acceptance in both the Protestant and Catholic churches whatever Hitler was meting out to them. One of Hitler's first achievements was a Concordat with Rome, a treaty which settled the relationship between church and state in a specific manner. As a result, many upright priests and theologians were persecuted, and only a very few in the church's hierarchy protested. No matter what we thought of the hypocrisy of the German church representative's vis-a-vis the Nazi party and the Third Reich, I carefully avoided making my strongest judgmental remarks in Friedrich's presence.

After a short period of rest and a few friendly soccer games within the battalion, the division was ordered to move back from Bulgaria to Romania by train. We found it unbelievable that we had wasted weeks hiking 500 kilometers across the country and two towering mountain passes, only to be told we would not be needed in Yugoslavia anymore. On the train, Friedrich and I relived our experiences in Bulgaria. We had been able to rest and the friendly attitude of the Bulgarians had helped us forget our blisters and the hardships of the hike. The Bulgarians had been hospitable and they were cautious, never allowing the battalion to be quartered with Bulgarian families. We slept on straw in our tents. No German soldier was to come close to their young women.

The Bulgarian newspapers turned this pro-Hitler phase of Bulgarian history into a journalistic hype. They repeatedly praised the discipline of the German foot soldier and compared the friendly invaders from the North with the mythological concept of "Siegfried." For me and my company, it was a big joke.

Our battalion was loaded on a Bulgarian railway train and as usual the game of guessing the destination began. There was a tremendous upswing in the general mood among the soldiers. The invasion of

Yugoslavia, Greece and the Island of Crete appeared to have been just further proof of the seemingly invincible "Blitzkrieg." In Africa, Rommel had reached the Egyptian border. Everybody was sure that the war was as good as over and there were rumors we would all be transported back home to Berlin and the units would be disbanded. This had happened to some of our friends after the victory in France. For the moment, we were on a slow train into never-never land, or so it seemed. Berlin as a destination had to be discarded quickly because we were going east for days and days ending up in what could only be the delta of the river Danube. Nobody had a map, nobody spoke Romanian, so we bored each other to tears discussing possibilities in a news vacuum. Finally, in Constanta near the Black Sea, we found some German Red Cross workers who told us that all these little trains were moving north towards the Russian frontier.

The snail pace of the military train movement was not enhanced by the stops to take care of the poor horses. They had to be walked fairly often for relief from traveling in their cramped quarters for days at a stretch, but one hour of horse walking cost us half a day of unloading and loading. The handlers, sick of being the butt of vicious jokes, were in a foul mood. The recent embarrassment of their charges vis-a-vis the mountain passes was still in everybody's mind. "Totally useless" as a description was perhaps the gentlest of the graphic characterizations we heard about these horses.

The movement of the train was so slow that my boys made up fictitious battalion orders such as, "The picking of wild flowers from the moving train is strictly forbidden." Particularly in the river delta someone could get off the train and re-board it without any effort. Lieutenant Fuchs, my occasional partner at cards, got so frustrated and upset with my repeated misplaying my moves (I'm hopeless at cards), he jumped out the door and walked alongside on the gravel for a while to cool off. Since ours was not the leading train of this transportation movement and there were no sanitation facilities whatsoever, the gravel held the residue of thousands of men and horses. It had occurred to me that from the point of view of a Bulgarian farmer guiding his horse and plow in sight of the slow-moving train, it would have been as though the Germans were mooning him *en masse*. Fuchs did come back into the compartment fairly soon because the walk had not been entirely pleasant.

My company was down to two-thirds of its standard size because on the hike from Romania to Yugoslavia, one-third of the more mature grenadiers had been sent home by hospital ship. The ordeal of hiking 500 kilometers over two massive mountain passes apparently had been too much for them. They were easily diagnosed as having a severe form of tendonitis by the battalion doctor. He and I were very glad to send them off with all our best wishes for a speedy recovery in Berlin. Later I found out, through some friendly gossip, that the regimental commander Colonel Rodenburg at the time had been toying with the idea of a court-martial for me. The colonel called my behavior irresponsible and accused me of decimating the fighting strength of my unit by sending them home in so cavalier a fashion. He claimed these ailments might have been taken care of with local rest and treatment.

It turned out all the rumors about going home and the war coming to an end were false. The battalion was unloaded after a long train ride in northeastern Romania and was billeted at Botosani north of Jassy. Friedrich and I immediately suspected that the unspeakable, the impossible, was about to happen. A break in the relationship between Russia and Germany seemed imminent.

After ten days of rest, thirty-five strapping and rather well trained youngsters from Berlin appeared on the scene and my company was the envy of all the other officers in the battalion. The boys were young, of course, and tremendously enthusiastic. They brought with them a refreshing piece of optimism and a kind of urbane sophistication that one found only in Berlin. Three of them had mouth organs and played the latest Anglo-Saxon tunes beautifully, the latest jazz from "In The Mood" to "Alexander's Ragtime Band," "Blueberry Hill" and "The Nightingale Sang On Barkley Square." Friedrich and the boys tried to imitate Satchmo Armstrong's version of "Blueberry Hill," which became the anthem of the company, as it were.

Friedrich and I together with the adjutant to the battalion commander celebrated the most wonderful jam sessions with them, enjoyed sun-bathing, sports and all kinds of practical jokes. You couldn't do much to train or practice or do anything about the military readiness of the outfit because every inch of the Romanian soil was being used agriculturally. We were in a friendly country, as I had to repeat over and over in the weekly company instructions, but I as well as Friedrich and many of the soldiers and some of the Romanian peasants and some of the Jewish merchants had an eerie feeling that this was the quiet before some dreadful awakening.

The news came that Hess, Hitler's right-hand man, had flown to England and had surrendered to the British. Officially, he was declared insane by the Nazi propaganda, but everybody started to wonder. Why would Hitler's most trusted friend and most loyal follower even conceive of an idea like this?

Friedrich and I never spoke to anyone else about our concern that war with Russia was imminent, however my anxiety grew whenever I imagined having to take this so youthful and exuberant bunch of boys into something like a shooting war against of all people the Russians without proper battle readiness. Friedrich and I spent long hours talking about our forebodings, discussing *War and Peace* and the historical facts concerning Napoleon's ill-fated attempt to make war on Russia.

By the middle of June, our worst fears were confirmed. One day Colonel Rodenburg, the officer commanding our regiment, took his monocle out of his right eye and instructed us officers that it was only a question of days now. It was not going to be warfare as usual. It was going to be an ideological struggle to the death. He explained to us that the Russian army had gone through a devastating process of purges in the past decade and that every military leader was now being accompanied, watched and evaluated by a political commissar of one rank or another. He added Hitler's strict orders to summarily shoot all Russian commissars and political leaders found among Russian prisoners.

Friedrich, in particular, as a devout Christian, was immensely troubled by this barbaric order, but both of us agreed that it probably didn't matter much. We expected it to be a confrontation of a bestiality never experienced before because both of us had read the various books about the Russian Army in World War I and in the Civil War following it, particularly the books by Dwinger, *Between White and Red* and *Army Behind Barbed Wire*, a story about German prisoners in Russian hands, which had been on the best seller list prior to the war. We promised each other that in the event of an incapacitating wound or worse to do everything needed to prevent that either one of us would fall into Russian hands alive.

Friedrich especially had forebodings of being killed. His present battalion commander had missed out on the experience in France in 1940 and now was particularly eager to prove himself and, if possible, earn a decoration. This man's grasp of the basic military necessities and leadership on the battalion level was limited, to say the least.

●◆●●●◆●●◆●

On June 22, while the German invasion started in the North, nothing changed in the lush, peaceful plain west of the river Pruth. That meant that if we, together with the Romanians, would attempt to cross this river, it would be no surprise for the Russians who would undoubtedly give us a warm reception. All the triumphant news about the fast progress in the Ukraine and in northern Russia did not do much to change our mood.

Each time Friedrich talked about his death premonitions, he apologized and labeled these thoughts ridiculous. Yet, he gave detailed instructions to me what he expected me to do if and when I would return to Berlin. It appeared his older sister was being harassed by a certain staff officer at her job situation with the headquarters of the German Army in Bendlerstrasse. He described proudly how he had put on his dress uniform and gone to straighten this man out. I admired him for I had never worked up the guts to stand up to a man in the rank of a major with any success.

On Monday, June 30, 1941, we two ended a long hot frustrating day in Friedrich's billet. It was a peasant hut with two big adjoining rooms. The highly pregnant wife of the Romanian veterinarian was living in the other half of the house. Here it was, my 23rd birthday and the order had just arrived that on July 2 the battalion would cross the river. It was a gloomy atmosphere and for the third time I had a chance to describe in great detail how all my Christmases and birthdays took place at a low point in my life and were accompanied by all kinds of disasters.

Sure enough, Tuesday night we started moving east. We were ordered to try to disguise our preparations, which included placing elaborate straw galoshes over the animals' hooves to make a ludicrous attempt to muffle the sound of their movement. For the first time in my military career, I found out why a company commander had to put up with a horse. It was for cross country mobility, of course. After having been useless in the mountain passes of Bulgaria, "Jackie," my pampered horse from a private riding stable in Berlin, had his big day.

The battalion commander, Captain Dietz, obviously feeling like a cavalry general, summoned the company chiefs and took them on a wild gallop, without straw galoshes, along the marching columns towards the river. The horses were left in the shrubbery and we six officers cautiously approached the water. He introduced us to the exact spot where A and B Company would have to cross the next morning.

It was largely a wasted journey because it was dusk and we could not see much of the terrain across the water. There wasn't a sound on the Russian side and I noticed with grim satisfaction that the straw galoshes didn't make much difference because all the other noises were there. I heard the whinnying of the horses, the rattling of the wagon wheels, the metallic sound of the gas mask containers clanking against bayonets and other metal parts of equipment.

The captain was barely rational in his excitement and enthusiasm. His narcissistic display of his military deportment was sickening to me. It was as though he was enjoying playing a role he had not been allowed to play in France and now saw his chance to fill. He would now "lead." I saw him as all bluster, attempting to cover up the fact that he was a former police officer and way out of his element.

We rode back again at breakneck speed and I caught myself thinking that my horse, having stumbled several times, would finally break his bloody leg and probably render me unconscious and ripe for the hospital train. I was now quite sure that conducting warfare under this battalion commander would be punishment for all I had ever done wrong in my life. I pitied Friedrich to have to be at close quarters with this man from morning to night.

Back with the company, I had the pleasure of walking the same distance to the river on foot by myself and thought about the orders for the next day. My company was relegated to be in reserve and to perform the part of ammunition carriers, as it were. We had to leave our own machine guns and mortars in Romania and have one box of ammunition in each hand just in case A and B Company might experience a rough going and run out of ammunition.

At 3:30 a.m., the crossing began. There was very little resistance and only a few rounds of artillery were there to greet us. Inflatable rafts and small boats were used and there was little trouble to reach the other side of the Pruth. As the sun came up, A and B Company moved through a huge field of chest high maize still luscious green. After two or three hundred yards, the attackers were met by rifle and machine gun fire and it became obvious to me that since the battalion commander had moved practically into the front line that nobody had any kind of idea as to where to find and pin down the Russians or know, for that matter, how far the Germans had advanced.

Everybody was engulfed in a sea of green maize. There was no communication with the battalion until the orderly officer Manthey arrived and told me that apparently they were stuck and he had no way of finding the forward observers of the German artillery. He told me to just wait for further orders.

On my left, suddenly, B Company of a different battalion started moving and shooting. I dashed over to the company commander and asked him where he was going. Schultz, a former master sergeant, said that he had orders to get the attack going by establishing contact with A Company.

I was shocked! "Who the hell are you shooting at?"

The man turned puce in the face when I told him that it wouldn't be very helpful to open fire until he had a target and was sure that there were no friendly troops ahead of him. This, I told him, was extremely probable. Schultz, looking decidedly sheepish and embarrassed, took his bunch 200 yards to the left.

By noon there was shouting, relaying the rumor that A and B Company were stuck and that the battalion commander and Friedrich were killed. I told Lieutenant Michael to stay put with the company of ammunition carriers and I advanced with two of my runners in the direction where Lieutenant Manthey had suggested they would likely find the battalion staff. The hostile fire was now down to single shots probably coming from a few sharp shooting riflemen with telescope lenses. I found two German corpses killed by single shots in the forehead. The closer we came, the shooting intensified and we dared only short jumps.

My worst fears were realized. The battalion commander and Friedrich and two other soldiers were on their backs staring blankly into the glaring midday sunlight. A small trickle of blood came from each of their head wounds. A sniper had carefully picked them off one by one, by the look of it. Friedrich felt cold already. A lifeless shell sprawled on the ground next to the battalion commander. His lips were slightly parted as if the bullet had interrupted him in the middle of an utterance. His eyes were wide open staring into the hot sun.

I dropped down next to him to avoid a single incoming projectile. It must be an antitank gun, I thought. It had a very flat trajectory very much like the French Ratsch-Bum we had experienced on Stromberg. I remained in the dirt pressing my face to the soil close to the stem of a corn stalk. I saw the top was shorn off probably by a ricocheting bullet, an almost ripe cob was slashed. I observed some yellowish dew was dripping down from it.

Suddenly I caught myself. What am doing here? Is there nothing more important to do than to stare at this mutilated cob? Who cares about trajectories? Nothing really matters, Friedrich is dead. In the distance, I heard voices and small arm fire, some detonation of hand grenades. I turned back to Friedrich. Tears welled up and I began shaking convulsively. I wiped his face with my soiled hands when I heard steps.

"Sir, do you want me to take over?"

"Yes, Mr. Michael, please do. I'll catch up with you later."

Now that I was left alone again, grieving turned into a torrent of abuse. Why did you have to do this to me? Couldn't you have found a way to let this stupid captain act out his death wish by himself? You promised to find a way to distance yourself from this bungling ignoramus. I was raging against fate, the army, Hitler and all the people in power in the last thirty years who had a hand in creating this situation. What business did we have to be in this corn field, in this country, for that matter? I kept cursing and walking up and down, coming back to the dead soldiers and looking at Friedrich again. I found myself hallucinating, being quite sure there was some sign of life after all. By now, I was totally oblivious to the noise and the people around me. I tried to close Friedrich's eyelids to no avail.

Lieutenant Hoppe from A Company brought me back to reality. He personally drove half a dozen prisoners towards the river, kicking, beating and cursing them. He had foam in the corners of his mouth. "Hoppe, what in hell are you up to? Have you gone mad?" I yelled.

"Sir, these bastards killed some of my best men!"

Hoppe raised the butt of his rifle against one of them. I was barely able to intercede by restraining Hoppe's raised arm with his Tommy gun near the left elbow. Hoppe collapsed moaning. I apologized and sent him back to his platoon. The Russians watched this scene without much animation in their faces. They were a scraggly looking bunch, not one of them wearing a complete uniform. Some of them were even barefoot.

Lieutenant Michael came by and took charge of the prisoners. I realized now that for a whole day just a few stubborn defenders had stopped two fully armed companies with all their fire power. I tried to convince myself that all the dead soldiers I had seen had come to rest in roughly the same way and there was nothing to indicate that they were victims of friendly fire from the back. Now my own boys came by single file with their heavy loads of ammunition boxes. Lieutenant Michael waved. I waved back and watched his men trudging east through the tall corn stalks. I sat down again. There was total silence for quite some time. I was unable to focus on anything concrete. Friedrich was dead. Nothing else mattered. My men had taken in the scene and had averted their eyes once they realized what had happened and stared ahead with an embarrassed expression on their faces.

I recalled a quote from Goethe's *Faust*, "And so I sit, poor silly man, no wiser now than when I began." Since the early days of our friendship in 1939, I had used this quotation jokingly each time Friedrich had been able to convince me that my immature way of seeking confrontation rather than persuasion and compromise had limited benefits, if any. Friedrich was mature for his age, street wise and a splendid negotiator. I had seen his influence on the "*Miles Gloriosus*," the blustering bragging Major Günther. I knew immediately that from now on Friedrich's influence would be sorely missed.

When I finally was ready to leave, I covered Friedrich's face with my handkerchief to keep the flies off it. Two of my runners got up and joined me. One of them was Friedrich, the half Jewish soldier from Hanover. Lieutenant Michael had left them to accompany and cover me on the way to catch up to the battalion. This thoughtful gesture by Michael I found moving, I felt close to crying again.

We caught up with the battalion at dusk and discovered that Lieutenant Fuchs was in command. Fuchs of all people. I excused myself, took a short rest and then again with the same boys who had volunteered went back to the field by the river. As we approached we saw some civilians whom I drove away with a few rounds in the air from my Tommy gun. A detail of grenadiers was lining up the dead for burial. Someone had helped himself to Friedrich's boots. I realized now, I should have made sure that Friedrich's belongings were safeguarded.

On the way across the field, they found a few of the Russian foxholes with empty cartridges strewn all around them. The spots were chosen rather cleverly to overlook the slowly descending hill, I thought. It was too dark to get a detailed impression. The group walked back in an easterly direction. A new battalion commander greeted me, a kind middle-aged captain of the reserves who was a professor of economics in civilian life. Manthey became his adjutant. I was too exhausted to even exchange small talk. I wrapped myself in my greatcoat and tried to sleep.

◆ • ◆ • • ◆ • • ◆ •

The next day our regiment continued moving toward the river Dniester, which was reported to be heavily fortified on the eastern bank as a continuation of the so-called Stalin line. My battalion followed "in reserve" while First and Second Battalions pushed the slowly withdrawing Russians ahead of us.

Once or twice a day my boys had to comb through a sunflower patch or cornfield to flush out alleged Russian stragglers. There were no losses. All they found were some wounded Red Army soldiers who were hoping to survive. These received some first aid and were transported to the rear mostly carried by horse-drawn carriages owned by the local peasantry.

Each evening, I caught myself being unable to account for what had happened during the day. Lieutenant Michael was tactful in bringing up questions whenever he felt that I might have missed something or done something without realizing the possible consequences. I felt like I was sleepwalking through each day. Sometimes they helped me on my horse hoping to give me some rest because they knew I wasn't sleeping well at night.

The third day, a Russian fighter plane, one of those plywood Ratas, attacked the marching column and was shot down. There was anti-aircraft fire from many different sources. Of course, Lieutenant Fuchs claimed the kill for his company. So did the commander of the 8th and 14th Company, the 2nd Company of the Artillery Battalion 176, and the light anti-aircraft unit attached to the regiment. As a result, one dead Russian pilot multiplied, as it were, within minutes and the Austrian division commanding general had to write a number of commendations. I was sure that the division in its turn would report half a dozen plywood Ratas shot down.

My condition worsened. I was told by my orderly that I was tossing and turning all night, talking in my sleep, answering myself in my sleep. Sometimes, half-awake early in the morning, I would summon the orderly, give him all kinds of instructions only to be told later by the totally confused young man that nothing really made sense. When I was asked about it, I had no recollections of having given any orders. I conferred with Lieutenant Michael about this and we both instructed this orderly not to be afraid to come to Lieutenant Michael and ask for advice.

◆ ◆ ● ● ◆ ● ● ◆ ●

August 1941. Those furlough days with Gundel in Dresden were the happiest times I had seen so far. She was being well looked after. Her landlady Gebhardi showered her with extra attention, food and comfort. It was fascinating to be able to watch her at work at the Wigman School of Modern Dance. She was not particularly athletic in a strong muscular way, but she had the perfect graceful body and expressive face for dancing.

It was there I met Mary Wigman, who was then the most important artist of the German modern dance scene. Fascinating to hear the old lady describe her travels all over the world. Her fondest memories were the dance routines she was invited to perform in the United States where there was a lively dance scene with Duncan and Graham, people like that. During those two weeks I often joined Gundel in walking the few blocks from her apartment to the theater where she was one of the dancing slaves in the current light opera. This was one of the ways she and the other students earned extra money.

I was evaluated by the White Deer Sanitarium as a walk-in patient. They didn't find an ulcer, but something close to it, some kind of nervous stomach reaction to the nervous strain I had been under. The doctors gave me another ten wonderful days for recuperation. Gundel and I used the time for long walks in the beautiful surroundings of Dresden, visited art exhibitions, went to concerts. It was a city of peace.

When the extension of the furlough had run out, my first concern was to report to the 203rd Replacement Battalion in Berlin-Spandau. I did not want to add to the long list of demerits I was sure I had earned during my various earlier contacts with them in 1939 and 1940. Of course, I found the same group of people in charge I had learned to mistrust a year earlier.

I phoned the Count von Kirchbach. His youngest daughter, Carola, answered the phone and when I told her I had on me the personal belongings taken from the body of her brother, she told me to come over in two hours when her parents would be back. They lived on Schlüter Strasse not too far away from the place I had been staying with friends in 1935.

When I got to the house, I found it a sort of high class rental, which contained between five and eight huge rooms with a lift going up to it. Carola and the maid came immediately to the door and ushered me in to the large hallway dominated by huge paintings of family ancestors. They all seemed to have the same name on the brass plates at the bottom of them. Most appeared to be generals or some other high rank and many stood with their beautifully coifed wives.

"Is this the whole family tree?" I asked.

She nodded and pointed towards one that had been a renowned artillery general in the 1870-71 war. She apologized that her father needed some time to calm down her mother.

So there we were, "Wonny" and I. After a pause she said, "Friedrich talked about you after he returned from France. I feel that I know you somehow." She pointed to the corner where there was a huge ceramic stove about six feet high and either side was a painting of Friedrich and his brother Tony. Her mother had just commissioned an artist to copy two photos and turn them into these magnificent portraits. There was a black ribbon on one of the corners of each. Everyone in the house were wearing black.

"I heard about your older brother's ups and downs in the infantry. I was pleased to hear that since he was such a fine skier he had finally been admitted to the mountaineers. Friedrich and I admired Tony's courage to fight the bureaucracy to get this transfer."

"Of course," she smiled. "Having a father working in the general staff helps."

Another pause as she led me toward the window in the living room. For a short while we both watched the autumn shower hit the street below us. "I will have to leave it to you how much you want to tell my parents," she said.

I assured her, "Unfortunately, I have become used to visiting the families of fellow officers who have been killed in action." I didn't add that these direct personal experiences made it much easier for me to notify the families of fallen soldiers by writing to them.

After a moment she commented, "My sister Margo is working in the Berlin Army Headquarters and can't get away to be part of this conversation."

"Yes, Friedrich told me about her."

"You know we received the trunks of both my brothers a few weeks ago. Would you believe that when we opened them the contents were crawling with lice? No one had taken the trouble to delouse them."

"They were?"

"Yes. It took quite an effort by the exterminator to clean the hallway where the trunks had been opened."

"You can be quite sure that this had nothing to do with your brother because his death occurred within the first 24 hours of the Russian invasion. The persons who stored and finally mailed the trunks must have been infected."

I was relieved that she could remain calm and talk in a relatively objective way about these trivial, but disturbing matters. However, I knew I soon would be having a very hard time talking with her parents. At that point, they both came in to the room and thanked me for going out of my way to meet them. I assured the countess that for me it was understood that I would want to talk with Friedrich's family. They asked me a few personal questions and were interested to hear that I was on my way back to the front.

There was a long pause during which I could hear the loud ticking of the antique grandfather clock behind me. The countess sat upright on the edge of her chair, studiedly composed. Her reddish eyelids gave away her state of mind.

"Allow me to express my sincere condolences to you for your loss." I could hear my voice trail away out of my control. All four of us were now grieving silently together and I wasn't ashamed of my tears.

Then the count asked me, "Panny, whenever you feel like it, would you be willing to tell us how it happened?"

I decided not to go into too many details and restrained my impulse to single out the inexperienced and foolish battalion commander for any comments to them. They thanked me again and told me that the other son Tony had died a week earlier than Friedrich within 300 miles in the Ukraine near the town of Unan. Suddenly the countess broke down and started berating Hitler, whom she blamed for this whole stupid war. I listened to her uncomfortably since I had no idea how her lieutenant colonel husband, now in the general staff, felt about this. He got up and put his arm around her shoulder and tried to calm her.

"Angelika, Panny will have to go back to the front in a few days and maybe we should consider that."

She nodded. Then suddenly she asked me, "Aren't the Americans coming into the war as well? They are practically in it, aren't they? What do you think?"

I replied, "It looks like it. Oh, I brought Friedrich's personal belongings that he carried with him. Is it all right if I put them on this coffee table?"

The count said, "Go ahead."

I laid out the few letters, one from his sister Margo, a couple of photos, a pocket knife, some Romanian money, and a compass.

The count glanced at the letters. The countess excused herself. At the door she turned around and said, "Where will all this end? Well, if the Americans do get in it, then God help us. Looks to me like 1917."

When she was gone, the count who had been glancing at the letters and the photos suddenly turned to his daughter saying, "Panny might like to have a cup of tea. Would you see to that?"

When she was out of the room he pointed to one of the photos asking, "Who would that be?"

"That's Ilona in a ballet costume. She was a member of a dance troupe who entertained us when we were stationed near the Russian demarcation line last year. Her group was traveling all over East Prussia and Friedrich and Ilona had been corresponding to see how they could meet again."

"How intimate did they get?"

He must have seen that I was taken aback by his question and he apologized for being so crude about it. I assured him that I had no way of knowing any details about their relationship. I did know they were fond of each other.

Then he asked, "Are you staying in Spandau?"

He was amused to hear my answer, "Not if I can help it."

"Wonny will be able to show you a good pension right next to the S-Bahn station."

Wonny came in at that moment with the tea. I took a few sips of the tea, she had poured and then excused myself. Wonny put on her coat and rain cap and walked with me those two blocks.

On the way she asked me, "Do you have any photos of Friedrich taken lately?"

"Yes, they are in my luggage," I replied.

The formalities in the pension took only a few seconds. I had a room for the night. After I registered, I picked up my bag and Wonny and I continued walking in the direction of my room. The receptionist suddenly commanded, "Excuse me, sir. We can't have a lady visitor in the upstairs."

Wonny blushed and we both suddenly realized the situation we were in and felt righteously indignant about the tactless way the receptionist had spoken to us. I looked at Wonny's face. Her eyes gave away her recent emotional trauma in spite of her composed demeanor with me. Anything this receptionist might have had in mind as to our purpose in going to my room together, in reality was the furthest thing from both of ours.

My first impulse was to return the key with a nasty remark and leave this place to this tactless woman. I stopped that impulse though, because for some reason I did want to stay close to the Kirchbach residence. My nerves were on edge from what we all had just been through and I felt protective towards the Kirchbach family and especially Wonny.

In the time remaining to me Ivan and I traveled back and forth between Berlin, Hamburg and Dresden to say goodbye to friends and relatives and to try to organize storage for my belongings. There was bad news wherever I went. Tutta's fiancé JR, my old friend, was wounded near Wjasma in central Russia. According to a postcard written by a Red Cross nurse, he survived the amputation of one leg and could not be transported to a hospital in Germany. Another card arrived that he was now in Posen, Poland. One of my favorite girls in the class at the Lichtwarkschule had lost her husband in Russia and two more boys from the same class had also been killed in battle.

I visited Alice Pollitz at the basement of a neighborhood school in Hamburg where she had to spend one night a week as an air raid warden. She even had a World War I steel helmet. We were commiserating with each other. Particularly the death of Hans B. got to her. He had been a handicapped child who needed and received much of her attention while we were at school. He died in an air attack while he was on guard duty in a POW Camp with mostly British prisoners near Bremen.

In Dresden Gundel was troubled about our impending separation. We had to realize that there was very little hope for a young woman with a single child born out of wedlock and a lieutenant in the German Army to receive the required army permission to marry. At the time, her little boy was staying with his grandparents somewhere in former Poland where the grandfather who was an architect had been commissioned to rebuild one of the destroyed cities.

I received a telegram calling me back to Spandau-Berlin immediately as I was ordered back to the front as of October 27. In addition, there was the news I was supposed to lead fifty noncoms back to their regiment in Russia. I was stunned. It looked to me like intentional harassment by the battalion commander with this attempt to cut three days off my furlough and furthermore expose me to this unpleasant duty. More than once, I had voiced my opinion that a soldier is confident only when he is with his own unit. I had no way of knowing what to expect from these strangers.

I told Gundel that my only hope would be to ignore the telegram. On impulse, I decided to put it back into the envelope and forward it to Regensburg where I had agreed by letter October 15 to meet Jutta for our goodbyes. Gundel was skeptical and said, "I smell trouble."

She saw Ivan and me to the railway station. I remember thinking that Ivan must be getting sick of all this traveling.

Gundel and I had barely kissed goodbye when a military police-man who checked my travel papers gave me a dirty look and said, "Just a minute, sir." He left for a moment then returned with a middle-aged captain in charge of the facility who pointed out to me that something was not correct on my travel orders. When I told him I was on my goodbye tour on my way back to the front, he said, "Well, I'll let you go, however I'll have to report you."

The trip to Regensburg was uneventful. Jutta made the twenty-four hours comfortable. She had baked some cookies and saved up some ration cards so we had enough to eat. When I complained about her shortchanging herself of food, she told me to mind my own business and besides I had given her all my coupons for leather goods and cloth-ing. Over the telephone, we talked to Tutta in Hamburg who was trying to move mountains in hope to find out where her fiancé JR was. Her letter to the field hospital had been returned marked, "Wait for the new address." I felt rather helpless because I could not give her any practical tips on how to find him.

A second phone call to my parents was even more depressing. The old man was so sure that the Russians were beaten that I told him to go and see the movie news reel that Wonny and I had just seen. Jutta was quite optimistic that she would be accepted by the Munich University to start studying chemistry. Otherwise, leave-taking was a rather subdued affair.

On arrival in Berlin-Spandau, I was informed by the staff sergeant that the report from the Military Police in Dresden had arrived and that the battalion commander was trying to put together his case against me. It was the shortest goodbye of the whole trip. I didn't say a word to him. He did not wish me well and to make it worse I could see a trium-phant gleam in his eye.

The final straw was the news that I would have to travel together with Lieutenant Müller-Hofmeister. Of all people it had to be Müller, the man who was generally referred to as "Müller -yes-sir." or "Müller-Keitel" (a disrespectful reference to Marshall Keitel who among the officers was known as "*Lakeitel*" (lackey) because of his blind obedience to Hitler's every whim. Müller had climbed up to the position of the orderly officer of the regimental staff, once the regiment had been reorganized after Major Günther and his battalion had left for his newly created division somewhere in France. The only contact I had was during the last two big parades in Berlin: Hitler's birthday and the parade honoring the Hungarian Marshall Horthy, both in 1939. In both cases, Müller and I had to flank the three battalion colors. I remember he thought this was a great honor and that I, at the same moment, was hoping fervently that nobody would notice that I had quite a bit to drink at Schölers'.

We were given a second-class compartment on a military train leaving from Spandau. The first day and night were passed with small talk and not very much of that. I was dead tired after all the traveling I had been doing the preceding weeks, so if I wasn't sleeping at least I pretended to sleep.

Through my mind's eye, passed all my current anxieties: my big concern of the Russian winter to come, the thought that I was going to be cooped up with someone as boring and ingratiating as Mr. Müller for weeks, and the uncertainty of whatever happened or might happen to JR, not to mention all my other friends and relatives.

We were handed out rather meager traveling rations and I had to share many a Red Cross soup containers with the dog. Finally we detrained at Rowno and reported to the Armed Forces Headquarters. There we were told that from now on we would have to hitchhike with some help from the respective military office in each town. Now I couldn't pretend to be asleep any longer. I remember we did a lot of walking in the mud and riding on open trucks. Unfortunately, none of these vehicles showed the insignia of our division and each time our ride could only be for a short hop.

Up to then Lt. Müller and I had only been impersonal and polite to each other, that is, until he happened to mention my comeuppance with Colonel Rodenburg. That bit in Ostrolenka was a sore point with me. This Müller had been ordered to witness my official reprimand. The gist of it was that I had canceled my scheduled training routine without asking permission, but there was more to it than that.

❖ ⬥ • • ◈ • • ⬥ •

The company had been scheduled to go through an approach to an assumed enemy line, which meant we would move into a cover of a small forest to prepare for an attack and then to move out to commence the attack. I had changed the plan because the temperature had unexpectedly dropped that night and we had neither the necessary winter equipment nor preparation to deal with this kind of frost. When Colonel Rodenburg gave a surprise inspection visit that morning he caught me connected to the regimental headquarters with the telephone receiver in my hand. He had found the company had fallen in, but not to carry out the scheduled exercise.

Immediately he started yelling. "Why aren't you on your way as scheduled? You're late!"

"I was just preparing to explain to you, sir, on the telephone."

This would take some of the bluster out of his indignation, I thought. Here I was at least trying to explain that it would be irresponsible to go out there as planned. It didn't work and he ordered us to go ahead with the scheduled exercise as planned, period. I tried to point out that it was the first cold day, and it was an exercise that called for a long wait before the attack could be launched. He, again, raised his voice and ordered me to proceed immediately.

It was an absolutely miserable January morning in the middle of that mild winter of 1941. Nevertheless, the company did well and he didn't have much of a negative criticism. I noticed with interest that his nose, which had been reddish now showed white spots of discoloration, unmistakable signs of taking frostbite. I respectfully suggested that the colonel should have someone vigorously rub his nose with snow. His accompanying officer soon confirmed my impression about his nose. The colonel was furious. He immediately ordered me to take the company back to Ostrolenka and turned away.

I ordered the platoon to have everyone's face, nose and ears inspected to look for serious frost damage. I did not mount my trusty horse, I walked the few miles with my company because I had ominous pains in both feet. I told my platoon leaders that while the colonel is sitting in his office having his nose rubbed and considering how he could possibly punish me, we should go from room to room and inspect everybody's toes because mine were hurting tremendously. There were immediate reports of various degrees of frost damage and we phoned our doctor to come by immediately. Then I sat down, took off my boots and socks and contemplated the discoloration of both my big toes.

The corporal, who had been looking after my horse, saw my feet and said, "Just a minute, I'll be right back with some hot water and horse manure."

I yelled. "What!"

"Lieutenant, that's the only thing to do. There's a lot of ammonia in those little apples."

He wasn't joking. He came with a large tub and a shovel full of horse manure saying, "It's A-1 manure and from your own horse."

I really did put both feet into this tub, while holding my nose, and then repeated the treatment when the discoloration wouldn't immediately disappear. The minute I felt relief, I told him to go from room to room and offer his services to anyone who needed looking after. At least no one had to have their toes amputated. Our Third Company did have to learn to take some kidding when we were referred to as *"Hot Rossäpfelstampfer"*.

❖ • • ❖ • • ❖ •

"How did you feel when you heard and saw the colonel reprimanding me?" I asked Müller one night when we were ready to go to sleep in one of the peasant huts. It was my first experience of this kind, staying with a Russian family, as it were. Our truck driver did not want to go on any further and told us to just knock and go inside. I wondered for a second why knock, but I let that pass.

"The Russians are used to this," he claimed.

So we knocked. When the door opened a huge cat met us and just barely made it past Ivan who couldn't do anything about it because I had him leashed. Only the leash saved this fat feline. A relatively young peasant man climbed down from above the stove and brought some straw and began to gesticulate. Since his Russian welcome was incomprehensible to us, he mimed putting both hands flat together and then against his right cheek, which I thought was meant to wish us sweet dreams or something. The dim light of an oil lamp revealed the huge sleeping place above the stove. Curious eyes peered over the edge of the bunk, faces of all age groups who were mostly interested in the dog.

We stretched out on the straw. Müller answered minutes later, "Well, you had it coming to you."

That made me wide awake. "Just what do you mean?"

"Objectively speaking, you took it upon yourself to change your schedule. That was an infraction."

I could not sleep for a while. I was cursing my fate to have to put up with this chap and faulting myself at the same time for engaging in this puerile discussion. Meanwhile, the occupants of the bunk above the stove kept making all kinds of noises. There was a constant commotion up there. After a while the thought occurred to me that we were rather trusting to just bed down right in the middle of a Russian peasant hut and go to sleep. Dog or no dog, there could be someone hostile hiding up there, for all I knew.

This thought kept me from falling asleep, and with this thought I got up and surveyed the scene. The weak battery of my flashlight allowed a not too clear view of a bunch of kiddies sitting around two people who were going "at it." The children were watching with some detachment while the partners in this activity did not even let the flashlight disturb them.

I thought I was dreaming. I had never seen anything like it before. While I was standing and feeling rather foolish, I put on my coat, took the dog and went outside to clear my head. It was a beautiful night. No clouds, limitless Russian sky, lots of stars. The moonlight allowed a view of our hut behind me. The thatched roof was hanging down its front in an uneven fashion, like the unruly ash-blond hair down the face of the muzhik I remembered seeing in Greta Garbo's *Anna Karenina*. It had gotten pretty cold. I stomped out my cigarette on the frozen ground.

The stench inside was overwhelming. I don't know why I hadn't noticed it before. A mixture of human sweat, borscht, and buckets full of fermenting cabbage. Müller-Hofmeister was snoring peacefully.

Our driver called us out at 5:00 a.m. to make use of the night frost when the German trucks still could move before the daytime thaw set in. The conversations between Müller and myself stayed at the same level for the balance of the trip. Only during our stopovers at Poltava and Kaliningrad was I able to avoid him. By and by, I found out from him what kind of reputation I had with the regimental establishment.

To wit: my behavior during the pogrom on the November 9, 1938. My keeping the dog with me against regulations, wherever I was going. My making fun of the foxhunt on St. Hubertus Day in Ostrolenka where all of us, pretending to hunt an imaginary fox, a gentlemanly activity among the upper classes, in reality ended up having to let a group of stampeding horses have their own way. Mügge fell off his horse, he was laughing so hard. Then there were my contacts with Polish girls and Polish families in Ostrolenka. My musical activities, teaching my platoon the songs of the youth movement to relieve the drag of The Phony War in 1939. Müller dished these things out one by one.

Unfortunately, more often than not, I tried to argue my side of the story, rather than just ignoring it. He kept repeating. "An order is an order and a regulation is a regulation."

"Of course, you must have obedience," I said without any reservation. "This goes especially for combat situations. That's the basis for all soldiering, unconditional obedience. I did not disobey. I made an adult decision in light of a weather emergency. How can I totally disregard a severe cold snap when I know my boys are neither dressed for it nor prepared for it? Have you used a weapon at ten degrees below zero? Have you started an engine at fifteen below? Only our alpine divisions have had winter training. Apropos, the basic regulations say the soldier must obey all orders with one exception: he can refuse to carry out an order, which entails illegal or criminal activity. Any soldier, no matter what rank must refuse illegal orders, remember?"

"Of course," he snapped.

"Well, Rodenburg read us the order introducing the attack of Russia. You were there. Everybody had to be present."

"Sure," he said. I could tell Müller was really getting irritated.

"When he came to the passage about this being an ideological life and death struggle and the shooting of any political commissar and Jew in our hands as POW..."

"Yes?"

"Remember that stir in the room, do you? The immediate murmur of dissent and revulsion."

"I did not hear it that way." Müller replied.

"Dissent and revulsion, man. I very much doubt that any of us would order the 'liquidation' of prisoners of war. I certainly would not! Rodenburg looked up from his text and started to shout about abusing the Russians as pig's intent to destroy western civilization, enemies we had to hate. We are soldiers, man. We don't shoot prisoners who have submitted themselves to our protection and we don't hate. We carry out orders, but we don't hate." I felt exhausted and a little sick.

● ◆ ● ● ◆ ● ● ◆ ●

The mud became our main concern. Daily we saw the superhuman efforts of men, horses and machines to negotiate the roads to bring supplies to the front. The original dirt road had mostly become a sea of mud, which was mostly ankle deep. Often it became 100 yards wide. The night frost lately made some movement possible in the morning. Once the sun came out or it started to rain, there were huge traffic jams. A hostile plane would have had a field day. I persuaded some drivers to start up at 3 or 4 a.m. to make progress and get this over with.

The closer we got, the more I had to think what was waiting for me. Would I even know the company? I left them in July and this was end of November. By this time, they had covered 500 miles as the crow flies marching day in and day out, probably 1,000 miles moving, taking detours and maneuvering for battles occasionally. They had to put up with heat and dust in the fall and now with mud and frost.

Poltava was a busy little place, a never-ending stream of traffic going through. There were wooden signs nailed to a pole in the center. Among them we discovered our divisional icon, the silhouette of a helmet of a Royal Prussian Guard Regiment around 1750.

Müller-Hofmeister and I saw the same movie Wonny and I had discussed a few weeks earlier. He was not impressed. He went as far as saying, "Look around you. We are in a fight for survival against world communism. And what all are we supposed to feed *Unwertes Leben*! Masses of people unfit for life! Mental and terminal patients, Gypsies, prostitutes, homosexuals, habitual criminals and those muzhiks. Look around you. They're subhuman!"

I just mumbled, "Why do I even talk to you?"

There were rumors. Berlin and Cologne had to go through heavy air raids again. The Allies met in Teheran. If true, that would mean Stalin could be supplied on dry land. Allegedly, General Udet had died in a plane crash.

Finally, on November 19, we reached 76 Division and the following day reported to the regiment, which had just finished a short withdrawal under superior Russian pressure. I barely had time to hand Ivan over to my trusty Corporal Hans Müller, who had been looking after my horse in my absence. Every time I looked at that horse I saw only a worthless creature from a West Berlin horse stable where it had cut quite a figure daintily carrying females around the Grünewald, I presumed. Hans and the dog were howling with pleasure of meeting up again. They hadn't seen each other since February 1941.

A new battalion commander, wounded this very day, came by on a stretcher. This was putting Fuchs again in charge, perish the thought! I went straight to the company, which was under fire. Word went around, "The chief is back."

Fifty-four grenadiers, that was all that was left. During sporadic fighting I jumped from platoon to platoon, or better, from squad to squad. The men looked ill-kempt and exhausted, but in relatively high spirits. The cold east wind was getting to them and to me. I suddenly remembered I was still wearing my Berlin Kurfürstendamm uniform, state of the art riding breeches, tightly fitting riding boots of a nondescript color. Weeks of mud and ice had ruined them during the last twenty-eight days.

Lt. Roethe appeared together with the new 01, the new orderly officer doing Lt. Hans Müller's former duties. They were both out of breath.

"Urgent! Do you see those guys over there behind that mortar?"

I took a look through my glasses, "Yes."

"They are Russians. They have pushed Fifth Company out of their position and you have now no contact with the Second Battalion."

"Oh, shit."

"Yes, here's your order: Third Company immediately counter attacks with all available force leaving a screen on the line. We cannot offer artillery support. Sorry. It's all up to you - and please hurry."

A nice how-do-you-do. I had no orientation. No map. Nothing. The only thing I was sure of was that my boys were facing east, or were they? I left a few riflemen and one mortar on the line and assembled the others behind a huge stack of straw. We formed two squads with one mortar each.

"Left, right, left right, walk in file. Remember? Once they shoot back you are to take cover for reloading purposes only. Here's some additional ammunition."

They looked apprehensive.

"See here. I haven't got a clue, having just arrived, and I'm just as afraid as you are. I could only make them out with my glasses so let's get it over with. Move out."

So we went, silently, until we could see them with our naked eyes in the haze of dusk. The Russians were moving and firing and ignoring us completely. When we got close enough I gave the signal and we commenced fire. They still ignored us for a while taking casualties. The closer we came, the darker it got, and when we finally saw their faces they fired back and started to run. It all dissolved in a route, we saw hundreds of earth colored shadows disappear in an easterly direction leaving some mortars and some machine guns.

A while later Fifth Company elements came and joined us and of all people, "Mr." Müller-Hofmeister. He looked like a real soldier, he even wore a steel helmet. I, however, still looked like a Sunday afternoon stroller who had fallen off his horse. I was covered with mud. There was a short silence. I told him he couldn't be blamed for getting cut off, if anyone could be, but he owed me one.

By 3:00 a.m. I was satisfied with setting up a defensive perimeter. The hot soup came, lukewarm it was. To me it tasted like gourmet salmon mousse. The bread and the sausage were frozen and not edible. Anyway, I never could eat that kind of sausage without mustard. I tried to sleep in a ditch on some leftover thatch cuttings and trembled with the cold east wind all night. The temperature never fell below twenty-seven or twenty-eight degrees, I guessed, but that wind was beastly. I did not get more practical things to wear till the following evening, that is to say, GI pants and a corporal's tunic. Hans Müller brought my steel helmet and some personal items and even a razor.

The Russians kept probing in battalion strength hoping to find a weak spot, however by November 24 all was quiet. Colonel Rodenburg came and commended me for the so-called decisive counter attack. He ended, as usual, by saying that, of course, nobody had expected anything else from me and offered one British cigarette. Lt. Roethe, who was standing behind him, watched with a sarcastic grin in the background and gave me an encouraging wink.

Rodenburg had barely left when incoming mortar shells brought me back to reality. Another one of those surprise barrages at dusk, I thought. Two houses were set aflame and immediately burned brightly so now we could see the oncoming muzhiks better. They came in company strength, I guessed, and they soon gave up after taking some losses. Our only casualty was Behrends who died before anyone could have helped him. We spent the night waiting for more to come. Nothing happened.

The next day, we had to move back another six miles in a southwesterly direction. There were rumors that Rostov and the Don bridges were *fest in Deutscher hand* (firmly in German hands). Hitler's SS bodyguards supposedly had done it. My right-hand noncom, Orje, said dryly, "So what?" Infantry was hardly ever impressed with the heroic deeds of elite Panzer units.

We weren't concerned with Rostov. Our problem was the frost. Around dawn the temperature sank to its lowest point of the night. We had taken to waking up even grenadiers off duty to make sure nobody had taken frostbite in his sleep. What was left of the company was a sorry sight to see in those early minutes of the day. Most had learned to fashion themselves some overshoes mainly out of straw and the baling twine taken from those combines that were rusting in the open. Their uniforms were filthy and torn, the gloves issued in fall had been worn through by October. Now, they used bits of rags or socks to cover their fingers. Even the reserve pair of socks found some use in this way very much against regulations. Still, most hands were cracked open in places with chilblains.

A wretched lot, I thought, but it was better to be here with the people I could rely upon in an emergency. Back home, I found it to be unbearable having to sit in air raid shelters surrounded by panicking humanity. I felt helpless wedged in with those mothers, children and the elderly knowing there was nothing I could do for them in case we had a direct hit.

So clusters of our men stood tramping or jumping around in the accursed snow behind the cover of a haystack, or house ruin. Hans Müller and two of his boys had just come on horseback to bring some lukewarm ersatz coffee and odds and ends requested by the platoon leaders. He said the fall of Rostov was official. While I was talking to him, moving and jogging in place to get warm, as it were, I suddenly felt something warm and wet on my left leg. I stood quite still for some time. Was I bleeding? Ridiculous. There hadn't been any shooting since last night. I put my hand in my pocket, then knew immediately that I must have lost control of my bladder. While I was still trying to sort it all out Hans Müller asked, "Is there anything else, sir?" I was tempted to tell him about this condition I was in, but I let it pass. I hoped this was just a single mishap, some temporary infirmity, nothing to make a fuss about. So he left.

An hour later I wished I had told him or somebody. I needed a change of pants as soon as possible. To function with this kind of predicament at below thirty-two degrees in a howling east wind was another matter. There was to be no hostile action all day. Unfortunately, I could not contact Müller so I knew I would not be able to have a change until twenty-four hours from now. I walked around in a daze, I don't remember specifics. Twice more it happened that day. Twice more the wonderful warmth dissipated after a few minutes and then my left trouser leg started to freeze. The humiliation was complete. I cursed myself on and off for not having told Müller right away, this same Müller who had saved my toes with horse manure. He would have understood and known what to do.

As in Lübeck in 1937, I started watching my men's suffering with more intensity: the frostbite, the first cases of dysentery and even jaundice, or hepatitis, as we found out later. The healthy ones, interestingly, were not necessarily the strong masculine types. Physical strength seemed to be meaningless. The clever, the more circumspect boys kept out of these troubles, god knows how!

The overriding problem as far as morale was concerned was abject disappointment. We felt we were being betrayed and discarded, the army had let us down. They kept asking me if I had seen any trains with winter equipment on my way. I had to reply that if there were any winter uniforms on the way I would have found them on the supply units who would have helped themselves first.

November 28, 1941. Postcard to Jutta:

> For seven days now I'm back with my own company, thank god! Lt. Michael, my substitute, was wounded the day I arrived. We cannot complain about boredom, there's quite a bit going on here. Otherwise, 25 marks are waiting for you at your postal address. Please give me your new one as soon as possible. I don't want to bother Hildegard, she has enough on her hands.
>
> So you will spend Christmas in Munich? How are all your friends? Champagne is getting more expensive, I hear. That will dampen your frivolity, won't it? Please excuse the postcard, I don't have any other stationery at the moment.
>
> Love, Vince

On the top of the army issued postcard in small print was an excerpt from Hitler's note to the Soviet Union. It read, "The German people are aware of their duty to save the western culture and civilization from the mortal dangers of Bolshevism and to blaze the trail for genuine social improvement in Europe." Since I hadn't even heard about a note to the Soviet Union, I didn't take it seriously. It looked like propaganda, or maybe an attempt to rationalize our position. I didn't think much of it.

By the end of November, Hans Müller was bringing or sending a daily change of pants each time he came. I wondered how long I should continue this. I was still hoping against hope that I would come back to normal. We treated my skin damage with Vaseline, which so far had been reserved for our cracked hands.

The temperature warmed up for a few days and it was then I discovered that around my neck and my belt line the first family of lice had settled in. I was now in complete despair, being among those reasonably educated Germans who had read books on World War I where lice were strongly associated with the loss of life for millions of people who died a slow and painful death from typhus.

During the short period of warmer weather neither we nor the Russians launched any hostile action. Word came that the proud SS divisions of bodyguards were forced to withdraw from Rostov after all, to my mind the first setback of some significance for the German army.

I found time to write to my sister on December 6. I could sit in the warm winter sun to thank her for her little parcel with excellent cookies and describe to her the great time Ivan was having with Hans Müller behind the lines. "He has plenty of food and any number of cats, dogs and rabbits to chase." I included another check for 25 marks just as pocket money and wished her luck with her studies at the University of Munich. I didn't tell her about my infirmities.

Colonel Rodenburg had another surprise for us. The advanced guards of Second Battalion had left their positions prematurely. They reported an imminent Russian attack as a reason for their withdrawal. Thus, a valuable lookout that had a commanding view of some lowlands had been abandoned. "Eleventh Company sends a raiding party to hill crest, coordinations follow and re-establishes positions of advanced guards. Engage only if fired upon." This was the third time we had to stick our necks out for some other unit's mistakes. To some it might have been a flattering assignment, but to me it was rather an inconvenient one considering my personal condition. Moving about over distances with one frozen trouser leg was not without consequences. However, there were only a few young noncoms left so there was nothing for it. I had to do it myself.

"Wendlandt, you'll go and see a doctor tonight, O.K.?"

The young noncom I had addressed protested. "Some of my men are worse off than I am, sir."

"I won't argue that point, but I have not caught them in the act. I watched you just now. If this turns into dysentery you might not make it home, you're nothing but skin and bones. Possibly, you're already dehydrated. What are you drinking?"

"Snow, sir."

"You go tonight. For now, you and your squad will look after our perimeter, is that clear?"

"Yes, sir. May I ask a question?"

"Why don't you do the same and go see the doctor when I come back?"

The idiotic advanced guard people joined us looking sheepish. I had warned my men not to make any cheap shot remarks about their "heroic" premature withdrawal. After all, we were in no position to judge their conduct, not having been on the spot. The Russian's behavior was still a source of puzzlement.

Moving in combat across the industrial area of Russia meant being able to use electric power lines for orientation. All we had to do was follow the line. That meant a net reduction of my anxieties by one, a big one at that. The Ukraine plains were seemingly endless and mostly without landmarks.

While advancing in the open a few well posted sharp-shooters can pick you off at random. This kind of assignment was not my favored sport, but then danger was so permanent everywhere. With a suddenly heightened sense of awareness, we moved. I felt my vision slightly blurred. Was it excitement? Everybody was sweating profusely. I could see the cold sweat on Orje's hands. With each step, I thought I was breathing faster and thought I could hear my heart beat, or was I imagining things. The tiny hole in my ear, which a shrapnel had pierced the day before, started to bleed again, or had I merely touched it. The solitary intruder in the air, a Russian plane, which came every night had dropped its bomb close to our position. We called it the sewing machine because of its odd engine noise. We were sure the pilot in that one-seater of World War I vintage threw bombs out by hand. We allowed ourselves to feel fortunate. If there were any hostile combatants in the area, they did not show. We put the advance guards back into their foxholes and wished them well.

After an uneventful return, we noticed a sudden drop in temperature. Wendlandt was waiting for me. We shook hands. "Take care, man," I said. "We have put a well-deserved EK for you, the basic metal for bravery. It will catch up with you in hospital unless our bureaucracy screws up again. Well done. We'll miss you. We need you back healthy."

"Thank you, sir. By the way, I asked my uncle about your predicament."

"Which one?" I made it sound as if I had hundreds.

"He is a urologist, sir. He thinks your stay here ill advised."

"How did you know?" I had lived with the illusion that I could keep this under wraps and I was sure Hans Müller would not talk.

"We all know, sir. We didn't think your daily change was mere vanity."

"I'll let that pass and I'll put your uncle's tip under advisement. Ciao."

It turned cold fast. Snow fell the next morning. A howling east wind created drifts of giant proportions. What was days ago the carcass of a horse was now shaped like a sand dune on the beach of the Baltic Sea, ripples and all. I was glad the carcass was covered. The sight of the four or five little piglets feasting inside it turned my stomach. Somebody said that a few of the piglets had been eaten and they were found to be delicious.

Just before Christmas, a very tough glaze of ice covered all these snow drifts so hard we tore the skin of our hands if we would fall into it or touch it. By now the numbing cold really had gotten to me. I functioned on instinct and was almost unable to think critically. Orje became even more valuable and reminded me of whatever had to be done. All forty-two of us just went through the daily challenges in some kind of primitive stupor, thinking only of survival, snatching a moment of warmth however we could. The Russians could only be heard in the distance. They must have left nature to do the work of destruction on us.

Orje was a *Bretterträger* by trade, a man who carries stacks of wooden slats or other building material up the ladder into a given house under construction. He pulled another beauty in my presence one day. One of the fresh replacements was having fun putting his initials into the snow. "Why are you wasting it?" he asked.

"What do you mean? Urine?"

"This is the only warm thing you get to enjoy these days, stupid. Good for healing chilblains too." Spoken as he rinsed his hands in front of him.

◆ ◆ •• ◆ •• ◆ •

December 24, 1941, near Artemovsk, Ukraine, Russia. There was a lull in the fighting. I was sitting in the half dark in a small railway hut. It must have been a signal box of sorts belonging to the lone industrial track leading to Artemovsk. Like all the houses I had encountered in Russia, the room reeked of fermenting cabbages and beets. I looked at my watch. About this time in the afternoon children back home in Germany would be standing in front their Christmas tree or at least some candles on some evergreen branches. The glow of the candlelight would reflect in their wide-open eyes. They would be singing or reciting some poem addressed to Father Christmas to earn their gifts, at least that's what the grown-ups made them believe. Later, Christmas music from the gramophone would be heard in the background. I kept staring in disbelief at my half open Christmas parcel from Hamburg, which had just arrived. It had come together with the long overdue rations of frozen bread, frozen sausage and a lukewarm liquid smelling faintly of coffee.

There he sat, our 250-pound sergeant major, out of breath, red in the face, perspiration dripping from his forehead and his hands. This was the first and only day we had ever seen him on the line, since I had been back at least. This very day as he carried out his plan to play Father Christmas, the Russians would come in force and throw everything they had at us. For the first time their superior T-34 tanks showed up. The sergeant-major's beloved German anti-tank guns turned out to be totally useless. Since 1940 he had been bragging about them to us, starting the minute he was transferred from the motorized anti-tank company to ours. I felt for him at the time. Frankly, I didn't think this transfer was meant to be a reward. While he was talking to me my mind was on the Russian tanks, the first ones I had encountered myself. "How would my boys react?" I wondered. Digging a foxhole in this frozen ground was hard labor, to say the least.

I told our visitor that I thought it was a nice gesture to hold back mail for Christmas and bring it in person on December 24, but would he kindly take off before the tanks take a right and display their wares to us. He, the sergeant-major, would be of much more of use to us where he belonged. So off he went glad to obey. He turned around and yelled, "Beketovka. They are in Beketovka, the tanks!" He pointed to the hamlet where Second Battalion was taking quite a pounding at the moment.

"Yes, we can see that," I shouted. "Thank you. Get moving!"

I could hear the yells of joy and surprise from some of my men who certainly had not expected any Christmas surprise out here thousands of miles from home in the Russian snow. I got to thinking about the sergeant-major holding back the mail for this moment. It was meant as a thoughtful gesture. Of course, what the men really needed would have been winter clothing and equipment to at least be able to cope with this first merciless Russian winter. It was no consolation that our allies, those Romanian soldiers around us, were even less equipped.

For the moment all my concerns, even the isolation, the shortages, the growing number of dysentery cases, the daily losses to frostbite or hostile action seemed irrelevant. I was looking at my Christmas gift from home, a carton tightly packed with Christmas cookies. All of them were burned to a crisp charcoal on the bottom side. No attempt had been made to scrape off the worst. The almond halves on the top of each cookie were singed to a sickening yellow gray.

I was stunned, not sure whether I wanted to scream with laughter or with angry frustration. I decided to stash the parcel under some garments I found in the corner of the switchman's bunk above the fireplace. I did not want to let the boys see my surprise gift from Father Christmas. It was too embarrassing.

I went outside all around the perimeter to check the positions. The lull in the fighting still continued. I did my work almost mechanically; my mind was still fixed on those damned burnt cookies. B Company on my right was exchanging fire with the Russians. I registered the pitiful "clunks" each time one of those useless anti-tank rounds from our German guns bounced off those T-34 tanks. I could hear clanking of the Russian tank treads in the distance, a sound that normally would cause paroxysms of fear or even panic. Not this afternoon, though.

"How did I deserve this mess?" I wondered. Surely I had eaten some burned cookies as a boy. Nobody else in the family would have done that. Then it was a matter of quantity over quality for a growing boy. To be sure there was no food rationing in 1935, but there were bottlenecks and Göring had asked, "Do you want guns, or do you want butter?"

"Guns!" the idiots had yelled back.

On the way back to the hut I thought about my helping with the Christmas baking until 1935 when I was age seventeen. The yearly baking tradition of a German mother and housewife required a muscular effort beyond my mother's strength. This kneading, mixing, stirring, rolling, molding, rounding, dividing and forming paid a handsome dividend at times for a young man who was in an almost constant search of chewables and I enjoyed sampling the various types of dough while handling it.

The Danish Browns were the most valued cookies within our family's Christmas baking tradition. It was by the quality of these cookies that excellence was to be determined. The various households in the family mailed samples of their baking efforts to each other. It was almost a competition every year. Of course, single family members, widowed uncles and less fortunate friends received a Christmas parcel with baked goods too. These Danish Browns were so thin that they became easily scorched if someone did not pay attention to the oven. No matter. I was willing to eat the burned ones after scraping off the worst. Ah, this must be the link.

I was a bit out of breath having had to run across a clearing. Once inside the hut, I even remembered the recipe. The women were so anxious to avoid mistakes that I had to recite the recipe to them ever since I could read. As I walked up and down in the hut I recalled the details. First, you melted butter and added sugar or syrup and then you added flour, crushed almonds, candied citrus peel, grated lemon and orange peel, some cinnamon, cloves, cardamom, potash (yuk). I still shuddered remembering potash. Kneading this took hours, or so it seemed. The dough was left standing for twenty-four hours, rolled and sliced very thinly. Now in 1941, I still could remember the recipe. Triumph!

I was about to throw the parcel away when a direct hit from a T-34 smashed the stable behind the house. Within minutes we were fighting for our lives trying to stave off a cleverly arranged surprise attack. During the afternoon we had to abandon the railway hut and take new positions behind the mound rimming the railway track. Contact with B Company on the right was lost. It was not until midnight when the fighting finally died down and the Russians withdrew.

I still wonder if any of those Russians found the burned cookies. And if they survived World War II, by some chance, they could have spread the story around confirming the old Russian saying that the Germans had invented the devil. Here was the proof: burned cookies for Christmas to their loved ones.

December 25: The enemy kept throwing men and tanks at our people around Beketovka throughout the following week. We were mere bystanders watching all day from our positions. The attack ran from left to right. We could make out command posts and mortar batteries and I could watch the traffic on the battlefield through my field glasses. Somehow the enemy kept ignoring us, while staying out of our range of fire.

Every once in a while, two or three tanks turned our way and lobbed a few blasts at random. No infantry accompanied them and they turned away after a while. After the second intrusion I told my friends of our anti-tank company to take their little toy guns somewhere else, clean them, oil them and then dump them in the river behind us. The noncom in charge eagerly agreed. He felt very bad about yesterday's disaster. He was heartbroken and complained loudly about not having been warned that his guns were obsolete when real tanks became involved.

We kept warm by digging a ten-by-eight hole with two supporting walls with our little shovels. Some of the boys had found some railway ties to use as support for the side walls and to be laid crosswise for the ceiling. I had never seen the men dig and build with such eagerness. They needed some cover and even more for protection from the night cold. We made sure that all excavated dirt was covered with snow immediately, otherwise it could be seen from the ground or by plane.

From then, on each night, they slept tightly packed in that dugout like sardines in a can. Every two hours the unavoidable change of the guards disturbed everybody else's sleep. It was like pulling out a fire log from the middle of a big stack and pushing another one in its place. This change was accompanied by outbursts of salty language, but in spite of this annoyance this was a warm shelter.

The next morning the sun again illustrated the importance of white camouflage gear for warfare in the snow. We could see the Russians standing out against the white background, apparently their winter uniforms had not arrived yet either. I left a note with the sergeant major the following evening to order, buy or steal forty white bed sheets. The spectacle in front of us illustrated my point.

On December 27 there was a dramatic reshuffling of sectors. It took place without warning. I was incensed by the hectic amateurism of this procedure. Were they trying to free troops for Beketovka? All of a sudden, there were total strangers on my right and I was with half of my men attached to the First Battalion 178 Regiment, our friends from Potsdam.

My assignment was changed to be an assistant to the forward observer of the divisional artillery. His name was Theo and he was an old friend from Spandau. He trained me, or tried to, in directing range finding while viewing the action from the side rather than from the front. We were very busy. I was given even better field glasses and was fascinated to see the Russian soldiers in much more detail. I could not believe the almost total indifference of the Russian soldiers facing artillery fire. I watched them taking losses, unmistakable hits, yet they kept moving about, bombardment or no bombardment. There was a tall chap standing in the middle of some mortars accenting his commands by raising and lowering his arms. You could see the wounded all around him, but he just stood there and worked.

I asked Theo, "This is incredible. What do you make of it?"

"They are not like us," he said. "Life is not precious to them, or something like that. I've seen them step on mounds of their own dead without any hesitation. It's gruesome. Remember Franz, the Austrian?"

"Yes."

"He shot himself when he found himself surrounded by Russian soldiers. He had always maintained he would never become a prisoner of war of these people."

I couldn't believe it. "How did you know it was suicide?"

"We retrieved the body later. There was a small-bore hole in his temple, one bullet missing in his revolver."

"Oh, my god. He must have read Dwinger, *Army Behind Barbed Wire*, the book that described the fate of German prisoners in Russian hands."

"Yes. He talked about that a lot. Frankly, each time I am forward observer I make sure my infantry friends have enough ammunition to protect me."

The Bekatovka attack must have exhausted our supply of ammunition. The next morning, we were told to go easy on the ammo and save it for emergencies. That evening, we turned back the one night attack on our sector. The enemy used no fire preparation, they just came across the field amid a flurry of dry stinging snow, the kind of snow where you barely dare open your eyes. Luckily, someone started shooting early and alarmed the whole front. The enemy withdrew after a while, certainly not as a result of my amateurish range finding.

At dawn, we went out. The bodies they left were covered by snow already. We rescued two wounded Russians. One had a facial wound and couldn't see much. The other one had a big slash on his left foot. We caught him hoping to crawl away for safety. Both had frostbite. The open foot had stopped bleeding. It was neatly opened. You could see what you could normally expect to find in a book on anatomy all the sinews, muscles, ligaments, bones laid bare. Had this been one of my boys, he would have been in shock and in very serious condition. All this Rusky did was chew on a piece of frozen bread we had offered him and mumbled, "*Cholodno*" which meant, I'm cold, I was told. There is a threshold of pain that we could not fathom.

As we approached New Years, the fight for Bekatovka petered out. We heard that Second Battalion was still there and intact and Mügge, my buddy, had been given the Knight's Cross of the Iron Cross for his part in leading the defense. I was delighted. What a turnabout. The black sheep of Spandau-Ruhleben, thick glasses and all, is now a hero! Major Günther, eat your heart out.

All this time, one miserable week, there were no pants to change into. I was in pain most of the time, sores were all over my legs and the lice were irritating me to no end, mainly around the belt and neck. I forgot time, place and my assignment. I have no recollection how I spent the time between December 27 and New Years. The only worthwhile event was the daily telephone with the artillery. They had all the information and told me that the German spearheads were stuck outside Moscow, that Hitler had now taken personal command of the army, that Goebbels had asked the German public to give up winter clothing for the troops in Russia. Sebastopol was still in Russian hands.

Hans Müller sent a note that he could not come anymore, they were looking after and feeding two or three hundred boys from another unit. Fortunately, the note was wrapped in a pair of pants. That gave my spirits some lift. I had barely changed into these pants when Colonel Rodenburg sent a personal invitation over the artillery telephone. He wanted me to come to a New Year's dinner at regimental headquarters at 11:00 p.m. sharp. RSVP not necessary, it's an order. His invitation was "wrapped" in a written order that we would be pulled out on the same day, December 31, and that I was to report to the doctor at the Divisional Infirmary on January 1, 1942. The irony wasn't lost on anyone hearing about this. The two black sheep were riding again, one was to go home on furlough with his Knight's Cross and the other on his way to a roast duck at the colonel's table.

So, this sore, smelly, unshaven lieutenant limped out of our hell hole on his way to civilization. I wished my men a Happy New Year, and found my way in the dark to Hans Müller, following the tracks of the nightly supply teams. It was about a ninety minute walk in the snow, but Hans was in a warm hut and after a sponge bath and a shave he and I took off for the regiment.

The regimental headquarters was a former school house. Rodenburg, the adjutant and Lieutenant Roethe even had bunk beds, a table cloth, knives and forks and a formidable roasted duck. Just seeing all the fat nearly made me sick. It smelled so good, I forced myself to eat some along with some sliced green beans from a tin and potatoes with gravy. The wine was wonderful and I got so comfortably warm under my pullover, I asked permission to take it off and then placed it on a bunk bed. Rodenburg made his usual attempt at sincere praise. I liked it better when he said it the first time after my return to the company. After that the conversation was not too cheerful, the news from Moscow didn't sound good.

My stomach rebelled after this unusual midnight nourishment and the wine had my head spinning. I excused myself early and Hans and I went on to the infirmary. By 2:00 a.m. I was in a real bed with a high temperature, a gastric problem, and still lice. The only positive facet of this first day in the New Year was that my bladder, my stomach and the lice allowed me to sleep until 11:00 a.m. the next day.

Roethe came by two days later concerned about my condition at New Year's dinner. I told him everything was fine. He grinned and informed me that I had apparently placed my pullover on the adjutant's bunk bed and they now all had lice.

January 1942, MASH. They put me into a small single bed unit with all the modern conveniences: a sink, a central heating radiator, and one electric bulb dangling from the ceiling. However, the scorched earth retreat of the Russians had reduced the above items to mere ornaments: no water, no heat, no power. Considering the size of the Ukrainian industrial area, the dismantling effort must have been surprisingly well organized. No matter, the bed was warm and I felt very much relaxed and taken care of, at least for now.

The medical personnel in dressing places this size mostly were restricted to cleaning and dressing wounds. Of course, bullets and grenade splinters were removed whenever possible. They did do emergency operations in serious cases as with oncoming gangrene. However, after preliminary care, most wounded were passed on to the field hospital in Artemovsk when they were fit enough to travel. Considering the state of the roads, they had better be fit. Often the cars had to be towed by tanks or by other tracked vehicles or, when all else failed, by horses.

For my urological problem, there was no qualified doctor available. At my request Colonel Rodenburg had asked the chief surgeon to put me up for a while pending further developments. The doctor, a bald forty-five-year-old jolly giant from Lake Constance, came by at 12 p.m. to welcome me personally as well as to give me a urological how-do-you-do. He had just finished operating and was still wearing his black rubber apron. Not a pretty sight. His term for what he did was, "Surgery in the raw." He told me that I had undoubtedly the most enlarged prostate gland between Leningrad and Sebastopol and that it had been irresponsible of me to drag myself with this problem through the snow for almost two months.

We had an immediate rapport and I considered myself lucky to be in his care. Since he was not a specialist, all he could do was keep me relatively warm and feed me some of those new wonder drugs every four hours day and night.

I discovered that he was even more critical of the army than I was. The numerous cases of frostbitten limbs had him seething with anger. During the Beketovka crisis rumor had it that he had operated seventeen hours at a stretch. His skill was so well recognized that often colleagues from other units would come to watch him at work.

My room was a haven of privacy, if nothing else. I could chase lice any time I felt like it without an audience of critical experts. I admit I could not be called proficient at this game. Even when I had one and was about to smash it between my fingernails it often escaped. Hans Müller brought some of my books, so when I wasn't chasing lice I was reading or writing letters.

The day after Roethe's visit, the colonel stormed in crashing another "hate the army" session between the doctor and myself. In his hand he had the file that had originated with the military police at the Dresden Main Railway Station and that had been lovingly inflated into an AWOL charge at Spandau. The colonel was fuming, his monocle was twitching. He even turned on the doctor suggesting that my medical predicament had to do with a "promiscuous rail hopping orgy" between Dresden and Munich, not to mention Hamburg.

"We are men of the world, Doctor. Tell me the truth."

The doctor assured the colonel that sex had nothing to do with it and that eventually we would be able to control my problem. Rodenburg, while taking notes and mumbling a few vicious threats, continued to give me a hearing.

All the while he was talking I was looking for signs of my own personal discomfort. How were my lice doing? Was Rodenburg aware of the fact that I knew about his lice problem since New Years? When he asked questions, I tried to hold my ground, my final argument being that, after all, I had not tried to avoid my duty and I had arrived way ahead of the transport of the fifty noncoms I was originally supposed to accompany. However, I did not put my foot down, figuratively speaking, because inwardly I had this nagging fear that Friedrich von Kirchbach's blank travel orders, which I had used, might become an issue and that I possibly would cause some harm and embarrassment to the Kirchbach family.

Rodenburg finished this official hearing with the remark, "If we lose this war, it will be because of people like you who interpret orders and regulations rather generously and to their own satisfaction. Of course, we'll win it, but if, ..." He didn't finish his thought.

After he had left I said to the doctor, "I don't think this was a very nice note on which to finish his official action."

The doctor was conciliatory. "I can't help liking your monocled big daddy and all his bluster. I suspect he has some kind of love-hate thing for you." The doctor suddenly excused himself and I was left wondering what he meant by that.

According to an old Prussian military rule the army requires an officer to always sleep on any decision concerning a given issue. So Rodenburg came back the next day to give his judgment. Again, I had to endure a lengthy monologue from him before he pronounced that I was to receive twenty-one days of severe house arrest. No visitors. To be carried out here and now in bed.

Normally one receives this kind of pronouncement standing at attention so I was tempted to stretch out as smartly as I could in the horizontal. The whole thing seemed so ridiculous. Even after my sentencing, he kept harping on my potential for causing the loss of World War II. He was walking up and down my small room chain smoking and tossing me a cigarette each time he lit his own.

"*Da! Rauch, du Schwein!*" (There, smoke, you pig).

None too soon the doctor joined us for my daily checkup. "Oh, there you are, Doctor. What is this idiotic 'prostatitis'? And tell me what is really wrong with this bum here?" Rodenburg challenged.

The doctor shrugged off the innuendo by ignoring the question. Rodenburg did not really expect an answer, by the look of it. I suspected that Rodenburg knew that he had to respect the doctor's discretion. As I watched and listened to Rodenburg, I couldn't help feeling he was preoccupied with something else other than my predicament alone.

After a while I asked him, "Are we getting winter clothing soon, sir?"

He stared at me and then answered with a totally different tone of voice, "That is what General Guderian is supposed to have asked early in October when the first snow fell. He would get it in due course they told him and he was not to make further unnecessary requests of this nature. That was in October. Now they have minus sixty-three degrees up there near Moscow and Guderian has been fired together with a goodly number of other generals, mostly for disobedience. Keep that under your hat, gentlemen, do you hear?" We shook hands and he left.

"Odd to see him go like that," the doctor remarked.

"Yes, quite," I said. "His face was ashen and in an artificial way devoid of expression, which to me betrayed some anxiety." I breathed a sigh of relief that Rodenburg had left and told the doctor how glad I was that Friedrich's blank travel orders had not been mentioned in the indictment.

Whenever I allowed myself to think about it, I had been noticing lately a subtle shift in my perception. What seemed to be draining away was my youthful naive optimism concerning my survival, and along with that was the resolution to do my duty no matter what happened. I said, "Rodenburg was hiding some of the same fear I've been having."

The doctor nodded knowingly. Then he changed the subject. "I still think he has a weird mix of love-hate for you, does he not? Are you that close?"

"Are you kidding? I hardly know the man. This is the first time he has been almost human, as far as I'm concerned. Come to think of it, whenever we have met in the past, he either embarrassed me with too much lavish praise or he cursed the hell out me."

In my six-page letter to my sister dated January 4, following this discussion, I told her roughly what had been said showing how concerned I was about the disciplinary action. I neither mentioned my physical condition, nor my rapidly sinking spirits. I guess this older brother was still feeling protective 1,000 miles away. I applauded her for enjoying academic life in Munich to the full. Bad news that JR was in a Hamburg hospital, but it was good that Tutta could now see him daily. He had to have two more amputations on his leg. Somehow he had not been able to adjust to his new situation very well and his frustration often resulted in his terrorizing the whole ward.

My company was in good hands with Lieutenant L. He and I communicated frequently. I needed something productive to do. He asked if I would please make a start on notifying next of kin and, of course, I accepted. I did want to honor those kids, but also, I wanted to be useful. I was also glad to be asked so that Colonel Rodenburg and my doctor could give me two days leave from my hospital bed. Hans Müller vacated his billet so that I could stay there with all the information and the typewriter. His landlady and her daughter both had been unemployed since the dismantling of the industry in the area so they were looking for ways to earn their livelihood.

The two women had known about me. They had washed my pants since my problem had first developed. Also these were the women Hans Müller had asked to experiment with the idea of developing a white camouflage cape for the company. All that would have been needed were the forty white bed sheets I had asked for. We still hadn't found them.

Writing those letters to the families of our fallen was a difficult task, since I had not been around enough to know where and how they had lost their lives. Only some of the names were familiar and I could recall faces and contacts, but in most cases I had not even known the person in question. After all, I had been gone from August to November. When I was finished I said goodbye to Ivan, Hans Müller, my two hosts and reported back to the dressing station.

The very next day, Lt. Roethe arrived with a flesh wound in his upper arm. Having seen him being guided through the door I stayed with him during the whole operation. A bullet was removed and he was given a good chance for a speedy full recovery. I held his hand, while he was put under and talked to him. The doctor encouraged me to do this bedside duty more often and even if the patient was unknown to me. This would not apply in serious cases, he said, but he thought my questions might distract the wounded and help them get through the first realization of their plight. Not a very cheerful assignment, but it gave me something to do.

Around January 20, Sartorius, one of my noncoms came to the dressing station. He had had dysentery when I had last seen him in December, but since then he had recovered only to catch jaundice. This was his ticket for months in German hospitals. Colonel Rodenburg had sent me a bottle of some god-awful plonk, so-called German brandy. Sartorius and I shared a few glasses at my bedside celebrating his departure for a safer climate. He warmed up considerably when we talked about his family and his fiancée until suddenly they called him out to mount the truck.

When he was gone I noticed one glass was missing. I thought he must have taken his with him. I had two more shots and went to sleep. Two days later the doctor explained the difference between jaundice and hepatitis. I guess I didn't really listen to him and I have forgotten what they were. Perhaps I was too overcome to even have it register. "Hepatitis," he said, "that's what you have." He put his shaving mirror up to my face and sure enough I was all yellow. What had been the white of my eyes was now dirty yellow and I had the feeling that something was pushing against my diaphragm, a nauseating fullness.

"When do you want to leave?" he asked.

"Leave?"

"Yes, of course. You need special treatment and a special diet right away."

I protested. "Just a minute. If you kept me here with a urological excuse, could we not handle this the same way?"

"Well, if you think you can subsist on porridge and canned fruit since that is all we can offer. You will be rather contagious to your environment, you know that?"

"Do you mean I got it from my noncom, who merely shared a drink with me?"

It was at that moment I saw the second glass on the floor where I had somehow dropped it two days before. The doctor said, "Give me some time to think this over. You know our rations. Do you think you could put up with all this for four more weeks?"

Four more weeks in limbo! I was devastated.

January 23, 1942. The Signals Detachment of the 76th Division was in our neighborhood and it was here I found Lt. Heise, Berthold, called Berti. As he was from Spandau too, we had shared Hitler's warlike speech in January, 1939 in the chancellery of the Reich. He and I had been sitting on the floor of Hitler's Tearoom singing all the White Russian, counter-revolutionary songs or any other songs of the German Youth Movement we knew. To meet up with him here in the Ukraine was a godsend, or was it?

For someone as ill and morose as I was, Berti's daily news was no help. It seemed to depress me even more. He was a tinkerer and had fixed a radio, which enabled him to listen to short wave and long wave transmissions, albeit unlawfully. If caught, the authorities would have pounced on him like a ton of bricks. Concentration camp would have been the minimum punishment. I never saw the radio. Berti told me he only set it up during the night, but I had no reason to distrust his stories or most of his sources except, of course, Moscow. The BBC repeated that Hitler's assumption of the post of Commander-in-Chief had made Field Marshal von Brauchitsch the scapegoat of the German winter disaster. From the beginning, the CIC von Brauchitsch had been sort of a role model, even at my age then. I had found his presence a reassuring guarantee for professionalism in this field. Two documents with his signature were in my possession. The first was my commissioning, which read in translation the following:

"On behalf of the Führer and the Reichs Chancellor, I herewith advance the *Oberfähnrich* Vincenz Panny to the rank of a second lieutenant as of September 1, 1938. This document is given with the expectation that the above named will perform his professional duties faithfully to his soldierly oath of allegiance and in a conscientious manner and that he will justify the trust placed upon him with this advancement. Likewise, he may always be sure of a special protection of the Führer and Reichs Chancellor.
Berlin, August 31, 1938.
CIC of the Army, von Brauchitsch."

Until I heard the Countess von Kirchbach denounce Hitler and his crazy war and curse the leadership of the Reich, I had a relatively good feeling about the top generals. Because of Berti's news items, this trust was burst wide open. In a few days, I learned that it was not Hitler who had invented the strategy for the 1940 invasion of France, neither did this idea come from the top generals. The man with this brilliant idea was von Manstein and his idea had been ignored by everybody. If it had not been for some accidental indiscretion that required a total change of plans, the German Army would have repeated the World War I stupidity all over again, albeit this time with dive bombers and tanks. Brauchitsch, the BBC said, by now was a second Keitel.

The other document was just as worthless, a commendation for alleged bravery in France signed by the CIC von B. It will be remembered that it was Major Günther's hype that almost got me into the Army Bulletin of the day. I knew it was a fraud, my boys knew it was a fraud, but we accepted it without protest. Besides it got me an advancement in rank, wiping clean the slate of "Spandau's black sheep."

Berti had more bad news. All four German group commanders were gone, retired or fired. Even Guderian had been fired, the *Spiritus Rector* of the German tank forces. I was shocked to hear of his dismissal. Berti knew all about Rommel's ups and downs and about the tremendous losses in shipping supplies to Africa.

"What about that huge Italian Navy?" I asked.

"Forget it," he exclaimed. "They are totally helpless since they have no radar. Each time they meet the British they are practically blind and get picked off one by one."

"What about the Japanese?" I wanted to know.

"Yes, they are all over Asia and approaching Australia via New Guinea. There is total mobilization in Australia."

"And Russia?"

"Oh yes, the Japanese have a comfortable arrangement with them. Neutrality, would you believe? That's why we have those wonderful ski divisions defending Moscow."

"And our winter clothes?" I couldn't refrain from asking this again.

"They stopped collecting them as of January 11. Those darling female fur coats will be here in June together with the confounded skis they began to confiscate as of January 1."

I trudged home worried and had another sleepless night after this first batch of news. It felt like someone had pulled the rug from under my feet.

February 1, 1942. I took part in the burial of five soldiers, one of them from my company. The Lutheran chaplain officiated. Three grenadiers, two Russian POW's who served as grave diggers and I were in attendance. Military funerals were mostly very short so why on earth did the chaplain have to launch into a lengthy patriotic sermon? It left me puzzled. Afterwards when he wanted to know what I thought of his speech, I was hoping to be diplomatic when I suggested a little less might have been more. I never could stand this man's glorification of war and death on the battlefield.

That afternoon, the Roman Catholic priest called upon me. At first, I thought he might have come to make some attempt to comfort me. As if on cue, however, he made a move to exonerate his Lutheran brother.

Father Kayser was certainly a different representative of the cloth from any I had ever known. He and I often had lengthy discussions about the meaning of this war business. I, personally, found his openness and his sense of humor refreshing. He was a huge man with unruly black hair (what was left of it), big black eyes behind horned rimmed glasses and lots of black chest hair coming out from under his collar. *Der gebenedeite Orang Utang* (The blessed orangutan) they lovingly called him. He was highly respected by the men because he was not afraid to speak up on their behalf. He was known to put his foot down without regard to rank or power when he saw abuse or irregularities. The main story that circulated about him had to do with his experience in France when he couldn't be stopped from joining the stretcher bearers. His actions concerning the recovery of those wounded during that ongoing battle earned him the Iron Cross for bravery.

Lately, our sector had seen very little action. I found it embarrassing when I had to admit to myself that I had been around now for almost a month without showing much interest in the company base behind the lines. The rumbling artillery duel in the North around Charkov must have reminded me to pay attention. I couldn't help but notice there was an appalling laxity in carrying out the most basic provisions to maintain security. No matter how much I personally was interested in getting to know the Russians and finding out more about these wonderful Ukrainians, this was not the time to fraternize. After all, this was war we had brought them and we had no reason to assume that their attitude towards us was entirely friendly.

The original enthusiasm that we had encountered came from the peasantry, the people who had suffered the most under Stalin. Now, we were in the industrial part of the Ukraine. Our presence had cost this population their jobs; all the important machinery had been removed so the people were very concerned about their future. I went from the supply bases to the barns where the horses were kept and set up security zones wherever I saw a need, much to the disgust of most of the staff sergeants, mine in particular. They resented someone, other than the battalion commander, being critical about their inaction.

February 2, 1942. Father Kayser came again inquiring about my state of mind. I admitted I had been bad company lately. The last time we had met on January 27, I had been more argumentative and sarcastic than usual because of the associations I had with that date - the Emperor's birthday. To us, in the *Jungenschaft*, the Emperor had been the personification of all that we associated with the ugly side of German political history. And I had just discovered we were being called "Huns" again in Allied propaganda, just as in World War I. This expression was justly credited to the Kaiser who sent off German Marines to China against the Boxer insurgents with a speech worthy of a rabble-rouser. To quote His Majesty verbatim, "Give no mercy. Act like the Huns of yore." These days I felt the analogy 1908 to 1942 was not too far off the mark.

"Why are you so down in the dumps, my learned friend? There has not been a meeting between us to my recollection," Father Kayser said. "Without you being irreverent and making fun of something or anything, including papal infallibility - and in pig Latin at that!"

I had no answer to that question, even to myself. For days now, I had brooded over my anxiety to get away from this accursed snow, this murderous winter, the army, the war. Was this the result of my being idle while being sick, or was my whole existence on the wrong track? I wanted out.

Maybe it was not a good idea to spend long hours reading Rilke's *Malte Laurids Brigge* again, the novel I had discovered in 1934 at JR's place. It had belonged to his older brother, a candidate for the Lutheran ministry who had turned Anthroposophist, much to his father's disappointment. When JR's brother saw what this book meant to me, he told me to keep it. I don't think I have enjoyed any other gift more than this one. It is an autobiographical account of the life of a young Dane, mostly consisting of his Paris diary. All through puberty I memorized long passages without trying, just from reading and rereading it. I identified with this young nobleman, his physical and spiritual disintegration, and his unsuccessful attempts to find any meaning in life whatsoever.

* ◆ • • ◆ • • ◆ •

Yes, I wanted out. I cannot possibly remember after fifty odd years all the details, but this much is clear, I wanted out. And I started to play out various scenarios how to do it. Since I could not face the reality of this winter any more, the killing, the maiming, the mindless stupidity of it all. All the self-doubt that had caused so much pain in 1937 in Munich came back. Only this time I felt sure I was in the wrong profession. Here, in Russia, I saw it quite clearly, but now it was wartime and it didn't really matter. I was trapped. I had come face to face with the insight that I was not cut out to take it, yet there was no escape. It was either Siberia as a POW or a meaningless death as a soldier for something I had completely lost faith in. If I were wounded, I would again be at the mercy of those people in Spandau. Suicide had entered my mind, or what if one could catch the convenient bullet, the proverbial "million-mark wound." But how? I had heard of cases where soldiers had shot themselves in the foot or hand. Naturally, most of them got caught and were either condemned to death outright or sent to a penal battalion. These people were frequently sent as cannon fodder to provoke hostile fire or something else of high risk. I followed up these fantasies and withdrew into myself, talked very little, and became so disconsolate that the doctor gave me a physical and diagnosed walking pneumonia. For days I had a high fever.

February 7, 1942. A dreadful night again. I slept fitfully, woke up at 7:00 a.m. in a cold sweat. I had very little recollection of what I had done the previous day. Had I eaten anything for supper? I wasn't sure. Hans Müller had been in and out mothering me as usual, even scolding me. He complained I had again made incoherent utterances upon waking up, given orders that made no sense whatever. I did not even try to deny it. I had been there before. It meant stress and it meant trouble just as in August last year. Am I losing my mind? Often, I would start a sentence and find my voice trailing off. When I catch myself, I am unable to remember what I wanted to say.

❖ ◆ ❖ ◆ ◆ ❖ ◆

This morning, my mother's last breakdown haunts me. It was spring 1935. It plays out in this daydream in all the details. I come home from school, meet my sister in the hallway. She just had arrived too. We start the long climb of four flights of stairs. The bicycle on my shoulder hurts as usual.

Half way up we are met by our little brother. "Man o man!" he says. "All hell is loose up there. I am supposed to get a locksmith."

"What do you mean?" I ask.

"To change locks in the front door, keep the devil out."

"Oh no, not that!" I cry.

Mother had been rather restless lately. Religious questions were on her mind and the need for her to do something to solve certain problems. She never let on what they were. Her religion, she is a sister in a fundamentalist sect, which gives her great support and for her something to hang on to. So, none of us ever jokes about it as Father sometimes does. But this is different, I can tell.

Sure enough she is irrationally trying to find a fitting key for the locks when we enter. She has smeared them with graphite and oil to try to make them fit. She talks in whispers, mostly to herself and moves about in short hurried strides. She is clearly not herself. She is someone else who is called upon, she says, to sacrifice herself in order to protect her loved ones. It has to be done immediately, before the Messiah returns. A whispering, babbling person in her negligée, disheveled, and the graphite and oil is on her hands and arms.

Jutta and I tried to calm her down and persuade her to go to bed. She is shivering with cold. Most windows are wide open for no reason whatsoever. While I try to wash her hands, Jutta makes Mother some chamomile tea and we humor her along by joining her fantasies with questions. Somehow, we get her to go back to bed. She calms down and cries softly.

Suddenly, she sits up straight in her bed and a torrent of disjointed self-indictments and complaints follow. What to me are gruesome details about her marital problems, about Father's frustration about being a breadwinner and businessman, and the hostility of certain relatives. She vows never again to go to a hospital where all they have for her is electric shocks.

Carola comes home, takes one look and throws herself hysterically over the bed rail, crying like a banshee. We tell her to get a hold of herself, stop crying and make some sandwiches. I find it odd that she understands the situation at first glance. Does she know anything I do not? Was she privy to Mother's last breakdown after Rolf was born? Thirteen-year-old Jutta is tearful but calm, a great help. She and I sit uncomfortably on the edge of the bed. Mother hangs on to my hand and keeps talking. This goes on for hours or so it feels. By now, all three of us are perspiring heavily. I suggest we take turns to freshen up, which I do after Jutta has given Mother a sponge bath.

By 6:00 p.m. Father comes home at last, reeking of schnapps. He collapses on the foot of the bed fighting for breath, clutching his chest. His face is ashen with fear. Mother doesn't want him in the room, so he goes to start telephoning relatives for help. Auntie Julie, the rich self-appointed family moderator, comes by taxi around 7:30 p.m. Still, no one has eaten anything. The sandwiches never appeared. I know because I talk to Auntie Julie on an empty stomach.

The grown-ups decide on hospitalization. I object saying that we can surely take turns to care for her at home. To hell with school. It can wait. Let's find a doctor and some medication. Of course, I am overruled. The nurse arrives at 10:00 p.m. and the ambulance comes at 9:00 the next morning. She is put on a stretcher and we walk her down the four flights of stairs past the curious eyes of the gossipy neighbors. I keep holding her hand, after I had convinced her that we would have to go to the Hamburg airport where Hitler is expected to arrive at any moment. Hitler, the new chancellor, who stands right next to her Messiah at this moment. All her hopes for a recovery of the country, her family and herself rests on these two. But Hitler, at the moment, seems to her more tangible. She knows he is expected that morning. In the ambulance, she still holds my hand and worries about not being dressed properly for the occasion. What might Hitler say? She feels naked. Meanwhile, Father sits in the back of the ambulance still having trouble breathing and keeping some bearing. She does not want Hitler to see him in this state.

At the clinic two competent looking nurses receive her, catching the situation correctly and responding to her fantasies in kind. I feel vindicated, as it were, for having done the same for the last dreadful hours. She lets go of my hand. A last look. Some realization that she knows where she is. She accepts it like a little girl full of trust. She is in a room with fifteen other patients.

We drive home in a taxi. The old man cannot walk. Not much conversation. All his attempts to make me talk go nowhere. My eyes are blinded by tears and my thoughts toward him are very unkind, though the full impact has not hit me as yet. My only consolation was that last afternoon. Her remarks about her relationship with Father were restricted to moments where my younger sister was not in the room. Her sensitivity gave me the hope that the hold on reality that this represented in my mind might indicate a quick recovery. When I handed the parental note to my teacher Alice Pollitz twenty-four hours later, she was taken aback by my appearance. I felt her hand on my shoulder. "So sorry, take care Vincenz," she whispered.

•◆•••◆••◆•

So, now here I lie in this dressing station asking myself if this was more than a manic depression or schizophrenia? If so, is it inheritable? I understand that my grandfather had a number of those breakdowns. Could that explain what is happening to me now? Am I fit to be in charge of my company? All those young men depending on my judgment. Good god! Can I do this to them?

February 10, 1942. Hans Müller, with the help of an interpreter, found an old man who was willing to show me the inside of the local coal mine. Ivan circled far ahead of us up and down various steel ladders. In the dim light the dismantling of key parts by the retreating Red Army plus some destruction by dynamite made for a macabre atmosphere. The Ukranian shrugged off any question regarding the repair of all this damage.

I cut short the trip when climbing down a stairwell incontinence hit me again - now after weeks of improvement. Ivan and I went home to Hans Müller to get a change of pants, but Hans was gone with the food detail and there were no pants. I trudged all the way back to the dressing station, stopping briefly at the horse barn where I had to put Ivan on leash because he wanted to run off hunting rats or something. I felt utterly disconsolate. I placed my cheekbone against the strong shoulder of the dog, and cried softly. This renewed humiliation was just too much. As usual, Ivan joined in. He became so noisy I had to stop our duet unless there was some horse-groom around somewhere.

I took the dog with me to my room leaving a note of explanation at the doctor's desk. He came by to tell me it was okay to have the dog with me for one night. "After all, we are not an antiseptic clinic. I envy you. What a wonderful dog! What are you going to do when you have to go home?" This was the final straw. I had forgotten that I couldn't take the dog with me if it were to be decided that I must go to seek treatment.

By February 18, I was determined. Something had to happen. I told Jutta in a cryptic one page letter not to write any more until I could give her my new address. Suicide or self-inflicted wound, I wanted out.

* ◆ • • ◆ • • ◆ •

Dear Jutta,

Thanks for your magnificent parcel and above all, for the American cigarettes. I was overjoyed about it all. Please do not write any more for the time until I give you my new address. I will not write either for the same reason. Please be patient.

* ◆ • • ◆ • • ◆ •

Our sector was quiet. Both sides were digging in deeper. Why would I change address? The doctor intended to keep me until my hepatitis had ebbed away, so no change of address was planned here either. This letter documents for me that I was determined on some level of awareness to do something drastic and that I saw no simple way out of my dilemma.

Each time I walked back to the company base, I stopped at the big barn to have a quiet warm place to think my situation over. The horses had seemed like good listeners and it helped to verbalize what was going on in my mind. For some reason, I had picked early a big Hannoveraner. This particular horse tolerated my visits and ignored my soliloquy without creating a disturbance. After our first "conversation," I offered him a carrot and that became part of our bargain. I often buried my face in his mane and felt the warmth of his winter coat. His lower lip kept searching for my pocket flap while I was talking either to him or to myself or crying, all very softly in case there was a driver on duty after all.

I found out that the stable was unguarded at night so I spent some time in there almost every evening. There, I began to experiment. I fashioned myself a piece of string with a loop on the end, placed this string over the notch of my hand gun, barely touching the front sight. Would I be able to pull the trigger without losing this lineup? In the dark? I went as far as attaching the string to a vertical post instead of my hand and actually pulled the trigger. It worked. The bullet sat right above the aiming point in the post. I tried again. Not quite as accurate as the first time, but good enough. It would have pierced the dorsum of my left hand. Did I know what I was doing?

Thinking about this now in 1993, I find the story incredible, but here is the letter to my sister from February 18. I have it in my hand. She mailed it back to me the other day with all our war correspondence she had been saving. This February 18 was the date I had set for myself.

In retrospect, why did I take these nightly walks back to the company base all by myself? Why were there no guards at the stable? For what reason did we allow a steady stream of peasants, mostly women and children, to cross the lines every day? It was a total neglect of any kind of sensible precaution, almost as if we had not quite understood what kind of war we were in. I should never have taken these walks in the middle of the night all by myself.

February 24 was a day like any other. I worked at the company base and returned at night. I was wearing a driver greatcoat and had a book in my left hand. After a short visit with my four-legged friend, I came out of the barn, putting my right hand glove back on. If it had not been for some fluffy clouds, it would have been a moonlit night. Some machine gun was being tried, apparently after a repair job.

Suddenly, a dark figure turned the corner of the building. I instinctively raised my left hand when I saw a weapon. There was a shot. My hand was whipped down and felt heavy all of a sudden. The man had turned back and disappeared. I went after him, but by the time I had my gun out of its holster and had opened the safety catch, not a trace, not a sound. I fired the gun three or four times to alert a guard. Either there was no guard in the barn, or he was asleep, or he was afraid to come out.

I wrapped my shawl around the hand, which had not let go of the book. The bullet had entered the inside edge of my hand and had exited through the back of my hand and apparently smashing the bone below the ring finger knuckle. I rewrapped the hand, this time without the book, and stumbled home, frequently stopping to turn around to be alert to further danger from my attacker. When I arrived at the dressing station they woke up the doctor who took care of my hand and gave me some painkilling shots. I must have slept almost twenty-four hours rather violently talking to myself at times. My simple little bed was in complete disarray when I woke up.

I have very little recollection of what happened the following day, but on February 26 the doctor had time to talk to me at length. He did not consider me fit for transportation until February 28. We spent some time trying to sort things out. I tried to share with him whatever had gone on within me for the last thirty days and told him how much I dreaded the long-haul home to hospitalization and finally the return to the Spandau replacement unit. Of course, I was particularly sorry to have to leave this remarkable surgeon and counselor. I did not include my fooling around with bits of string and my gun in my confessions. I just couldn't bring myself to do it.

It turned out that he too, like JR's brother, had turned Anthroposophist after attending a Waldorf School in Berlin. His reservations and/or open antipathy regarding the Nazis was based on their anti-Semitism and the ruthless repression of the Rudolf Steiner Movement throughout Germany almost immediately after taking over absolute power. This was then the second acquaintance with an "Anthro" as I called them, both of them memorable ones at that. We promised each other to keep in touch, even while fully realizing it would be difficult.

Before my departure Lt. Blümel came by, and next, Müller-Hofmeister, my favorite aversion. He gave me all the propaganda line about the coming victorious offensive in spring and proudly announced that Rodenburg had taken over the Division 76. He added it was too bad I would not get the German equivalent of the American Purple Heart. Significantly, ours was a black piece of metal with a German steel helmet and crossed sabers on it. "You won't get it because you were not wounded in action."

"Too bad," I said with all the sarcasm I could muster. If he didn't see that I was in no mood to think about medals or for that matter Rodenberg's career, I certainly was not going to engage in any kind of conversation with him. I was under sedation and my bandaged hand, my allegedly disqualified wound was the least of my concerns. It was exactly the kind of remark I would have expected from him.

"Wound infection," the doctor said later. "Traumatic fever. That's all you need now, good luck."

He gave me detailed instructions on what to do and what to avoid. They would have a tennis racket shaped frame for me, which would serve to put all my fingers under attention which would help the bones heal properly.

Thank god the dog was nowhere near. Hans Müller and I shook hands and off I went. A small group of wounded and sick people left in a truck. It was a short hop to Artemovsk where we were loaded on a Russian freight car normally used for cattle transportation. It was filled with straw for bedding purposes. One of the sliding doors could not be closed. There were twenty-seven stretcher cases and a number of men who were able to move. We were given one blanket each. It was beastly cold, particularly in the rear half of the car.

The slowly rolling train was attacked twice by our nightly intruder, the plane they called the "sewing machine". The bombs missed badly, thank god, but the emotional effect was immense. A freshly wounded soldier is looking forward to peace and safety at home and is in no mood for further hazards, particularly not from the air. We traveled practically three feet up in the air in a moving vehicle, there was no hole in the ground to hide or find cover and nobody had any weapons.

The train kept rolling. A stop here and there, some soup, some medical attention for serious cases. Two days later, we were strafed by fighter planes. Again, there was not much damage, but we were in near panic, particularly the stretcher cases.

In Berdichev, we were transferred to a train with a European gauge, this time in Polish cars. The same discomfort, but nobody cared. We were rolling. My hand was throbbing badly. They gave me pain pills. I couldn't make myself very useful having only one hand available.

I began to notice the countryside, the hills near Krakow and my thoughts went back to my company, to Hans Müller and the dog. All of them "in good hands," I told myself. In Krakow, we were driven to a proper hospital and deloused. I felt clean for the first time since I started out with Müller-Hoffmeister in October 1941.

They put me in a room with about two dozen men, mostly with hand and arm amputations. I felt totally out of place and humble looking at these victims of landmines. They were in a wonderful upbeat mood, ready to be transported to their hometown hospitals. Some even had their girls with them already. To hear them talk the winter hadn't been that bad after all. Human nature, I thought. They were convinced victory was assured in the spring. Their war certainly was over; their naive optimism saddened me.

No doctor could be found to look at my hand apart from having it freshly bandaged. I got rather impatient and phoned all over the hospital, but I was told it was the weekend and there was nobody around except for emergencies. One nurse quite frankly let on that her doctor was skiing. I would have liked to hear more about that tennis racket bandage, but considering my comparatively minor problem it didn't seem right to raise a stink about the lack of attention.

March16 we finally made it across the border of former Austria. Each of the wounded received his destination separately. When the other gentlemen in my compartment heard I was bound for Gmunden, a white-haired police captain who was old enough to have been my father exclaimed, "*Masselbauer!*" (You lucky peasant). It struck me as being ironic as the Jews had been disenfranchised since 1935, the influence of Yiddish in conversational German was undiminished.

The train stopped at a tiny station high in the mountains and I was called out. The big sign said *Gmunden am Traunsee.* I may have seen a picture postcard of the place previously in passing, but what I saw through the window of the train compartment was absolutely breathtaking. After the constant stench of blood, gore and pus and the discomfort of frost, lice and dysentery in the dressing station and on the train, I thought I was in some kind of fairy tale landscape. Wherever I looked, there were the mountains framing the Traunsee on all sides. The water was glistening in the morning sun. What a glorious warm spring day it was! I waved goodbye to the others, climbed into a car and found myself in a rather luxurious bed of the former Kur Hotel, a spa in peacetime reserved for well-to-do patients.

For the first time since February 25, my hand was properly taken care of. It was still infected and throbbing, but the doctor mumbled something encouraging. When I asked whether this was it, he nodded. I brought up the question about the reconstruction of the bone with the help of the tennis racket frame. The doctor said, "Yes, we do that in peacetime, but now your bones have grown together in some odd way and it would be risky to break them again while the healing has not been completed. As long as there is pus, we'd better not experiment. We'll clean your hand as well as possible, put it in a plaster cast, and send you home to your loved ones. Would that be all right with you for the time?"

I wasn't going to argue. The thought of being in Dresden or Hamburg in a few days distracted me and made me forget my discomfort at the prospect of my hand being somewhat crippled. Long walks in the beautiful surroundings, excellent food, friendly nursing staff and the idea that in two weeks I would be back here for some time. Then they would look at the damage again and see whether anything else can be done.

I phoned Gundel in Dresden and suggested we both meet in Hamburg to celebrate my confrontation with JR. For me to become his brother-in-law was the last thing he or I would ever have wished. We arranged to meet at the Hamburg main train station on March 18 and hung up.

Once in Hamburg, we took the fast commuter train home, and sized up the new situation. Not only was her mother in the house, but JR and his fiancée were about to be married. This was the first time all four of us would be in one flat since 1940. She was concerned about her sister's problems adjusting to her invalid husband-to-be and I was concerned about JR's bad temper which, according to Gundel, he often let loose on his fiancée. Her family's house on the edge of the university campus stood undamaged by air attacks.

The elevator was in working order, thank god! I would not have enjoyed four flights of stairs with my throbbing hand. There was a big "Hello" in the doorway. Tutta was particularly moved; she hugged and kissed me and said, "How glad I am you are here. We need you to help plan the wedding."

Mrs. Eplinius, Teddy as everybody called my future mother-in-law, gave me a hug and asked whether I had brought her any cigarettes. Everybody tried to be tactful and encouraging whenever JR became the center of attention. He was just a shadow of his former self, nothing but skin and bones hobbling on crutches. He told us his stump still wouldn't heal properly, so they might have to operate again.

We all missed Ivan, of course, still in Russia with little hope of getting him back, for the time.

JR and Tutta were acting most unlike a loving couple. JR just found it impossible to adjust to all his physical problems, and with self-pity, the notion that the world owed him something and a vicious resentment of anyone who did not constantly assure him of their understanding. Tutta suffered the most, obviously. After all these months of waiting to hear that he was all right, and the weeks and weeks in the hospital in Hamburg with more than one further amputation; she was at the end of her tether.

When JR made one more of his whining self-justifying complaints, Gundel blew her stack, "Since nobody in this house has the guts to tell you, let me give it to you straight. We are all trying to understand what you have been through. We all know "your lovely war" has hit you a little too close to home. (She had always labeled him a militarist.) If you keep rubbing our noses into your stump the way you do, you make it impossible for us to be around you! Your self-pity will destroy you, and anyone close to you will see his or her empathy turn into disgust. Man, the world is going through its most harrowing disgrace and all you can do is to think of yourself."

I had never seen her like that. Of course, she was right, but then she hadn't been around to watch him bathe in his own reflection in the mirror. I remember distinctly the sudden insight I had that here was not only a destroyed human body, but a narcissist deprived of his perfection.

Vince with sister Carola (seated)

Vince and Carola on father's lap, beach outing

Primary school class, teacher Mrs. Ottens, Vince in second row
from back, seated second from left

Class photo at the Johanneum school, Vince in third row from front,
second from right

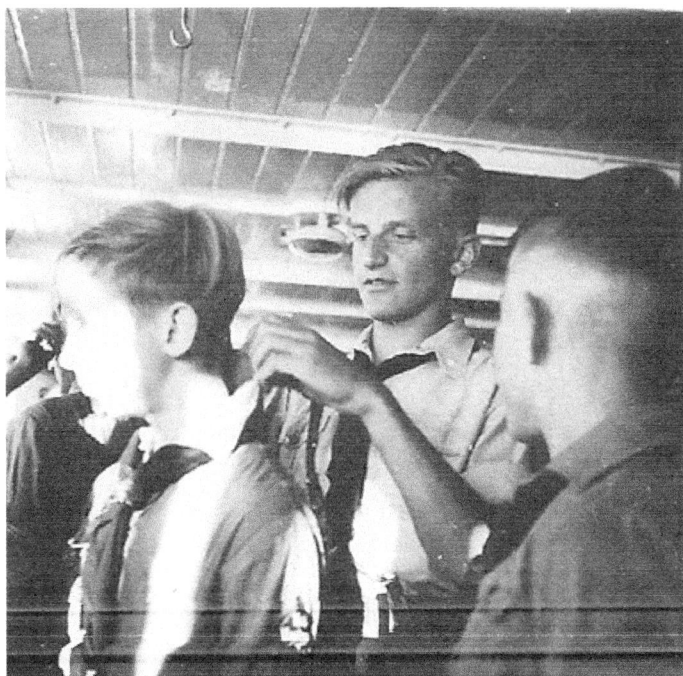

Vince as youth leader

Vince and best friend Jürgen Remé (JR)

Youth group outing

Youth group outing

Vince sailing on the Alster, Hamburg

1936, age 18

Nazi party rally, Nuremberg, with his father Ignaz Panny

Alice Pollitz

Ivan, 1944

Vince, back row, third from right

Vince, front row, one left of center

Image from handmade Christmas card, 1944

Egypt, POW camp, 1946

Vince playing the fanatic Catholic priest in *Jugend*, POW camp, Egypt

On stage, POW camp, Egypt

Post war image

CHAPTER V

THE RECEPTION IN SPANDAU WAS MIXED, TO SAY THE least, but the young people, my friends and the officer candidates were glad to see me again. The bane of my existence, Captain X continued collecting a file on me as before and I gave him plenty to work on. After almost every workout in the field, I found some reason to complain. The methods of training, to my mind, were removed from the modern reality of modern war. I find it tiresome to even think about it, but here is one example:

I had to watch over and over as one recruit after another charged a straw-filled scarecrow, meaning the communist enemy, which was waiting patiently to be bayoneted by one of our young warriors. Soldiers were taught to rotate the bayonet when pulling it back, which they did do with some gusto, except, having thrown themselves into this pleasure full force, most of them had trouble controlling their forward momentum. They overshot their jerkily dangling dummy opponent and couldn't get the damn knife out of the straw body.

The following memoranda I found in 1984 when my whole military file was handed to me. I had gone to the archives near Aachen to find information documenting my social security claims. I knew already that I would not get the promised pension, but would have to make do with partial social security payments. The clerk on duty, a delightful woman in her fifties, surprised me with the announcement that they had all my military files and I would be welcome to copy any I wished. I was surprised, elated and occasionally shocked at what I read.

To wit: March-September 1942

Spandau, 9/17/1942 Confidential

Re: First Lt. V. Panny

Inf. Ers RGT 218

Attention: Commanding Officer 218 Reichert

Lt. Panny shows an attitude on duty as well as off duty, which is unbecoming a regular officer of the German Army.

1. An oral presentation he was assigned to give was carried out completely "off the cuff," although he had ample time to prepare and certainly has no lack of ability.

2. Substituting for his company commander, he hardly ever showed up for duty.

3. Lt. Panny displays arrogant patterns of behavior, which sometimes are even insulting less through speech than by facial expression and by body language.

4. He hides behind an alleged stomach and intestinal problem, which prevents him from carrying out his duties. This problem does not ever seem to prevent him from enjoying his private life or from pursuing his personal plans.

5. He spends whole nights in Berlin. Moreover he travels even to Romania where he certainly will not find diet

food and/or medical attention. Early August, he requested another furlough from our doctor in order to have ambulant treatment in a hospital in Dahlem where he allegedly had a chance for a daily routine of treatment. He received medical leave. The day he was supposed to start the course of treatment, he appeared at the battalion office and declared he would have to do without the ever so important treatment. Instead, he went with Colonel von Kirchbach on an extensive trip to Romania. He did have official permission, but he went without the required documentation from the battalion.

6. Another example. Lately Panny was suffering from stomach cramps, which were caused by my official reprimand for his behavior. Now, he had to go to hospital every day and could not participate in the routine and always arrived late for dinner. When, unexpectedly, an order from General Command arrived, which again required his presence on a trip to Romania, Lt. Panny all of a sudden was healthy again. There were no more stomach cramps and he didn't need any more treatment in a hospital.

I attach a medical evaluation for Mr. Panny's state of health (Exhibit 1).

The fact that Lt. Panny has shown similar patterns of behavior early on and that disciplinary actions do not seem to have any effect can be seen from the following items:

A. July 20, 1942. Lt. Panny allegedly was incapable to participate in a short administrative procedure in Döberitz. He did not timely excuse himself, nor did he really report sick. (Exhibit 2)

B. Lt. Panny was given ten days house arrest because: #1 he did not report to the battalion commander in Spandau, even though he was assigned to do this by his hospital in Dresden. #2 he continued onto Hamburg without having permission and, #3 he told the authority in Hamburg that his furlough papers were in his luggage in Dresden, which was not true.

C. Lt. Panny, furthermore, was given twenty-one days of house arrest in autumn 1941 because he did not obey the telegram calling him back to duty.

It can easily be seen that there is a certain lack of moral integrity as well as weakness of character, which seems to point to a lack of maturity. I think it is urgently necessary to place Lt. Panny in a situation where he cannot set a bad example to the ongoing officer candidates and where he will be in the hands of a staunch disciplinarian. He does not have the necessary qualities for an advancement to the rank of captain, which he claims to expect daily.

This man had really done everything in his power to ruin the surprising turn in my career by the look of it. I always knew he kept a file on me and this was the proof. In my file I also found the official transfer of a certain Sergeant Major Stachowiak who was supposed to report on August 20 for a special assignment by the German general staff.

I met this young man in my office where he had located me. He was all excited and told me that he was supposed to go and show Colonel von Kirchbach the grave of his son and explain the circumstances of the lieutenant's death. Stachowiak had no idea how he was selected for this honor and frankly had no idea what happened on that day because he had been a sergeant major and spent all day near the field kitchen. He said, "Please try to contact Colonel von Kirchbach and see whether he will take you too, for after all, you have been on the spot. Frankly, I wouldn't be able to say much. Please try to come with us."

This was electrifying news. I just had finished a very trying week putting up with the open hostility of the battalion commander. I didn't think I would have much chance even though I had met the colonel and felt we were on friendly terms.

The next morning, I walked into headquarters at Bendlerstrasse and was shown to the officer on duty. I explained my problem to the lieutenant colonel and asked for permission to phone Colonel von Kirchbach. Friedrich's father was surprised and delighted that I could be available. He promised he would take steps immediately to have me posted.

The officer on duty who had been watching me smiled and said something complimentary about my going straight to the crux of the matter and we chatted for a while. On the wall they had a huge map of Russia and I had to show him where Friedrich had died. I couldn't help observing the divisional symbols in blue, which indicated the positions the German Army had reached as of the preceding day. It looked like two rows of blue pearls, one moving in the direction of Stalingrad and the other one turning to the Caucasus. Behind them there was just an empty map that made me ask, "Is this it? No reserves?"

The lieutenant colonel said, "No reserves." His face changed to a very serious expression. "We don't bother to show the Romanian Armies, the Hungarians or the Italians." I couldn't believe how widely strung out these German units were and that there were two big offensives going on in two different directions. What was worse, according to the lieutenant colonel, there were no reserves behind either army group. I just couldn't believe this splitting up the available power, such as it was. I thought about this for the next day or two until my transfer arrived. This was the first time I had seen the German situation map with the incredibly vast distances involved. I felt humbled and dumbfounded.

The battalion commander had another item to put into my file, meaning Stachowiak had the proper documentation, I did not. Good thing I didn't know that the battalion commander had commented on the irregularity of my transfer by teletype, juxtaposing it to the proper documentation that Stachowiak had.

Stachowiak and I met at Bendlerstrasse with very light packs and food for ten days. We shared a railway compartment for the long journey to Vinnitsa in the Ukraine in a special courier train and the sergeant turned out to be pleasant company. I learned all about his family and his army career. We compared notes.

Arriving in Vinnitsa after two-and-a-half days, we each had a room in an abandoned school house and reported to Colonel von Kirchbach the following morning. Then we traveled in two cars, von Kirchbach and a captain as orderly officer with two well-armed drivers. In Jassy, a Romanian major joined us and we spent the night in a hotel. The Romanian, our host, who, no doubt, knew that the count had lost both his sons, still insisted on offering some female companionship for the gentlemen. I saw one of the prospective partners who was a cleaning lady. I employed her to get me plenty of hot water for a much-needed sponge bath. That was the extent of my interest. When I told the colonel of my experience, he just shook his head and said, "Other cultures, other mores. I don't want to spend time thinking about this tactlessness."

The following day, we drove to the River Pruth and crossed it in small boats at exactly the same spot where the battalion had crossed on July 2. The captain took many photos contrasting the small well-cared-for corn fields on the Romanian side to the overwhelming horizon-spanning mass of sunflowers on the Ukrainian side of the river. We slowly walked up to the point where I had found Friedrich and reached the cemetery behind the hilltop. A white picket fence surrounded the well cared for graves. There was a huge cross in the center under which the battalion commander and Friedrich were resting. By and by hundreds of villagers came and a Greek Orthodox priest conducted an impressive religious service, which ended in the usual manner, everybody sitting down on the graves eating and drinking. The wooden cross that we had brought with us was put in place and then the Romanian.

The major excused himself and our two cars struck out for the grave of Friedrich's brother Tony, which was near Uman. This time I sat next to the colonel and the captain took my place in the other car. Von Kirchbach and I engaged in a detailed analogy of Napoleon's war and the present one. He had a tremendous knowledge of military history and described the one and only big battle at Borodino and how Napoleon actually got into Moscow, an empty capital. There was no one to meet him and discuss peace, as he had hoped. When the city started to burn, set afire by the Russians, the disastrous withdrawal of The Grand Army began. He said that Stalin was stupid to sacrifice millions of soldiers in 1941, but now the Russians were withdrawing just as they had been in Napoleon's war. I told him about my impression seeing the map in Berlin and he agreed and expressed his concern.

I couldn't help pointing out that Napoleon had very little help from his Austrian, Prussian and other allies who turned against him once the remnants of the French army reached Poland. The count said he'd hope there were no analogies to be drawn and we both nodded knowing that even with the utmost good will, our allies would be no match for the Russians. It was not a very encouraging talk, but I enjoyed his well-balanced evaluation that confirmed my anxieties.

※ ◆ ※ ◆ ※ ◆ ※ -

The grave near Uman was a different story. We were all by ourselves. This part of Ukraine was under German administration. The Ukranian farm workers were not even told that we were coming to look at the graves. The second wooden cross we had brought was put into the ground and again the count asked me to join him in the car. I could tell he was very tired by this emotionally wrenching experience.

He suddenly lowered his voice and brought up his intention to have the last male members of his very old family exhumed and brought home to the family plot in Silesia. Hearing this, I checked to see if the driver could possibly be aware of our subject matter, but the count smiled and dismissed my concern. Besides, it was a noisy open army car. Before I had time to speculate why he had told me all this, he suddenly turned facing me and asked, "Would you be willing to do that for me?"

This was much more than I had expected. We both were aware of the strictly enforced regulation that prohibited bringing German war-dead home. I was so touched by his trust in me that I didn't even inquire how he was planning to go about this. I just said, "Yes, of course, sir." We shook hands.

At this point he said, "We are planning to have an expert in handling metal coffins and a grave digger with a driver and you in charge. Leave Vinnitsa by truck, contact the local gendarme in Moravia, exhume Friedrich's body, cross over to Uman, do the same with Tony, both coffins soldered immediately, arrive at Vinnitsa at some agreed place and time. When the soldiers have been dismissed, you and the coffins will be put into a railway cattle car that will not be opened until you reach the destination in Silesia. There some orderly officer will contact you and will be in charge of the necessary security. Do you think you can do that?"

I said I would try and I would trust that I would be able to find Tony's grave. Everything else being equal, that would be my only concern. He continued that, of course, this would be strictly confidential and he had already seen to my transfer to the headquarters of the German Army. The details I would get after this project was taken care of.

I was overwhelmed, flushed with this immense sense of seeing a new direction, new skills, new possibilities. The outlandishness of this plot! It sounded like a covert conspiracy. It was against all reason, but it was an affront against the bureaucracy I hated so much. Here was a chance to do something that expressed my feelings towards this god-awful war.

Far removed from any utility, I knew that this plan was based on some kind of Christian sentimentality and at this moment it didn't matter to me. The whole thing was an outrageous idea. To do it for these wonderful people was exhilarating and I was caught up in this dream immediately. For the rest of the trip, I had great trouble to act normally or talk to Stachowiak as I had before. My thoughts were on the impending project.

Returning to Berlin, the battalion commander had some more dumb questions about improper documentation. I was so polite to him, he almost became suspicious. I kept looking at him straight in the eye thinking I know something you are not to know. The next day, another transfer order arrived from September 10 to September 20, 1942. Again, no documentation and I took off like a flash, which made him put in my file, "He had no documentation from the battalion." Little did he know and little did I know that I had already been transferred as of August 26 to the general staff of the German Army as an orderly officer.

The battalion commander must have taken further steps to thwart me, and if he didn't somebody else did, because on September 26 the III Army Corps inquired who had nominated me for this transfer. In lieu of an answer on October 1, I was permanently transferred to *Fremde Heere Ost*, a section of the German general staff concerned with intelligence - Russia. There is more. On October 7, the personnel department of the German Army repeated the question who had nominated me, under what procedure, and for what purpose had I been transferred to *Fremde Heere Ost*. The personnel section had not released me for this transfer. There is a footnote, "We point out the questionable record of Lt. Panny."

Outside of Spandau, I felt fine. Well, there was some stress too. Gundel and I, after this wonderful summer, were not doing too well together. She thought I was trying to become a martyr of sorts, marrying her and adopting her son against all odds. She was sure I would forfeit my last bit of credit with the army. I was still sure I could find some way to get around army regulations; however somehow a chill had set in. The increasingly devastating air attacks against civilian targets put everybody on edge and Gundel had received notice that she was about to be drafted to work in a munitions factory. That didn't help either.

Of course, I "spent whole nights in Berlin." In Spandau, I had a single room without running water. The former officers' flats were taken by noncoms with families. All wash and shower facilities smelled like mildew and were in constant use by singing or yodeling males. Often the songs were not in German. I presumed these songs were the expressions of the "volunteers'" homesickness. I was lucky to find a flat near the Dahlem Hospital where my urological and internal problems were under observation.

As luck would have it, I ran into Irmel's friend Wiltraut von Brünneck whom I had befriended at Irmel's wedding. She was having one glass too many and I had taken it upon myself to shield her from insensitive males who claimed to find her state most charming and who continued to offer her more to drink. What a reunion! I was happy to find company in this god-awful town. I learned that Irmel was a widow by now. Her husband had been killed in France in 1940. She worked for the German Foreign Ministry as an assistant to the press attaché in the public relations section. Her sister Wiltraut was about to begin her judicial career. So we three spent time together in Berlin as well as in Hohenlübbichow, the family estate where Irmel's mother and two brothers made us feel very comfortable on weekends.

It took a long trip by slow commuter train each time, which entailed crossing the River Oder. They corrected my shortcomings as a horseman and taught me to jump properly. The two young women and I had a wonderful time, swimming, boating, and playing tennis.

Irmel's mother was a delightful hostess. At times, we must have been a little bit too noisy and rambunctious for this former lady-in-waiting at the Royal Court of Saxony, but she never showed any irritation. Her face always had a smile. She seemed to feel curious as if anticipating with graciousness whatever was coming her way. Even the shocking rudeness of her younger son, she never acknowledged.

One or two of these weekends at Hohenlübbichow were spent together with the nine children of the other branch of the family, which resided in Marienburg, East Prussia. Each year, I was told, the whole group descended on this peaceful village east of Berlin and stayed sometimes up to four weeks. To share a meal with a family of such numbers was an experience all by itself. Mrs. von Keudell said grace and from then on the long dinner table, extended three or four times its normal size, became a showcase for Prussian lunch style as you would never see it. The people and the hordes of children talked quietly, in groups. Food was being passed around politely and the total impression was that of wide open family communication, the exact opposite of the Prussian family stereotype which implies children at the table are seen and not heard. June and July passed very quickly in this enjoyable company.

◆ ◦ ◦ ◆ ◦ ◦ ◆ ◦

The war in Russia became fluid again. Every day the loudspeakers everywhere intoned blaring victory claims, always preceded and followed by fanfares. Irmel's brothers mailed postcards from Ukraine where the Soviets were giving ground, retreating to avoid losses, 1812 revisited.

Irmel, Wiltraut and I were the automatic weekend team spending hours on slow trains with innumerable stops between Berlin and Hohenlübbichow. Nobody was allowed to use cars for private purposes, obviously, and you could get gasoline only on the black market. Her mother became very friendly and helpful. She was particularly amused by the constant interplay between Wiltraut and myself. At times, when I had again admitted that everything was my fault, she got up laughing, patted me on the shoulder and said, "I'm glad chivalry is not dead. As you were." She left the room.

So much for my weekends. My life during the week was frankly humiliating. I didn't make many friends in Spandau. One outcome was that an innocent joke, one of my intended to be humorous one-liners about the black market, induced one of the culprits, a canteen contractor, to panic and partially confess. At issue were black market activities and illegal slaughtering and sale of meat. As a result of my being allegedly instrumental in this embarrassing scandal, the commanding officer, the bane of my existence, tried and almost succeeded in spoiling my leave for JR's wedding in Hamburg.

That was some wedding. We all met at Teddy's flat and I was delighted to see Gundel and her mother and the prospective bride and groom. I must admit it took quite an adjustment for me to go from Irmel's family estate to the crowded apartment in Hamburg. I didn't have time to reflect much about this because Gundel and I had to plan the entertainment of the wedding guests.

The schedule called for the formal visit to the town hall. The civil wedding there was a joke. Gundel and I had a difficult time to keep from laughing out loud when a nice pudgy gray haired little man intoned a lengthy diatribe on the importance and the meaning of the marriage vows. He kept repeating, "These are particularly important now in the Third Reich." In the taxi on the drive home, still laughing, we acknowledged that at least he had not included in his speech an encouragement for Tutta and JR to immediately have a son for the Führer.

We changed and then we all drove to the Fährhaus, a landmark restaurant right on the Alster, the lake facing downtown, to arrange for the wedding banquet. We all had to mail in so and so many food stamps from our ration cards, particularly meat stamps. We earned this food by going through the religious ceremony, which was celebrated by Pastor Knolle.

The banquet table was comprised of Mr. and Mrs. Remé, Tutta's mother, Pastor Knolle, two officers representing JR's anti-tank company, Hank and Strick (two members of the *Jungenschaft*) and JR's two little sisters. No bridesmaids or other wedding conventions. Over coffee and ice cream, JR's father made a moving speech. At least he thought it was moving, he cried. It hurt me to see this wonderful old man talking about "the final victory" when only a few years earlier he had opposed Hitler's solution for the Lutheran Church.

The informal part was mostly Gundel and myself. We collaborated on two mock radio interviews concerning the childhood of bride and groom, created an organ grinder's ballad based on the stormy ups and downs of their courtship. We did another mock radio interview on the achievements of the German anti-tank weapon. She was the reporter and I was the lieutenant colonel who praised the battle worthiness of the German anti-tank gun. Instead of the *Panzer-Abwehr* (defense against Panzer), I called it *Panzer-Anklopf Gerät* (the gun that politely and ineffectively knocks at the protective shield of the Russian tanks). The representatives of JR's *Panzer-Abwehr* Company were pretending to enjoy this interview as much as the rest of the audience did. By that time I was somewhat high on the bubbly and so was Gundel.

We all took taxis to continue the festivities at the family flat where we danced and caroused until 2:30 a.m.. My last contribution called for my changing into a dress of the roaring twenties along with a wig. I suddenly appeared in the hall and began to dance in a parody of Mary Wigman's modern "expression" style to the "Dance of the Sugar Plum Fairies" from Tchaikovsky's "Nutcracker Suite." When I woke up, I was fully dressed on my mattress in Tutta's study, Gundel in my arms. Great party.

◆ •◆•• ◆•• ◆•

Having lost her husband in France, Irmel, now von Wallenberg, kept suggesting that the brothers and sisters would be together for the last time. We met in downtown Berlin one weekend hoping to enjoy a drink in a posh historic restaurant. Irmel knew all the restaurants that still had reserves of excellent French red wine. As I saw them approach me on the street, I was struck by what an odd picture it was. The small young woman on the arms of her two unusually tall brothers. I had never seen them together in public.

We had a good time and then on the way to Irmel's office we met three Jewish women and one little girl and noticed they were all wearing the yellow star. Siegfried ignored the spectacle, his brother, Irmel and I fell silent. It was as if a shadow had fallen on our conviviality of the ten minutes earlier. Siegfried must have noticed something. He shrugged off Irmel's reference to the scene and became somewhat defensive. He even quoted the party line that we are defending western civilization against the hordes of the East.

On the way back from another weekend in August, Irmel and I sat on our luggage in the open-air section of the train. We passed up the dreadfully overcrowded compartment, which stank of cheap tobacco. Starting again with a sudden jolt, Irmel sank into my arms almost losing her balance. She stayed there for quite a while, her hair still emanated that mixture of pine and the tar smoke her blacksmith had used in changing the horseshoes two hours earlier.

We got out of the train into the S-Bahn when we heard early warning. The loudspeaker in the train station stated, "Expect possible attack in 30 minutes." I told her I would take her home and she accepted. We made it home to her flat just in time. Mrs. von Keudell was just coming down the stairs to go to the air raid shelter and was still not quite awake.

Then the bombs started to come whistling down all around us. The woman from the downstairs apartment started shaking and screaming. She had seen Lübeck go up in flames, she yelled. The two-story building apparently had some windows broken. We heard glass fragments falling into the stairwell and we found a small incendiary in the attic. I felt like a fool carrying it down in the lid of the garbage can. It had not done much harm while resting on some masonry.

Some fire could be seen through the attic window. Irmel thought it might be at her friend Ruth's place a few blocks away. She changed quickly and we both went over to the burning building. It was as she had thought and we joined the battle with a conflagration that had almost gone out of hand. Everybody helped rescue valuable books and furniture. Ruth's father seemed to be in shock. He kept bringing down odd potted plants of some kind and we let him go ahead until we had to tell everybody that it had become too risky to go back in. They took their valuables into the shelter of the house next door and left their furniture in the open.

Back at Irmel's, we looked at each other and collapsed laughing. With her blackened face, she looked like she had minstrel make-up. She gave me a long "Thank you my boy" kiss and started to wash up. The telephone was operational. There were no more trains that night to Spandau we found out. "Could I leave my luggage while I hike across Berlin to Spandau?"

"Are you joking? It's 2:00 a.m., you'll sleep here." Mrs. von Keudell was definite in her invitation.

In the morning, we found the S-Bahn working and I even arrived on time in Spandau. It was my lucky morning. It was the day when Stachowiak connected me with the project of Colonel v. Kirchbach.

●◆● ●● ◆●● ◆● ●

Irmel had a flat in Zehlendorf and had to go to work every morning, we shared the commuter train. She was again effective showing me how to avoid further confrontations with the battalion commander and she and I became close friends, as one thing led to another.

Irmel was quite encouraged by the sudden turn in my "career," which seemed to motivate her to do all she could to improve my chances to get along with fellow officers, the higher ranks in particular. "Stop putting on this not too well cashiered act of humility and tolerance," she advised. "Whoever you are talking to will read you like a catechism and if you add your subjunctive contrary-to-fact gimmick, they will be suspicious of what you really might be thinking. I watched you talking to Colonel Boysen at my wedding and every time you said, 'Yes sir,' it looked to me that he understood you to mean, 'if that is what you think, sir.'"

"And when you are drinking with them, try to look more animated, no matter how dumb the conversation gets. In Spandau, I heard somebody complain that you just sat there, giving probing looks to everybody. Some of them said they felt they were under your observation and they didn't like it."

I took her maternal musings seriously, only occasionally under protest. Not since 1934-1935 with Alice Pollitz had I received this kind of constructive feedback. It was appreciated from both of them, even if it was painful at times.

By now Irmel was in the habit of calling me "Vinzelchen" mixing the adjective *winzig* with my name, which made it into a double diminutive. I had to get used to that one.

* ❖ · · ❖ · · ❖ ·

These conversations reminded me of how it was when we had our first relationship in 1938-1939 when she had tried to teach me tap-dancing and common sense. Then, as now, her occasional advice seemed to me very helpful; I never resented it, bruised male ego notwithstanding.

The plan to visit the von Kirchbach graves struck Irmel as odd. She suggested only a very few people in very high places had the means to pull off this sort of thing. She ascribed this religious fervor and stress on strong funereal tradition to the Silesian brand of pietism. It far exceeded that of the Lutheran Church. She did not understand von Kirchbach's kind of motivation. As for her own adjustment to grief, she did not seem to have any resentment or blame for having lost her husband and was not obsessed by her ignorance as to what had happened to him. However, she had seen her husband only three weeks after the wedding at the most, she reasoned, so maybe she shouldn't compare her loss with the one von Kirchbach had incurred. I admired her willingness to examine her reactions.

Before I had left for my trip, Irmel had encouraged me to get an impression of life in the occupied Ukraine behind the front line where no reporters were allowed. She had heard stories of successful food production on the one hand, and of terror by the SS on the other and she wanted to get some idea of what was really going on. Now, both she and her mother had to be disappointed because this first visit yielded very little information for them. I couldn't tell them anything much of importance. I had been constantly around the colonel busy making arrangements on his behalf. The two women did find the graveyard

service touching, even though the whole thing was a command performance arranged by the new masters of Moldovia, the Romanians.

My description of the tactless behavior of our Romanian host
appalled them. Not only had he tried to provide 'female company' for
us that first evening, he had even approached me for information as to
where he could find male prostitutes in the German Army or, for that
matter, in the embassy in Bucharest. Mrs. von K. exclaimed, "Our allies!
May God help us!" She immediately apologized to me, but Irmel told
her that I was not an uninformed idealist like her little brother Siegfried.

I did not say a word about the plan for the second trip, feeling
strictly bound by my orders. When I was again posted, this time by
myself, I had a hard time explaining the purpose of my trip to Irmel.
She claimed to understand, but her unspoken questions were hanging like a cloud between us for those few days before my departure on
September 10. Wiltraut immediately sensed a certain tension and, of
course, arranged for a party.

The evening was hilarious. Playing "Murder" and other silly games,
this time with students of law and medicine, turned out not to be so
naive as the ones we played back in Hohenlübbichow.

During the party, I met a distant Baltic cousin of mine, Sylvia, a
beauty with blonde hair and dark brown eyes. She looked at my injured
hand and told me she could be assisting in the operation to repair it
a few blocks away at her hospital when the time came. Now, that was
interesting news. I contacted the hospital the next morning.

The guests went home around 1:30 a.m.. To top the evening off
either Wiltraut or Irmel suggested that we go swimming in the Krumme
Lanke, a pond a few blocks away. I agreed to go provided that I would
not again be made solely responsible by Wiltraut if anything "untoward"
happened. The wartime blackout did alleviate some of our concerns
about propriety in our dressing or undressing. There was enough moonlight to at least help us find the water. The two girls insisted I turn away

until they were in the water and only then was I allowed to undress and join them.

It was an adventurous end to a wonderful evening September 10, 1942.

◆ • • ◆ • • ◆ •

I began to think it might be a reasonably pleasant trip when I discovered that I had a whole compartment to myself in the courier train, but when I woke up the next morning everything in the compartment was covered with sand and swirling dust. It certainly spoiled any enjoyment I could have had looking out of the window. The very fine sand was oozing into the compartment wherever there were cracks or small openings in the wood paneling. After arriving in Vinnitsa, I had to spend some time making myself and my uniform presentable. I was able to take a sponge bath with very cold water from a well behind the house in which I had been billeted.

The next morning, September 13, von Kirchbach and I had brunch with his boss, General von Zielberg, who happened to be in a splendid mood. The day before he had been promised the 28th Ranger Division, an active unit of good reputation. Nobody mentioned my assignment so I didn't bring it up either, expecting to be briefed privately at some later time.

Later I met my crew. The driver, Tad, a twenty-four-year-old factory worker from Posen, now Poznan, spoke some Polish, some Russian and some German. He was supposed to handle the grave digger, a Russian POW from Tuapse on the Black Sea. I've forgotten this man's name, it was unpronounceable for me anyway. He himself was a linguistic nightmare who introduced all his explanations in whatever language with the German *muss man*, meaning "one has to do this or that," followed by a quick succession of phrases in Russian, Ukrainian, Romanian or bad German, which Tad, the driver, had to interpret. He was a very likable, soft spoken undertaker, or so we were told, who had had some education. I was assured by von Kirchbach that he was reliable and loyal to the anti-Communist cause and had quite a bit of personal dignity.

The iron worker, Willy, who was supposed to solder the coffins was a married man in his forties and not very communicative. I decided I would not "go and try to steal horses depending on him," quoting a Teutonic adage, yet his papers gave him credit for his having been a reliable and circumspect soldier in combat. That was more than the driver's papers attested, which referred to him as being "flighty".

So, Tad looked after "muss man," Willy carried the second machine pistol and sat on the box containing the ammunition, and I sat next to the driver staring at the inaccurate map for orientation. We started at 10:00 a.m. in splendid fall weather. After 150 miles of dirt road, we crossed the River Dniester near Mogilev-Podolski. I kept hoping that we would not come upon rain since I was fully aware that it took only one healthy shower to turn the dirt road into a morass of mud. No German truck was fit for service in Russia once the rains started, ours included.

At Balti we had to report to the district agricultural advisor who confirmed our arrival to our people back in Vinnitsa. It wasn't long before we reached the River Pruth where a white-haired former Austrian civil servant from Bukovina was waiting for us. He, his wife and his daughter spoke German, Romanian, Russian and Ukrainian, or so he claimed. The constable proudly showed us his property and then billeted my crew in the place next door. I noticed the house was another unusually large, mostly brick building, which appeared oddly misplaced in a village where most of the indigenous population lived in much more primitive whitewashed huts with thatched roofs.

I just had time to wash my hands, then immediately I had to sit down and eat. Dirt still formed a crust on my face. Each time I moved my arm or when my ebullient host slapped my back, a cloud of dirt dust swirled around me. At such times my host declared himself my comrade-in-arms, for indeed both our countries had been allies in World War I and now World War II. He turned increasingly folksy under the influence of the dreadfully sweet wine that he claimed he had saved for this special occasion. Mother and daughter were too busy fetching and serving to take part in the conversation, but their German was impeccable, apart from the Swabian accent. The mother kept hinting she would soon send Dorothea to a Swiss boarding school for her education - and for safety, she added, as she crushed her pork rind between her gold-filled teeth.

For the night they showed me to the room reserved for the daughter's hope chest, that is to say, the room where the family had accumulated linen and blankets and boxes of household goods stacked all around the walls. This room was seldom used, I was given to understand. It was some kind of honor that I was going to be allowed to sleep in her prospective matrimonial bed. It wasn't long before I began to be uneasy with this family's pretentiousness. If all this display would make me feel that way, how much more would it be likely to frighten a simple peasant boy from the next hamlet as a potential groom?

Dinner over, I would have preferred to take a rest in my room or even just to relax by sitting down in the car, but no. The daughter Dorothea helped by two servant girls carried buckets of warm water into my room and then left, all three smiling coyly. I couldn't turn down this invitation of a sponge bath in spite of its being offered in the middle of Dorothea's hope chest and I tried valiantly not to splash too much.

Since I had never been waited on hand and foot quite like this, I wasn't sure what to expect. I had just washed the upper part of my body when the two servants came back bringing more clear water and taking out the first buckets. I began to realize this situation was going to call for some delicate timing. I never knew which of the two doors would open next, or when. It also made me a little wary that Dorothea insisted on being present to supervise the girls' activities when they were in the room. For that matter, I didn't see any necessity for her to come in with them at all. At one point, she grabbed my soiled clothes and stated she would wash them. When I was about to stop her by suggesting we were hoping to leave early in the morning and there wouldn't be time enough to dry them, she said, "Yes, yes. I will iron them dry," and promptly left with them.

After all this, I did feel wonderfully clean. I also felt very tired, but this family was not going to allow anyone to give into that. The "down home" part of the evening then began with pastry, coffee, whipped cream, cognac and champagne from the Crimea. Then, I was obliged to dance with the daughter while the mother and father watched proudly. The only record in the stack I could cope with happened to be "In the Mood" with "Boo Hoo" on the backside. The other records including mostly Balkan folk dance stuff, left me cold. The mother came up with her favorite tango record "Jealousy" with *"Blauer Himmel"* on the flip side. Not until 1:30 a.m. was I finally allowed to retire and then not without being kissed good night by both mother and daughter. Of course, there was one last cognac with the father as he continued to insist that this night was the beginning of our "friendship for life."

Alone at last, I could not sleep - my boys were still singing in the house next door. Concerned about what they might be led into, also about keeping our mission as unobtrusive and as discreet as possible, I got dressed and went over there to check. It cost me another brandy, but everything was okay. They and their hosts were about ready to break up the party anyway. I noticed that they too were being cheerfully looked after by pleasant looking young females.

Back in the hope chest, I pursued my earlier train of thought, which included observations concerning the situation of my host and his family. This bragging constable could not have owned this place for long. Bessarabia had been ceded to Russia in 1940 with Hitler's consent and that was the time about two years ago when the Romanian army and any civil administration had moved out. The Romanians had reclaimed it a little over a year ago, which was when my host had been posted here.

Who were the original owners of this mansion and where were they now? All of these large houses standing on either side of the main thoroughfare were an enormous contrast to all those small Romanian whitewashed huts with thatched roofs lining the side streets where the indigenous population lived. I remembered seeing mansions of this type in villages on either side of the River Pruth, in western Romania and all through the Balkans. The contrast between the two types of houses was most pronounced in the Polish towns. These great houses, I was told, were owned by the doctors, lawyers, pharmacists or successful merchants of each community and all these people had belonged to the Jewish segment of the population.

So, did the Russians deport the former owners along with other people of standing, as we were told, or did the Romanians deport them at the behest of the SS? Was this what Mrs. von Keudell referred to when she asked me to keep my eyes open in the occupied territories?

I was puzzled and glad, in retrospect, that I had gone to the next house to make sure that nothing untoward was happening or would happen. I was also relieved that at least my better self had restrained me from asking pointed questions about these opulent houses. No doubt, the Romanian government had given them to these civil servants who would not appreciate to be confronted with questions about the former owners and when and why these people had been forced to leave and whether they possibly had been Jews. To summarize my thoughts, at this point it merely seemed odd that this simple constable was living in a house ten times too big for his pay check and that the original owners were somehow missing. I concluded that I was on a delicate mission and my responsibility included not arousing attention of any kind. So, I put my uneasiness aside.

"Mum's the word," I told my boys the next morning. "Let's be on our best behavior and bring those two coffins to Vinnitsa without publicity. We are conspicuous enough at it is, having a Russian prisoner with us." Soon the constable-host stamped my papers and we took off early to dig in the relatively cool forenoon. When we arrived at our destination "muss man" explained to us, or better demonstrated, his procedure. He would dig and then probe from the side starting at the foot end and a tarpaulin was made ready to receive the remains. He began digging. My mouth ran dry with apprehension. What would we find? What if it wasn't Friedrich under the big wooden cross, which we had unceremoniously just pulled out? What if the grave markings were mistaken?

As I watched, I began to experience a feeling of hostility toward the deceased like that which had bothered me so much on July 2, 1941 sitting in the dirt next to his corpse. My mind began to churn. If only Friedrich had been able to control the impetuous behavior of his battalion commander, I would not be in this godforsaken cemetery at this hour. I knew I was being unreasonable, but I kept focusing on this mindless captain whom I blamed for this whole mess.

Our Russian was probing with his gloved right hand. "Knee," he pointed out. Very slowly, shovel by shovel, he uncovered a skeleton in a uniform. Yes, those were Friedrich's remains, all right. "Muss man" explained there was very little left because it was a shallow grave and in sandy soil. It took quite a while for us to assemble everything which had been primitively wrapped in a blanket a year ago. I wrapped his rusted handgun in oil paper as one proof of his identity. The Russian was very conscientious and showed great sensitivity. He knew this dead soldier had been close to me. Having soldered up the coffin, we returned to the ex-Austrian gendarme who had been drinking already in broad daylight. He embraced me and declared himself a friend for life.

This time it was a quiet dinner at the constable's family table. We did talk, however, but in all our conversations I seemed to detect a certain uneasiness. I had the impression that our hosts did not at all accept the judgment that the war with Russia was practically over, as the German and Romanian propaganda had been telling all of us. The old man had served so many masters: the Austrians, the Poles, the Russians and now the Romanians. I could understand that he was looking upon all this as temporary, not as a final political solution and he had no illusions about the preparedness of the Romanian army.

The next morning we took off in a northeasterly direction to reach the ferry at Rybnica. I was in a pensive mood still thinking about the old man and his remarks about a possible return of the Russian army. It wasn't defeatism, he protested, but he remembered 1918 and so did I. Again a clear, very hot day to ride through Ukraine. I felt relieved.

We found the graveyard and began to dig for Tony's remains. This time we had to go three-and-a-half feet deep before we found anything. In this case no cloth had been used to wrap the corpse, but even so, the corpse was well preserved, which meant it was extremely heavy and difficult to handle. We all had rubber gloves and helped to lift the remains into the coffin. Our muzhik was not a big enough man to handle this weight by himself and appreciated our assistance, constantly warning us about poison from contact with the corpse.

* * * * * * * *

From Uman we drove back to Vinnitsa. Wherever we encountered people working in the fields, they waved and we waved back. My driver apparently considered this as part of his public relations duty, he kept waving and praising these wonderful Ukrainian peasants. Ever since we left on September 13, I was very much aware that we were in occupied territory and I also remembered very well being shot at around midnight only a few months ago; however, on this trip I was very careful not to let this anxiety become visible.

On the last leg of the trip, we had some personal contact with agricultural workers who offered us beautiful ripe melons. These were the first melons I had ever seen in my life, let alone tasted. It was a tremendous experience, and in the end we had about a half dozen melons between us in the back of the truck.

Outside Vinnitsa we had contact with a group of marching women who were returning to their camp after some road work. "Ukrainians," the driver said. Some potbellied soldier at least fifty-years-old trotted behind them. I asked him, "Why do they have to be guarded?" My curiosity was aroused. We talked to some of them who spoke German; however, I became mindful of our delicate mission and since the sun was about to go down I knew we needed to go on. I certainly did not see any yellow stars. I never found out whether they had been pressed into the service or in what kind of camp they were being kept.

In Vinnitsa, I called von Kirchbach who welcomed us back, sent the truck to some depot. I found a bottle of cognac in my room and passed out after two glasses.

The colonel sent a note around 9:00 a.m. telling me to get freshened up and then relax. He would call again in the afternoon. While shaving I found some skin inflammation under my chin with a watery discharge which made me feel rather uneasy. The question was what I had picked up and where? Half my instructions to my company in Poland, Romania and Bulgaria consisted of dire warnings concerning infectious materials and plants. So, here I was, trying to imagine what kind of nasty bacteria had now nestled in the roots of my beard.

It was heart-rending to tell Kirchbach the particulars of our mission and to watch the old man break down and cry. He admitted that he had thought carefully and concluded that he could not possibly take the responsibility of sending me on the additional mission we had previously planned with the two coffins. I could easily end up in court-martial and so, of course, would he. He asked me to forgive him and took me to the grave in the local cemetery where the two crosses were standing over the final resting place of the boys.

He presented me with a photo of the grave in a family heirloom frame. Of course, I was let down after all the mounting tension that had accrued in the last two or three weeks. Yet, human nature being what it is, very soon I was beginning to feel some kind of relief, which was helped considerably by his order for me to dash back to Berlin, collect my belongings and return with the next train. There was a job for me at FHO, *Fremde Heere Ost*, Foreign Armies East, (Intelligence East). Colonel Gehlen was waiting for me and they had a shortage in one section. I could hardly believe my good fortune to finally be out of the clutches of the Spandau battalion commander.

On the train back to Berlin, I felt the letdown again and it was hard to shake it. Our mission, such as it was, had consumed all my thoughts and had even haunted me in my sleep. It had to do with my emotional ties with the von Kirchbach family, the conspiratorial preparation of the trip that smacked of an aspect of Karl May, i.e., "wild west romanticism," meaning, in my case, the good guy overcoming all kinds of difficulty to bring two other good guys home to the family. I kept thinking what could I as the accompanying officer inside in the locked cattle car have done, if something had gone wrong. Then again, I had moments when I doubted if I had been adequate to the task. Had I not compromised this undertaking by getting caught with Friedrich's blank papers half a year after his death? These inconclusive ruminations went on and on while I was packing my luggage for my new destination. I hated myself for giving in to all these questions and doubts. Thank god it was soon to be over and I found myself thinking that it was so simple to move without having to consider the dog.

At the train station I was finally able to phone Irmel at work. She had just returned from an assignment in Rome and she was excited and pleased about my new job and sad not to be able to wave me goodbye. I rather numbly took in her reactions.

This time I had to share the compartment with a *Sonderführer*, an agriculture administrator in the occupied Ukraine. He lectured me during my waking moments on Germany's impending victory in the Russian war - shades of Müller-Hofmeister, I thought. I pretended to sleep whenever possible, particularly when he insisted on going all the way back to World War I, talking ad nauseam how Germany hadn't deserved the bad treatment she had received since she had not really started the war, how we then found ourselves groveling before the victors, how we had lost our respect in the world because we had not had self-respect, and what a miracle it was that the German flag was flying on Mt. Elbrus in the Caucuses.

●◆●●◆●●◆●

Fall 1942. Vinnitsa probably had been a university town in peace time. On the edge of it in a campus like setting, I found the OKH located in what seemed to be former school buildings. All of them were relatively functional structures, solidly built with high ceilings and large windows letting in natural light that we truly appreciated, having been used to living and working in dark low *dachas* with small windows. The one-story buildings could have been laboratories or offices. A few were two story houses fitted with almost modern plumbing including cold running water hand basins in the loo. All of these school buildings originally had been fitted with electric lights, but no power was left in town. The army had brought in huge generators to provide electricity for the compound.

We were billeted in comfortable rooms kept clean by a maintenance crew of a dozen Ukrainian females. Much to my disgust my room had a mirror. I couldn't help but notice my blond hair was much too long and since I had never seen myself unshaven it was somewhat of a shock that my beard was black. I looked like I was a U-boat ensign transferred to the infantry by mistake. Not everyone in my new situation swallowed my *Bartflechte* (barber's itch) story and I received some good-natured ribbing. This did not help to create the good first impression that I had intended, but it did help to establish some kind of camaraderie. The closest dermatologist was in Krakow, I was told. My problem was when and how was I going to get to him. I was needed here and my boss, Capt. Grüner, was good enough about it also. He told me he needed one more warm body, clean-shaven or not. Besides, I was sick of traveling, especially all the way back to Poland. I had done that trip five times within a few weeks.

I found I was teamed up with Lt. Uwe Letchert, a tall Friesian reserve officer who was hoping to study law after the war. Soon after we met, he remarked, "I suppose I can forget about that kind of a career; one year from now I will be in charge of 500 Mongolian slaves in outer Siberia." I enjoyed his great sense of humor and we became trusting friends in a matter of days. I took some comfort in the open way Uwe talked about Hitler. He blamed him for the loss of some of his toes in the winter of 1941 and called Hitler the *Gröfaz*, which was the intentionally mixed up abbreviation of the Nazi propaganda phrase, *Grösster Feldherr aller Zeiten*, meaning "Greatest Military Genius of All Time."

Our boss, Major Wessel, who was in charge of daily intelligence-Russia, taught me how to approach my job. Every night when I was on duty, I had to phone the southernmost Army Group "A," the one that was moving into the Caucasus. I had to transcribe, sift, compile and condense the telephone messages. We relied on the wireless communication, POW statements, reports from infiltrators or spies from behind the Russian lines and the daily air reconnaissance to sum up the enemy situation. From time to time, we had to sum up and evaluate possible trends or changes behind the Russian front. All this was jotted in telegram style on the big situation map and Capt. Grüner brought this about 8:00 p.m. every night to Gehlen and Wessel. They in turn passed the newly updated map on to the chief of the general staff who added his commentary to our texts.

Since much of this by its very nature had to be conjecture or assumption, the subjunctive had much use. That was no problem for me since I had studied the high art of the subjunctive during the number of years I had taken Latin in school. We easily arrived at sentences like: "They might do this or that and then again they might not do it." Apparently, Hitler did not appreciate Gehlen's analysis. We heard he was infuriated by the vagueness in our messages and by the professional honesty and realism of Gehlen's warnings, which he labeled defeatism. Hitler could not stand Gehlen's insistence on recognizing the seeming inexhaustibility of Russian manpower and the overwhelming quantities of war materials that were coming from the United States. Hitler, following his own obstinate vision, was reported to have yelled, "The Russian is finished! Dead! Do you understand?"

To give one example of our work routine: Army Group "A" reports an uncoded communication between a Russian military policeman and someone in 29th Guard Division. (We were always grateful to the blabbing of the MP's who apparently had not been trained in any kind of security attitudes.) So, I recorded this conversation and looked up FGTC on our list of known or assumed Russian units, and lo and behold it was last confirmed as a unit that was almost destroyed near Wjasma in 1941. Conclusion: the Russians must have reconstituted this corps. Until further confirmation, it will now appear on our map opposite German Army Group "A" among the list of units assumed to be in reserve, but possibly ready for deployment. The next morning when my twenty-four hours of duty were almost up, I passed this on to Lt. Ritter who was in charge of a huge data bank entailing the most minute, the most trivial bits of information regarding the Russian Army.

Twenty-four hours' duty meant in some cases being up all night on the telephone. To be honest, when not communicating with Army Group "A" it was with Irmel and with my sister. These calls when there seemed to be nothing to do were permissible, but strictly monitored. There was a day bed for the man on duty in the room, but it wasn't used too much. Army Group "A" had high drama going all the way in the Caucasus and our neighbor on our left had Army Group "B" with potential disaster brewing in Stalingrad. Between the two army groups there were a few motorized reconnaissance groups around Elista, along the Caspian Sea, a gap of at least 500 miles, which gave me chills when I had to think about it. So the days passed. Food was better than average and we had a small account for canteen goods.

Downtown Vinnitsa was mostly destroyed so I took long solitary walks in the colorful fall scenery in the outskirts of town. I walked alone because I needed to sort out my anxieties. I was shedding the last bits of the front-line soldiers' naive confidence in the military structure. You take orders and give orders and are responsible that they are carried out. You rely on every one of your fellow soldiers and convince them that they can rely on you because you all share alike in everything that happens. This is a tremendous source of strength and your outlook by necessity is optimistic. Here, I was just a cog in some gigantic wheel that was grinding inexorably in a direction that looked increasingly like disaster. Here, I had to face the big picture and it wasn't pretty. The gap between propaganda and reality was glaringly apparent. Now that I was looking at the total picture, I saw that what the public was being told was not the truth by a long shot.

Our position worsened day by day. Our Field Marshall List had been fired early in September. Hitler had taken over the Army Group

"A" himself. It did not make any difference, of course. While 6th Army (Army Group "B") was bleeding to death in Stalingrad, our troops reached neither Groszny nor Baku. General Halder, Chief of the General Staff since 1938, was fired too on September 24. In his place Hitler appointed the rotund bundle of energy General Zeitzler, a "yes-man without substance," I was told by Uwe.

Everything was collapsing around us. Both the 6th Army at Stalingrad and our army group were burned out. We read in a report from Army Group "A" that German soldiers were dying of sheer exhaustion - not the front-line soldiers - the people who were trying to get food and ammunition to their comrades. This happened near Tuapse where these poor guys got stuck in mud up to four feet deep. They had to abandon their mules and their supplies, then shoot the mules because there was no way to get them out of that mud. At the same time, the German papers reported that Stalingrad was nine-tenths in German hands and Hitler had occupied the rest of France at El Alamein, Rommel was forced to order immediate withdrawal, the allies had landed in Morocco and Algiers and, last not least, the Americans decisively beat the Japanese in the Battle of Midway.

Week after week, we had stared at the map showing the Russian build up on either side of Stalingrad. Gehlen's warnings, of course, had been ignored. Even a rank beginner could have drawn conclusions considering the troop concentrations and preparations opposite the two Romanian armies on either side of Stalingrad. Sure enough, on November 19, at 5:00 a.m. superior Russian forces burst out of the Don River bridgehead northwest of Stalingrad and swept the Romanians out of their defenses. On the following day, another Russian offensive south of Stalingrad destroyed the other Romanian Army. The two pincers met south of Stalingrad at Kalatsch and almost 300,000 soldiers were trapped. Our friends from the operational sector in charge of our Army Group "A" and "B" came over to our office at midnight to look at the new situation map. They were stunned. Some were almost admiring this encirclement as a classic success.

The next morning, Hitler relieved the leadership of Army Group "A" and soon afterwards we found out that the whole headquarters would be moved to East Prussia. I felt like I was sitting on a time bomb. Headquarters, Hitler's and ours, were in no immediate danger, but at least you had to conclude that somebody had woken up to the seriousness of the situation. Moving two headquarters for thousands of miles under optimal circumstances would be a giant undertaking. At the time, I compared what was happening to be moving a whole division with all the attendant services and supply units. Grüner and Letchert were sent to East Prussia and I was left to ensure the smooth transition until they got there. For the time being, everything came to me until they had arrived and they were ready to take over.

Of course, I was not allowed to tell Irmel anything about this move on the telephone. I'm afraid I disregarded security when the head office asked us whether we knew someone back home who needed domestic help. Allegedly, there were twenty-eight Ukrainian women who had applied to work in Germany.

I asked Irmel outright, "Are you interested in a household helper?"

There was a long pause and she said, "Are you kidding me?"

"No, I have just been interviewing Katinka with the help of an interpreter and she has assured me she would love to go to Berlin to work." There was some static on the telephone line I couldn't interpret.

Then she said, "You know I almost fell off my chair, I was kneeling on it. Could you call back in ten minutes?" I agreed to do that.

I assessed the situation and didn't think I was doing anything illegal, after all it was a private business matter. This pause gave me a chance to find out what their motivations were. Katinka said simply that she didn't want to be around if the Russians ever came back since she had heard what had happened to people who had collaborated with the Germans.

Katinka and her girlfriend assured me if it came to agricultural work on the estate of my friend, they would be just as willing to go.

I called Irmel again and she was overjoyed, even ecstatic, because her job kept her away from home at an irregular schedule and all her housework had been neglected considerably. She continued, "Did you say you had more than one? Remember Ruth Wirth whose house was on fire the other day? She needs one too."

So Irmel gave me the details of the second place of employment and what kind of job her friend had and what kind of necessity it was to have household help. I had to sign some papers and the deal was clinched in twenty minutes. I felt a bit like a slave trader, but in a positive sense. I knew Katinka would have a good time in Berlin, as anyone would from Vinnitsa, bombs or no bombs. I heard from the interpreter that from our FHO all twenty-eight girls had found employment and would be sent by army train to Berlin with the names of their future employer and destination written on some kind of card around their neck. The interpreter assured me that all these candidates were in perfect health, good workers and had good reputations.

Now that there were only a few of us left, we had more contact with Gehlen. I remember one discussion with several coworkers over a cup of coffee one afternoon, our topic was centered on euthanasia. My mind was not on that subject at the moment so I just sat there and observed him in action. Short of stature, slight build, pale, thin hair on a head disproportionately big for the narrow width of his shoulders. The prominent feature was his large ears which stuck out, as it were, but the minute he started to talk in his soft-spoken, elegant diction, he immediately had our attention. He was lucidity personified. He never talked down to anyone and he never showed that he knew so much more than you did. For instance, at the end of a long discussion with Lt. Burkhardt, he tried to give the young man some credit as if his ideas had been helpful in reaching a practical, feasible solution. When General von Zielberg joined the group and proposed a different solution after a few minutes, Gehlen had little trouble to convince his superior officer that he was wrong without making him feel like a fool.

I must admit that for the first time since 1936 I thought I had found someone in the army to look up to, and it struck me as particularly fair that while the beginning of the Stalingrad crisis was on everybody's mind, not once did he hint that he was tempted to say I told you so. When we finally broke up to travel to East Prussia, I was sorry I could not have more of those very encouraging encounters. I heard that Gehlen was a tireless worker much at the expense of his health and he had stomach problems for years.

● ◆ ● ● ◆ ● ● ◆ ●

About four weeks earlier I had approached Gehlen at one of these informal sessions in a typical German fashion taking him completely unawares, "Sir, I understand you said we are welcome to nominate a friend or a deserving regular officer who happens to be an invalid."

"Oh, yes," he answered. "Do you have someone? It so happens that Graf Ritteberg needs help in his group too." When I told him how far back JR and I went, he smiled and said, "A good thing Ritteberg is in a different group. We don't need a Castro and Pollux act."

Gehlen must have moved immediately on my proposal, because when I came to East Prussia there was JR, who had been very glad at my suggestion over the telephone that he might consider such an appointment. It took him only a fortnight to convince the whole section that he had the temper of a choleric - good old JR.

◆ ◆ ● ● ◆ ● ● ◆ ●

The huts at "Camp Fritz," telephone code "Exchange Anna," were deep in a largely coniferous forest called Mauerwald. The structures were predominantly one story high and looked from the distance like industrial sheds. They were nestled along narrow streets and/or wooden walkways. Once I came close enough I was struck by the modern design of the structures. They had large windows with screens and all the modern comforts inside of the huts like central heating which came from a distant heating plant, hot and cold running water, fluorescent ceiling lights and desk lamps. Our main office building housed Gehlen and section I. Section II was in a smaller hut behind us, and a third building housed the kitchen, the mess, registrar and the map printing shop. Personal quarters were about 200 meters away at the foot of the hill accessible only by wooden walkway. One step off the grate and you were ankle deep in mud.

Only a few roofs had camouflage paint or nettings. This surprised me since I had seen in Hamburg where the trouble had been taken to construct a phony bridge in the middle of the lake, hoping to fool the Allied Air Reconnaissance. Letchert had a simple explanation for the fact that neither the Russians nor the Western Allies had ever tried to bomb this jewel, our little town. "They have every interest in keeping the present German High Command alive and working undisturbed, working right into their dirty little Allied hands." This was spoken two months before Stalingrad became a topic.

Hitler was in some hideout, "Wolfschanze," near Rastenburg. We reached the German High Command (OKW) by means of a diesel rail car, which carried commuters back and forth day and night. Security was in the hands of some middle-aged reservists who never had reasons to become active while I was there; even their dogs looked overfed and close to retirement.

My attention to my work in Section A was consuming. The shift started when the corresponding officer at Army Group "A" phoned in their report about 6:00 or 7:00 p.m. I had to comprise it and dictate it to the clerk. The telephone connection to the foothills of the Caucasus worked impressively well considering the distance, which was at least 3,200 miles as the crow flies.

I had a good rapport with the people in the Army Group "A" staff, a Captain Felding in particular. He said right off, without knowing me well enough to be that trusting, "At last I'm hearing the voice of someone who understands that we are connected by some technical miracle so we don't have to shout. Could you please help me to explain that to Grüner?"

"Well, I could tell him, sir, but since he has two more pieces of metal on his shoulder than I do, it might not be wise."

Captain Felding agreed, "You may have a point there."

◆ • • ◆ • • ◆ •

Letchert, Ritter, JR and I became quite a foursome. We had almost daily contact. However, our conviviality petered out November 8, 1942, when we saw Rommel's burned out army overwhelmed by the British at El Alamein. November 11, I became involved when the Americans landed in Algiers and Morocco.

My command of the English language, such as it was, landed me the job of giving a daily rundown of the events in Africa. Unfortunately, it turned out that my shortcomings in English were rather unimportant. Gehlen and von Rönne winced each time I tried to pronounce French terms and names pertaining to military and political developments in North Africa. By the time I had procured an up-to-date dictionary in French, the show became of secondary interest upstaged by what had happened in Stalingrad between November 19 and November 23.

When the Cyrenaika region was finally lost, all interest switched from Rommel to Stalingrad. Obviously, my own anxiety centered on my division and my company. Irmel wanted to hear about her brother's fate and last, not least, Mrs. Müller, Hans Müller's wife, approached me over the phone. She still had kept my sister's address and had written to her that she had not heard from her husband since the end of August 1942. So now I had three people to talk to on the midnight phone. Yet, of course, I could not say much; all calls were being monitored.

⁕◆⁕ ⁕⁕ ◆⁕ ⁕⁕ ◆⁕ ⁕

My goose arrived. I had ordered two geese before leaving Vinnitsa. One was safely here and was immediately eaten by our foursome. The companion bird was on its way to Hamburg. Letchert, Ritter, JR and I had a feast - roast goose and toasted army bread. All of us had stomach problems afterwards. After years of food rationing, our system didn't take it well. The other goose arrived in Hamburg in a sorry, smelly state; it had to be thrown away. Apart from saying that I was sorry, I couldn't at the time explain why their goose had spoiled. In retrospect, the train from the Ukraine to the headquarters was a fast-moving courier train; the journey from Vinnitsa to Hamburg may have entailed many stops and delays. My family was not only disappointed, they were crushed.

I watched for every bit of news from Stalingrad by going to my coworker in the operational section on my off day. Neither Irmel nor Hannelore Müller had any news and had become apprehensive. In each case, there was a chance that their man could have been somewhere outside of the encirclement the moment the Russian ring closed. Irmel finally had a postcard; her brother was in Stalingrad. No news from Hans Müller. The late-night conversations with Irmel and Hannelore, frustrating as they were, since we could not openly discuss anything, these talks became some emotional high points, of sorts. In all this uncertainty and despair, Hannelore was expecting her first baby and put up a tremendous show of courage.

Irmel's ex-brother-in-law died as a fighter pilot in Africa. She was now faced with the burden of having to look after her husband's three sisters. She started searching frantically for solutions and was very glad and relieved when they accepted jobs in munitions factories. That was the last I heard about them. Irmel's friendship with her domestic helper from Ukraine, Katinka, became a very important factor in Irmel's mind boggling, stressful life at the foreign ministry.

The truth about Stalingrad was kept from the public. Instead we had to read about the heroic battle of vital importance for the "Final Victory." "Victorious up to the moment of utter destruction," I told Letchert. Motivated by solidarity, not too well defined, some of us tried to live on Stalingrad rations. We were advised to discontinue that. "No demonstrations in the OKH, thanks." The Operations Sector had been ordered to follow that diet by the commanding officer. It was a miserable failure and the order had to be rescinded. People were unable to work. On the evening of December 17, the chief medical officer in Stalingrad had reported the first case of death from exhaustion.

My General Rodenburg became notorious for forbidding suicide, but it wasn't all his idea. On December 12, an order was issued from Sixth Army Headquarters saying that no officer was to allow himself to be taken prisoner. "Should he be in danger of falling into enemy hands, he was to shoot himself." Premature suicide was also forbidden. "When a unit has been overrun it is the right and the duty of an officer to shoot himself."

One report read:

"On December 19, thirty men of the 2nd Battalion Infantry Regiment 178 were taken prisoner by the Russians. They had fought until their ammunition was exhausted. In his daily report, the battalion commander mentioned this fact. Two days later, he was standing at attention before his divisional commander, General Rodenburg.

'You report thirty of your men taken prisoner. How did this happen? Are you and your people unaware of my very firm order that there is to be no surrender?'

'We are, sir. I and all my men are fully acquainted with your order.'

'Then what has happened? How do you explain this utterly filthy business?'

'I issued your order to my men, sir, and I added that so far as I am concerned, a man who is honorably taken prisoner is not automatically a coward.'

'You're out of your mind. This is a clear case of insubordination. I shall relieve you of your command and have you court-martialed. I will not tolerate any sabotage of the Führer's orders.'

'I shall welcome a court-martial,' the battalion commander retorted.

'And you, as an officer, would you choose captivity rather than shoot yourself?'

'I should, sir. I regard suicide as an ultimate act of cowardice.'

'Get out of here! I'll think about what to do with you.'

Nothing was done."

I told Gehlen about this and read the report to him adding that Rodenburg was my former colonel. Gehlen blushed and covered his face with both hands. He said, "No German officer has ever been subjected to this kind of dilemma. Try to understand both sides, would you?"

Towards the end Rodenburg allegedly reversed himself and forbade suicide. "Postwar Germany will need men who can lead," he is supposed to have declared.

A Major von Zitzewitz was flown in to Stalingrad with modern communication facilities to give high command up-to-date truthful reports on the situation. This too was an exercise in futility. The Air Force was less and less successful in supplying Stalingrad and it was too late for breakout schemes since there were no more horses, not enough gasoline, and since they had thousands of wounded on their hands.

News from Irmel's brother and my division talked about an imminent end to resistance. The troops sometimes had days without food and shelter. Discipline broke down. 364 death sentences for looting and desertion were carried out. It was every man for himself. Frequently, the supplies dropped from the air were spirited away and hidden by whoever happened to be near.

I don't remember much about the end of 1942 or January 1943. I did my job mechanically, though it was interesting and suspenseful. The big question was since Stalingrad could not be relieved, would at least Army Group "A" be able to retreat from the Caucasus in time and in good shape? The Russians did not spare lives or materials to threaten Rostow, the narrow bottleneck for the retreating Army Group "A". My good friend Captain Felding told me at the height of this crisis that while everybody else was scrounging up supplies and gasoline, a bunch of SS caravans with plenty of gasoline were found meandering around the Caucasus searching for archeological and anthropological proof that a German tribe, some Goths, had been living in this part of Russia.

Irmel took a leave of absence and stayed with her mother, who was, of course, having a very bad time. We agreed on a telephone moratorium to pacify whoever was listening to our conversations at the censorship office. The good woman had interrupted us once or twice because we were coming too close to talking about the true situation.

Hannalore Müller had a vague statement from a former kitchen helper that Hans had been seen armed to the teeth sitting on a big new German tank on the way to a counter attack near Abganorovo. Finally, she received a postcard from Hans saying that horse and dog were fine when he left them; he had to go with a crisis unit made up of shoemakers, cooks, paymasters clerks and tailors. These temporary battle groups were thrown in to the big gap between Voroshilovgrad and Voronesh.

By this time I had lost weight and I was sleeping badly, upsetting friends in adjoining rooms with violent outbursts at night, railing invective against Göring and the whole bunch responsible for this mess. Letchert and JR at times woke me up because they were afraid someone else might hear me.

The general mood was moderately upbeat when von Manstein started to attack in his drive to open a corridor for the Sixth Army. His advance had to be stopped the very moment when the Russians knocked over the Italian Army along the Don River. This was then the end of all hopes. They had come within forty-eight kilometers of the encirclement, but now they had to disassemble to defend Rostow and Army Group A's retreat. The rest is history. By December 29, Army Group "A" was in full retreat, i.e., 17th Army towards the Crimean Peninsula and the 1st Panzer Army through Rostov. Stalingrad was ordered to keep fighting with ten percent of the promised air support.

CHAPTER VI

JANUARY 12, 1943 BROUGHT THE NEXT RUSSIAN OFFENSIVE. The Hungarians accounted for themselves somewhat better than the Romanians and Italians, and they lost 30,000 killed that first day. Ukraine was wide open and the Russians clearly had Kharkov in mind, which would open the possibility of another Stalingrad on a much larger scale.

While I was staring at the map contemplating the Russian options, von Rönne came into my room and asked for a quick translation of President Roosevelt's press conference. He immediately pointed to a given paragraph and asked me to translate, and I had to read to him that America would continue the war with the clear goal to achieve unconditional surrender for Germany, Italy and Japan. Roenne nodded. He, of course, had understood before I confirmed it and he said, "If Goebbels needed a morale booster for his next speech, this is it."

January 18. Leningrad was reached by Russian supply columns and Stalingrad lost Gumrak, its last airport, while Rommel and the Italians were retreating from Tripoli.

January 24. Hitler forbade any talk of surrender of Stalingrad and Goebbels made his big speech in the Sports Palace in Berlin asking for total mobilization and nationwide call-up for work.

January 31. Paulus surrendered with his southern pocket and three days later the northern part of Stalingrad surrendered. Three days of national mourning were called by the government and Gehlen gave a short address to the whole section to pay homage to the sacrifice of the 6th Army. He did not use this as a patriotic appeal - we all understood what he had in mind. I remember walking around for the next ten days or so like everybody else. We were all like sleepwalkers avoiding each other's eyes. At least we had some good news that von Manstein finally got through to Hitler getting his okay to withdraw to the Mius-doetz Line, which was the line we had achieved in winter, 1941.

February 15. Female clerks appeared and many of our soldiers were posted with fighting units.

March 18. Goebbels finally gave the big speech everybody had been waiting for. Using the unconditional surrender as a motto he asked thousands of enthusiastic people in his audience, "Do you want to fight to the last drop of blood to achieve Final Victory?" They yelled back to him, "We do!"

He had about ten of these leading questions:

"Are you and is the German nation prepared, if the Führer gives that order, to work ten, twelve and if necessary, fourteen and sixteen hours a day and to give your all for victory?"

"We are!"

"Do you want total war?"

"Do you want it and, if necessary, more total and radical than we can imagine it today?"

"We do!"

"Then, now nation arise! Storm, break loose."

This same minister of propaganda wrote, regarding the announced policy of demanding unconditional surrender, "As for us, we have burned our bridges. We cannot go back, but neither do we want to go back. We are forced to extremes and therefore resolved to extremes. We shall go down in history as the greatest statesmen of all time or the greatest criminals."

A friend of mine in the personnel section let me know that since November '42 we had lost one million men killed. I don't know how the month of March passed; it was a lot of hard work because Manstein had success in his counterattack. The early part of April was taken up mostly with the discussion of the massed graves that had been found behind the German lines at Army Group Central. So far 4,100 Polish officers had been identified. The Army called in neutral experts and Goebbels launched a tremendous propaganda campaign, which Stalin countered on April 18 saying that the Germans had killed them.

On April 19, the staff clerk suddenly approached me to produce a spring party for May 1. He said that Colonel Gehlen thinks we should do something to lighten the general mood in the department. I co-opted JR, three corporals and one female clerk to do some collective creativity. We had about a dozen of these women who had been working in civil administration in Berlin and were quite enthusiastic about their change of scenery. I proposed to write a radio interview satirizing the work of Group 1. One of the corporals co-operated and promised to perform a stand-up act as a British agent dressed in a jumpsuit of a paratrooper and we planned other miscellaneous sketches.

JR was in a rather giving mood and told the others about my dance parody at his wedding. He made me phone my former teacher Alice Pollitz to ask her if she would please mail her dress again and a wig. And I let her have my address on an army postcard. She was pleased to hear from me and delighted to play a part in an attempt to cheer up my outfit. Miss Goll promised to find a not-too-small bra for me.

We found a vacant hall big enough to take the whole department of about 200 people and had a wonderful time putting it on. The most applause was achieved by the paratrooper British spy from "London" standing on a table in full gear reporting on each of the Sections. The climax came when he mentioned Lt. Colonel Nauck who keeps tab on Russian tank production. The agent said, "According to Mr. Nauck, the last Russian tank was destroyed last Christmas and he couldn't for the life of him explain where all these other Russian tanks were coming from." And he ended using Letchert's quote.

"The reason why we haven't seen air attacks around here is:

A. That Gehlen is really not in charge of the department. The real power is Corporal Hundt who has a tremendous influence on his peers in the German High Command (relating to Hitler and his having been a corporal in World War I.) Mr. Hundt is never here, so there is no point in attacking when Hundt is not here.

B. London doesn't want any harm to come to your local security forces because the British know that these forces are Hitler's secret weapon."

The German propaganda had kept harping for months on secret weapon development that would decide the war. If Hitler ever tried to use this secret weapon he would be rather disappointed, wouldn't he.

As for my dance number, Alice's dress celebrated another success, the wig she had mailed was believable in the context of modern expression dance, and Tchaikovsky rotated in his grave.

Gehlen came up to me afterwards and after complimenting me on this production, expressed for the first time he wondered if I had chosen the right profession. I wasn't sure if this was a compliment or not, or if he meant I shouldn't be in theater, or if I shouldn't be a soldier.

❖ •• ❖ •• ❖ •

May 10 was the scheduled operation on my hand in Berlin. My lovely distant relative, Sylvia, took extreme care to push a needle with what I think was atropine in me that made me beautifully drowsy and turned our conversation into an absolute riot. She then pushed me into surgery and I went under.

Sylvia assured me that the nasty bone splinter that had given me so much trouble had been removed and she then took great pains in explaining the x-ray. She wished me a good "cast-furlough" in Zürs and we parted company, reluctantly, as far as I was concerned.

The following day, Irmel, her mother, and I traveled to Austria and began our fourteen days in a posh ski hotel far distant from the railway station. We had to ride in a horse drawn sled for three-and-a-half hours. It was wonderful. Irmel and I tried to be available to Mrs. von Keudell, but she kept assuring us to go our own way. She still was taking the loss of her son very hard.

The following Tuesday, I had to go back to Berlin so the cast could be opened and everything could be checked. By this time we had made a number of acquaintances, among them was one of the secretaries in Hitler's Chancellery who made at least one big mistake per day. The day before I was leaving, she put herself right into the hot sun without any protection and she came back to the hotel looking like a lobster fresh out of the kettle. I tried to be helpful and I avoided joining in with the critical voices who called her foolishness just plain dumb.

Whatever I deserved for doing an errand for her at the local pharmacy, I certainly didn't expect her at my bedroom door at 10:30 p.m. covered with Nivea cream. She was stalling, so I invited her in. She said, "Oh, I just came by to give you a little note for my colleague in Berlin. Would you be so kind as to mail it for me?"

I was only too eager to accept her assignment so she would be retiring soon, but with my luck there was another knock on the door and there was Irmel. She looked distinctly nonplused, "Oh, you're busy?" Before I could try to explain, our little Nivea-covered friend stammered some excuses and left. It didn't take long before Irmel was enjoying the comedy in this situation as much as I was. We talked about the possibility to bring my sister Jutta with me on the way back from Berlin. Irmel thought it was a good idea, anything to provide distraction for her mother.

I picked up Jutta in Munich on the way back from Berlin and we had a joyous reunion in the train. She bubbled with enthusiasm about her being able to stay a week in such a posh resort. After that topic was more or less exhausted, she did her best to give me an idea what it was like to try to study in a big city at this stage of the air war.

While the train had stopped for a moment I leaned out of the window, enjoyed the beautiful sun and smells of spring. Jutta kept talking and among the anecdotes she had to offer, there was a rather unfunny joke in the hilarious North German dialect.

Question: "What is a motet?"

"Well, if you just sing, 'Hand me that ax from the cupboard,' that is not a motet. But if you sing, 'Hand, oh hand, oh hand me, oh hand me that, etc., etc., etc.,' that is a motet."

Of course, I didn't laugh. Then suddenly I realized she had been singing that as one would hear it in a motet by Bach or Palestrina and she had done it in such a fashion that I had to turn around and ask her to do it again. I couldn't believe this was my sister.

Half a day later she was sleeping in my bed, I was sleeping in the bathtub and we all woke up completely snowed in. It was May.

Mrs. von Keudell was enjoying my sister's company and kept saying that all three of us would be worse off if we didn't have her fresh input and her stories from the University of Munich. On the second evening there was a lull in the conversation, and I rather inadvertently brought up the silly motet story. "Oh, yes, Jutta, what was this thing about the motet?" and she did her stunt again. I had no idea what it was that made the people at our table yell with laughter, asking her to do it again and again - at least three times. I don't know whether it was her timing or the way she rolled her eyes - a parody of religious ecstasy, the way she was singing it, or was it the North German dialect that made us laugh so hard and brought people from other tables. She had to do it again and again. This made her vacation. Everybody from then on called her "Motet, darling" and the soldiers who were there convalescing kept asking her to dance whenever there was a dance tea or whatever. When the two weeks were over, Jutta left by herself with lots of gifts in her luggage and a wide grin on her face.

• ◆ •• ◆ •• ◆ •

I reported back to Gehlen at OKH the next day. To my pleasant surprise I found out that my old division, 76th Infantry, would be refitted in France and that I would be assigned to it. I would be reporting on June 1, 1943.

The news coming from the front was so grim that the atmosphere around the department those last few weeks was subdued, to say the least. At times the almost mindless routine of our daily chores came to a halt and we began to catch ourselves staring into space. The tables were turned, the Russians were now coming at our lines with a great superiority in men, tanks, planes and fire power.

Since early spring there had been talk about a German offensive near Kursk, allegedly planned and scheduled, but constantly postponed. Here the Russians had held for some time a salient of seventy-five miles with Kursk at its center. This was a relatively deep indenture of the German defensive lines, which seemed to invite a surgical pincer attack from both shoulders, north and south.

My friends and I discussed this on and off. We had no knowledge whose idea this was, but we had read intelligence reports of Russian preparations for just such an attack. Gehlen had presented various items of information and had some reliable indications that Russians were making defensive preparations, were moving forces there and were building up supplies in anticipation. According to one of our friends in the Operational Dept., Zeitzler had been pushing this project since early April. Allegedly, the army generals involved in this plan had been summoned by Hitler to Munich early in May where most of them had spoken against such a big undertaking. The only consensus they reached was that if adopted, "It must not fail."

Gehlen had done his best to warn the Supreme Command of the Russian preparedness and the resulting absence of the surprise element. The German insistence on this surprise element had played such a big and often decisive role in successful German offensives in the past.

In light of the memoranda leaks and presumptions mentioned above, my friends and I tried to piece together how an offensive move of this scope actually was decided upon. Ritter was able to offer the only available first hand impression as to how such high level tactical decisions were being made. Early on, Ritter, as an orderly officer, had been assigned to accompany two generals on their visit to Hitler at his Wolf's Lair for consultation on a given plan. His description of the experience to Letchert and myself was illuminating:

"When I called for the two Generals at the airport, they were engaged in an animated conversation about the coming discussions with Hitler. They rehearsed their arguments, as it were, by which they hoped to convince Hitler that the planned attack was an unsound proposition, since it had by now lost the element of surprise and the Russians would be well prepared and waiting.

When we drove back to the airport, the same two generals were two different persons. For a while they were sitting in back of the car in silence. Then they started assuring each other that they had done what they could, but it had been to no avail. I heard them abandon their previously firm convictions one after another. I heard expressions like, 'Well, if you look at it his way, he may have a point,' etc. As usual, Hitler must have run over them with one of his well-known monologues".

It wasn't the first time I had heard this kind of story. It meant that the opinion of the professionals on the spot counted for very little. Of course, not knowing enough about the whole situation, I hesitated to make a judgment at this point. I left the headquarters with this not very encouraging insight into our leadership. From now on we had to get used to bad news. El Alamaine, Tunisia, and Stalingrad, whole German armies had been left to destruction.

◆ •• ◆ •• ◆ •

Near the end of May 1943, on my way to Redon, I had to change trains in Paris. I had a few hours to enjoy a beautiful spring day. I saw women in German uniforms walking arm and arm with their French boyfriends, and the German soldiers doing the same with their French girlfriends. I remember asking myself how much longer this illusion would be allowed to last. England was reported to be one huge military encampment, the invasion army getting ready.

On June 1, I arrived at Redon near the coast of France. General Abraham welcomed me then ordered me to report to my sector of the coastal defense where the commander of my regiment, Colonel Günther, would be waiting for me.

"Colonel Günther?" I asked, "The one from Spandau?"

"Yes, Panny, I take it you know each other," he said with a smile and an expression that I had trouble interpreting.

"Günther told me all about May 10, 1940, where you were the very left wing of the German invasion, you with your First Company in particular. How come you had a company?"

"The commander of First Company was on furlough in Germany at the time." I was beginning to feel I needed a transition to some other topic, away from Major Günther and my allegedly heroic deeds. "I was very pleased to find so many familiar faces, Sir. Will returning veterans be assigned to their former companies - at least as much as possible?"

"Yes, as far as I know." He paused as he enjoyed the flavor of his cigar. "Damn fine cigars, these - a present." And then he continued by telling me all about his recent birthday celebration. "All the anti-aircraft guns and the navy's coastal artillery gave me one big booming five-minute salute, would you believe? At 10:00 p.m. from Vannes to St. Nazaire we had some fireworks! Did they tell you about it?"

"No, Sir," I said.

"Fifteen thousand rounds of all calibers went out over the water. How's that for fireworks? The population started packing. They thought the invasion was about to happen."

He looked pleased with himself and proud of his popularity with the anti-aircraft and the coastal artillery people.

"Yes, Panny, we all co-operate, we are one big family here."

Now it was my turn to celebrate his birthday; one cognac followed another served in a huge snifter. In the back of my mind I tried to imagine what quantities 15,000 rounds of munitions would represent. He continued to ask me all kinds of questions about my job under Gehlen including how the Stalingrad disaster could have happened. I think I gave him my honest opinion and did not mince words.

I had to be very careful in my dealings with these ex-police officers. Most of them had a chip on their shoulder, a feeling of inferiority, having first been rejected, then now needed because there was no choice. The shortage of noncommissioned officers and regular officers meant that reactivated police officers suddenly found themselves swept into positions as company or battalion commanders in the framework for the German Army expansion. From a 100,000 man *Reichswehr* in 1933 with wooden guns and dummy tanks, the forces had expanded to three million by 1941. Some of the police officers had tried to stay in the army after World War I, but had been rejected. Now, the army wanted them urgently and they gladly accepted their respective commissions. General Abraham had been one of these *Landespolizei* too, a former policeman from Brandenburg, the same as Günther. From my experience at Spandau, I found these chaps always supported each other, at times to a fault. The chip they often had on their shoulders was understandable, after all they were surrounded by the smooth mannered sons from nobility background. Jokingly, Regiment 9 from Potsdam was called "Count 9" (Graf 9). In my experience, people like the general often behaved as though they had to prove something.

I was left with a bad taste in my mouth. Fifteen thousand rounds! It was as though Stalingrad had never happened, and these people on the French west coast had not realized at all what the consequences of this defeat might be. His questions about the function of Gehlen's intelligence apparatus showed that he had very little idea how vitally important this work was. I knew that no one in the German Army was told more than he needed to know to do his job, but the ignorance displayed by this general was rather disquieting.

•◆• •• ◆• •• ◆• •

On the drive to Vannes, I met a number of my former soldiers. The most pleasing aspect of the trip was a short visit with Wendland, the noncom I had sent to the hospital in January 1941. He was a healthy sergeant now and was assigned to run my first platoon. It was an auspicious beginning. He told me he had been wounded in late fall near Kalach crossing the River Don, and thus he had avoided the Stalingrad encirclement.

Colonel Günther. There he was again - same size glasses, same double chin, and same beer belly. He opened a bottle for the two of us right away and began talking about what had happened to him, his experiences since he left Poland in 1940. He was surprisingly well informed, and was able to tell me with details what had happened to many of our former comrades as well as many of the fellow officers from our peacetime garrison. What was also a pleasant impression was that he did not seem too displeased to have me back under his command. I was beginning to feel more optimistic for a successful third go-around with him.

It was a good thing I had some food after my talk with the general. Colonel Günther, as was always his habit, insisted on "bottoms up" and making sure his guest kept pace with him. Very soon we were back in the winter of The Phony War on the Moselle River, and he kept rambling on about the great time we had. Soon perspiration collected on his forehead, his voice dropped down to a rich *basso profundo* and the discussion invariably turned to his favorite topic which was Colonel Günther. I was so familiar with his scenario I was tempted to finish his sentences, whenever he paused for deep thought. Sure enough, there it came - how he had made me, almost broke me in order to save me, and how his battalion garnered all those well-deserved medals.

"Well-deserved - of course, it took some writing," he said.

After an hour or so, I was finally able to wrestle myself away, giving my need to see Sergeant Wendland as a reason. "Wendland, a great soldier. You are lucky to have him back."

With this positive note, I excused myself and embraced the hot sunshine. I have always loved sunshine, summer or winter, unless, of course, I was filled up with cheap liquor. How fortunate that I was being driven to company headquarters and my billet. My new landlady had some real coffee for me and some home-baked croissants, a second breakfast and very much needed.

When I was finally sober enough to assume command over Eleventh Company, I was able to recognize seventeen of the men as having shared at least some experience with me. They were still young, but they all appeared much older than I remembered them from two years ago. Right away I had a good impression of the platoon leaders, all sergeants, but I had some concern about the sergeant-major, an ascetic looking professional soldier in his forties who immediately prepared me for some unspecified problem he would be facing at home. He appeared restless and at times had trouble concentrating.

The company defended a rather large sector of the coastline. We were spread so thin that there certainly was no depth to our defenses. Thank god! there was really not much going on. The Allied attack on St. Nazaire to the south of us was still on everybody's mind, but our sector remained quiet.

The horse I was assigned to ride was a young, immensely strong, skittish black gelding from a posh stable in Berlin. It was difficult for me to establish any kind of a relationship with him. Had Hans Müller been here, he would have taken good care of the horse, exercised him daily, etc., all of which might have improved my experience with that horse. I could soon tell that the young man who was now in charge was not the expert horseman that Müller had been.

My hopes for a well-planned schedule of training were soon dashed. We were in occupied France and were ordered not to interfere with agricultural production in any way which meant that we were forbidden to cause any damage to the cropland and the roads. We still needed some kind of training: many of the new soldiers had not yet practiced digging a foxhole while lying flat on the ground and under fire, as it were.

The company was an odd mix of seasoned veterans, some of them had just recovered from fairly serious injuries and some were definitely weary of war. Among the new recruits were some older men who had until now been deferred from military service. Their skills had been considered essential for the defense industries. Suddenly, their deferments had been terminated by the *Heldenklau* (*Held*, hero; *klauen*, to steal), which was the nickname for the new authority which sifted out people whose jobs could possibly be handled by invalids or women. I remembered Gehlen saying that Manstein's successes in the summer of '43 did not yield large numbers of prisoners because the army lacked manpower to "close the bag" and masses of Russian stragglers had slipped out. Everyone was well aware of our manpower problems by the time I left the general staff in East Prussia.

When we were not manning our coastal defense perimeter, we were in reserve near Vannes, billeted close by with mostly cooperative French peasants. We had reasonably good relations with the populace until one of my men went berserk and shot a teenaged girl. This tragic incident happened exactly one month after a corporal from 230 Regiment had been convicted of attempted rape, summarily court-martialed and then executed on the spot. In our case, we were not able to find out exactly what had led to the shooting, only that our man was severely disturbed. His statements made no sense, and the French family involved was not much help either when we were trying to find an explanation. However, they were willing to come to the court-martial and testify and so were other witnesses, French and German.

As a matter of fact, I recognized the accused as the same person from my earliest platoon who had been captured May 19 by the French when we had run into a heavily armed stronghold while on reconnaissance. The French had released him after the armistice and he had reappeared in Poland in 1941. At that time, we had to send him to a mental hospital for observation. Now here he was for the third time, I regret to say. I had never been able to fully communicate with him on anything because I was never sure he understood what I was asking. I did not ever find out what happened to him after his arrest.

I learned only a few things about the girl - that she had been brought up by a distant cousin who had become her foster mother, and that both parents allegedly had perished at sea when the girl was four-years-old. That was all. This incident changed the so-called emotional climate in our village for the worse.

Thus, it was a relief when the battalion received orders to be shipped to Coëtquidan, a large military training ground of the French Army. Among other installations, it included the well-known French War Academy, St. Cyr. I was going over these orders the night before we left when a big tan-colored dog appeared at my office door. From the third day here, I had first noticed this boxer on my daily walks past the barbed wire fence that surrounded a nearby compound. Some coastal artillery unit was said to be in position inside, and it was patrolled by Dutch SS volunteers as watchmen. The dog had been free to move around in the compound - not on leash as the other watch dogs had been, so occasionally I had talked to him through the fence.

Was it possible these frequent contacts might have encouraged him to call on me? Of course not, the dog wouldn't know where my office was, but I was so pleased by his visit that, quite irresponsibly, I adopted him on the spot. I should have sat down to think about this, but I'm afraid I didn't. His name was no problem, because I knew it. I had heard the Dutch call him Winston. He could not be blamed if he wanted a change of scenery; his Dutch SS guards treated him just as shabbily as they treated everyone else. Twice I watched them kick the poor dog hard, just as they had been seen kicking some French children who came too close to their field kitchen. It didn't surprise me that no one came looking for him; the SS had at least half a dozen trained police dogs, which they no doubt preferred. God knows how lovable Winston got into that crowd. Anyway, I had a dog again.

The new camp at Coëtquidan was in good shape. It had the appearance of a regular garrison, French style. As in peacetime, each company had its own hut where the men slept. We ate at the central mess hall. Since the whole battalion was concentrated around these five huts, I had a chance to rub shoulders with my fellow officers from the other companies. The battalion commander was a captain about my age and he and I got along fine. The same could be said about my relations with the other company commanders. Wachsmuth, who commanded the machine gun company, had been a corporal in Spandau in '38. I had not seen him since then and was struck by his disillusionment, which was obvious. This first meeting we did not have much time to talk, but he said that before he had been flown out of Stalingrad at the end of December '42, he had seen the worst.

We all worked hard to turn our units into a viable battalion. Colonel Günther was soon showing that he had noticed and appreciated our efforts. Jokingly, I told my friends that he was very good in writing positive reports to his superiors, and I would not be surprised if his hyperbole would end us up in the Daily Situation Report from Berlin.

How right I was! In the end our battalion was singled out as the *Füsilier* Battalion of the division, a high honor on paper. At first, we thought this was meaningless, but in the long run we were given more of the latest weapons and materials than the regular battalions.

The training ground was so spacious, we were able to train with live ammunition. We began on troop and platoon level and then the training was extended to company exercises. We tried to emulate active service standards and use live ammo, whenever that was feasible. I had to apply for a certain space with the camp commandant giving date, time and the details about the purpose of the shoot. The camp commandant gave the okay and took the responsibility for closing down all highways and lanes around and behind the allotted area. Only then could I go ahead, observing strict adherence to safety regulations. Accidents still happened, of course, here at Coëtquidan.

The colonel came unannounced to one of my "wild west" shows, as my boys called them. I'll never know what made my soldiers put up such a tremendous show. It could have been that the adrenaline my anxiety released communicated itself to my platoons. The coordination of forward movement and supporting fire was the point of the exercise. Each platoon in turn had to attack over a sizable terrain, where every 200 yards cardboard enemies suddenly came jumping up. These target figures were manipulated by other soldiers hidden in relatively safe dugouts. It did not faze us for a minute that these cardboard enemies were still wearing German helmets.

Since this exercise was one of Günther's specialties, he was smiling from one ear to the other. In fact, he was so taken with it and at the same time so afraid of accidents that he stopped watching, sat down on the ground, yelling and laughing and beating the dirt with some cudgel he had picked up. In his final critique, he was full of praise, but he commented it got too realistic for him. "These things can get out of hand, you know, and end up in accidents, lengthy court-martials and heaps and heaps of evidence on paper."

Thank god! nothing went wrong. Günther had praised me - I could hardly believe it.

Towards the end of June, we were just finishing exercises at platoon level. I had taken my precious horse with me for once in order to facilitate moving quickly from one platoon to the other. By noon, horse and rider had had quite a workout and were bathed in perspiration. As a matter of fact, the horse was covered in foam and I was looking forward to the end of this morning's work. My strong but skittish gelding and I had finally come to terms, or so I imagined. Returning to our quarters we suddenly heard a tremendous explosion somewhere near the barracks. We never did find out what it was. My horse panicked and bolted, depositing me in the branches of a young birch tree, which happened to soften my fall. Just the same, I had to collect myself and walk home bruised and aching.

When I arrived at the office, one of the sergeants informed me that the sergeant-major had shot himself in bed that morning. I was shocked. I was concerned that I possibly had not taken the warning he had given the day we met. Sergeant-Major Stelter had never mentioned his personal problems to me and I had almost forgotten about them. Had I been delinquent in one way or another? I had the office produce all the rules and regulations applying to such an emergency.

As I looked at the poor chap lying there in his blood, I again had to control the feeling of hostility similar to that I had felt with Friedrich's unnecessary death. We had to collect all his belongings, among them his correspondence. One of his friends told me that the sergeant-major had occasionally let on that his marital problems were too much for him to bear. It turned out he had been married for ten years, most of them happy enough, but that neither one could stand being separated from the other. We found some merciless taunts in her letters directed towards his pride and his manhood.

I signed the report and was about to stretch out for some needed rest when we received orders to move. Within a couple of hours, we received the light khaki uniforms of the Africa Corps and a time table for outfitting every soldier. We were ordered to be ready for entrainment by 10:00 a.m. the following morning. I was furious. I did not consider this company ready for all eventualities and this haste allowed only one conclusion: there was an emergency somewhere.

How many freshly outfitted divisions had I watched arriving in Russia after some hurried transportation, detraining in unfamiliar surroundings and being thrown straight into some crisis situation. Most of them had their baptism of fire before they were even fully assembled and against superior forces. In the process, they lost men and material and never had a chance for a true test of their effectiveness as a fighting unit. The only comforting thought was that we were to fight in tropical uniforms, so that excluded the Russian cauldron.

I realized that since June 1, I had concentrated solely on my company and had registered the big news from the fronts only in passing. Under Gehlen, I had been so spoiled by a constant flood of reports about the big picture that I now felt the absence of information disquieting.

When I finally had a quiet moment, there was a lot to consider. Tunisia had surrendered in the middle of May, so we would not be needed in Africa; however, what about Sardinia, Corsica, Gibraltar, Sicily? On July 7, the German offensive near Kursk had begun after all, but on July 13 Hitler aborted it in light of the fact that Sicily and Italy clearly were about to be invaded by the Allies. As predicted in May, it was a costly mistake. What might have made sense in May, by July was like running into an open knife. The Russians were just waiting, supported in great depth by anti-tank guns, artillery and rocket launchers. I had hoped against hope that Hitler would not undertake this project. It had long been an open secret for the well-informed Russians. Ukraine was crawling with spies, infiltrators and partisans. The sudden invasion of Sicily forced Hitler to shift whole divisions to Italy from Russia and France. We were apparently part of this large slow movement of military transport heading southeast.

In our compartment, we were typing up the rest of the required paper work from the suicide when a former cook from my company, who had escaped from Stalingrad, knocked on the door. He was on his way to his 2nd Battalion section of the train and stopped by to give me some incredible news. He was sure he had seen Ivan at Berdichev, Ukraine! I questioned him extensively again and again and he stuck by his story and explained why he was certain of this dog's identity. While we were talking, I couldn't help noticing poor Winston. He would be eaten alive if Ivan would ever make it back to us.

I immediately wrote to Hildegard, Ivan's former mistress, and told her of the possibility that Ivan could be found and that I was about to send someone to recover him. Hildegard was so happy that she saved the letter and passed it on to my sister who sent it to me in 1993.

The train moved into Monaco, about the same time I had my letter to Hildegard ready to be mailed. We came to a stop at a crossroad where I jumped out and joined a group of civilians who were waiting for the train barriers to go up again. These people didn't seem threatened by my approach, but they certainly showed a guarded curiosity as if to consider, "This wouldn't be the invasion of little neutral Monaco, would it?"

I turned to a young woman who luckily spoke German and she said she wouldn't mind mailing the letter for me. She did not want money for the stamps, but did eagerly accept my two packs of British cigarettes. We parted wishing each other good luck and the train slowly started moving again.

I made it back into the compartment and Wachsmuth scolded me for not getting the girl's name and address. In retrospect, I was not setting a good example for the men who had been watching my illegal escapade and cracking jokes about the Lt. Panny trying to invade a neutral country by *coup de main*. I certainly hoped that they didn't see that I was trying to mail a letter, which was an outright offense against the rules of security.

Moments later, we were in Italy. It wasn't the same Italy I remembered. Mussolini had been voted down by the Fascist Council, arrested by the king, was awaiting court-martial, and Badoglio became prime minister. This was just another news item that I had but barely taken in while I was so occupied with my company. For the Italians, it was the abrupt transition from a dictatorship to a kingdom ruled by the parliamentary system. Needless to say, we were all keen to see what this would mean in terms of our relationship as allies.

We detrained north of Genoa and were billeted in schools and dance halls along the highway leading to the Mediterranean. My host was a director at the state-owned Italian shipping company who had a German wife. She must have left Germany decades ago. Her whining in broken German got on my nerves. Her husband stayed hidden behind a newspaper most of the time. I tried to stay away from them as much as I could.

Our new orders were for us to get in shape for mountain warfare, at least twice a week we had to hike up and down the steep hills around Genoa. Even in khaki uniforms, this was hard labor and I lost a number of boys again through tendonitis. Everybody was sore at the end of the first week.

On the hilltops, we visited with the Italian anti-aircraft units. They invited us to share their rations. Our experience with their food helped to explain the Italian soldiers' lack of enthusiasm. We were served masses of wartime flour - only pasta, barely chewable rigatoni, if I remember correctly, almost indigestible, while the Italian officers had their usual gourmet cuisine prepared for them. All the Italians were hoping for a quick end to their war, here we saw another reason why.

◆ ·· ◆ ·· ◆ ·

On July 25, the German High Command reported heavy air attacks on the city of Hamburg. I felt concerned and definitely thought I should go to find out what happened to my family. Colonel Günther and the Italian commander came by the following day and had a proposal for me that I could not refuse: if I could be back in a week, they would let me go on an emergency furlough. Von der Decken was very understanding and added that there was a daylight attack in Hamburg as we were talking.

Günther suddenly stiffened and asked, "Since when are my battalion commanders listening to the BBC?" We all laughed and I used that added information to up the ante. "How about August 2, that's a whole week of waiting." Günther gave his permission.

Time went very slowly until I finally could take off. Decken had more bad news about an attack on July 27. The mail from home I received was all dated prior to the attack on Hamburg. In spite of myself, I was getting anxious.

•◆•••◆•••◆•

The ride in a very crowded train was a matter of standing most of the way. I ended up shoved against the door to the restroom. I did learn the meaning of the Italian word *permesso* on this trip. I made room for one passenger after another, who opened the door and were startled to see two Sicilian refugees sitting on the floor of the restroom. That was too much for most of them; they closed the door, returned to their seats, suffering in silence.

In Milan more southern Italian refugees squeezed into the train. Allegedly, they were trying to get to some refugee camps in the foothills of the Alps. Once we got to Germany, the trains were running on time and there was enough seating space available. I overheard snatches of conversations, which let me know that the Hamburg population had been encouraged to leave the burning city, particularly families with children.

South of Hamburg the train came to a stop. From then on everybody had to walk. I quickly found the highway and was fortunate to hitch a ride with the TN, the Technical Emergency Organization. The driver, on his way with badly needed plumbing equipment, painted a gory picture of what he had seen so far across the river, "Sodom and Gomorrah was a kindergarten picnic compared to this," he said. "Hamburg is wiped off the map."

We joined a long column of emergency vehicles coming from all over northern Germany. Our truck inched its way across the river Elbe, burning and half sunken ships on either side of the bridge. We came past an area that was closed off altogether - only rescue teams, i.e., soldiers, prisoners of war, inmates of concentration camps and police were allowed inside. The driver explained that all this acreage had been searched for survivors and now had been left to burn itself out. We drove along this sprawling tomb for miles. At Lübecker Strasse, I thanked my driver. All I had to offer him were cheap Italian cigarettes.

Our street, Mühlendamm, and the whole neighborhood lay in ruins. Only a few of the two or three story houses were still standing, some appeared still inhabitable. Near the northern end three four-story houses, ours in the middle of them, were still standing, while the old folks home and the houses behind ours were gone. There was only rubble and smoldering ash heaps all around.

I cursed myself for bringing a suitcase heavy with food and sweets when I knew I had to carry the blessed thing up the four flights of stairs. I had to be very careful finding my footing amidst broken glass and grimy puddles of wet ashes. On the way one door moved slightly ajar, and out came one of the most gossipy neighbors, "Oh, Mr. Panny, what we have been through!" She talked incessantly, while trying to keep up with me. "Your parents got out, I don't know how. They sent word from Poppenbüttel. Your brother was here too, just for a day. He and his comrades in the Labor Service had to work in the ruins."

Our door was not locked. The luggage and the containers, which normally were taken down to the air-raid shelter, were standing in the hallway, untouched. Most windows and doors had been blown out, but there obviously had not been any looting. The kitchen was a mess - no power, no gas, no water. And if there had been a note, my brother must have taken it. There was nothing. I pushed my suitcase under a bed and decided to go and look around.

"Leave the doors open," she said, "That is what we all are supposed to do." I thanked her and she went downstairs.

My mind went back to my visit in '41 when I had offered my parents to use my salary to help them move out of town while the going was good. "Traitor of the family" they had called me then, and "defeatist." That scene was so firmly engraved in my memory. As the air-raid siren had started howling, I watched my father don a huge Czechoslovakian steel helmet he had been issued as a symbol of his importance. With his flashlight around his neck and his shovel in his left hand, he began alerting all the people in the building for them to promptly grab their emergency suitcase and move down to the air-raid shelter. He looked like a shepherd gathering his flock. Puffed up with self-importance, he was enjoying every moment of his power. Only now did I find out that there was more to it than I had anticipated in 1941.

Halfway down the stairs, I met Helga of all people. "What in the world are you doing here?" I asked.

She burst into tears and buried her face on my shoulder. There we stood for a while. It could have been half a minute. "Oh, Vinci, is this the end?"

We sat down on the stairs and smoked some of those stinking Italian cigarettes; the British ones were three flights up in my suitcase. She explained that my brother had been here two days ago and she was hoping to find him again. "He reminds me so much of you." I just smiled to myself, I didn't know how to take this. I felt this was not the time to ask questions about her relationship with my brother, my mother had hinted as much in a letter. Anyway, I was more interested in finding out what had happened.

We walked down the street towards the water and sat down near the bridge. Our former house on Immenhof was gone, so were all the other buildings around, except for the church and the two vicarages flanking it. I suddenly remembered I had a flask of god-awful Italian brandy. I brought it out.

Helga talked haltingly, often correcting herself, "The attack that first night, you see, that was bad enough, oh no - there was a false alarm that noon on Saturday, July 24 - but shortly after midnight the planes came by the hundreds. When I went down to the shelter, I noticed our search lights were acting in a very confused manner, different from earlier attacks."

"That night most of the damage was incurred on the western side of the river, except for Barmbeck. The open-air zoo was destroyed and they were hunting wild animals, many injured, all over the city. I heard that 2,000 people died that night. Transportation, water, power and gas were locally out of action."

"That Sunday we woke up to find no sun, the otherwise bright sunlight couldn't pierce the smoke. That afternoon before 3:00 p.m., about 100 American bombers came to attack the harbor and the eastern part of the city. There was no night attack that Sunday. July 26 went off without any disturbance. Around midnight on July 27 came the most devastating attack - right here all the way up to Wandsbeck. That's when the fire storm was created."

"Firestorm?" I had never heard of such a thing.

"Yes, you see there was no wind, so the heat of this huge conflagration went straight up as it would in your fireplace or blast furnace. All the small single fires became one huge inferno. The suction of this phenomenon was so powerful that whole trees were picked up and sucked into the cauldron and so were many people who were trying to find a way out."

"What about the shelters?" I wanted to know.

"Most of them got so hot, people died just sitting or lying down in them. Oh, my god! Mother and I just wrapped wet clothing around our heads and dashed those 200 yards to the water and sat shivering under the willow tree. Afterwards, we were told that six square miles just vanished that night."

"There were two more attacks, one on July 29 at midday by the Americans, and another night attack on August 2. Most people had left the town by that time."

"What about this phosphorous I've heard about?"

"Please, it's really hard to talk about it, it's too horrible." She swallowed hard and covered her face with her hands. Her explanation came in a monotone. She was breathing heavily. "You see, it splashes on impact. It sticks to anything, metal, wood, concrete, clothing, and your hair and skin. As long as it doesn't get oxygen, it will just sit there, but once you take your afflicted skin out of the water, it flares up. You start burning. These unfortunate people came screaming down past our street to reach the water - the only place they could find temporary respite. You could see their heads bobbing on the surface. Soon they became delirious, pleading for help. There was no help and the longer they stayed in the water, the more their skin started to blister and fester."

"We rowed out and gave them water to drink, but I could not go on. I could sometimes see the raw flesh. Some went insane cursing God, cursing Hitler, cursing their families. Late that day, we all had to leave the Alster River and military persons began moving out in boats mercy killing. I can still hear the shots and the skull crushing sounds when the ammunition had run out."

She wept quietly. We sat there smoking and emptying that little flask.

Later, we went to her apartment. Her mother had left her a note that she and her sister had left town. Helga promised me she would do the same.

I don't know how many hours I walked around. That evening, I tried our flat again. My parents were back. I had never seen them in such dazed despair. Father did feel proud to have found a rowboat and to have rowed the two of them up the river to get away from the heat. They did find some friends to stay with. I didn't feel like talking much. What could I say? My parents were plainly traumatized to a state near panic. Any loud report outside or the sound of a siren -any unusual noise - made them jump and tremble uncontrollably. In one week they had seen more suffering, more massed destruction of human lives, than I had experienced out in Russia in all those months of warfare.

Did I come on a special furlough to Hamburg to be humbled in the sight of these two-elderly people, my parents, in their pitiful state of helplessness? Not that I could have done much, I had to leave them as I had promised. I had to leave them in the knowledge they would get more and more of the same as the war would grind on. I realized that my proposal in 1941 to help them get out of Hamburg was just as unrealistic then as it would be now, for my father had to do his job at the bank. The alternative would have been unemployment and an uncertain welfare.

The trip back to Genoa was slow agony. All my immature criticism of my parents and family, the years I had spent hating and detesting my vainglorious abusive father or pitying my hapless mother, who throughout her marriage had allowed herself to be trampled on by Father, it all passed through my mind over and over. I felt I should ask their forgiveness.

I understood something new now. I had just seen what was left of my parents, two unfortunate human beings who had gone through so many disappointments, their hopes in China ending in internment and forced repatriation. Back in Germany, they had to endure the runaway inflation, the food shortages, only now to be exposed to all the suffering our town had to go through.

What right did I as a fourteen-year-old boy have to look down on his old man as an opportunist. I had been disgusted with his joining the Nazi party, but he had joined the party to be able to feed a family of six. My father, a 'fraidy cat' in many respects, had gone up into the attic on three different occasions during the air attack to extinguish and neutralize incendiary bombs. I now knew what it took to do what he had done.

Up until now the other tenants in the house never had liked my father because of his "uppity" attitudes. "I do not really belong in this milieu," was his claim all along, and if he didn't say so it was implied by his manner. Now, they all respected him for having been instrumental in saving these houses and their property. I still hadn't forgotten the frequent beatings and injustices, but I knew now our juvenile elitism at the time was just as wrong and detestable. If my belief in my own survival was the natural, albeit naive, attitude for a soldier to take, so he was entitled to his childlike trust in Hitler to find a way out and have the war somehow end well.

It was a long sad train ride. When I got sick of thinking about my family, I thought about the dog. Would I really have the guts, irresponsible really, to send someone to Ukraine for Ivan? What if something happened to the man? Wasn't I meddling with somebody's fate?

I had left my parents all the food I brought and wished them well. I was so glad now to have seen them alive. I could not help smiling when I remembered my father turn boastful again and describe how he had neutralized three incendiary bombs in the attic.

I made some inquiries to find a telephone connection to Berlin. No luck. Tutta, JR's wife, was gone, so was JR's father. I took the first available train back south, leaving my home town to an uncertain future. On the way, I could see large numbers of rescue workers protected by gas masks and rubber suits moving about, digging for more victims. The stench of decomposition, quicklime and the acrid smell of still-blowing ashes were my last impression.

The Italians were getting restless in anticipation of some change. They had not been told where Mussolini was, or if he was still alive. They certainly were aware of the fact that more and more German units had come across the Brenner Pass. Sicily was now in Allied hands. There was strong pressure by the Russians in the Ukraine, even Kharkov was threatened again.

I looked through the company list to find someone from East Germany - East Prussia, if possible. One of my best runners was a young chap with rosy cheeks called Karger, fresh out of high school, which he had completed in the expectation of later studying medicine. He was one who had his family in Danzig. I cautiously approached him to find out whether he would volunteer to take his furlough now and take a detour in returning via Berdichev. I would write him a ticket to travel by Warsaw, Lublin, Rovno, Zhytomyr to Berdichev. He would approach the station master, who allegedly had Ivan, with a letter from me and a photo of the dog. Then, he would return by way of Lwow, Krakow, Ostrowa, Brno, Vienna, Salzburg, Innsbruck, Milan, to Genoa.

When I told him of my plan, his face lit up and he wanted to leave to pack his bag right away. I immediately had pangs of conscience. Berdichev was about 1,000 kilometers behind the German lines, but traveling the occupied Poland or Ukraine was not without risk. There was now danger of sabotage, train accidents, or attacks by groups of partisans. The boy came back with some question or other and kept waxing effusively about how happy his parents would be to see him, a totally unexpected reunion because there was no way he could notify them in time, and they would understand my reasons for the detour on the way back. So he left the same evening with a letter to the station master and the photo of Ivan.

I don't remember the wording of my request to the station master. I think I tried to describe how I met the dog and under what circumstances Ivan and I had experienced the war together so far and how much the dog meant to me. So, if he was the kind man who had taken care of Ivan after the Stalingrad catastrophe, I would appreciate it if he would allow the dog to come back to me. Furthermore, if he would identify himself, I could thank him more personally for his generosity. I would be happy to reimburse him for any expenses he might have incurred. I knew he had no expenses for feeding Ivan because everybody was living on army rations, but I was willing to do the proper thing.

The boy had left on cloud nine. I spent a rather restless night and I was tempted to call the whole thing off while I could possibly still reach him. When I told Wachsmuth, he laughed in my face and said, "Forget it. You would only embarrass yourself."

On September 7, we were put on alert, took live ammunition and moved to a schoolhouse close to downtown Genoa. With this same order came a letter, which was sealed and not to be opened until a given cue word was given. The schoolhouse was in Sampierdarena. This was the part of Genoa close to the waterfront. Not knowing what this was all about, I gave strict orders to look noncommittal and refuse to be provoked. I had seen quite a number of intoxicated mobs running up and down the streets.

On the street, a kind old gentleman came by and told me what the uproar was all about. An armistice between Italy and the Allies had been announced and there were rumors of British and American landings in southern Italy. Salerno and Taranto were mentioned and so was another landing on the southern tip of Calabria. I thanked the gentleman, and the minute I did Genoa seemed to explode.

We watched, weapons at the ready, how this waterfront was celebrating the armistice. I took great pains to avoid clashes with the drunken mob. Whenever a group approached our boys, I joined with the group to ensure nobody on either side would do anything untoward. In some cases that meant accepting a glass of red wine and whatever else they had to drink and wishing them luck. The populace was milling up and down the streets and I didn't blame them in their naive conviction that the war was almost over.

At dusk the word came. Decoded it said, "Sixteen sailors will report to you before 8:00 pm. At 3:30 a.m., Eleventh Company will move down to the waterfront guided by the sailors. You will disarm and take over all ships and Navy installations in the western half of Genoa Harbor." There followed a detailed description of the demarcation line between my half and Tenth Company's perimeter.

So, this was the end of a very uncomfortable alliance between Italy and Germany. We felt we were being part of history in the making. We proceeded as ordered and found no resistance on the way to the harbor, although we picked up a few celebrators who might have had a pretty good idea that ours was a rather unusual way of celebrating the armistice. It is still a mystery to me how we managed to walk up and down these piers, enter each ship, wake up the officer on duty and have him help us round up his crew. Once or twice somebody tried to reach for his holster or gun, but one warning shot into the ceiling solved the problem. All our victims were still drunk or had such a hangover that they were cooperating easily.

On each ship, we left one of our sailors and two of our soldiers. With the balance of my men we arrived at the huge naval installation. We couldn't tell what the source was. It was possible that the anti-aircraft installations on the surrounding hills were still celebrating, or they could be fighting off the German intruders, or the German intruders had taken over the batteries and were doing some range finding, familiarizing themselves with the Italian anti-aircraft weaponry. So, I was on edge too because this could be the beginning of a free-for-all for the possession of the harbor of Genoa.

I wasn't very nice to the guards and the officer in charge. We disarmed them quickly. But then there was a fortunate turn: a white-haired, highly decorated officer came out, wanting to know what this shooting was all about. We struck up a conversation in German. He said he had worked to supply Rommel, lost many of his ships to submarines. I noticed he had the German Iron Cross First Class to show for it. With tears in his eyes, he apologized for the shame of the Italian nation and the Italian Navy in particular. I refused to accept his weapon and asked him about the situation within the installation.

"There is a total breakdown of order and discipline," he said. "There are about 2,000 sailors and technicians and, if you trust me, I'll try and talk to them."

I agreed, and he went back in together with one of the guards and the German sailor who spoke fluent Italian. The gentleman came back after twenty-five minutes and assured me that there were no hotheads insisting on shedding blood for or against Mussolini - or the king, for that matter.

Negotiating with a *soldateska* and 2,000 unruly Italians made me feel sort of giddy, but I trusted the captain and we found consensus. If they left all weapons and all contraband military gear, we would frisk them and release them to their families. Had I insisted on keeping them all as prisoners, I would have been in deep trouble. Since I had no contact with the battalion or the regiment and I had only two machine guns and fifteen men left, I felt it was a good bargain.

With the captain standing at my side, we released the whole bunch and retained only the captured ships we had taken over. Later, the adjutant of the battalion commander tried to give me hell over the phone. He would have loved to have added 2,500 prisoners in his report, but in the end I was proven right - even the battalion and the regiment had to let go of all their prisoners. Our part in this *coup de main* was even mentioned in the order of the day by the commander of the 76th Division.

◆ ◦ ◦ ◆ ◦ ◦ ◆ ◦

On September 10, we moved to our new headquarters, the office pavilion of some coal company from where I had a good view of the western half of Genoa's harbor. Disarming or even fighting a former ally is not a pleasant task. Many Italian friends were shaken up badly, especially those people who were anti-communist, had lost friends or relatives in Russia and now despaired of the crusade against Moscow.

In the afternoon, a young woman came by offering to lead us to the armories and secret hoarding places of the police. She proudly pronounced herself anti-communist and anti-Badoglio. She wanted no money or reward, just a piece of parachute silk for her wedding dress and she knew exactly where to find it. She kept the date we made and we were able to gather quite a number of weapons and thousands of rounds of ammunition. In one armory, a policeman voluntarily added 200 sets of first-quality male underwear to our collection, a bit of generosity our interpreter was not able to explain to me.

After two days, we had the bad news that Mussolini was rescued by German paratroopers. My boys were crushed - our former ally, then enemy, now friend again. He was flown to see Hitler and put in charge of the republican, that is to say fascist, government of Italy. Rumors were flying of impending American landings near or in Genoa. Frankly, had this been tried, an invasion force of reasonable size could have landed successfully since only one company was defending the western half of Genoa. We were totally out-manned. Our defense perimeter was much too wide for just one division.

We now found out that some Italians did put up resistance somewhere near Rome, and that thousands of Italian prisoners of war were being sent across the Alps to become slave laborers. All of this was none of my concern. I couldn't afford to think about it. Our job was to guard the harbor and specifically ships or shiploads that were intended for Switzerland. Twice a day we had to ferry food and supplies to the platoon defending the outer wall, the breakwater protecting the harbor.

The battalion commander went on his furlough, so I had to play his role for a fortnight. His headquarters was in the Olivetti "high-rise," six whole stories of it, so now I was billeted in a flat with access to a roof garden, while my new lieutenant looked after the company.

The adjutant, a law student reserve officer, was another Blümel type, a yes-man like the adjutant of the former Regiment 203. Daily he brought some paper work to my desk. One day, I found a top-secret folder containing the evaluation of First Lieutenant Graf, whom I barely knew personally. This was my first experience doing anything like this and I found the procedure amazing. His file held every detail of his career, from being a regular noncom to his present rank. I had to read the whole file and then proceed to pen my own "unbiased" opinion.

I rang up the adjutant and asked, "Are you serious?"

"Yes."

"Is this the way the Captain is doing it?"

"Yes, this is routine."

"Are you telling me that all German officers are evaluated this way?"

"Yes, sir," he answered, "every one of them."

After a moment I said, "Now I have an idea why my own advancement to the rank of captain is slow in coming. If you are a 'black sheep of the battalion' the first time you are evaluated, you remain a black sheep all your life."

"Not necessarily," he answered, "but I will grant you we are not talking about unbiased opinion."

I found this procedure hard to believe, and decided not to do the evaluation on the prescribed date, but rather leave it to the battalion commander to do it in his own time once he got back. I wrote him a note to that effect. When he did come back, I apologized and he nodded and said, "You have a good point. I remember how nonplussed I was when I had to do this for the first time."

A few days later I became a captain, but it was not connected in any way to this telephone conversation.

* ◆ • • ◆ • • ◆ •

With the fall, there came stormy weather. One morning the battalion commander woke me at 7:30 a.m. I was not too pleased, I had a hangover.

"Didn't you get the storm warning?"

"No, Sir." He apologized and said something about a communication mix-up, for which I was not to blame, but then he continued saying, "We have definite reports about soldiers being swept into the harbor basin in ours as well as in the 2nd Battalion's perimeter. I think you should check that out."

I took only a few minutes getting dressed and drinking ersatz coffee and sending for the most athletic among my runners, without knowing what had caused people to drown. We arrived at the wharf in minutes, took a canister with hot coffee and a first aid kit and some drinking water. We shared this load, but his was the larger one because he had the radio in his backpack. Even crossing over to the sea wall was bringing me close to seasickness. I hated inflatable dinghies all my life and here I was paddling with these ridiculous paddles for thirty-five minutes to cross over a stretch of 120 yards or so.

The sea wall or breakwater protecting the east half of Genoa harbor was a long concrete structure. On the ocean side it was at least twenty feet above the water level, toward the harbor that was reduced to about ten feet, so behind the sea wall there was a walking space ten feet lower than the crest. Along the water's edge, there was a row of pillars. My first impression was that these were intended for tying down boats or vessels, but they were too massive for that purpose, at least two feet in diameter. On this day, they were there to save our lives.

We had barely climbed up the rope ladder to the walking space level when a huge wave smashed across the crest of the wall almost wiping us back into the harbor basin. The noncom in charge of the pillbox watched anxiously to see whether we could find something to hang on to. This was the problem now. We had to move a mile to the east protected by the sea wall, and yet whenever one of these waves came smashing down we had to make sure we were hugging one of those pillars to stay anchored. We watched this phenomena for some time and decided to go singly. We would have to make our own decisions right after one of these waves had spent itself, run to the next pillar and hug it in anticipation of the water. I would go first.

The minute I had draped my arms around the concrete of the first pillar, there it came. Without the steel helmet, my head was shoved against the stone. Masses of water pressed down on my rib cage so vehemently that I barely had the strength to breathe. As soon as I could, I turned to my partner and yelled, "Press your cheek against the stone before it hits, and take a deep breath if you have time." He yelled back, "All right, sir." He didn't sound too confident. He had seen me disappear under the towering wave and come out of it with a bloody nose.

Somehow we reached the midway bunker where we met the six frightened defenders who swore they had seen the supply runner of the divisional artillery vanish in the harbor basin. The poor fellow had to carry a heavy back pack, which must have dragged him down. Half-an-hour later, our own battalion supply runner had come by, had left them their breakfast, and got careless on the way back. He too was swept into the drink. By that time, however, there was a powerful Navy vessel nearby, which was able to pick him up. He was safe, they said.

After a while we were ready to go on for the last leg, at least 500 meters of racing from pillar to pillar. The further out we went, the more violent the water behaved. My runner waved confidently each time he did hang safely on to his pillar, but I could see from a distance his cheekbone looked red and blue. We reached the outer edge. It was a roomy concrete pillbox where I found my men huddled inside in low spirits. They too had watched some drownings, mostly on the eastern side of the harbor.

One boy had a broken arm. He was the first one of the group who had been smashed against the pillar. He was quiet and did not complain when I told them we did not have any sedatives with us. After some time we had the radio working and I asked for a ship to bring a relief crew, take our invalid and the rest of us back to the headquarters. "No ship can come close to the wharf at the present time. Please hang on," was the reply.

So we spent a long day sharing our meager rations and drinking coffee or water. These were mostly soldiers from Berlin and Brandenburg and the biggest vessel they had seen was a pleasure boat on some nearby river. For most of them this day was a harrowing experience, none of us had any idea of the force and the weight of water in motion. Soon the topic switched to uncles and relatives who were sailors and how generally one had taken their stories with a grain of salt.

In one way we all agreed that the last thing we had expected from World War II was to sit in a wet stinking concrete pillbox for at least the daylight hours, being challenged by one thundering wave after another, feeling the breakwater and the pillbox shiver slightly each time. My runner said the final word: "If the Americans want to land here now, they can have me." Of course, he was from Berlin. By evening, a boat came by and brought us to safety.

Autumn in Genoa. At last I had some time to look around and get to know the city in the full autumn colors, a beautiful sight. I made some friends and they showed me restaurants where you could still get relatively decent food. We contacted a local variety show; the artists were pleased to entertain the troops once a week. I always made sure that the front and rear entrances to the theater were kept under surveillance, just in case an Italian resistance movement might spring up. Rumors were still flying that the Allies would land in Genoa any time. We heard reports of impending landings and suspicious movements out in the open sea.

I felt pangs of conscience about Karger and the dog. Everything being equal, they should have been here I thought. The boy left in late August and this was early October. Instead of Karger, Brunner reported for duty. He was the man who looked after my things at Gehlen's department in East Prussia. As a matter of fact, he had half a dozen officers to keep clean and tidy. He registered my surprise with a grin and explained that he had been asked where he wanted to join the front-line and he had opted to follow me to Italy. He was a remarkable young man who had taken a number of educational courses to get himself out of the proletarian environment in Vienna.

We had often talked about the "Red" district of Vienna where his family had been living for generations. Shortly before Hitler took over, his father had been killed by the fascist troops that had run the country since the end of the twenties. He still was a Marxist at heart, but he loved Germany with or without Hitler. I felt very pleased and assigned him to my headquarters where he was only too happy to again make sure that I get up in time in the morning. No mean feat.

Räder müssen rollen für den Sieg. You could read this slogan in every German train station - "Wheels must roll for victory," a reminder to the public to avoid unnecessary travel. Here I was worrying about Karger and the dog. The thought was in the back of my mind day in, day out - all the more since the Russians had crossed the Dnieper River and were making progress in the direction of Berdichev.

Then, one afternoon, the door opened and there they stood, Karger and Ivan. For a moment, I was speechless trying to control my emotions. The same could not be said about Winston. In response to Ivan's snarl, he took one look and started towards Ivan to attack him. I was fortunate in just catching Winston's hind leg before he could reach the intruder. It would have been mayhem. Many male dogs have the scars to show for mixing with Ivan - in Munich, in Hamburg, in Berlin, wherever we went. It was just as fortunate that Karger had not let go of Ivan's leash either. He understood my hand motion, retreated, and closed the door behind him. This gave me a chance to put Winston into my bedroom and phone Wachsmuth to send someone for his new dog Winston.

Now Karger came back in and stood there watching my tearful reunion with Ivan. He and the dog had lost a lot of weight on this trip, but both were in good shape and while Ivan and I were howling and hugging great big tears came down the corporal's cheeks, so moved was he by this spectacle.

Wachsmuth came himself and he too was quite emotional. "I always wanted a dog with me out here," he said, "This is too good to be true." He thanked me over and over and took his new friend back to the heavy machine gun company and out of Ivan's reach.

Karger was most enthusiastic about getting a chance to give me a day by day account of his odyssey. He produced a note from his parents who expressed their happiness about this unexpected reunion and another note from the station master in Berdichev who wrote he had been much concerned with what to do with Ivan. It appears he had to sell his geese and follow a transfer order to Poznan where an office job was waiting for him. He would have to live in a railway hostel where pets were not welcome.

Karger said that most military police shook their head when they were reading his traveling papers and some expressed their wonderment as to what an important dog this must be, but nobody gave him any trouble. He shared his daily rations with the dog and Ivan enjoyed some of the Red Cross soup offered at the stations. When he had found Ivan he was in a moveable compound, sections of chain-link fence around a large flock of geese, whom Ivan apparently was responsible for protecting. Karger didn't specify against what, there probably were foxes around or hungry people. Ivan had always hated geese and ducks, but I had never seen him tempted to chase or attack them. The station master was impressed with the whole undertaking. Speaking as a railway man, he found the names in Karger's itinerary impressive, but then he added that he himself had no scruples either, making good money on the side by raising and selling geese mostly for the black market.

Ivan and I took some walks and I kept him on the leash just in case. On one of these walks, the battalion sent a sidecar motor bike to bring me to a quick conference at battalion headquarters. I gave Ivan's leash to one of my men saying I would be back in a few minutes. We drove off and covered about a mile when suddenly Ivan appeared on the asphalt next to me. I stopped the bike, since I didn't want this spectacle to continue into downtown Genoa. But then I noticed that he was limping, the soft skin on his paws had been badly damaged by the run on the road. There was nothing for it, I took him on my lap, and so we arrived at Major Günther's meeting.

"Where in the hell did you get that dog? Isn't that your - what was his name?"

I apologized and explained why the dog had been with me on the bike.

Günther inquired afterwards, "Whatever happened to that fat Boxer?"

Wachsmuth piped up, "I have him, Sir."

Günther, "Where is he, didn't you bring him?"

"I didn't bring him; the two dogs don't get along."

Günther said, "Well, I've seen Panny's dog get along famously with the little Schnauzer of his company commander, but this is not what this meeting is about, is it? I have to apologize to you, gentlemen, there was a report of a sizable naval force approaching Genoa and I was supposed to take immediate steps. Turned out that this report was false and I didn't have time to tell you."

So I took my invalid dog back to the sidecar and home. Since the veterinarian was not available, we made little bandage shoes for him. Of course, he pulled them off as soon as he could and started licking his paws. Ivan's paws healed quickly, just in time for another train ride -back to the east, where he had just come from.

* ⬧ ⁘ ⬧ ⁘ ⬧ *

We received winter clothes, turned in our tropical uniforms and gear, and were ordered to entrain October 18. We all had a pretty good idea what that meant, the daily army bulletin spoke of heavy fighting in Ukraine approaching Berdichev. The only alternate route would have been Yugoslavia, which, to my mind, would have been even more unwelcome. I had followed the daily reports from there while I was working with Gehlen. The loyalties in this war theater changed weekly, if not daily. If a German unit was engaged in fighting Tito's partisans, they could very well have the Chetniks, the Serb loyalists, assist them. There was no reliable expectation as to how long this relationship would continue. Switching sides was a matter of mood, almost, except between Croats and Serbs. They were always killing each other. With the collapse of the Italian Army, everybody helped himself to vast stores of Italian weapons, ammunition and equipment. The few German forces now had to be spread over the whole of Yugoslavia since the Italians had been shipped as prisoners of war to Germany. In other words, it was a terrible mess, and being on the defense against heavily armed civilians is the last thing I would like to see a division involved in.

While passing through Vienna we heard that Genoa had been attacked by air with heavy damage and casualties on the railway goods station where we had entrained. The temperature dropped the moment we crossed into Ukraine. We took great care to keep Ivan and Winston apart. Every time the train came to a halt, we took turns at letting one of the dogs have a short walk. Wachsmuth was careful not to let Winston off his leash.

Unfortunately, during one of those stops at 2:00 a.m., one of Wachsmuth's men made the mistake to play with the dog off the leash. When the train started, relatively abruptly, the soldier made it back, but Winston had taken off after some creature and that's where we had to leave him. Wachsmuth was inconsolable and blamed himself for leaving the dog to someone else. He was sure whoever would find the dog would eat him. So there was no more dog problem, we could concentrate on World War II.

We detrained near Krivoy Rog, I vaguely remember. On the way to the front, we saw numerous Russian tanks, trucks and guns rusting away. As we were moving in a northeasterly direction, we could see that Manstein's counterattack some time ago must have cost the Russians dearly.

I don't remember much about time or geography because while the battalion was in reserve, I was singled out to leave my company in the excellent hands of Lt. Graf and form a mobile staff, one car and a motor back, to explore the terrain behind the line to set up defensive perimeters on the battalion and regimental level. I have yet to find out why General Abraham picked me for this task. If I had any expertise, it was in intelligence work. I certainly felt barely competent to make such vitally important decisions as defensive lines. If I were a battalion commander assigned to one of these, I possibly would have entirely different ideas and would not enjoy doing my job along somebody else's tactical judgment.

Again, I saw very little of my company or Ivan. This went on for weeks, while we were still in reserve. I took my assignment seriously and found the thought remarkable that Abraham had the guts to have me reconnoiter defensive positions in the rear. This was forbidden by Hitler in more than one case. "I forbid such thinking. Not one step back!" was his motto, only to be forced to give ground anyway, more often than not.

Early in November, we had our first cold snap. As I was afraid would happen, one morning my bladder let go again, as I was leaving the car. I had warned Brunner that this might come about again, so he had a second set of everything ready for me including the winter jump suit. With best wishes and two days of army ration, I was sent by car to a urologist who worked in a hospital near Headquarters, 6th Army. Same urological procedure, same diagnosis: Bad Wildungen, special hospital for urology. The doctor recommended to report there right after Christmas.

I was allowed to lead my company into its sector on the line four days later. I had to hand it over to Lt. Graf and report to General Abraham as the new orderly officer at Division 76 Headquarter. It so happened the present 01 (orderly officer number one) had overstayed his welcome by driving everybody crazy with his anxiety and resulting over-reactions. Half of all the false alarms in Genoa had originated at his desk, I was told.

Since there was a shortage at the division staff, Brunner made the move with me. It was typical for Abraham to deduce if Brunner took care of six officers in the Gehlen Department, surely he would be the best person to do the same thing here. His services were appreciated by my boss, the first general staff officer (henceforth called IA by my roommate, Bert), and by the IB (the major in charge of logistics). Brunner had used his long service in Russia to become quite fluent in Russian, so he was also used as an interpreter when it came to interviewing Russian prisoners.

I became the assistant to Major Klennert, the IA, with whom I shared many friends at OKH. This time I did the telephone reporting to the Army Corps every night and from there the report was passed on to Army Group and OKH. I was sometimes tempted to add a little personal touch when I knew the person who would receive it.

The reports came regiment by regiment and, of course, our *Füsilier* Battalion. Bert, a young artist from Cologne, became a very close friend and we helped each other through many hairy situations. He made friends with Ivan so fast, I had a few small pangs of jealousy.

Once the morning report was over with, I still had to travel around reconnoitering prospective defense lines to fall back to. I had to check bridges, god knows for what purpose - we didn't have any tanks - and record fording possibilities in rivers. We stayed in a small hut, sharing it with a family. The very attractive daughter was not having any attempts of clumsy male approaches and she constantly protested when our runners left magazines or pin-ups lying around, "*Nix cultura*," was her verdict. (No culture.) She loved Ivan and helped Brunner look after him whenever I had to be away.

My company reported that they had found my horse with a bullet in its neck in the company animal compound. A crazy paymaster from the artillery was hunting, shooting from his moving vehicle at anything that stirred. Of course, we had to destroy the horse.

Shortly before December 15, they put me on the train back to Germany. Another very short stint in the Russian winter. This time I had to leave the dog again, but since Brunner was due to take a furlough pretty soon, it was arranged that he would bring my luggage and the dog to my new address. The railroad trip was much shorter now, we were west of the Dnieper River.

I reported to the hospital, left my luggage and made it just in time for the traditional Friday before Christmas party at Alice Pollitz's flat. There weren't too many people. Three of the women were wearing black, having lost their husbands in Russia, but Alice Pollitz arranged for such a comfortable ambiance that we sat and talked and ate and drank until 2:30 a.m. when we all went to the air-raid shelter. It was a short attack, possibly by mistake. Since we couldn't find out whether the subway was functioning, I walked two of the women home and came back to my parents' flat at Mühlendamm Strasse.

Since Alice Pollitz was about to leave town to be with her sister, I couldn't be with her. I did not want to stay over Christmas with my parents and endure the heart-wrenching sight of their nervously waiting for the next shoe to drop.

◈ ◦ ◦ ◈ ◦ ◦ ◈ ◦

It was a first-class sanitarium, in peacetime a world renown spa. The doctors were very communicative and admitted that frankly they wouldn't know what to do with me at this point. One of them, whose sense of humor appealed to me from the beginning of our acquaintance, jokingly said that he knew a colleague who would prescribe leeches in such a case. I was given a single room after a few days, because somebody had complained about my nightly outbursts, always including an indictment of the Air Force and Herman Göring.

A young general staff major in the room next door had heard about this and we became fast friends. His name was Kuhn and he was an assistant in the Organizational Dept., which was mostly concerned with logistics. We had long talks about the hopelessness of the military situation, and we had a reciprocal dinner arrangement where we invited each other to one of the downtown restaurants where we had good food and good wine.

Kuhn had a telephone connection, which I used to approach Gehlen to tell him I was available again while I was waiting for an operation. The colonel was very responsive over the phone, but did not have a vacancy at the moment, so he said he would talk to General Heusinger and I would hear from him. Two days later I received a transfer order, and a week later I was back in Mauerwald and posted with Major von Bomhard. It was again the Army Group North Ukraine with which I had to work. By this time, they were defending the Polish border. My own 6th Army was in deep trouble in the south hanging on to Moldovia. The old man on the River Pruth, my "friend for life," had been right after all. The Romanians would lose Moldavia any minute.

The last weeks in hospital, Kuhn and I spent arguing the case against the German Army, taking turns in the roles of the proverbial "devil's advocate." He was well informed through his daily telephone connections. Our conversations were a useful preparation for my new temporary position at the Operational Department, Op. Abt.

It was during this time, I learned that Göring had lost over 1,000 fighter planes this January. Field Marshall Rommel was appointed Commander of Army Group "B" in France, north of the Loire River. Mussolini's son-in-law, Count Ciano, was convicted of treason and shot in Verona. The Americans landed at Anzio and at Nattuno, and the Red Army was approaching the Polish border; while the south of the Ukraine and Nikopol were still in German hands. As a result of the rigid defense tactics of the high command, 54,000 were encircled near Tscherkassy. The official daily report just mentioned something about a heroic defense.

I enjoyed Kuhn's insights. He came from a motorized tank unit and was able to give me striking examples how the former Blitzkrieg became so successful. Their motto was, "Boot 'em, don't spatter 'em." Now these units were used merely as mobile fire brigades wherever there was trouble, instead of bringing them to bear in a concentrated operation with two or three divisions together. The much-depleted infantry divisions could not prevent Russian breakthroughs anymore; their meager forces were stretched too far. By and large, the tanks were coming too late and in insufficient numbers. Mobile tactics were replaced by rigid "last stand" thinking.

The Tcherkassy pocket made a desperate breakout. Only 30,000 men made it, six divisions were lost with all their equipment. The daily army report now called it a defensive victory - the losses were not mentioned.

Kuhn had to leave to join General von Zielberg and his 28th Ranger Division. I missed him. I was expecting Jutta to come visit me and meet Kuhn, it wasn't to be; however, I had other visitors. One day when I looked out of the window, there was a wooden two-wheeled cart, the kind railway porters use. It was being pushed in our direction by a soldier and, by the look of it, pulled by a dog. It wouldn't be - it couldn't be - yes, it was Sepp Brunner, Ivan and my luggage. I excused myself, breaking off the conversation with our head nurse who said, "Of course, go." She came to the window and could see and hear us from behind the glass.

Ivan and I celebrated our umpteenth reunion and Brunner was watching with some self-satisfaction. The nurse soon gave me a stern lecture on clinical procedures in the hospital, which did not include a dog's presence. After she had taken a good look at Ivan, she relented. He was allowed to stay in my room as long as I took him out the back stairs and did all my medical discussions with the doctor in his office.

I offered Brunner a place on the couch in my room, but he refused with thanks. He had made other arrangements.

"Fast work," I couldn't help remarking.

"Big deal, sir," he said with a sly expression, "When I came by with that dog, no problem."

The head nurse shook her head and left the room. Our Red Cross helper, Renata, happened to bring my ghastly quantum of spa water and witnessed the whole scene. The taste of the water reminded me of the smell of a broken water main back home in Hamburg. That comes with being in a hospital in a famous spa - I had to drink their water. Anyway, she put down the tray with the water and knelt right down to Ivan. He was flattered and responded with his soft whine and licked her ear. As a result, Renata insisted that Ivan and I come and visit their farm a few hours outside Wildungen over the weekend.

On Saturday, the three of us took the short trip to Elmau by slow passenger train. Renata explained the source of the devastation we saw, while passing through the countryside. On May 16, 1943, the British in a night attack with special torpedo bombs had destroyed the Eder and Möhne Dams. The special bombs they used were built to sink down to the base of the dams and explode from the bottom up. She said it was a water catastrophe of biblical proportions; however, these were not the crucial power stations. If the British had picked some of the dams further north, they might have shortened the war considerably because in that case the Ruhr industries would have been paralyzed.

Renata's mother was a lovely hostess. When I expressed my appreciation, she said with a self-deprecating smile, "It's a result of years of practice. My seven foot Nazi husband is so boorish, he tends to drive all our guests away - he has all through our marriage, unless I had my wits about me. Excuse me for being so blunt, but I thought it better you know what to expect."

Renata added later, in tears, that the family was on the verge of breaking up. The father had gone so far as to threaten to report the both of them for making critical comments regarding the war leadership.

The farm was huge. Sugar beets were the main staple crop. They had quite a number of prisoners of war to work for them: Russians, Serbs, Italians and Poles. The old man ruled them with an iron fist and a very loud unpleasant voice. Renata and I took long walks in the beautiful countryside. Unfortunately, I could not let Ivan run off the leash. The police were still hunting runaway dogs that had been abandoned in the big flood and somehow could not find their way back to their original owners. These dogs were shot whenever they were found hunting for food.

I promised to come back to Elmau and bring my sister Jutta. There was a certain feeling of finality about saying goodbye these days. Renata's mother gave me a big hug with tears in her eyes. "Are we going to see you again? There is a lot of room for you in our hearts, Renata's and mine."

"Mother!" Renata protested.

"Never mind, Renchen, this is the time when you tell someone you like how you feel - you may not get another chance." I was deeply touched by this.

❖ ∙ ∙ ❖ ∙ ∙ ❖ ∙

A week later, I was back in Camp Mauerwald posted with Major von Bomhard. The arrival in Angerburg was made pleasant by my new department staff officer Captain von Bülow. He even came down by car to call for me. I learned from him that he had been Rittmeister in the World War I Cavalry and was over sixty-years-old. He had volunteered for this job as personnel manager of the department. My new section was still called "North Ukraine," which was ridiculous because most of the action was taking place in Poland. South Ukraine, on the other hand, was still hanging on from Krivoy Rog to the Crimean Peninsula.

There was so much going on that the two daily reports took a long time on the phone. I could jump in straight away, since nobody needed to show me the ropes. They were the same type of reports as under Gehlen, only this time concerned with our side.

Von Bomhard was a true Bavarian in the positive sense. He had a great sense of humor "under the gallows," according to his self-deprecating analysis - we got along very well. I had been in Munich often since 1936 - 1937 and we had many memories in common.

The only other contact I enjoyed was the lieutenant colonel who in November '43 had come to my room the minute Stalingrad was cut off, he and Bernd Freytag von Loringhoven from the Baltic family line. He could never hear enough of my Auntie Else's stories told with my version of the Baltic dialect. In speaking of mutual Baltic connections, I learned he was even acquainted with Sylvia, the young doctor and distant relative who had assisted in my hand operation in spring 1943.

As for the rest of the department, I just did not find the same calm thoughtful discussions at meals or whenever we met that I was used to from Gehlen's department. There was a certain tension at times. People seemed to be shooting poisoned arrows at each other, figuratively speaking. There were personal rivalries and even rival factions.

The right-hand man of General Heusinger was part of the problem. Colonel Brandt, known the world over for his horsemanship and gold-medal during the 1936 Olympics, had been a role model for young officers at that time. The one I met here had nothing in common with my sports idol. I put it down to tremendous ambition. He was a "Yes-Sir man" with the generals, but rather rude and uncaring with younger officers whom he often treated with stinging sarcasm.

A Major Sieber joined our section because we were overworked. As with Gehlen before, we had twenty-four hours on and twenty-four hours off until "Bommy" developed some telephone drama with his wife and started drinking. This meant I had to cover for him whenever he had sought too much solace in his whiskey. Sometimes my turn lasted forty-eight hours. It became pretty exhausting considering the stress of watching the disastrous development on all war theaters.

My personal interest was, of course, the *Füsilier* Battalion, 76th Infantry Division. They were fighting superior Russian forces around Jassy. The person responsible for receiving the Russian reports was my old friend Lt. Krämer from 1942. He let me know when my division was mentioned. He was as critical as he had been in 1942 - 1943, but he did not go around all day holding forth and lecturing and showing how he would lead and win the war as some of his younger colleagues did.

Sieber was one of those young snappers who knew all the answers and wasn't hesitating to let us know about it. Whenever he kept harping at me, I kept answering with a thoughtful, "Hm. Hm." I didn't trust him either.

When "Bommy" was sober, he played a terrific jazz accordion. Sometimes, we even walked all over the terrain following his music and imbibing a little. Down on the lake, we occasionally went swimming and Ivan had a ball retrieving things out of the water. Most of us had never seen a dog jumping into the water with such style and grace. He was a perfect jumper. Right before reaching the jump-off point, he would curl his body only to let it fly. It was a fantastic show.

Swimming and movies were our only group activities. Some played *Faustball*, akin to Volleyball, but on a larger field and without changing around positions. It was not fun because these chaps from my department fell into arguments over referee calls with great regularity.

On June 6, the invasion of France began and the daily army reports became vague; however, we saw some photos and soon had a good idea why the Allied operation, which was flawlessly prepared and supported, had to be successful. The air superiority was 100 percent; all German countermeasures were stifled and destroyed from above. They even used daylight carpet bombing against specific targets of such a destructive force as only German civilians had experienced so far. Now, Hitler had what he had been warning about ever since he had gone into politics in 1923. At the time, he had promised the German nation that never again would there be a war on two fronts and now we had practically four, counting Italy and Yugoslavia.

The first German miracle weapon was launched on June 12. It was called V1 "Revenge weapon." It was a flying bomb that could not be aimed at a specific target and it flew so slowly it could be shot down if detected in time. When it ran out of fuel, that's where the 1,000 pounds of high explosive fell. For instance, they aimed it in the general direction of London and washed their hands of it. None of us so far had laid too much store in the promised miracle weapons. This one certainly did not have the potential to become a decisive weapon, by a long shot.

Meanwhile on the Eastern Front, all hell broke loose. The Russians were gaining in Finland, they were approaching the Lake Ladoga, and Army Group Central was faced with a tremendous offensive starting on June 22. Hitler had also been warning about this since 1942. The Russians conveniently used June 22 as a starting date, commemorating the first German onslaught in 1941. By June 29, three German armies practically had ceased to exist, twenty-eight divisions had disappeared, at least 350,000 German soldiers were either dead or missing. As per usual, this would all come to pass in the end of June when our section celebrated one of the more gloomy of all my disastrous birthdays. Poland and East Prussia were now wide open for the Russians to attack.

On July 14, we were starting to move the whole headquarter to Zossen. It was situated in thick concrete bunkers on the edge of a military training camp near Berlin. Sieber took off with the move and "Bommy" and I were left to hold the fortress. We had just welcomed another helper, Lt. von Dresen, another invalid from Stalingrad. On his second day, July 20 at lunchtime, I felt I could go and take a walk around Mauer Lake with one of the more mature women working for Count von Kirchbach who was still working at headquarters. Miss Kessler and

I had met at Dresden where her parents had a flat near my posh hospital, "White Deer Sanitarium." I instructed Lt. von Dresen to leave a phone message at the checkpoint half way around the lake, if anything out of the ordinary had happened and he needed help.

It was a hot day and I almost regretted having suggested this hike, but we both flung our uniform coats over our shoulders, which made the heat somewhat bearable. She was well read and enjoyed concerts of various kinds. She had seen a number of dance concerts that the Wigman school had produced. She thought Gundel was tops as she most often had to dance character parts, witches and nasty queens, not the romantic parts, which were more glamorous but not very exciting. After an hour walk, we hit the checkpoint. Sure enough, my lieutenant was waiting for me on the line.

"Something stupendous has occurred, sir, but I can't be explicit over the phone."

"What the hell are you talking about! Am I needed for something?" I was hot and impatient in my question. "Your call must mean some urgency, does it not?"

"Yes, sir. Well, I don't know how to put it."

By now I was tense. "Why don't you try?"

"Well, sir, there was an assassination attempt against Bismarck at one time - but that did not succeed either, get it?"

"Either?" I felt somewhat slow on the uptake.

"Either," he repeated.

And at that point a female voice broke in. "Kindly be judicious about what you are discussing over the phone, sir. I'll have to disconnect you."

Kessler was watching me with an open mouth and I was dumb-founded myself. Lt. Dresen could only have meant Hitler, to follow his analogy. She and I speeded up our return trip. She insisted on joining me in my "forced march." We exchanged breathless speculations as to what might have happened and who would do this kind of thing to

Hitler or to anyone. I gathered that she always had reservations about the Nazi party, but Hitler still stood high in her estimation, so she was deeply concerned.

At the office, the lieutenant had only fragmentary facts. This much was clear, an assassination attempt had failed at "Wolf's Lair" and Hitler had survived it practically unharmed. We did not hear anything more until we were given the official version later that evening.

Once word got out that Hitler was not killed, some key conspirators must have decided not to carry out their assigned tasks in the plot, possibly as an attempt to save their hides. A good example had to do with communication out of "Wolf's Lair." The two generals in charge of Hitler's Signal Dept. did not cut off communication to the outside as they had agreed with the fellow conspirators. Because of their inaction, Keitel in Rastenburg and Goebbels in Berlin were able to communicate by telephone to the loyal officers. Then Goebbels was able to hand the telephone receiver to Captain Remer, who had orders to arrest Goebbels. Thereby, he was able to connect him to Hitler in person proving he had survived the attack. Thus, Goebbels and Keitel were in a position to issue orders countermanding the directives from the conspirators, preventing the success of the *coup d'état*. As for the effect of the bomb, the only definite news we had was that Colonel Brandt and one stenographer were dead.

I walked over to FHO to Gehlen's department, since it was my free night. JR, Letchert, Ritter and I talked for hours. None of the names of the conspirators mentioned so far in rumors were familiar to us. It appeared most of them had belonged to the ORG, Organization Department, with which we had very little contact at our level.

That night after midnight, Hitler's voice came in over the radio. If anything, it was more harsh and rasping than usual, unmodulated and with vulgar, guttural consonants:

"A very small clique of ambitious, dishonorable and criminally stupid officers had formed a plot to remove me and at the same time overturn the High Command of the German Armed Forces. A bomb planted by Colonel Graf von Stauffenberg exploded two meters to my right. It has very seriously wounded a number of faithful members of my staff. One of them has died. I myself am absolutely unhurt, except for minor scratches, bruises and burns. I regard this as a confirmation, a decree of Providence, that I should continue to pursue the goal of my life as I have done up to now.

No civilian authority, no military authority, no officer or private soldier shall obey orders from these men. On the contrary, it is everyone's duty to arrest, or, if they resist, shoot at sight anyone issuing or implementing such orders.

To create order, I have appointed Reich Minister Himmler, Commander of the Reserve Army.

Only a few can imagine what fate would have befallen Germany, if the plot had succeeded. I thank providence and my creator, but not because He has preserved me. My life is solely devoted to worry for my people. I thank Him, rather, because He has made it possible for me to continue to shoulder these worries."

Lt. von Dresen and I listened together to this speech, then went our separate ways, without talking about it. I thanked him for the telephone call and his historical analogy, which proved he knew some history, and at the same time could have aroused the Gestapo. If anything, we both might expect a reprimand. After all, how were we expected to know, there was a total news blackout clamped on all matters regarding the assassination attempt.

The next day, Saturday, my day off, we volunteered to go to the infirmary of the SS barrack compound to visit our General Heusinger, one of the bomb victims. This was my first opportunity to travel by the minuscule light-rail diesel between our "Camp Fritz" and "Wolf's Lair" running straight through the young evergreen forest.

It was strange to see all these badly burned or maimed officers lying there all in one room together guarded by SS soldiers at the door. These wretched victims, by the look of it, were being treated as potential suspects involved in the coup attempt. I certainly would never have expected to see about a dozen generals, admirals and staff officers penned up together in such an evil smelling infirmary as this - a humiliating treatment, to say the least. To me it was becoming feasible that the conspiracy had calculated personal damage or death to some of their own friends in the attempt to kill Hitler.

Heusinger was covered, as were most of the others, with a substance which looked to me something like mercury. He was one of the few patients who were alert and able to talk. He had a kind word for each of us and said he hoped to be back soon. He even asked me how Ivan was doing. We didn't stay long, of course. It was a sign of the new atmosphere in the aftermath of this crisis that during the return to Mauerwald none of us felt like talking about what we just had seen, or about the coup.

"Bommy" was on the phone when I walked into the room. Bernd was sitting near the map table, white as a sheet. He said to me, "Keep this under your hat. My uncle is missing." I could understand his concern because I knew how close he was to his uncle, the Colonel Freytagh von Loringhoven, and how highly he regarded him. All I knew of the colonel was that he was in charge of a section of Abwehr (counter-espionage) under the Supreme Command of the Armed Forces, *Ober Kommando der Wermacht* (OKW).

Someone came by and said, "General Stieff has been arrested." We looked at each other. It was only yesterday morning that we had been with Stieff. Over breakfast, he had condemned the conspirators and distanced himself from any rationality for their actions, even though some of them belonged to his ORG department. All this was happening while the headquarters was in transit to Zossen near Berlin. We left "Bommy" to do the last report from East Prussia, as we boarded the now familiar courier train.

On the way we stopped more frequently than usual so Ivan and I took the opportunity to get some fresh air. On one such stop, near Marienburg, I ran into Bernd's uncle. He recognized me and asked me all kinds of questions about who was arrested. I couldn't say much, but gladly informed him of the little I knew. He guardedly asked me not to mention to anyone that we had met on the train. When we got off at Zossen near Berlin I did not see the colonel.

The next morning, "Bommy" told me that he had heard that Bernd's uncle had committed suicide. I wondered if in our conversation near the train the colonel had indirectly warned me to distance myself from any known contact with him.

Having unpacked and settled into our new routine of duty we were ordered the same evening to pack our things to go back to our Camp Mauerwald. This was not a practical joke, it was symptomatic of the general confusion in the Supreme Command (OKW). We heard that Zeitzler had resigned and Guderian was now chief of staff. Colonel Von Kielmannsegg and our General Heusinger were posted somewhere else, we didn't know where. General Wenck became our boss and Colonel von Bonin became his chief of staff.

By now Letchert, JR and I came to the conclusion that the conspiracy had been vast in scope, much larger than up to now had been admitted. The analogy with the "stab in the back" myth from World War I immediately came to our minds. Potentially, from now on any defeat would be blamed on treason, instead of where the blame belonged.

A devastating bit of news: I heard from von Kirchbach that General von Zielberg had been shot because he had let Kuhn, his staff officer, get away when the Gestapo wanted to arrest him. Kuhn, my friend from

Wildungen, presumably had gone over to the Russians although that story could not be confirmed.

The sight of those badly burned generals cooped up all together in a small infirmary room did not leave me for weeks - the moaning of the dying ones in bed right next to those like my boss Heusinger who were wide awake and must have been aware of the fact that they were heavily guarded. There were SS guards all around the room for which there could be only one reason: they were all suspected of having been part of the conspiracy one time or another. The whole atmosphere was poisoned. I felt like an actor in a cheap mystery novel. I might as well admit it, I was frightened too. Kuhn's disappearance was at the crux of it.

I went to Colonel von Kirchbach to get the latest information. He was now in a different part of the headquarter named Quelle. I did not think it advisable to approach him by telephone. I knocked and the count yelled "Come in," and motioned me to sit down while he was finishing his telephone conversation. He gave me the additional earpiece. According to this voice, I don't know who he was, someone with a Baltic accent, General von Zielberg had been summarily executed for failure to keep Kuhn under guard until the Gestapo could get there and arrest him. I had to sit down, my right knee was twitching so badly.

Was Kuhn involved that deeply? My friend and mentor at the hospital in Bad Wildungen who was so gentle and so soft-spoken. I just did not see him as a conspirator in a deadly game of this magnitude. He had been critical of OKW as we all had been, but planning to overthrow the government and kill Hitler at this juncture of the war seemed a preposterous idea to me then.

Von Kirchbach put the receiver down. I quickly told him why I was so interested in Kuhn and gave him a description of our dealings in and around that hospital. The count frowned, "Oh, I see. If the Gestapo interrogates you, answer yes or no. Don't volunteer any information, let's have none of your anecdotes, no embellishments. They always start with some small talk about the weather, soccer, or your family, tempting you to think they are on your side. Then they will hint that they have all the information they need, they just need you to confirm their data. If you need any help come in person. I will not be giving telephone interviews. Let's hope you don't have to worry. Good luck, Panny."

The atmosphere at Mauerwald was depressing. I found it difficult to concentrate on my daily reports, which, of course, were nothing but bad news about those poor devils who were trying to stem the Russian tide. 6th Army was about to be encircled in East Romania in my own North Ukraine section, about 30,000 German soldiers were missing near Brody, presumably captured. Russian tanks were approaching Warsaw and in the west the Allies were about to break out of their Caen-Avranche bridgehead any minute.

In free moments my mind went back to Kuhn. I knew he was Stieff's assistant. I wondered how many people in the headquarter would examine their past contacts with one or more fellow workers who were now in the hands of the Gestapo. I began to trace my way back to the day I arrived at the hospital and met Kuhn. General staff officers are very conspicuous by the crimson stripes on their pants. Would the Gestapo be interested in Kuhn's contacts during that period, say, half a year ago? He and I had been seen together at all times, sometimes arriving way past curfew, and he did put a good word in for me when my roommates had complained about my nocturnal ravings against Göring and the OKW.

Apart from Kuhn, couldn't I have been overheard occasionally making irreverent remarks about our leadership, particularly after Stalingrad? What about that little booklet, the transcript about our satirical comments at the May 1, 1943, party in Gehlen's department? Didn't the registrar of the same department report me at one time for not using the Nazi salute entering the mess hall? Right this minute the

Armed Forces of Germany had been ordered to abandon the military salute in favor of the Nazi salute. Last, not least, did someone see me on the train to Berlin talking to Colonel Freytag von Loringhoven before he disappeared from the train and shot himself?

My preoccupation with such concerns bordered on paranoia. I even made an effort to apologize to the camp security when Ivan had used a few seconds off his leash to attack and badly maul one of the over-fed police dogs. "Service dog XYZ was unfit for duty for four days," the report said.

My new boss, General Wenck, showed me the document, "You see," he said, "if we didn't have to bother with all the domestic dirty linen, as it were, we might have won the war by now." I was relieved to see him take this attitude and decided to like him, at least for those few weeks I had left at the headquarters. Neither Wenck nor his aide, von Bonin, were Nazis, while all German units had to appoint NS *Führungsoffiziere* (political commissars, of sorts). We did not get any, or if we had one I certainly had not noticed the change.

The new team, Wenck and Bonin, did not change the department around completely. We just kept on with our work. I felt, with Colonel Brandt gone, the atmosphere in the group was improving a little, notwithstanding our having to endure the constant protestations of loyalty to God, *Führer* and country. Guderian's part in all this disgusted me, but he did one nice thing - he took Bernd Freytag von Loringhoven into his staff and we were told he had personally vouchsafed Bernd's loyalty as a general staff officer. That was a relief because there were rumors that even the families of the conspirators would have to suffer *Sippen haftung* (arrest through family liability).

Once more in Mauerwald, some of our mail clerks were posted to the front. As a result, a number of extremely good looking younger women who had been working for the occupation authority in France took over their positions. They certainly turned Mauerwald into a livelier place. My "godfather," Captain von Bülow, gave me the responsibility for entertainment which included ordering films. On my off-days, I checked out the movies that were shown in other departments hoping to make some reasonable choices. The German public was usually offered a pretty dismal selection of movies to distract them from the conditions under which they were living. I hoped to find more acceptable ones.

Our food was getting more and more inadequate. My jack-of-all-trades reputation had grown by this time to the extent that I was asked to go into the surrounding countryside to buy vegetables. There were moments of serious discussions on these trips because the populace in general had become aware that the Russians were poised to set foot on German soil. I attempted to lighten up the atmosphere with my jokes in the East-Prussian dialect. At least the peasantry and the people I dealt with on the estates seemed to enjoy my informal tone.

After a few days, I had another request: General Wenck had invited the SS leaders from Himmler's staff at Army Headquarters for a party. My guess was that this was an attempt to let bygones be bygones and somehow establish better relations. Stories were beginning to surface, which made us aware that in some cities, particularly in France, the conspiracy had succeeded in rounding up all SS and party leaders and detaining them, for a few hours anyway. Rumor also had it that when the coup had collapsed, they all had a drink and shook hands.

I had to find a room, some help and female clerks willing to participate in this party. Von Etzdorff, the *attaché* of our foreign ministry to OKH, very graciously offered his establishment, a full-size office hut. It was hardly ever used since our so-called secretary of state (foreign minister) shunned contacts with the army for reasons of his own. I rearranged two adjoining reception rooms, one cleared for dancing and the other set up as the party room with tables for refreshments. We brought my radio, turntable and swing records, and turned the place into a veritable speakeasy with low lights and lots of alcohol. I had the movies of the roaring twenties in mind for a theme.

I was told to invite a number of young officers of my age group just to make sure somebody was dancing. It became mostly a northern German affair. Among the new faces posted to this department with General Wenck was my childhood friend Jörgensen, now also a captain. He had been serving under Wenck, both in France and in Russia; it became obvious Wenck was still his idol. I noticed Jörgensen's right arm was badly crippled.

Rolf Lutteroth also appeared, an old classmate of JR's from Bertram Private School. He was now working under General Burgdorf, who had become the department head of Personnel Management (IIA). This move was the result of the death of General Schmundt from wounds suffered in the assassination attempt. I remembered hearing his groans from across the room, as we were talking to General Heusinger at the infirmary.

Letchert, a Lt. von Wiese and myself were quite a lively host team, although none of us had any illusions about our role. We were not supposed to talk to the SS staff officers, we were just to give the whole thing the look of conviviality. I made it quite clear to each girl how I felt about this, and they all said that they didn't care whether it was a command performance or not, they just loved to dance.

The first party took place in mid-September about two months after the July 20 assassination attempt. A good time was had by all. Once Bonin came by and commented, "What are you doing, Panny? This is a strange way of dancing the foxtrot. What the hell are you doing there, wriggling your behind?"

"Sorry, sir. Since I don't have a mirror, I don't know what you are talking about," and I kept dancing my version of swing and so did my partner.

I remember the party lasted until at least 2:30 a.m.. When everyone had left, we tidied up the place and emptied ashtrays. Most of the young people said goodnight and Jörgensen and I sat down and had another drink. Tomorrow, no doubt, would be another day of bad news.

During this period, Lt. Freiherr von Soden joined our group. He was the youngest son of a noble family that reached back to the 1400's. Two sons had died in battle, one was hanged the other day, so Colonel von Bonin had convinced General Guderian to pull this young man out of his cavalry regiment and assign him to the operational sector. He added a new perspective to our discussions because he had connections to occupied Poland. Rolf Jörgensen, Letchert and I were unsure whether to believe all his stories. They were too gruesome. He claimed first-hand reliability because his sister had married a well-known Polish horseman who was missing in action since 1939.

The accounts of effects of German colonialization in Poland were appalling to us. Moreover, the Poles in the Russian (the eastern) provinces underwent an even worse treatment. He said Stalin had staged a phony general election late in 1939 for the benefit of the western democracies. After that the area east of the Curzon Line was annexed outright and became either part of Ukraine or Belorussia. Most educated people, industrial leaders, technicians and civil servants were deported in three stages - February, April and July 1940 - to either northern Russia or to Siberia. It was known that most of the men ended up in gulags. Each of these deportations allegedly numbered between two and three hundred thousand people who could only take whatever they could carry and were dropped in a no man's land to fend for themselves. Universities, schools, theaters were kept open, but had to spread the Leninist-Marxist doctrine. Churches were closed, destroyed or turned over for public functions. The Polish soldiers were kept in internment camps where Russian noncoms began retraining them. The idea was the formation of a Polish army in exile, which later was supposed to join the Polish units who were already fighting in Italy or France.

From the beginning, the Russians gave no information as to the whereabouts of the likewise interned Polish officers. The investigation was obstructed by the Russian authorities until 1943, when the Germans published the photos of the massed graves of thousands of Polish officers near Katyn. The Polish government exiled in London did not openly state that the German claims were valid, but they certainly intensified their pressure until Stalin broke off relations with the exiled government. The Polish General Sikorski, who functioned as commander-in-chief of all exiled Poles and symbolized the Polish determination to continue the war, became very insistent and visited Stalin, Roosevelt and Churchill. As a result, the relations between Moscow and the Western Allies became very strained. Sikorski demanded the restoration of the eastern borders of Poland and some territorial gains in East Germany and the truth about the murdered officers. Sikorski's plane crashed immediately after takeoff at Gibraltar. Soden added that there were rumors in Poland that the same general had a number of accidents in British planes and that this one finally did him in.

Ironically, when the Germans overran eastern Poland in 1941, some of the people welcomed their liberation from the Soviet terror, being unaware what was in store for them once the *Sonderkommandos* under the command of Himmler's SS would arrive. While we were talking, beginning the first of August 1944, the Polish underground army had started the uprising which had been in preparation for years. The SS mobilized some of their worst units, mostly Ukrainians and Baltics, and began to lay siege to the city of Warsaw again. Meanwhile, the Russian Army was sitting a few miles away and did not lift a finger to help. After sixty-two days, the Poles had to surrender. In recognition of their valor, they were treated as POW's and interned. The Soviets did not even offer their close-by airfields to the Allied planes, who had been dropping supplies to the hapless Poles.

The news on September 14, 1944, in summary:

The Crimean Peninsula was lost. The 6th Army, including my Division, was destroyed near Jassy where the Romanians defected and went over to the Russians. The war in the East now took place in Poland, Lithuania, Latvia and Estonia. The Finns had been defeated, were suing for an armistice. Romania and Bulgaria had declared war on Germany. German forces were retreating from Greece and Yugoslavia and fierce fighting was taking place in Hungary. The Russians had just taken Ostrolenka, my 1940 - 1941 garrison.

And in Warsaw a Polish uprising was squashed by the SS, while the Russians sat in Praga, a suburb of Warsaw, not moving to assist the Polish. The Russians wanted no part in any activity that was directed from the Polish exiled government in London. Since the discovery of the murder of thousands of Polish officers around Katyn, the diplomatic relations between the Russians and the exiled government had been broken off by Stalin.

The 6th Army again had disappeared from the map. Since August 23 my men, my friends, are considered to be missing in action. Army Group North-Ukraine flew in a number of stragglers who had survived for a more thorough debriefing by Gehlen's interrogators. Among them was Lt. Reuter, whom I had seen for the last time when I assisted his first aid cleanup in Mash unit 1942. He had given an oral report to officers of the Operational and the Intelligence Departments. In the evening we had him in our dorm, and he retold his story to JR, Letchert, Ritter and myself.

When the regimental staff had been overrun by Russian tank units, he and three other soldiers had waited for the night to fall in a mossy hollow. They had argued among themselves about their next move, and he, Reuter, had prevailed. He had explained to them that it was no good in a westerly direction crossing the Carpathian Mountains and ending up in now hostile Romania. He insisted they try their luck following a small river in a north northwestern direction.

They had a number of close shaves the first two nights. They did not see or hear any German wherever they went. They moved all night, taking turns in leading. They were always lucky to find some growth, some place to hide to spend the daytime hours. Food and water soon had run out, so they collected berries, mushrooms and drank some of the relatively clean water from the river. After ten days, they decided that they had left World War II behind, and dared moving during the morning hours. They found frightened, but mostly friendly peasants of varying ethnic backgrounds who let them have some food and found rags and twine for them to replace their totally ruined boots and socks. The same argument they had at the outset caused another split-up when they had joined another group of stragglers. Reuter insisted that going west would mean Romania and unnecessary danger. So in the end, Reuter and one faithful corporal followed the river Bistrita and ended up about 100 kilometers west of Chernovtsy.

While he was talking and enjoying the cheap red wine we could offer, I had visions of the return of Napolean's Imperial Army. The thought didn't leave me for days afterwards. Reuter was given a generous furlough. After this survival, I hope he survived the war. He deserved it, I thought.

The entire crew of the Operational Department, with the exception of one orderly officer per army group section, was replaced. I was kept to show the ropes to some incoming major and two captains. The new team supposedly represented reliable and ideologically loyal officers.

Our department had been stressed before July 20, now it was a wringer. Each time I went to bed, I knew the next day would bring more sadness, but now I would be surrounded by people who firmly believed in a miracle. This unrealistic faith made everyone avoid the obvious conclusion that the end of the war was near and that there could only be unconditional surrender.

I did my routine daily reports, watching the Russian steamroller approaching the eastern provinces of Germany. There was a short stab by Russian tank forces into East Prussia beginning October 16, but they were driven back immediately, leaving numerous mutilated corpses wherever they had found German civilians of any age. Goebbels, of course, made the best of this propaganda opportunity passing the photos to the neutral press. For the soldier on the Eastern Front, these images of female corpses with fork handles rammed into them was one more motivation to fight on. To be sure, only poor people were caught. The "haves" at the last minute found ways to flee - by horse, wagons, or by even by car, in the case of the local party boss who most often led the way. This occurred in defiance of Hitler's strictest orders to stay where they were.

To my surprise, Major Sieber came back to take charge of our section. His substitute was posted somewhere else. Sieber must have been considered "reliable," after all. In retrospect, I was glad I had never engaged in any kind of intimate or political discussion with him.

Before I left for my hospital in Munich, I did all kinds of odd jobs like working with the daily *Bandenlage*, the section concerned with saboteurs and partisans behind the lines. There was a merciless struggle going on between our SS volunteers and Cossack units, and the underground partisans in Yugoslavia, Italy, Poland and lately Czechoslovakia. Losses of human lives on both sides were mounting. Unfortunately, peaceable civilians had to suffer in this maelstrom of murder and retributions. Keitel issued a specific order not to punish German soldiers who had gone too far in their brutality. Only once was there an encouraging bit of news: the Ukrainians under the SS Commander Bach Zelewski were taken out of the fight in Warsaw because of their excessively brutal procedures.

The Gestapo had taken photos of everyone who had worked in the general staff and had now been released. This was done for Gestapo files, we were told. "Why not some thumb printing as well?" was my reaction. My photo turned out to be respectable, I asked for a personal copy and got it.

My weekly attempt at foraging vegetables yielded less and less. The peasants were quite frank. If I could bring a little container of gas, I could buy the whole farm. Word had spread around the neighborhood that sooner or later we would soon be moving west. I couldn't blame the civilians for preparing themselves to trek to safety, the orders of the local party boss notwithstanding.

I took my furlough in short installments. In a three-day stint in Hamburg staying with Alice Pollitz, I met Tatiana at a tram stop. She came straight to the point, "Karlchen Schneider is in prison. A trial for high treason is impending. Could you do something? They arrested those "swing" boys, remember? And some people from two different underground groups, the Hamburg "White Rose" from our high school among them. My teacher, Miss Stahl, is in prison too."

She, her friend Maggie and I talked for a while in the freezing autumn wind. Her tram approached, we hugged and kissed and wished each other better days.

Back in East Prussia, I went over to my old department and phoned the Hamburg Gestapo from JR's office. JR used the second earpiece, he too had been a very good friend of Karlchen's. The officer at the Gestapo tried to turn the tables. Who was I? What was I? What was I doing there? etc. In the end, he refused to give any information and told me rather rudely to mind my own business.

Second trip to Hamburg unloading some of my luggage, Alice Pollitz and I had a solemn last dinner. She still had received some Red Cross parcels from her friend in New York. It was a somber affair with many questions not asked and no attempt to gloss over the threatening reality.

The next morning, I faked two more of Friedrich's railway passes and visited Ilka and Anne, both lately widowed and living with friends in the country. Alice, who knew that we had worked together the last school year, wanted me to find out how the two women were doing.

While I was near Kassel, I visited Renata. But when I got there I had a very high fever and they put me into a small chamber, which was normally used for domestic help. The doctor diagnosed a tonsil abscess and prescribed some medication. For three or four days I must have laid there with a high fever. I have no recollection.

When I got back to East Prussia, the move to Zossen was on. Jörgensen, with whom I had arranged two more of those god-awful dancing parties, reminded me of my offer to help him evacuate his in-law family. We both drove out to the estate to find his young wife going about like a sleepwalker. Her mother did all the packing and still had time to cook a fantastic dinner for us. She made no bones about the fact that her husband had "flown the coop," accompanied by the estate secretary. She was determined, she said, to move herself and all her help the minute we were gone. She took me to the window where we could see a highway other than that which we used to get there, crowded with the refugees in their slow move west.

While all this may sound pretty miserable, miraculously I had found a haven of support in Gundel again. I couldn't phone her at night anymore. She had to go to bed fairly early because she worked in a munitions factory. Since Goebbels had announced "Total War," all cultural activities, with the exception of a few big orchestras and the film industry, had to be closed down. The minister would not let go of his pet propaganda weapon: film. The movie industry turned out one *kitschfilm* after another to suggest escape from the beastly reality of war. Fluffy fairy tales and lots of schmaltz. After Stalingrad, they changed their tune and one movie after another sounded cheer-up messages and demonstrated the value of hanging tough. *Kolberg*, the fortress that did not surrender to Napoleon easily, was a prime example of this genre. Thousands of soldiers and horses had been made available for this venture. I never found out how many men and how many horses came to grief in this monster show.

Anyway, Gundel hated her factory and her forced retirement from dancing. She worked out every weekend at the Wigman School when she had at least a few free hours. She had become a voracious reader and wrote delightfully witty and mostly sarcastic letters to me. Her parents had been lucky to get out of occupied Poland in time before the Russians. Her father had been forced to retire for reasons of health. They lived now in the ruins of Hamburg, enjoying Gundel's little boy and finding Tutta's two "extra" boys an additional burden, since Tutta had to work too.

When I learned I had to go to a Munich Hospital, Gundel wrote me a letter. It certainly was a masterpiece: to send a patient to Munich in October 1944 for a problem of internal medicine seemed the height of stupidity. Dresden, on the other hand, was still enjoying nearly peacetime conditions and was full of hospitals. She said she couldn't believe I would follow my order, and called me a masochist.

A few weeks later when the Russians had come closer to her town, she changed her tune a little, and even had dark forebodings. All of a sudden, she doubted very much that the Allies had spared Dresden for some reasons of their own. According to the descriptions of her work place, I had to assume that she had unpleasant experiences with her Saxon countrymen.

Rolf Jörgensen's mother-in-law sounded the same warnings when she heard I was going to Munich the night we said goodbye to her. She too loved the city and could enumerate the various architectural and artistic gems that had been destroyed so far. She said, "Go to Sudetenland. The Czechs are the least likely targets for air attacks. What can your so-called specialists in Munich do that other urologists cannot do just as easily somewhere else in the country? The war is almost over, Panny, and you risk your life unnecessarily."

"He who has bad luck freezes to death in a sauna," was my routine answer to this kind of concern. I knew the Allied planes had nearly perfect control of the air and used it.

She continued, "You're not a stoic, Panny, you are a masochist. I knew that when I heard you promising my kids to help them to get away from this lost cause here in East Prussia." She was talking about her beautiful estate. It turned out she was right. Smuggling a civilian out of East Prussia was a nerve-wracking experience. 700 kilometers in an overcrowded train, military checks by police patrols who were awed by the phony papers Jörgensen had been issued through his idol General Wenck. Rolf did not show them to me - in a way, I was glad, I didn't want to share that responsibility.

I hastened back to East Prussia and made a round of "goodbye" visits. JR was in charge of Ivan, radio, record player and the damn jazz records. I made a trip to introduce my substitute to my "vegetable" community. These were short and hearty goodbyes. The unspoken tendency of these wonderful people was: if I or we make it out of here alive, I hope to see you again sometime on the other side of Europe. Many of them had come to terms with the so-far unthinkable and prepared secretly to give up home and the soil, which had been in their families for centuries.

●◆●●◆●●◆●

Munich was all it was reported to be, a stricken city trying to look alive. My former barracks, the old infantry school, was largely destroyed. The famous inner city was barely recognizable. The naked facades often had to be blown down for safety reasons. The monstrous subway project Hitler had started was under water and many churches had been condemned. Wherever I went, gaping charcoal blistered woodwork and heaps of rubble.

The hospital was alongside an old cemetery, which in a sarcastic moment struck me as a bizarre efficiency. I was given a single room again, after a few days, on account of my nightly tirades against higher-ups in my sleep. This time I did not ask which names I had mentioned. The hospital was probably built around the middle of the nineteenth century. The not-too-well-lit rooms had dingy white walls and many of the windows had been shattered by bombs and the makeshift cardboard repairs were flapping in the cold autumn wind.

After various tests, the doctor informed me that an operation was out of the question. The affected tissue had too large a concentration of blood, as usual when there is an infection. Even if surgery would have had some promise, at the moment there was no surgical theater in working order. Every time there was a nearby bomb, the remaining glass would splinter and fly around the room like bullets. The only one thing he could do for me, and would I please refrain from laughing, would be to order some leeches.

I couldn't believe it.

"Well, they will take a while to get here, because I have to order them from somewhere north of Hamburg. You know what shape transportation is in these days. Take your medication and spend your days walking around Munich and the surrounding areas. Don't stay in here, it's too depressing. Do you have friends here?"

"Yes. Quite a number. Thank you, doctor," I replied.

He was right. It was depressing there. Other ranks, NCO's and other officers were sharing the meager rations, the baths and the air-raid shelters. Some ardent Nazis were all over in the building. It was part of the daily routine to see them coming and you had better change the subject of your conversation. I had a seven foot Bavarian medic looking after me and he had warned me right from the start to take this seriously. One of the reasons, he said, was understandable. In a urological institution there obviously were people with GO and syphilis and he was quite sure that some of these agents were keeping close check on such patients to find out whether they were continuously re-infecting themselves on purpose to stay away from the front. He warned me about listening to the BBC. One story had it that these agents succeeded in catching one young man by switching on his radio while he was taking a shower. When the two informers heard the BBC pause signal, Beethoven's four beats on a kettle drum, the young man was as good as convicted and disappeared soon afterwards. A policeman came to collect his belongings.

One night in the oppressive atmosphere of the air-raid shelter, one of these characters came sniffing into our dark corner. He was told in no uncertain terms where to go and what to do with himself by a chorus of "anonymous" voices. He didn't pester us again.

November 26, a week later, was the big day. A six-by-six parcel had arrived and was solemnly unpacked by my seven-foot bodyguard. He placed the glass with five gray slimy creatures on my night table the very moment Linda, one of my favorite dance partners and dear friend from the operational sector, walked into the room. She brought cookies for me and best regards from the other girls and all of my friends, and she sat down on the edge of my bed. Why I was in bed at that time, I don't remember. So, she proceeded to talk all about Zossen where two people were killed, Susan had lost one eye, and what a good job everybody was doing taking care of Ivan, but her eyes never left the jar with those worm-like creatures. I told her that normally I was ambulant, and how long would she be in Munich, could we do something together? She replied, "No, Vincenz, I'm just on my way through. My parents are expecting me in Landshut."

In a way, I was relieved. Behind Linda at the door of my large room, I could see my medic and some of his friends who were obviously there to inspect the leeches. They were scheduled to be applied this noon and I had no intention to let my little secret travel back from here to Zossen. I asked her to excuse me and told her I would meet her at the front door in three minutes so we could at least go for a cup of coffee. She thought it was a good idea and would I please see her to her train.

With her out of the room, I told the medic that as far as I was concerned he could even charge admission for the inspection, but would he please be sure no one disturbed the jar. Having come this far, I didn't want anything to come between us. I'd be back in an hour.

When I returned, my bodyguard was still watching the jar. He had furnished me with a framed mirror, roughly one-by-three feet in size. In his best Bavarian High German he gave me detailed instructions. "You see, sir, I'll put this mirror propped against the pillow, and now you can see yourself from below. Here is a hand mirror. You can't raise up all the time to watch the beasties in action in the other mirror, you'll get a stiff neck. I'm pleased to see a patient, for once, to see the humanity from below. I have to do that day in, day out. I'm sick of it. And if you ask me, so are the doctors. We do an extra good job of washing you and then I will put them one by one where they are supposed to go to do the most good."

"What's the technical term," I asked.

"*Der Damm*" (perineum), he growled. "Don't touch the leeches, sir. They will fall off by themselves once they have their fill. Before they let go, they secrete a sealing agent that closes off the wound. That's important. They must finish the process their way."

For a moment, I was tempted to pack my things and leave. Surely there would be time to find some other than this medieval approach. But then again, now that I was here in Munich I wanted this problem solved.

He put the hand mirror in my hand, directed the floor lamp against my posterior and opened the jar. I was glad to see he knew which end of the leech was which. All five were immediately greedy and attached themselves to my skin with a vengeance. Every first bite did hurt and I used some foul language, but they settled down and so did I, watching them through my hand mirror or raising up to watch them directly until it got boring.

After a while, my tormentor came back and told me that I would have to stay here in the second-floor room during an impending air-raid. I agreed, I wasn't going to upset this procedure, as if I had a choice. The thought of my going down the stairs as I was with my load was not my choice.

"Take care of yourself, sir." Those were his last cryptic words as he left with everybody else for the shelter.

Franzel had left an hour glass gauged to run for two hours, just in case I wanted a visual reminder of how much time had elapsed. The electric clock on the wall had stopped running the same day when most of the windows had been smashed in 1943.

◆ ◆ ◆ ◆

Wednesday, February 14, 1945. I stood on the railway platform and checked my papers: "Berlin-Spandau to Army Distribution Center Italy, Brenner Pass. Stopovers at Zossen and Dresden." I had been up late last night packing and saying goodbyes at Army Headquarters - Zossen and was exhausted.

The train rolled past, car after car, until it came to a stop. As I walked beside it, searching for an available space, I saw it was so full that passengers in each carriage filled the aisles; the doors of the cars opened but nobody was leaving. It was obvious there was no room for me in any of the third-class coaches, let alone room for as much luggage as I was carrying - and a dog. The second-class compartments were just as overcrowded. I kept walking until I saw a family climbing out of a car close to the engine, three grown-ups and two children, one of them needing medical attention. Their misfortune created a space, and a few moments later I was standing in the aisle of the car with my baggage in the nets below the ceiling and Ivan curled up between my feet.

I knew it was not a good idea to ride this close to the engine, it was a favorite target of Allied fighter bombers. I had no choice. I wiped my forehead and decided this might be a good opportunity to test my newly found stoicism a la Marcus Aurelius, an approach Colonel Gehlen had recommended during the days after the Stalingrad crisis.

As the train started moving, a man close by announced with some gravity, "At this very moment, I expect the Americans are having their turn at Dresden."

Someone turned around and challenged, "And just how do you know?"

The first man drew up his shoulders, raised his eyebrows and said, "That's the way they do it since '43. The Tommies hit at night and the Amies the day."

There was silence, then a female voice asked rhetorically, "Why at this time and of all places should Dresden should be attacked?"

Somebody else remarked, "Well, I can't believe this is happening. Dresden has been spared so far, given a few minor bombings. Beside some barracks and railway facilities it has few military targets, the Allies won't do much damage. In any case, everybody knows Dresden attracts art lovers from all over the world and has for centuries. Nobody would destroy such a beautiful city."

This brought a few cynical guffaws. One man said, "Yes, Dresden will be spared because the Allies want to dictate our unconditional surrender in an environment that still functions."

A male voice in the back challenged, "Unconditional surrender, if we let them. But we have other ideas, don't we?"

There was an embarrassed silence. Then a woman nearby asked me, "You are in a captain's uniform, what do you think?"

"I know just about as much as you people," I said.

There was another pause until someone volunteered, "We in Essen had 20,000 casualties."

To which someone else piped up, "Only 20,000? In Cologne, we had 50,000."

I sighed. Not this macabre competition again. If there were truthful reports from the government would it limit the amount of this kind of conjecture and posturing? I wondered.

A man then said with a touch of controlled panic, "If you are right that the Tommies are going to be bombing Dresden at night and the Amies in the day, then it is likely Dresden is completely finished."

A woman appearing to be in her eighties burst into tears, "All those people. All those people."

"Quiet, watch yourself. Be careful," the first gentleman hissed, "someone might hear." We all knew what he was referring to. Gestapo informers could be anyone and anywhere. It was surprising this much talk had already taken place. Severe punishment was quickly available for "rumor mongering" and "defeatist talk." I made a mental note to stay out of any conversation having to do with the war. Keeping to myself in such public situations was my preferred tactic, anyway.

By nightfall, I expected to be in Dresden. I was apprehensive, to say the least, at what I might find when I got there, just as these people were. Last night, the Air Force liaison officer had used the word *Grossangriff* to describe the estimated size of the massive air attack then reported going on in Dresden. As usual, nobody in the Air Defense had any visual or instrumental data to go on because of the routine use of falling tin foil fragments to paralyze our German detection systems. Somebody must have heard the planes coming. I grimaced at the absurd simplicity of this. Under these circumstances, there was only one compelling reason for me to go on to Dresden at all and that was to find Gundel. Somehow, tomorrow we would be married and in my mind that marriage certificate would make possible a war widow's pension for her and her son, in case I would not survive. In spite of the weight, a few bottles of champagne and cognac were in my pack for the occasion.

I had to keep my mind occupied away from the train and Dresden. My new assignment in Italy was a reasonable topic. I was grateful that as some kind of parting consideration for my service at HQ, I had been allowed to influence the choice of Italy as my next assignment. Last night, I had made a few inquiries as to what I might be getting into, especially as to the reputation of the commanding general of my new division. This had brought some sardonic smiles. "Well, he wouldn't mind getting another cluster of diamonds on his Knight's Cross," was one comment that kept coming up, which didn't bode well to me. However, those same knowledgeable sources had assured me that the division had acquitted itself well during the slow retreat along the Adriatic Coast this winter. From what I was told and what I already knew, I could not help but have respect for how that army group had slowed down Allied advances, considering the odds against it. Since the Allies had almost total command of the air, supplies had slowed to a trickle. Reliable communication was almost an impossibility and the German High Command had to leave many tactical decisions to local commanders in the field. To be sure, without Hitler's meddling directives, the army group leaders were able to be more flexible, using their own professional military judgment and could avoid the kind of ridiculous blunders I had observed from HQ.

Unbelievably, with each one of the innumerable stops, more people tried to claw their way into the compartment of the train and only a few ever left. By now, no one was able to move in any direction, let alone go to the lavatory which was packed full of people too. Overall, I found it remarkable how calm and considerate everyone was being. I suspected most of them had been used to riding overcrowded trains, something like this one, whenever they could manage to get to the countryside to scrounge or barter for food.

For hours I had been keeping one hand in turn on the luggage rack above to keep from lurching into the people around me. Of course, the only body I really wanted to be conscious of was that of Ivan's against my leg. Under the present circumstances, he had to be off the leash; he would never lie down while on leash and I knew he could not sit on his haunches at attention for as long as this slowly crawling train might take. As a result of his freedom he was able to slip out of the car when the doors opened during a stop. I was so wedged in, there was nothing I could do and was chagrined to notice his absence each time he left.

When I heard the sound of the first door slam as the train readied for departure, I whistled to remind him to come and hopefully give him some sense of direction. The people standing near the door welcomed him with comments like, "Good dog;" nevertheless, I knew I was taking a big risk in losing him and each time I was grateful to feel his cold nose on my hand.

So, with luck, in a few days Ivan and I would be in Italy with the division I had requested. It included soldiers and officers from my own Berlin-Brandenburg District. I could look forward to the possibility of finding some of the men from my last two units, survivors from the battles of Stalingrad (1943) and Romania last year. Some of those labeled missing in action might have made it through the Russian lines.

My arms were numb from holding on to the strap above me, even though I tried to remember to change sides fairly often as the train continued on its slow journey. As the hours went by, some elderly people finally had to give up their struggle in trying to hold back their normal functions and had to relieve themselves where they were jammed in, whether sitting or standing. The stench became overwhelming. The doors being opened at each stop didn't help the smell all that much.

"I continued replaying images from last night, saying goodbye to friends, co-workers and supervisors. My childhood friend JR and I had worked closely together there, he evaluating reports concerning Russian logistics, I combining the daily situation reports from the front lines and from other sources of intelligence and then drawing the situation map accordingly. We had made some hollow jokes about how important our work had been, how Gehlen had delivered his evaluation of our reports and sent them through higher command to Hitler. Hitler could then refuse to believe a word of them and dismiss all the projections as defeatist pessimistic garbage, while he continued to demand that the army hold on to every inch of ground, no matter what the facts were. So, the army did hold on until it was too late for organized withdrawal and any possible counter-measures.

I had missed seeing my present boss General Heusinger at HQ because he was still recuperating. As a victim of Stauffenberg's bomb to assassinate Hitler, I knew his future was uncertain. I wondered what would become of him. The last time I had seen him, he and the other injured staff officers were being kept all together in a small hospital room, covered with zinc oxide and bandages, held as potential suspects with an armed guard outside the door. It was curious. As a result of Stauffenberg's "betrayal," from now on access to important information would be kept even more restricted, and all Heusinger's staff was being replaced by more ideologically dependable officers. I and one other had been kept to help the incoming group get oriented. Now, I was glad to be out of there.

My short visit last night, with now Lt. General Gehlen, had reminded me how fortunate I had been to get my position at HQ in the first place. For the past two-and-a-half years, whenever I had been wounded or incapacitated, I was able to call him at HQ and ask, "Any vacancies for me?" and get a desk job rather than do service at Berlin-Spandau Replacement Battalion, a group I was not particularly fond of.

Gehlen had been a source of stability for all of us, especially during the Stalingrad crisis. Day after day I had received the reports of the slow disintegration of those two Divisions. As I removed the numbers from the daily situation map, I saw their faces in my mind's eye, those of my friends in the officers' corps and many of the soldiers. As the reality of the situation began to dawn on us, there at HQ our sleep was fitful and during the day we functioned like zombies. Gehlen's example and advise somehow helped us still function and emotionally survive. At least he tried.

Last night, shortly after midnight, Gehlen had interrupted his conference with Colonel Herre and another officer to shake my hand and wish me well.

"Is there anything I can do for you?" he asked.

"Yes, Sir," I replied. "Do you think you might consider recommending my release from the service? As you know, I want to try performing arts in whatever way I can."

Gehlen's face was quizzical.

"When the war is over, of course," I quickly added.

We looked at each other in silence for what felt like minutes. Finally, Gehlen, with a wry smile, offered his hand. "Of course, and do take care of yourself." We looked at each other. No comment necessary. All over the room, maps and charts had shown the desperate situation of the German forces in all theaters of war."

It was becoming dark when the train came to a halt in an open field. Military police ran along the train yelling, *Alle aussteigen!* (End station). We would have to proceed to Dresden on foot from here. Everybody awkwardly climbed down. I had shooting pains in both feet as I hit the ground. I started to shoulder my pack, then dropped it immediately; my arms felt weak and sore, my legs rubbery. It was slow going for a while.

It looked like a hike of between eight to ten kilometers into Dresden. I carried my duffel bag in one hand and had the dog on the leash in the other. My backpack would have been heavy enough without the bottles. We somehow formed two loosely grouped lines, loaded down, stumbling through the stubble field. Ivan was eager to be on the move and I must admit for once I enjoyed his pulling on the leash.

When we reached a dirt road, a young woman pushing a bicycle joined the column parallel to mine. As the road narrowed we were walking together.

"S'gott," she greeted.

I do not need any small talk at this moment, I thought to myself, so I just muttered, "Unh-henh."

"What a beautiful dog! A German shepherd, right?" she remarked.

We stopped and I introduced myself. She had a pleasant face, hazel eyes that peeked out from under a thick shawl wound around her head.

"Nora," she said, and firmly shook my hand.

She suggested we walk together and resort our luggage making use of the bike to haul as much as possible. Nora offered to manage Ivan and I handled the bike. The dog took to her immediately and pulled with renewed vigor.

"I really appreciate this. You have no idea how tired I am." I said.

She replied, "You are really doing me a favor. I had been hoping to find company for some protection, as it were. There has been looting and rumors of ugly incidents around here."

Some protection I could provide I thought; I was so tired I could hardly keep my eyes open. I did wear a double shoulder harness, but the two ammunition pouches were not filled with ammunition, they contained cigarettes and chocolates. The only weapon I had was a little nine millimeter Beretta pistol with exactly four bullets in the magazine.

After a while, I couldn't control my curiosity and blurted out, "Where were you during the attack last night and what was it like?"

She just raised one hand in the direction of the ugly orange-yellow haze forming a dome over Dresden a few miles away. "What can I say?" At the catch in her voice, I noticed the tears in the corner of her eyes.

We walked on silently for a while and soon found ourselves alone because most of the other people on the train had been stopping frequently to rest the weight of their luggage. As we came closer to the river, the acrid smell increased. Each time a little gust of wind hit us, it swirled up ashes into our faces. It was a cold night, but the perspiration on my forehead made a place for some of the ashes to stick. I noticed it when I wiped my free hand across my head. I looked at her and saw the ashes sticking to her temples.

I asked, "Were you close to the city when it started?"

"No. My parents and I were at my relatives' place at Lössnitz. We wanted to discuss what to do in case the Russians would come to Dresden. The house was standing on high ground so there was a good view of the city. Somewhere between 9:00 p.m. and 10:00 p.m. I noticed those ugly flares, the markers we call Christmas trees, over the city. We heard no alarm sirens, although obviously there must have been planes in the air. There was no anti-aircraft fire either. Not one damn shot was fired."

"And then they came at about 10:15 p.m. I've never heard a more threatening noise in my life, hundreds of planes. The first explosions were so powerful that even where we were everything seemed to shake. After these, came the rolling thunder of bombs and the raining down of incendiaries. I don't know, I think it was about fifteen or twenty minutes and it was over. I guess the planes turned around and went home."

"How did your people take it?" I asked.

"It was awful. Mother turned away from the window and started shrieking. We had to hold her, trying to calm her down. My father and my uncle opened a bottle and sat staring at the sea of flames that filled the air over Dresden. Mother hasn't stopped. She's tossing and turning, cursing her fate, cursing Hitler, cursing the country, the enemy, the whole world. Poor mother. She never has recovered from my brother's death in Russia."

"Oh, no," I muttered.

"It was three years ago." She went on, "Anyway, around midnight Uncle Theo's son came by with a big truck. He was on his way to Radebeul to get gas and other supplies for his father's rescue team, which was still working in downtown Dresden. He agreed to take all of us back to our farm on his way."

"At home, we tried to calm Mother who refused to go to bed. Just as I brought her some Baldrian tea, the sirens in our village started up again. The radio announced, 'The fleet of bombers has just changed direction and is approaching Dresden.' Then there was silence.

"We could hear them coming almost immediately. This must have been between 1 and 2:00 a.m. Wave after wave rolled by our window, dropping their immense loads on the still burning city. A few of our searchlights were flashing around wildly above us, trying in vain to catch one of the intruders. There was hardly any defensive fire. After thirty minutes or so, they too turned away."

"Thank god! Our doctor came that very minute to check on Mother and he gave her an injection. Before she went to sleep, I had to promise her that I would go to Dresden-Neustadt this afternoon to find out how Grandmother was doing, she is eighty-years-old and has a heart condition."

"Sorry to hear that," I sympathized. Then, it hit me where she was going, "Did you say Dresden-Neustadt?"

"Yes."

"That's where I am hoping to find my fiancée. We were supposed to get married today, Ash Wednesday. Oh no, it's past midnight. Where does your grandmother live? Gundel lives in Melanchton Strasse."

"Bautzener Strasse," she said. There was a pause when we just looked at each other, recognizing the amazing coincidence. After a while Nora said in a caring tone of voice, "We know some of Dresden-Neustadt was destroyed. Don't set your hopes too high."

"I'm trying not to. How was your family when you left?" I asked.

"Thank god! Mother slept through the American attack, which came about 1:00 p.m. this afternoon."

"I almost forgot. Do you want to talk about it?"

"It's all right. We only could guess, there was so much smoke and haze we didn't know where or what they bombed, but we knew Dresden was hit again by hundreds of bombers. This was followed by numerous Jabo attack - fighter bombers, Mustangs - swooping down low to strafe or bomb, to hit with rockets anything that moved." Her voice trailed.

"Sorry, I don't think I'd like to go on with this. All I know is what Uncle Theo told me. He came home late in the afternoon after having worked around the clock. His hair had turned white and he walked with a stoop and was utterly exhausted. Each time we asked a question, he started shaking."

We stopped for a while to give her time to get hold of herself. She said under tears, "Let's see. Where are we going? You said Melanchton Strasse. We're now in Leipziger Strasse, close to the river."

We were not alone any more. This street was alive with a steady stream of trucks going in both directions, loaded with either the wounded or those for whom help had come too late. They had tried to cover these people, but not carefully enough. There were rescue workers on foot as well: civilians, Labor Service, soldiers, SS and foreign volunteers in SS uniforms and prisoners of war, mostly American or British. Only some of the prisoners walked under guard, many just came in little groups on their own.

One American airman stopped in front of us, "Where do you imagine you're going?"

"Dresden - Neustadt." I replied.

He shook his head and walked away.

I turned to Nora. "Do you think you could find Melanchton Strasse by taking a detour? Not only do I feel embarrassed not to be helping in the face of all this, but I would not enjoy explaining my presence here to an MP even though I have the proper papers."

She led me to a side street on the right and immediately we found ourselves in an eerie silence. The only signs of life in this deserted area were a few dogs and cats sniffing at the smoking ruins. The closer we came to the river, the more intensive were the signs of destruction. I recognized nothing standing in front of the street sign, "Melanchton." I didn't even know which way to turn.

It was 2:00 a.m. when I finally recognized Gundel's address, Melanchton Strasse 25. I took Ivan off the leash. We went cautiously around the ruin and found no clues, no messages. Across the street, outside a partially destroyed building attached to the front gate, we found a cardboard sign, "We all went to Meissen. Call Lotti," then a telephone number.

We turned around and sat down on the cold curbstone to collect our thoughts. Against the orange glow of the burning city center, we could get a broader view of what was left of Gundel's building across the street. Only the jagged outline of the left front corner remained. The roof and the third floor were gone completely and on the second story level, where Gundel had rented her room, there was only the bathroom corner standing, and of that only the toilet bowl remained, still on its pipes, dangling in the air. Every once in a while it would clatter against the wall in a gust of an early morning breeze. Far away we heard the siren of an ambulance, and closer by a jackhammer was at work.

I felt numb and lightheaded and was afraid I would be sick. Nora put her arm around my shoulder to comfort me and moaned, "Oh god! Oh god!" We sat there for some time as I tried to pull myself together.

I finally said, "Well, this is not necessarily all bad. If the house was spared by the first attack, they might have made it out of here. After all, we saw only a few blocks away some neighborhoods that were empty, but untouched and in good shape."

"Yes, Vince, that's what Uncle Theo told me. Many people living around the rim of the fire storm just took off in a panic once the first attack was over. They had never experienced anything like it. They just went anywhere as long as it was away from the city."

I folded my rubber coat to sit on and we settled down to a macabre picnic. The can opener worked. "Meat in its own juice," the label said. We opened the cognac and the dark army rye bread. There was not much conversation for the next ten minutes. We took turns sipping from the bottle.

Ivan had been investigating the neighborhood. After dropping a dark blue high-heeled shoe by my feet he settled down and waited for his share of the meat. He must have been hungry too, he readily ate the army bread which Nora had dipped in the can in small bits for him.

"Was your grandmother completely independent still?" I asked.

"Yes. She cooked very tasty meals for herself and occasional guests. The last days must have been a traumatic experience for her." Her eyes filled with tears. "What if, you know, we can't even use the telephone. What do I do?"

"Let's go and see," I said.

The food and the cognac had given us a second wind and we prepared to go. Ivan took off, then brought back another high-heeled shoe. Normally the items he delivered to me were part of a throw and fetch game we had; this was different, the second shoe was identical to the first one. It was an odd circumstance we both thought was worth our attention.

Nora said, "I think Ivan has been exploring around that porch." We both looked in that direction and noticed a concrete stairwell by the side of it, a place we somehow hadn't noticed before.

"I'll check it out," I said as I walked the few steps to the stairs. In the dim light I could see bits of debris and a crumpled mound lying at the bottom of the well which appeared to lead to a cellar. I went down the stairs and found the body of a woman stretched face down on a wooden grate. I didn't have to turn her over to know her condition, she was stone cold.

Nora watched from the top of the stairs. We looked at the body for a few moments then I asked, "Shouldn't we...?"

Nora covered her mouth with her hand and said with a quiet strained sound, "This is the first dead human I have ever seen ... you mean bring her up?"

I nodded, "Yes, if you wouldn't mind, I wouldn't feel right just leaving her down here."

Nora took two steps down the concrete. "All right."

I turned the woman over. "It's a Russian worker," I remarked. Her heavy quilted overcoat made it possible for me to grab her, but it was not as easy as I had imagined. I could not quite get her up and out by myself. Nora came closer and I gave her my gloves. "Would you take the feet, please."

She tried, "I can't hang on. She's wearing nylons."

I took off my belt and placed it around the woman's ankles so Nora had the belt to hang on to. We managed to get her up the stairs that way. Nora and I were perspiring with our efforts, breathing hard.

Once above ground, we noticed more details. Of course, her shoes were missing, she was dressed up for the evening, and she wore the patch identifying her as a Russian domestic labor volunteer. I said, "I saw something like that patch in Berlin in 1943, but the two girls I met did not wear their quilted coats out in public, knowing it would put their comparatively sheltered set-up at risk. They borrowed German coats from their employer even though their own coats were a lot warmer. Look, she has cleverly covered her identifying patch. I wonder if she did that to avoid the curfew and go to a movie. I can't help thinking this poor kid was sure she would avoid Russian retribution by volunteering to work in a German household in peaceful Dresden."

"How do you know that's what she was doing?" Nora asked.

I replied, "If she had been in one of those forced labor camps she would have a different patch and would not have had access to the black market to buy nylons."

I had no way of judging for certain what had killed her, but the closeness of some buildings that were completely blown away indicated it might have been one of those air mines. I didn't think my conjecture was worth mentioning to Nora who was tiring visibly and wanted to leave. I was ready too. We were both shaken.

We took off in a north-easterly direction and quickly came to Bautzener Strasse. After a few miles, we stood in front of a deserted apartment house. There were no messages anywhere around on the outside of the building. Her grandmother's apartment door was half open, and by the light of an oil lamp Nora found, we saw that the flat was empty. Of course, there was no electricity, no water, no gas on the stove, no central heating. Ivan found a bucket with some water and decided it was drinkable.

Nora was not heartbroken to find her grandmother gone and no note. She gave me a hug and then with tears in her eyes said, "I can only hope someone has taken her somewhere safe. I must admit I am relieved I don't have to face another crisis tonight. I have to get some sleep," she said.

She showed me how to arrange the sofa into some kind of bed and went into another room. We didn't say goodnight. I just sat down on the sofa, put up my feet on a chair and opened the cognac again. When

I was about to pour the second shot, Nora came back into the room and said she couldn't sleep either. She nestled down next to me and we sat, talked, drank for some time, until we both fell asleep, hand in hand.

Thursday morning wasn't really a morning. There was no sun, hardly daylight. Smoke hung like a curtain over Dresden-Neustadt. Nora found some bread and some fruit juice and the three of us went back to Melanchton Strasse. What seemed to be a long walk in the night was now hardly more than a mile. The street was still mostly deserted. It was an eerie quiet. In the distance, we heard the digging for survivors.

As Nora and I checked again in the neighborhood for anything that might help us know about Gundel, we heard a few alarm sirens howling from far off. The dolorous drone of the Flying Fortresses immediately gobbled up the siren's whining. They were turned on much too late to do us any good. "Take cover," I yelled. Barely visible through haze and smoke, there they were as if in a peaceful exercise, formation after formation. My throat went dry. A huge bomb load crashed down some distance away leaving Nora and me shaking with the tremors. Earthquakes must feel like that, I thought to myself. Ivan snuggled up to the back side of my knee. He hated the sound of explosions. It stopped as fast as it had come, and now there was silence. I noticed that again there was no anti-aircraft fire.

Nora hammered the ground with her fists, sobbing. "When is it going to end?" I couldn't think of anything to say, put my hand on her shoulder for a moment and then reached for the cognac bottle. More army ration, more cognac.

It wasn't long before a few inhabitants returned to see if any of their belongings could be salvaged. One man was helpful; he did remember Gundel for her long light blond hair and suggested we inquire at her school on Bautzener Strasse. It turned out to be a good idea. The caretaker of the Mary Wigman School for Modern Dance assured us that Gundel and two friends had safely left for Hamburg before the

Americans came for their daylight attack. There was the relief I had been hoping for. Nora rode her bicycle back to her grandmother's apartment, while I looked around the school and reminisced.

Nora soon returned. "I found out from a neighbor that grandmother was evacuated. Look," she continued, "it's obvious you won't be able to get a train out of Dresden. There's nothing more that either of us can do here. Come back with me to our farm near Radebeul and from there you can more likely find a train to Meissen and southern Germany."

It was a long walk and Nora did most of the talking. "Why do you want to go to Italy to certain disaster? I could hide you here until the war is over. Please, don't go to Italy."

I tried to avoid a direct answer for a while, tired and frustrated and foot-sore as I was. It occurred to me that in choosing my footwear I had not considered the possibility of all this hiking. As luck would have it, halfway to Radebeul we saw one of those old fashioned public bath houses. It too was deserted, however we found it still had water so we washed up. In the room next door we discovered built-in tubs for washing feet. It was luxurious to sit there opposite each other with our feet dangling in the lukewarm water. It must have been hot in the heating tank before the water supply was cut off.

I touched a painful spot on my foot, but couldn't quite see what it was. "That's a big blister that burst and it's bleeding," Nora said. I took out my first aid kit and we cleaned and padded it. While we were at it we cleaned an abrasion on her right heel and bandaged that too. After our foot bath and first aid session, we both felt better. We even found a way to wash Ivan to get rid of what he had been exposed to on the floor of the railway car.

With the comfort of fresh socks and for me, better shoes, Nora again brought up the subject of hiding me there in her district. I had no intention of deserting, no matter the pressures, the risks, as I saw them, were too great to consider seriously. I decided I had better be direct and quietly responded, "Nora, you are the most wonderful Samaritan anyone in my situation could have found. I will always cherish the memory of these hours we have been together. Please, let's not discuss such life and death matters until we have a chance to rest and calm down. I am too vulnerable at this moment, too distraught. Did I say I am fond of you? I love you, but this can only be a short encounter. To be sure, I would not have been able to accomplish by myself what we did together with your help and guidance. I can only say I cannot be party to a scenario which would put you or your folks at risk, regardless of what I might think of deserting the army. Just recently, I saw a photo of a young woman strung up on a street lantern with a poster hanging around her neck which said, 'I helped to hide a deserter.'" Nora was silent and looked away, biting her lip.

On our walk to Radebeul, Nora talked about her family with an uncustomary frankness. She conceded her family was so exposed to public scrutiny that they must have made enemies. Nora didn't approve, but could understand the opportunistic motivations for her parent's involvement in the local Nazi organization.

"My mother is the leader of the local NSDAP (Nazi Women's Organization). My father is in charge of the local chapter of the Nazi Party Farmers' Organization, which oversees seeding, harvesting and delivering according to quotas. I know my parents have enemies among the villagers and among the POWs working for us as well. Those men get three good meals a day, all right, but my father has been known to be abusive and hit some of them occasionally, particularly the Slavics. Vince, I never thought to hide you on the farm, only with my friends out in the country. Since my brother died, Father drinks around the clock and Mother has one depression after another."

"Why is it you talk without a trace of the Saxon accent?" I asked, suddenly noticing.

She looked away for a moment, then turned and looked me straight in the eye and replied, "Everything centered around my brother. At grade five, they farmed me out to an *Internat*, an expensive boarding school for girls. I felt as stifled as if I were in a convent, tomboy that I was. I couldn't stand it and complained to Mother. She became furious and said that one day when I would marry an industry captain or a Party District Chief, I would be grateful to her. You can imagine, Vince, what this did to my chances of blending back into this rustic setting. The local men find me a bit overwhelming."

Nora wanted to know more about Gundel and I became evasive. She could see my increased anxiety when Gundel's name was brought up, so she changed the subject back to Italy.

By the time we reached Nora's family farm, there was barely enough daylight to get a general impression. Nora turned off to the left, handed me Ivan's leash and put the guard dog, a big Doberman, into its doghouse and disappeared into the main building. I noticed the Doberman's leash was connected to a ring on a guard wire leading straight in our direction. The two dogs snarled at each other, and Ivan was spoiling for a fight and pulling at the leash.

Nora returned and led us to the biggest barn on our left, passing the typical central European dung heap in the middle of all the buildings. "These are our POWs," she explained pointing to a group of farm workers standing on the opposite side of the heap. The men had turned around and Nora responded to their friendly greetings. The workers were wearing odd bits of uniforms under half-open military greatcoats from various European armies.

"How many of these men do you have here?" I asked, slightly out of breath from the steep climb up the ladder to the second floor of the biggest barn.

She replied, "Between twelve and fifteen, mostly from Poland, Yugoslavia and Russia."

We carried all our gear into a spacious room that had the appearance of an office with a daybed under the window. "Our manager used to stay here when he wasn't able to go home after work. He's the man on crutches you saw in the middle of those prisoners. He lost a leg near Moscow."

Apart from the bed, there was a table, two chairs and a washstand. "Sorry, this is the only room left. All available rooms are occupied by refugee families from Dresden; the lucky ones who could get out after the first attack on the 13th.

"How's your mother?" I asked.

"We'll have to watch her continuously, she is still disoriented, talks to herself incessantly. Will you be able to get some rest here?"

"Thanks a lot, Nora, but I could have slept on straw near a horse. This is great. Thank you."

Nora put out some towels and soap. Two pitchers of hot water were brought up by a female worker. The room was warm thanks to the heat of the horses below. Nora looked around, "I'll fix some supper for you, you must be hungry. What about Ivan? Is there anything he should not be offered?"

"Sometimes he and I had to exist on Red Cross soup and bread, he'll be fine with anything," I remarked.

After my sponge bath, I sat down and scribbled some notes to Gundel and fell asleep at the table.

"Oh! you finished the Cognac. Thank goodness!" That woke me up. Nora had a tray with hot food. "This is rabbit stew," she said. I opened the bottle of champagne and had my first good look at Nora, who looked beautifully feminine. Her ash blonde hair was loose to her shoulders; she looked relaxed and quite a bit younger than she had. Over a stylish woolen dress she wore a silver gray quilted jacket, knee length.

"You look great." I stopped right there and shifted position. I had to take stock of my situation and soon. Here I was, with the letter to my fiancée half-finished on the table, and at the same time was being lulled by the comfort of this clean warm room, the delicious smell of well-prepared food and the charm of this lovely woman. We had shared an unusually intense experience during the last two days and this situation alone, I realized, could make us vulnerable enough to go along with the feelings of the moment.

Fortunately, she somehow sensed my backing off from her and she acknowledged her awareness by a gentle smile. We hugged tenderly. Then she said, "I must ask you to excuse me again, uncle and his crew are overdue. I must relay a message by telephone."

She was back in a few minutes, her face flushed from coming out of the cold night air and climbing up the ladder. She unbuttoned her jacket and said, "Wouldn't you have liked this warm coat at times in Russia?"

"It's wonderful, where did you get it?" I asked.

"A Volga German nurse who made it for me soon after she first came here about a year ago."

I had read at Headquarters about the fate of the ethnic Germans in Russia since 1941 and asked, "Did she have to go through one of those mass deportations?"

"Yes, all the Volga Germans were corralled by the Russians and driven in open trucks toward Siberia in the winter of 1941. Having endured being raped several times by the soldiers, she finally found an opportunity to escape using her World War I nurses uniform. Wearing it, she was able to mingle with the guards and then she found an opportunity to get away from the transport. After Stalingrad fell, as you know, the German army in the Caucuses had to retreat and many ethnic Germans who had been living in the foothills took off ahead of that retreating German army. Some of these helped her to end up in Krakow, where she worked as a volunteer in various hospitals. When the Germans had to give up Ukraine and the Russians advanced towards Krakow, she hitch-hiked to Dresden."

"And what did she do here?"

"Oh, she worked around the farm and looked after the welfare of the Russian prisoners, interpreting whenever there was a problem. Father resented her meddling, but he had to admit she was very useful."

"And when did she leave you?" I asked.

"When the Russian forces entered Poland, she again felt it was time to put some distance between herself and the front-line."

I saw this as a perfect opportunity to express my concerns for her welfare and said softly, "The Russians are about eighty miles from here, Nora. Didn't you say your parents and some relatives had a discussion on the 13th as to what to do when the Russians came to Dresden? It's none of my business, but what are you planning to do?"

She shrugged. "I have no illusions about my parents. Like all the other party leaders they will carry out Hitler's orders. Nobody leaves his post, but they will surely have some vehicle hidden away along with some black-market gasoline, and they'll drive off when the time comes leaving the ordinary people to their fate."

There was a knock on the room door. "Sorry, here we go again. I told them to knock when I'm needed again with Mother. Rest up, will you? I'll be back as soon as I can."

When she was gone, I jotted down names and addresses in west and southern Germany where she might find temporary shelter. I decided I had better be careful about teasing her about her idea that she might be able to hide me and how foolish I thought it was. What was really important was that I must not fail to impress upon her what everybody knew since Gumbinnen in early 1944, that the Russian soldiers were encouraged to abuse women as revenge and to create fear and terror among the civilian population. It would be soon open season for all women and no matter what her parents did, Nora should leave immediately.

She returned looking disturbed. "Mother doesn't want to face it any longer. We will have to watch her day and night." I had her sit down, I moved my chair closer and put my arm around her. So, we sat there as we did on her grandmother's couch, weary and tired, enjoying a moment of tenderness.

Again that confounded knock at the door! Even Ivan showed signs of indignation. Nora gave the dog a pat and trudged warily down the ladder.

I continued fishing for suitable persons she could contact. Hildegarde, Ivan's former owner, still seemed to be the most promising choice. She was with at least three children all by herself somewhere in the foothills of Bavaria. Her husband Walter came by only rarely because he was constantly traveling on Nazi party business. Walter and I had become friends when I was schooling at the military academy in Munich. I very much appreciated his critical stance and his honesty when it came to discussing Nazi party corruption, although he was wearing the gold membership medal reserved for only the oldest and closest followers of Hitler.

He had seemed to appreciate my reservations about the mushrooming German Army and sometimes expressed disbelief how they could have made me a lieutenant. I never found out what his traveling was all about, but it must have been diplomatic work and behind the scene negotiating. Anyway, it was top secret. While Hildegarde was still in Munich, her two sisters could still help her. They were now house-sitting in a badly damaged house; their upper floor was practically gone.

Nora came back to Ivan's usual energetic welcome; he had a crush on her and I didn't blame him. All his food had come from her since Ash Wednesday.

"Good news," she said. "I found a *Holzgas* truck. They are burning wood for methane for it to go on. It's slow, but it could drive us to Meissen. There we heard that there is a goods train on a single-track line that is being shunted and scheduled to go south. It's far removed from the main line rail traffic, so it should be relatively safe from U.S. Mustangs. It has mostly flatbed cars, so do you have warm enough clothing to ride in the open air?"

"When I packed the rubberized coverall for my journey, I must have anticipated this. I think I will survive." I tried to joke, "It didn't do much for our appearance on foot, but it will look okay on an open-train car."

I hugged her as a silent expression of my relief that she would not try again to propose hiding me somewhere. She understood. "No, don't worry," as tears came to her eyes.

In the morning after breakfast, Nora and I set out on our way to Meissen. We found the train siding without trouble, Nora and I embraced, she said a short goodbye to Ivan. I flung my luggage onto the last car and Ivan and I climbed aboard. I didn't bother to size up the train as to contents or purpose, I just noticed that they were all open cars. Nora's friends had found a train for me, that was enough. As it started moving I sat down on the last crate, my feet wedged against the tailgate of the car.

◆ ◆ •• •• ◆ •• ◆ •

I discovered there was an SS man with a Tommy gun on the front gate of my car. Behind him was a car with an anti-aircraft gun sitting about four feet higher than my car. As we rounded a bend, the curving train revealed an SS guard on each of the cars and a second anti-aircraft gun behind the vintage engine, which puffed out huge bellows of black smoke.

All this military presence led me to check what I was sitting on. I'd read accounts of blown-up ammunition trains from World War I that were horrendous disasters. I tried to read the description of contents on the crate, but they were coded and illegible. I didn't rest any easier.

Ivan asked for attention, as was his habit whenever he saw me down-cast. He pushed his face up my leg with his cold nose. After a while, he gave up and stretched out between the hinged tailgate and the crate. There were three of these crates on my car, all tied down to the car floor in the center, each two feet high, ten feet long, maybe six feet wide.

I woke up from my stupor and decided to follow Ivan's example. I stretched out next to him and we had some protection against the icy wind. This time Ivan's body warmth couldn't do much for me because I had this confounded rubberized coat on. It would have been foolish to sit on that crate in the wind, although it was only twenty-six degrees.

I couldn't get to sleep. I asked myself silly questions like, "Will the train come to a halt if we have an air attack?" I dismissed that when I remembered how much time it takes the air brakes to really make a train come to a stop; we would probably just keep moving until the engine got a hit. At this not very comforting thought, I must have fallen asleep.

Suddenly, there was a confusion of battle noise and Ivan was pulling on the leash hysterically. The god-awful anti-aircraft guns didn't start firing until after the plane had already strafed the train with rounds of various caliber and was disappearing in the distance. I saw that we were standing on a side track letting another train run by in the oppo-site direction. It was now that the anti-aircraft gun started firing a new magazine right above me. I could see the muzzle flashes and was hit by the deafening noise. He was obsessively trying to hit that distant plane on a very flat trajectory - much too late.

I screamed and waved to the men to stop firing. "Hey, are you out of your mind? You could hit the other train!"

One of them nodded and gave his friends the order to stop. Now, I could see that these dunces were mere boys in blue uniforms, "Air Force helpers" in huge World War I steel helmets, Hitler Youth age.

Ivan was still trembling and shaking. The "Air Force helper" yelled something like "Thank you." Whatever it was, I couldn't hear a thing and became concerned that with these detonations, they might have damaged my ear drums.

I asked the SS man, "What did he say?"

He came very close to yell, "Their gun was jammed." I offered him a cigarette and postponed any conversation. The train started moving. When I could hear again, the SS man told me there were some refugees on the cars near the head of the train who had shrapnel wounds. They would be taken off together with their families at the next railhead twenty miles away.

Ivan at last quieted down and began licking his paws. Although he never had liked detonations, I had never seen him so hysterical. I remembered that in my absence he had been with the baggage train that narrowly escaped the Russian encirclement of Stalingrad in 1942. I wondered if these circumstances might be triggering traumatic memories of that time.

A few hours later, we again found ourselves shunted onto a side track and word was passed along that we would have to wait at least ten minutes. I took Ivan for a walk and he became more relaxed. We were about to climb back up on the car when out of the sun two Mustangs swooped down on us starting to fire the same instant. The train had started to roll but now the brakes were put on rather vehemently which increased the confusion all around.

The train we had been waiting for appeared at this moment attracting one of the Mustangs. Now, all the refugees on the train jumped off to seek cover. I gave a desperate lunge to grab the satchel with my important papers in it and as I did Ivan took a tremendous leap and pulled the leash off my arm. The plane came again and I jumped into a dry ditch and pressed my face into some evil smelling weeds.

The "Air Force helpers" were still trying to put their helmets on, while our train was being worked over by the remaining Mustang. It soon joined the other one to concentrate on the train heading in the opposite direction northeast to the Russian front.

There was damage to the engine and the first three cars. Parents desperately tried to find their children. A number of people were hit badly. The boy in charge of the anti-aircraft gun passed on the radio directive, "Stay where you are. Try to make the injured people comfortable. The emergency train will be here in one hour at the latest."

I gave a hand wherever I could by placing injured people under protection from the wind, family members pulled out covers. A few people had first aid experience, although there were hardly any medical supplies. After a while, I felt I could concentrate on looking for Ivan. I walked up and down the train asking anyone I passed if they had seen him. Nobody had. I kept looking, whistling, calling.

The emergency train arrived and crews started getting our train to move again. The injured people were loaded on the support train and taken to a hospital. Word was given to get back on our train. I asked the train commandant for three more minutes, hoping the noise and commotion of the loading might lure the dog back. No Ivan. I had spent too much of my leave time in Dresden; there was no way I could take more time off to hunt for the dog. I had to force myself to give up and climb back to my perch on the car.

I remained seated on that crate in spite of the discomfort of the icy air stream as the train picked up speed. After a while my grief turned to fury. How could Ivan do this to me! I berated him for his hysterical desertion and then all the indignities I had suffered on his account since 1938. I'd had to separate him from his victims in numberless dog fights; just a few days ago he had been on report at HQ for mauling a guard dog who was unfit for duty for days after the fight.

I don't recall how long my anger at Ivan's behavior had hold of me. It cannot have lasted for more than a few minutes, that is until I fished for my handkerchief with my right hand and I looked down on the sleeve near my left hand splattered with blood. Was this Ivan's? Had he been hit? Was he in shock?

It was difficult to reconstruct those first frantic seconds; however, it soon came to me. The blood must have been from the peasant woman we had carried off the train and laid down in a hollow. She had a cut at the base of her neck, probably a flesh wound. Whether she had any other wounds I didn't know. Her sullen patience had impressed me, as I watched the medic taking care of her.

I tried to calm down her crying children, but it was pretty much in vain. How long, I wondered, had these children together with their mother been searching for some kind of safety. Their despair brought home to me again the terrible plight of civilians touched by this war. What kind of mad thinking was this, to even attempt in the first place to open up a colonial empire in Eastern Europe in the name of Germany? All the suffering I had seen in Dresden was just a microcosm compared to the millions of lives the war, our war, had destroyed. What was the loss of Ivan, merely a pet, in light of the world-wide tragedy we were witnessing? What was the temporary loss of Gundel? She was probably safe. What was the loss of Nora? I'd barely got to know her. My grief was giving way to rage and shame. What the hell did I think I could do with Ivan in Italy anyway? I would be in my foxhole and he would again be somewhere near the field kitchen, a few miles back and just as exposed to hostile fire. I should have left him with someone in a more stable situation like Nora's.

Here I was on my way to Italy accepting orders, ready to carry them out. I had better recognize that I have judged numberless generals guilty of spinelessness for their obedient performance of duty, when they must have had knowledge that whatever they did was militarily worthless and as well often wasteful of human life. In my lesser position, I was just as afraid to disobey and be alone as if I were to follow my own conscience wherever it led. How much fun we officers made of Keitel when we saw his name rubber-stamping Hitler's orders. Colonel Gehlen had repeatedly said that it was irrational to believe that this whole thing could come to some kind of an acceptable ending. I thought of that same impulse toward blind optimism that keeps the front-line soldier at his station.

It got so cold I unpacked my luggage and got out the battle dress we called the winter coverall and hid my face behind my ski mask. In reorganizing my pack, I brought out Ivan's emergency rations from the duffel bag. I grabbed the hard tack, compliments of the Royal British Army (World War I Gallipolli vintage or else Tobruk, World War II) and threw them by handful over the tailgate. It was followed by his spare leash, his muzzle, his food bowl, brushes, combs and other paraphernalia including his flea powder. As I reached the bottom of the bag I was surprised to find an envelope, which turned out to be a note from Nora.

"Dear Vincenz,

When you unfold this little note you will probably be across the Alps enjoying a peaceful sunny day near Bolzano, or thereabouts. (Do I wish I could be there with you!)

How will I remember you? Oh, yes, you told me about Bernard Shaw's Captain Bluntschli, the Swiss mercenary who had his ammunition pouches filled with chocolates and other goodies instead of bullets. Well, you had that - and cognac. So, I will remember you as my 'Cognac Captain,' not that there is anything wrong with cognac, it helped me over some of the worst moments of Ash Wednesday, 1945. Thanks for being with me, cognac and all.

I do have news. Uncle Theo came up with a plan whereby I accompany Mother to a renowned psychiatric institution in Bad Viessee, Bavaria. I will go as a Red Cross nurse, uniform, proper papers, everything authorized and legal. I hope this starts soon and comes off without a glitch. I added the little snapshot, it was taken two years ago and out of date - just in case we do meet again, two survivors having a difficult time in recognizing each other.

Please take care of yourself. If the general situation is as gruesome as you told it, then you will be needed after it's all over. Love, Nora"

The train was rolling through pretty ever changing hills and valleys of Thuringia. The forests looked lovely, still partially covered by snow. The clouds came lower and lower promising a relative quiet and safe journey without any more air attacks. Just as I decided, I could sense by smell that it would start snowing, flakes began to strike my face.

It wasn't long before the train was being shunted on to a side track. The Air Force soldier I had talked to early on came climbing over his tail-gate and brought me a cup of hot black coffee.

"Real coffee?" I asked.

"Yes, sir." He struggled with his massive winter coat. "Air Force, you know."

"I see Hermann (Göring) is looking out for his kids," I observed.

He nodded. We talked for a few seconds and then he came to the point. "I wonder how far it is from Saarbrücken to Heidelberg. Would you have any idea, sir?"

"Sixty, seventy miles, I would guess, I mean as the crow flies."

"Sixty, seventy miles?"

"Yes," I answered. "Why?"

With a sheepish grin he said, "We just heard on the radio Patten is approaching Saarbrücken."

"The Amies, eh?" I was immediately on guard.

"Yes, Sir." he blushed.

I said, "Look, whatever it is you are listening to, don't share that with just anyone, okay? You're likely to find yourself hanging from a lamp-post with a cardboard poster hanging around your neck saying, 'I listened to the BBC.'"

He nodded, snapped to attention, "Sorry about your dog, Sir, and thank you."

He left, and I slept fitfully as the train kept rolling and stopping in turn until we reached the outskirts of Nuremberg. I heard the familiar shouts, "End Station. All refugees bound for the south have to walk through Nuremberg. There will be guides to help you find transportation to Munich."

It was hiking again. I was glad to be able to move. In these early morning hours, it was cold. Backpack and duffel bag felt much lighter, which was just as well. This time I was alone. It was pretty depressing passing through the ruins of this medieval town and at the same time remembering the optimism and the holiday atmosphere among the people who watched those of us in the Labor Service during the 1936 Party Rally at that same location.

After half-an-hour, I noticed I was walking past some military barracks. It was about 7:00 a.m. and the soldiers were singing - on orders, no doubt. "Oh no!" I said to myself as I recognized one of those off-color songs, that raunchy thing "Anna Marie."

Then there was a pause and I heard the voice of the noncom in charge, "*zwei, drei*" and the next song started. This one had been played over and over since the war started. The refrain: "For we are sailing, we're sailing, we're sailing against England." I was appalled. As I walked, I thought of all the thousands of German sailors who had been sent to their death, while the leadership was fully aware that the Allied Navies, due to their superior technology, would beat them at every turn. There was by now nothing much left of Hitler's Navy except a few units used almost exclusively for the rescue of refugees and Army units from East Prussia.

Another song followed. Oh god! I felt nauseated. I didn't know the lyrics of the verses; however, the refrain was unmistakable. It had been burned in my memory years before Hitler had taken power when I had heard the SA and some of the teenage Hitler Youth gangs sing it as they marched through the streets of Hamburg. It was a protest challenge to law, order, to the capitalistic establishment and all decent human behavior as well. My friends and I had thought it was a perverted bit of ugliness then, which nobody in his right mind would take seriously - the bragging of thugs: *Und wenn das Judenblut von Messer spritzt, dann geht's noch mal so gut* (And when the Jewish blood squirts off the knife, then it feels twice as good).

No regular Army, as I knew it, would ever have sung this garbage. Then I noticed, as if to confirm my suspicion, the SS insignias on both sides of the wrought-iron gate to the compound. My pace quickened and I soon passed the partially bombed out barracks on the southern end.

◦ ◆ ◦ ◦ ◆ ◦ ◦ ◆ ◦

February 20, 1945. At Munich the railway system had been repaired and was functioning. I phoned Gerda and we met downtown over ersatz coffee. I learned she was still working with Allied prisoners in the hospital north of Munich, and said that if she didn't have that job in the hospital as a Red Cross volunteer she would have to work in a factory or dig trenches. She told me that she was even more aware of the impending doom since a conversation with her older sister's husband who she said was "still pretty high up in the Nazi hierarchy." He had lately stopped by for half a day to take a few more household goods to his family now staying in a nearby village. For the first time, Gerda heard him express the idea that there was no hope for any change in Germany's fate and there were no "miracle weapons." When she heard that I was on my way to Italy, she gave me the Military Mail number of her husband. We both felt the loss in Ivan's disappearance.

I continued by train to the Italian border. Again, no window panes. The Brenner Pass was in deep snow and it was beastly cold. I was well on the way to my new division, the only place where I, as a front-line soldier, could feel safe, a place where I belonged. The train did not stop except for Innsbruck. Remarkable that they still tried to keep a fast train, I thought.

I approached the check point at the Italian border with some misgivings because in the snow all around me I could see bomb craters and broken vehicles of all kinds. The MP told me to continue by hitch-hiking since the constant air attacks on railway lines and bridges had blocked all further rail traffic. The rotund officer of the watch, a fatherly sergeant, asked me, "Have you been in this country before?"

"Yes, in 1943," I replied.

"Well, you'll find a few changes. They have total command in the air and you better constantly observe the Italians around you, especially when riding in a car. As pedestrians, they are not encumbered by engine noise and they are clever in recognizing danger from the air."

"What do they do?"

"They warn each other and you by using hand signals." He demonstrated with his right hand and said, "This means take cover, the planes are coming." He wished me luck with not just the usual theatrical send-off, "Break a leg," he said in the more thorough German way, "*Hals und Beinbruch*" (Break your neck and your leg). He seemed to enjoy his educational assignment. As he returned my papers, he said, "*Immer Deutscher Grüss und Deutscher Blick.*" His men grinned as they too watched him in his mocking demonstration, strutting around almost in place while giving the Nazi salute and staring into the air, mouth wide open. I hope nobody reported his disrespectful parody.

At dusk a German supply truck stopped for gasoline on its way to the troops near Bologna which, I had been told, was in quarantine for some typhoid epidemic. But since I only needed to go as far as Ferrara, the driver allowed me to climb up to the top of the load and ride in the open air. He apologized for the drafty condition of my accommodations by saying that the protective tarpaulin had been irreparably torn and thrown away.

To me the situation looked acceptable enough since I was wearing winter combat clothing. For added protection against the icy mountain wind, I built myself a nest using the cardboard cartons I found in the back of the truck. Forgetting for a minute about the clattering of the wood walls containing the load, it was a beautiful way to cross the Alps. Stretched out on my back in this cardboard trough I gazed at the clear winter sky. The stars appeared more numerous and much brighter than I had remembered them to be in northern Europe. Did Hannibal riding across the Alps on his elephant have time for contemplating this sort of thing? How many days had it taken Hannibal to reach Italy anyway? I expected to get across in one night. Then again, Hannibal hadn't taken this route, had he? Ah, yes. Those invaders had come from southern France. I must have dozed off and woke up when the truck had to steer around some smashed-up vehicles and was stopped by another MP.

A few minutes later, I was joined on the truck by a young woman who claimed to be an Italian nurse. She spoke German with a Viennese accent and was so talkative that I instinctively was on my guard. Besides, her pungent perfume bothered me, and I was suspicious about her expensive fur coat.

She let me know I should have stayed in Dresden and gone into hiding since the war was practically over anyway. The woman said she knew that the average ammunition allowance for a German frontline soldier in Italy was not more than five rounds per day and all vital supplies and gasoline were limited by the constant Allied air attacks on the few single supply lines through the Alps.

The truck finally stopped in Ferrara to allow me to get off. The woman motioned goodbye. I tossed down my bags and awkwardly jumped. It hurt to feel the cobblestones under my feet after such a long cold ride. As far as I know, the woman went on with the truck to Bologna and I was relieved to be rid of her. Our conversations had made me feel uncomfortable because I thought she could easily have been part of an intelligence setup.

It must have been around 2:30 a.m. when I found on the medieval city square the only open hotel. I didn't bother to undress, but straightaway stretched out on the creaking bed and stared at the single dim light bulb in the ceiling. I smoked one of those awful Italian cigarettes and finally must have fallen asleep.

Allied planes woke me with a bomb attack at dawn. The building was severely damaged, but no one was hurt, as far as I could discover. It was just another day.

I felt lucky to find a sidecar motor bike going on to Imola. It was a relatively safe trip. The low cloud cover limited air craft activity and only three times we had to hide the machine and throw ourselves to the ground.

At the divisional headquarters, I was received with disbelief. Clearly, I had not been expected. No wire or written order had preceded my arrival. The officer in charge of personnel turned out to be Major Fuchs from Spandau.

This same Major Fuchs was greeting me with what appeared to be some relief saying he knew exactly where I should be placed. I thought he was a bit condescending in his magnanimous gestures. After all, we had been in command of a company in the same battalion since spring '41 and he had even been the temporary battalion commander once our commander and my friend Friedrich, his adjutant, had been killed on that first day in Russia. After our exchanges, he excused himself to turn back to a group of freshly arrived replacements he had been addressing. To these he extolled the virtues of blind obedience in light of the coming "final victory" for the German forces.

In peacetime this Major Fuchs had trained with us as an Olympic Pentathlon contender for the 1940 games in Stockholm, which never took place. Some of my friends and I had been used as pacers for this would-be Olympic team. My garrison in Berlin was located next to the 1936 Olympic facilities. At the time, we idealized these talented athletes. One of them, Fleckner, had even been my company commander from 1939 to 1941, that is to say, all through the French campaign.

As I stood there listening, I was shocked to realize that this man now was one of these new "ideological supervisors," a veritable Nazi political commissar of the same type that the Russian officers always had breathing down their necks. I felt that no self-respecting German officer would take such a job because it meant spying on his fellow officers; however, I knew that after the foiled assassination attempt at Hitler's headquarters on July 20, 1944, every army unit had to have one of them. Nonetheless, I resented his hypocrisy. He knew full well that the Americans were near Giessen, the Russians were encircling Berlin, and almost all transportation within Germany had been smashed.

In the evening, I was taken to the First Battalion 992 Regiment. I relieved a middle-aged captain of the reserve who seemed under a nervous strain and spoke somewhat incoherently. He left as soon as he could. Later, I learned this man had previously broken down under stress and was barely holding together. When his battalion was nearly over-run near the Solerno River, he had convinced himself that there was no way out. This had happened three weeks before I came and now he could be sent back for some observation and counseling.

When I found some of my men from our various former units, I felt immediately at home. The hope of such reunions had motivated my choice to join this division in the first place. Some of these men came from the company that was destroyed in Stalingrad in 1943 and some came from the new unit rebuilt in France in the same year, which had ceased to exist in Ukraine in 1944. All of them were the lucky wounded who had been shipped home before their companies were completely destroyed. During our reminiscing, I was able to inquire as to the fate of friends. Not all of my questions could be answered. I was conscious of repressing my growing sense of guilt at having survived by my legitimate, but in the light of what had happened, somewhat trivial reasons.

It was only now that I gleaned from the divisional roster that each regiment had only two battalions instead of the three I was used to. So, what looked like a division on paper now lacked one third of its conventional strength. Typical of Hitler's self-delusions, I thought, here we had only about fifty men left in each company anyway. We were so shorthanded that we were depending on the Hiwis, the Russian prisoners of war who had volunteered to serve with the German Army to get out of the death-trap prison camps. They cared for our horses and supplies extremely well, carried food and ammunition to the front lines and helped with the logistics in general. We couldn't have done anything without them. We appreciated them, treated them well and they never presented any problems. Unfortunately, some of these became casualties since the British had a habit of shelling the supply routes indiscriminately at night on all roads leading to the front.

On my second day, I had to go back and attend a veterinarian checkup of the ninety-odd horses of my battalion. While watching the veterinarian making his rounds I wondered about the survival of those horses. I could not imagine another withdrawal where these horses would be useful. To keep horses when the opponent is relying almost totally on mechanized forces seemed silly, but that was the German Army. Only ten to fifteen per cent of its divisions were motorized.

The unwieldy horse-drawn divisions of World War I vintage still had to deal with feed and then hide about 4,000 horses from each division, and these horses had to be fed with precious oats and other expensive and rare grains. I just couldn't believe it. The more I thought about the sheer transportation problem of getting these supplies, the more grotesque it all seemed to me that they were there in the first place. We nurtured them and then we exposed them to the destructive forces of the battlefield. I had often seen them suffer in action. The screams of those wounded horses still haunt my dreams.

The end of the German Army in Italy could be only a matter of days or at most weeks away. After all, the Russians were outside Berlin and General Patton roamed around Frankfurt. Horse inspections at this point were pointless, I thought. At the moment I was painfully aware that we were at the mercy of highly mechanized and motorized armies and here in Italy we had thousands of horses to contend with.

That same night the young orderly officer guided me through our perimeter. To my amazement, I saw for the first time the Allied search-lights illuminating the Italian sky from Rimini on the Adriatic across to Livorno on the Ligurian Sea - a continuous chain of light, I was told. I had just come from the typical World War II winter night, where there was no light whatsoever except when the searchlights blazed during an air attack. Even the cars had their front lights dimmed to a narrow slit. Because of the darkness many people came to grief in accidents while driving or just walking.

Here, I was standing in front of a dome of light comparable to the one Albert Speer had invented for the Nazi party rallies at Nuremberg and later for the Olympic games. It turned the night into something fantastically unreal. Obviously, it was to the advantage of the Allied troops. They could easily see the illuminated Germans, but we stared into their blinding light. Of course, at the same time it also helped us. We didn't have to grope around in the dark among those foxholes and shell craters to go about our business.

It was my duty to welcome some new replacements from Berlin. Among them was a famous young actor who I knew from newspaper accounts between 1936 and 1941. His career interested me and I hoped to get to know him to hear more about it. They all gave me their names and answered questions about their families and what experience they had as soldiers. I decided to tell them that the Americans were near Kassel and the Russians were fighting in Berlin, and here in Italy they could expect only limited resources including ammunition. At the moment, the average was only five rounds per man per day. This should not be interpreted to mean we all were unimportant or expendable. I asked them to do their duty and I also pleaded with them not to engage in last minute heroism - risking their lives needlessly and possibly that of their comrades. The young actor gasped in disbelief. I nodded and said, "Yes, only two weeks ago in Berlin, Major Count R. was hanged for saying that the war was lost. You draw your own conclusions."

Every night after that, when I made rounds of the perimeter, I had an enjoyable time talking with this young actor about Berlin and the stage. We had many things in common including the love of Shakespeare and Kliest. I was glad to hear that nowadays more earthy translations of the former were used on German stages. The Shakespeare translation I had read at school did not do justice to the poet, I thought.

March 9, 1945, our battalion moved over to Tossignano, west of Costa, a dream of an assignment. We had a perfect view deep into the Santerno Valley, while defending the steep rocky cliff. I entertained some wishful thinking that if only the war could come to an end right here and now, it would be a perfect place to receive the news of it. I wouldn't have to withdraw for miles and miles and possibly have to cross various rivers such as the big River Po.

The battalion headquarter, however, was on the back slope two miles north and that was a different story. The Tommies must have spotted us there and shelled us day and night at irregular intervals with solid projectiles, that is to say, shells without detonators. The rounds were possibly steel casings filled with concrete or something like it. There were no direct hits on the primitive dugout or the casa in which we stayed, but the stress was tremendous on the nerves of those soldiers who had to stay inside with their communication equipment. At irregular intervals, a single grenade would howl into the ground around us. Day and night we were waiting for the other shoe to drop, as it were. I was not as affected as the others since I spent most of my time in the open air staying in contact by telephone. Two of my confined wireless operators had to be relieved because they could not stand the stress.

One day, our General came to inspect the Battalion. He was a loud, stocky type who had come up from the ranks. I resented his constant spitting into the fireplace, while giving inane cheer-up speeches. After two or three of those dummy grenades had slammed into the ground close by, this general nervously left. I chuckled to myself when I thought about being told earlier at the Berlin headquarters that he was one of those Generals who had aspirations for getting the Knight's Cross to wear around his neck.

On April 6, 1945, this same general congratulated all units. He said that our division had been promoted to 278 Volks-Grenadier-Division. I recognized this as a nominal gesture. This did not give the unit any special privileges or, for that matter, enough ammunition or better rations. Neither, I noticed, did the general get his Knight's Cross.

Three days later, on April 9, I was in Imola studying the military signposts on the city square trying to find a dentist, when suddenly the long-awaited offensive began. At 2:00 p.m., the ground all around us seemed to groan and roll with detonations some miles east of us. I had no visual perception of exactly where this was happening in the distance, but I could see several hundred big planes coming from the south dropping their bombs at a given location and then sharply turning east toward the Adriatic Sea - a seemingly endless chain of metallic birds glistening in the sun. The explosions created a huge wall of dust and smoke which slowly rose and stayed above the ground like a curtain. It was obvious that the carpet bombing and the massive artillery shelling of the final offensive had started.

What then went through my mind were those reports from the German High Command concerning D-Day in Normandy, which detailed the total destruction of German tank divisions trying to assemble for a counter-attack. Thousands of bombers destroyed numerous tanks by simply upending them with their carpet bombing of hitherto unknown force.

Needless to say, I cut short my search, assuming I would be needed immediately at my battalion. The driver of my one-horse buggy was impatiently waiting for me. Leaving the town, we noticed the air above that curtain of smoke and dust became alive with fighter bombers, which remained after the big bombers had disappeared. A few minutes later, an artillery barrage of tremendous concentration began lasting about forty minutes. I said to myself that I wouldn't like to be one of those Mustang pilots over the target area, while the artillery shells were raining down all around. Once the barrage had stopped, the artillery remained silent for about twenty minutes, then another barrage started. This went on until about 4:00 p.m., when the general battle noise became audible.

I found the battalion staff packing to be ready to move. We had orders to relinquish our beloved Tossignano ridge at dusk on April 10. At this point, I had no idea how serious the situation was with our troops to the east of us, which made it necessary for us to leave Tossignano.

In his book *Die 278 Infanterie-Division in Italien 1944-45*, the commander of our division Lt. General Hoppe describes the last battle of Sesto Imolese April 13 through April 16; and he describes the action of April 9 as having resulted in a "deep penetration" near Lugo. As we know now, the German defenders were pretty much wiped out. So, in retrospect, I find it hard to understand why the general is trivializing this disaster. I had to study Caesar's account of his activities as a Roman general in France, a welcome break from grammar and vocabulary. Our teacher made no bones about what he thought about generals writing books after a military campaign to either justify their actions, blame others, or blame circumstances for defeats, all of which makes life very difficult for historians searching for the truth. I tend to agree with him, particularly after comparing many such works written after World War I, and especially after World War II when I had first-hand knowledge of a given situation. I was surprised to receive this book in November 1954 from General Hoppe with a hand-written dedication to: "Captain Panny, *tapferen 'Kommandeur'* of First Battalion Grenadier Regiment 992 from his Divisional Commander." I have no idea what makes him use the adjective "brave." Up to this afternoon, near Imola, I had not seen any action whatsoever. I had inspected the 400 horses of the Battalion, inspected the line every night and signed every required report that my staff put in front of me, all this required bravery? I bring this up as another example of the habit of gratuitous glorification of the military culture by exaggeration, which I hope to have demonstrated amply in dealing with Major Günther in 1940 and General Abraham in 1943.

General Hoppe's book has been invaluable for the purposes of checking my memory for dates and locations. In spite of my disagreeing with his account of our last battle, my first and last battle under his leadership, I am very grateful to him for his resource and his attempt to do justice to the "brave" men who were involved.

At sunset, the following night April 10, we stole away from our ridge and were directed to join 94 Regiment in the so-called "Hermann" line halfway between Santerno and Senio River, where we spent a quiet day. Apparently, nobody had been following us. I requested to be driven to our next assignment to the "Laura" line along the Santerno to be reached during the night of April 11-12. I hated hiking through the countryside at night along lines of regimental guides, without having any personal impression of our new perimeter. My request was denied.

I was told that our regiment would be pulled out altogether for a rest period at Sabbioso.

So rest we did, hiding from the Mustangs and the slow observation planes. We camouflaged our weapons, ammunition boxes and such company vehicles that had joined us, for example the field kitchen. For once, we had a hot meal even if it was mostly beans and that leathery wartime pasta.

Those of us who were not "resting" in Sabbioso itself had to hide under trees and shrubs all day. We could not even wash anything. It was said that Mustangs had it in for military underwear hanging in the open to dry. The planes bothered us all day. Some rumors disturbed our rest as well. "Reliable sources" had reported the death of President Roosevelt. If true, this could have been part of radio newscasts, either Italian, German or BBC. Wild speculations were rampant. Would the United States opt out of the war now? Would the western Allies break up their uneasy marriage with Stalin? Would they subsequently invite us to join them in a war to finish off the Russians, correcting this amateurish effort we had been making?

Ever since we had left Tossignano, we were all very much aware of the fact that with each step we took, we came closer to the "eye of the cauldron." (This was one of my better mixed metaphors, it amused Heymann no end.) Very soon, it would be our turn. Even our walking one man entertainer, Corporal Bönike, twenty-two-years old, Iron Cross First Class, the man who always cheered us up with his cutting Berlin humor whenever we were low, even he quieted down noticeably.

Most roads and trails were now almost around the clock under harassment fire. On April 13, as we took off to our new destination, Heymann saluted walking by, "*Ave, Caesar, morituri te salutant!*" (Hail, Caesar. We who are about to die salute you!) Again the regiment declared it impossible to bring the two of us battalion commanders to the front of the strung-out column of hikers. The "Paula Line," where we had to relieve 993 Regiment, was running parallel and close to the Sillaro River where our next opponents, the New Zealanders, were about to arrive. So, I had to slosh through the wet grass right along with my grenadiers who, of course, were used to being herded around like this. They named this practice *Marsch ins Blauer* (hiking into the blue yonder), a take-off on the so-called *Fahrt ins Blauer*, the popular weekend trips the Nazi party organized for workers. Those were train or bus trips ending up at some surprise destination.

Tomorrow upon arrival, presumably I would have to ask my company chefs just to follow the Regimental Guides since I had no idea where we were going. I would not have made at least some assessment of the state of the battle, no idea about the topography, the size of our perimeter, and whether or not the terrain behind us would lend itself for my idea of a defense in depth. If anyone came by and asked me a question, I would have to tell them, "Your guess is as good as mine." In all fairness, this was an emergency, but I was very disturbed just the same.

The last leg of the hike, we moved under occasional hostile fire parallel to the river. I moved our column fifty yards to the left because I saw we were exposing ourselves continually to the Tommy artillery fire. I couldn't help but be reminded of famous gun battles in sea warfare where ships were moved parallel to an enemy line firing "broadside," to use a navy term. In addition, the preceding battalion had trampled the grass into a path no doubt visible from the air. We traipsed silently along, forty feet apart, stopped frequently by incoming grenades or fighter planes. Again, and again, flares on parachutes turned the night into a pale orange, which mingled with the mist that was rising from the wet grass.

I felt like I was walking into a police line-up. The string of powerful flood lights behind the Allied lines made us feel very visible from the air and very vulnerable. The closer we came, the more often machine and mortar fire joined the cacophony. We had to fling ourselves on the ground so often we were dripping wet, covered with mud. There were losses stopping the progress of the line each time for a while. I had placed all the available noncoms at more or less equal intervals, so they could see to it that we never lost contact.

We passed the Field Headquarter of the Second Battalion outside Sesto Imolese, where I found the battalion commander, my friend Captain Dörwald, standing near the trail. We shook hands in passing. He too was furious and bewildered by this frantic maneuver. He said his was a choice piece of real estate, smack in the line of the New Zealand advance. Did I know what the Tommies had unleashed to force their breakthrough on April 9? He quoted, "800 super fortresses, 1,000 fighter bombers, 1,500 artillery pieces, and he added, 'The BBC doesn't lie.'"

We had barely passed by Dörwald when the Tommies started an artillery barrage on Sesto Imolese. My men were moving as if in a parade, "eyes right" staring at the gruesome spectacle. Some of them were entirely oblivious to their footing, stumbling and falling every now and again, their eyes never leaving the fireworks. I had to force myself away from this in order to contact the battalion commander to be relieved.

At dawn, the thundering roll of the barrage moved closer and then died down followed by mortar and small arms fire around Sesto. Just then, I met the commander of Third Battalion 993, a major who fell all over himself apologizing for the botched-up relief operation. He had no idea where all of his units were. Rather than getting upset, I tried to stay calm and I told him I realized he had only been there twenty-four hours and he had been led by the nose just as I had been. It took us all day to finalize the matter. In the end, he and I still weren't sure whether we were fully in possession of the left bank of the Sillaro, if at all.

I sent 1st Lt. Peichel, the adjutant, and Carlo the orderly officer, to try to contact our companies. Heymann sent word again prefaced by "*Ave Caesar*" that he had contact with 993 on his left. Carlo came back exhausted and said that his sector was in a mess. The runner who had accompanied him was wounded and had to receive first aid.

The unresolved relief operation lasted all day. Peichel came back empty-handed. The situation close to the railway line and 993 Regiment was unclear after all. One company commander, Lt. Keyl, reported that they barely avoided being subjected to friendly fire from 993 holdovers who had no idea what was going on. At last the major disappeared after complaining good-heartedly that I had held him hostage with my unanswerable questions.

We were bothered by range finding artillery fire and Mustangs all day. Every once in a while, single stragglers and small groups of disoriented Panzer grenadiers came filtering through the New Zealander lines indicating that the Kiwis had not occupied the river dike in a continuous line. General Hoppe had told us that the Tommies had achieved a "deep penetration" in the Sector of the neighboring Corps. These stragglers were the living proof that it was a rout, some of them came without their weapons and complained about broken eardrums and clearly were still suffering from the shock of their experiences.

The fighting around Sesto subsided. An eerie silence settled over the perimeter where my friend Dörwald last was seen. Carlo alerted us to the fact that our own artillery had not been heard from all day. According to Hoppe, the Second Battalion on our left and 993 Regiment on our right, locally had lost some ground. When our artillery at last was ready, a counter-attack regained the lost ground and pushed the New Zealanders back over the river. All we knew at the time was what we heard; nonetheless, since Stalingrad, German soldiers were extremely sensitive to the impression that both of their neighboring units were in trouble.[5]

---

5. The General wrote in his book that during the counter-attack, "First Lt. Gmelin was killed leading his men, standing victoriously with his Tommy gun on top of the dike." Lt. Gmelin

The next day, April 14, we heard that the New Zealanders had broken into Sesto Imolese. I was going about my usual duties when suddenly I was handed an uncoded wire directive from our General H.: "Taking advantage of the new situation, First Battalion 992 Regiment prepares to counter-attack," etc. He was giving the exact map coordinates of our counter-attack!

I was, at first, confused. The use of radio communication, let alone an uncoded one, had been strictly forbidden for weeks. We had become increasingly aware of the sophisticated Allied electronic intelligence. Not only were they able to get the Command Post's bearings immediately, they were even able to listen in on telephone conversations. The content of this order in no way could justify breaking radio silence unless the general had information that I did not have. There were no "new situations" to take advantage of. The Tommies were still range finding and keeping us low in our foxholes by their incessant shelling, bombing and rocketing.

In my disgust, I dictated an answer back consisting of one disrespectful rude retort, "Taking advantage of what situation?" I was pretty sure I would not see the general again. When the wireless operator timidly asked whether he really was supposed to transmit this, I

---

was standing on top of the dike when he was killed? In retrospect, when the general had mailed his book to me in 1954 complete with a flowery note about my alleged bravery, of which, of course, he knew nothing, since Sesto Imolese was my first contact with the enemy. I should have penned an open letter to the editor of the Frankfurt newspaper, the retired General was most likely to read. In it I should have expressed my disgust at the general's misdirected creation of phony military images. Gmelin was an intelligent soldier and a gentleman who would have had sense enough to keep low in newly occupied territory. It is conceivable he didn't get down fast enough, but Hoppe made him look like a "Rambo" type macho firing a weapon with an inexhaustible supply of ammunition making one last heroic gesture. I didn't write the letter because, in 1954, I was about leave Australia to start a new life. I wanted to get away from this kind of glorification of the re-militarization of Germany. I must admit I did not read his book at that time with any kind of concentration and left it with my younger sister.

shouted, "Yes, damn it! What the hell does it matter. Look around you. We're getting it any minute."

In the afternoon a young peasant woman appeared out of nowhere, or so it seemed, shouting excitedly. Carlo,[6] my young orderly officer from Argentina, stopped digging his foxhole on my left and took over the interpreting, proud and eager to be useful. It turned out she had her tiny baby with her grandmother in a dugout nearby, which the Germans had not discovered when they evacuated all civilians a few days earlier. She knew she had no business still being around, but she felt she could not leave. She had heard that all evacuees were being pressed into the service of the new Italian government and were being made to dig ditches for tank traps. Some would even be sent further up north to work in industry, and she could not do that because her baby was too new and frail. There was no one to help her. Her husband was hiding to avoid military conscription by the North Italian Republic. Her father had been reported missing in action in Russia in 1943, and her feeble-minded grandmother was not much help since she needed care herself.

She answered Carlo's questions with an amazing amount of aplomb for a young peasant woman, I thought. I was struck by her poise and dignity, but I had the feeling she didn't fully understand her situation. I then tried to point out to her how the hostile artillery was range finding all around us at this moment, and that the clouds of smoke left by the impact of incoming grenades provided colored markers for the observer in the low flying spotter plane above us to see, record and report. Either today or tomorrow, all hell would break loose followed by Allied troop movement into this sector. I stressed to her that there would be an artillery barrage of immense force, very soon followed most likely by tanks

---

6. Carlo had interrupted his college studies in Argentina to join the German cause, when the outcome had been considered promising. His parents were naturalized Germans, who settled in La Plata where he grew up in an Italian immigrant neighborhood.

and flame throwers. Low flying planes would carry out ground attacks all through the battle.

Only now, did she begin to fully realize the seriousness of her situation. She was quiet for a moment, she bit her lower lip, her grimy nose twitched, but she did not cry. Finally, she decided that if I would let her stay, she would take her chances. She trusted that her dugout would hold.

I had been told that peasants such as these had become quite clever at constructing primitive but surprisingly strong structures for protection. Above a dugout hollow, they placed layer upon layer of timber arranged crossways tamped with dirt and straw. It was conceivable they could survive. I pointed out to her that if she wanted to stay she had to be on her own since we would be preoccupied with our own casualties once the attack started. I could not do more for her than to pretend I never met her.

She was leaning forward to reach for my hand when a sudden incoming round made us all take cover. As I watched, she quickly returned to her shelter. I became aware for the first time of its cleverly disguised entrance hidden by grape-vines and bushes some fifty yards away.

Later, in the afternoon, Zoschke made some sandwiches for me. Since Sabbioso three days ago none of us had had any chance to wash ourselves or even brush our teeth. Under these conditions, normal hygiene was impossible; nonetheless, Zoschke was preparing my sandwiches as usual.

I always enjoyed watching the elaborate cleansing procedure he employed in order to put some corned beef or whatever on our black bread. Since he had no water, he spilled some coffee on the ground, picked up the wet dirt and massaged his hands elaborately. Then he rinsed the palms of his hands with another drop of coffee, drying them on the cleaner parts of his tunic above his belt. This time he did all this, while registering every incoming round.

I started eating, which Zoschke took as the signal to begin thinking aloud. "Captain," he said. (He always used the British term whenever we were alone.) "Captain, this is it. This is *Götterdämmerung*! I've never counted so many different batteries engaged in range-finding. We are going to get it right in the ass."

I nodded in agreement.

"*Wir werden verbraten*." (It's time for our final stand.)

Of course, I recognized it too. Yet, there was nothing to be done. If I could have had my own way, I would have left a few observers shooting green flares at irregular intervals to mask our withdrawal out of range; thus, forcing the Tommies to waste ammunition. This, of course, could only have taken place last night; so, why fuss about it?

Again a Mustang chose us with all its fire power and everybody hit the dirt. When things finally quieted down and there was no cry for a medic, we all came up. No casualties, except my sandwich. I usually ate Zoschke's products in spite of our lack of proper hygiene, but I couldn't abide sand in my mouth. Zoschke made a new sandwich and became quite talkative again.

"This is our turn now," he said confidentially. "My parents always voted Communist before 1934, but then like so many others my old man switched parties when Hitler took charge. All of a sudden, there were all those job opportunities. Mother never quite forgave him – especially, after my brother was killed in Yugoslavia. If I survive the war I'll join again - and mark my words - Berlin will be Red."

I gave him no argument. It was clear to me that there would be chaos if Germany collapsed. Conditions would be much worse than after World War I. I knew, furthermore, that Stalin did not trust his allies at all and was convinced there would soon be a falling out. The western intrusion into Russia after World War I had given that man a hefty case of paranoia. At that time, the Reds came close to being toppled by the right-wing counter-revolutionaries. "V-mann Max", a German spy in the higher Russian echelons, kept reporting about this to General Gehlen as early as 1942 and 1943. I was privy to these reports, when I worked in the German General Staff during the Stalingrad winter. There were people who maintained that Stalin was about to come to terms with Hitler, rather than wait for the active participation of the Western Allies. The Russians were more than tired of having to carry the whole burden of the war since 1941 and they had been wanting a second front in France for years.

Another series of range finding shells brought me back to matters at hand. I told Zoschke to guide the supply detail this night and make sure they would steer clear of Sesto Imolese. We could still hear the fighting going on there. Zoschke saluted with mock precision and suddenly offered his hand, which surprised me but I shook it firmly. In the month we had known each other, we had never shaken hands and had seldom engaged in this sort of military pageantry. Perhaps because of that, I was struck by the trust and emotion involved this time.

Sporadic shelling.

I had never been exposed to British forces so I welcomed the inter-pretive hints my Austrian adjutant was giving me concerning the last-minute preparations the British were taking. He too kept saying that this was the largest artillery preparation he had ever witnessed.

I kept wetting my dry lips with my tongue. It was like the minutes before my first action in France 1940. The utter confusion of the battle-field, the total helplessness of the battalion commander. Only this time I was among those who were hunted and humiliated from the air. I was forced to take to the dirt at any time and burrow into the ground like a rodent for the sake of a few inches of protection. My Tommy gun was a relic, an outdated piece of equipment for which I had maybe thirty or forty rounds of ammunition left.

At last around 8:00 p.m. the big barrage started. Whenever I had time to look around, it seemed that Sesto again was getting the worst of it. I registered that our Second Battalion in Sesto took the brunt. I felt an obscene relief that the shelling wasn't concentrated on us, but over there instead.

The barrage lasted about twenty minutes. Then, all of a sudden, there was a pause. Unsure of what to make of it, I tried to find contact with Lt. Heymann whose First Company should have been pretty close. Against common sense and military procedure, I started to go all by myself.

The evening mist was rising from the freshly shell-plowed soil. I smelled gun powder and saw smoke from burning wood, some the splintered stocks of rifles. The runner from First Company joined me and offered to act as my guide. After a few minutes, he said, "Everything looks different. I've lost my way." I was disoriented myself and so we decided to go back to our foxholes and start all over. A volcano of deafening concentration erupted all around me. I jumped from one shell crater to the next and clawed the dirt to hang on.

Suddenly, there was Carlo. "In here, Sir. All our foxholes are smashed and useless." I realized I had just barely made it back to my men. During the smoke and confusion, Carlo pulled me into what turned out to be the dugout belonging to the Italian girl. It was pitch dark except that somebody had a flashlight. I could recognize the Forward Observer of the Rocket Battery who had also helped himself to the shelter.

"The cable of the field telephone leads to the entrance door, but not much further," he said. "The line is dead." He informed me that his battery had just spent their last rockets and that his presence in this stinking hole was totally useless and he saw no point in being stuck here, and then he left. I heard Carlo softly talking to the girl, while she fed her baby trying to stop it from screaming.

The outside roar seemed to have reached its peak. I was sure that we had taken a couple of direct hits. Lying flat on my face, I felt the continually falling dirt on my back and legs and was almost overcome by the smell of human sweat and unwashed bodies. Images of my experience in the Dresden disaster began to pass through my mind.

There was a sudden silence. I looked around and asked Carlo for his interpretation. The young man said he would go look and I agreed. The minute Carlo had left, the shelling started again. I couldn't see the Italian woman, but I waved just the same as I crawled out of the hole. The landscape had totally changed and I was confused. Mortar shells were detonating all around me. Instinctively, I turned away from Sesto Imolese, which was now burning brightly.

Suddenly, I was hurled by a tremendous explosion into something solid - it could have been a tree stump. I never would be sure. My ear and the right side of my head felt wet. I vomited helplessly. Somehow, I found the telephone wire and slowly crawled back to the dugout following it. Without that wire, I might never have found the entrance. They had lit a small oil lamp and I could see the grandmother slumped whimpering in the corner protecting the child with her shoulder.

The Italian girl was horrified at the sight of my face. She kept repeating, she didn't have any way to help me. "*Non medicantes, non medicantes,*" was what I thought she was saying. I pressed my dirty handkerchief against the side of my head. Then I must have lost consciousness.

When I came to, the girl was standing in the opening of the dugout yelling, "*Civile, civile.*" I remembered a clean handkerchief in my breast pocket and struggled to reach for it. I crawled the few feet to her and motioned for her to wave it and then I vomited again. I told her to say, "*Civile, tedesco malato.*" I didn't want her to pretend there was no one in there but civilians, and I surely didn't want to mislead any eventual Allied soldier who might discover us.

I had no idea how many minutes or hours I spent in the dirt on the floor in that condition. Or whether I was hallucinating. I had visions of being with that wonderful young woman standing in the door. There were short episodes of sheer fantasy - walking together, sitting together, being together there in the Campagnia. There was no language barrier. Whatever I experienced did not need any language to share.

When I came to and felt in charge of myself, the thought of this being the last moment of my life became acceptable. It seemed this calm mental state lasted for quite a while.

At last, a huge man appeared in the door, took my gun and asked, "Can you walk?"

The girl pointed to the ear and tried to make him understand that I had something wrong with the right side of my face. The Tommy helped me out of the dugout and stood me up against a tree. Having seen the telephone he looked around.

The girl said, "*Capitano.*" At that moment, an elderly Italian man appeared out of nowhere and exchanged a few words with the young woman. Whatever she said seemed to enrage him and he tried to attack me. He was raising his fist to strike my face when the Tommy sent the little old man flying with a tremendous kick, yelling, "Take your fuckin' hands off him." The girl told off the old man as well, who remained seated in the dirt muttering to himself something like "*Almuchi.*" Maybe something to do with his cows.

The battlefield was absolute quiet. I suddenly realized that I had not heard or seen any heavy weapon in action on the German side for a long time. I had no idea from which direction my captor had come, nor did I have much of an idea where he was taking me. Part of the time the huge Tommy practically carried me, since I was still fainting on and off. Soon I realized we were heading toward the Sillaro River, which my battalion was supposed to have defended and I had not seen one

German soldier. On the river I saw a huge bulldozer cut right through both embankments to make way for tanks and trucks.

I was led into a peasant's house where in the basement an officer presided over five or six different soldiers with walkie-talkies. He gave each one in turn instructions for their counterparts in the front-line. I was tremendously impressed with the way they used technology in achieving smooth communication with their advancing units.

Somebody drove me to the Divisional Headquarter. As if to charge a fare, the driving sergeant took my medals and my wrist-watch. I was so glad that the whole business was over and I was still alive, I didn't mind. I had only one desire, to get away from the actual battlefield. Shortly after he had pocketed his souvenirs, we were caught in artillery fire of some heavy German guns. Everybody hit the dirt. When the attack was over I scrambled up next to an American medic. This was the first and only American uniform I experienced in World War II. I have no idea how he got into this New Zealander division.

I was placed into a wire compound and there were some of my people. Heymann greeted me, "Sir, you're late." So we were six in all in this chicken yard surrounded by barbed wire, Heymann, Peichel and two other lieutenants from my battalion plus one artillery observer. When Heymann saw my face, he said, "Whatever happened to you, look at your face."

"Sorry, there was no mirror."

He urged me to lie down. I did, on my stomach. I was about to vomit again.

When I came to, it was morning. Around me were my shivering fellow officers doing calisthenics to keep warm. I was numb with cold. Our cage was now filled up with mostly soldiers from other units. Next to us, I saw a group of New Zealanders washing up or shaving, displaying their well-fed muscular torsos. They used gasoline field stoves to heat up the water just for shaving. Some made tea on the same kind of stove, boiling water in blackened food tins with wire handles on them. I was sure the tea would taste of gasoline. Matter of fact, the whole compound reeked of gasoline. They spoke to each other in loud cheerful voices. I could understand most of it except for the constant "f" word, which seemed to proceed almost anything.

In time the bright morning sun warmed us all. In some distance hundreds of our men were kept in a barbed wire quadrangle, too far away for us to communicate with them.

A huge New Zealander came to call me out. First, he led me to a doctor who checked eyes and ears and had someone dress my lacerations. Then he motioned me into a trailer. A middle-aged officer was sitting behind a table. After looking at my papers, he said in German, "Well, Herr Panny, this is not exactly the way you expected to come out of this war, is it?"

I mumbled something in the affirmative. He showed me a map. "Where were you taken prisoner?"

"Even if I thought it would be helpful I couldn't tell you. It was somewhere northeast of Sesto."

"All right, where are you from?"

"Grew up in Hamburg."

"My home town," he said.

"I noticed that, sir. Your 'r' gives you away."

He smiled and became quite interested. "Has Uhlenhorst been damaged?"

"Quite a bit, sir."

It turned out that this man was a Jewish dentist who had left Germany in 1937. He brought up the name of another dentist, Dr. Keitel, a Lutheran Jew, who had been an active member of our congregation. I knew of him, remembered the sign with office hours in front of his ground floor apartment, and I had talked to his daughter playing in front of this building as I passed with groceries on my way home. So here he was, in the uniform of a British officer, interrogating German prisoners of war. It was an awkward moment, but I was glad that he did his job with civility and objectivity, without resorting to any malicious gloating. The families of my Jewish schoolmates had been disenfranchised and felt under such pressure that most emigrated from Hamburg between 1934 and 1938. I certainly could understand any resentment they might have about it now.

In front of this man I was embarrassed, and yet elated to finally be out of it. Embarrassed, because of the treatment of German citizens like him who had lost everything, their homes, their friends and their cultural inheritance - some families respected members of the German community for centuries.

Personally, I felt elated and liberated. Although it was the end of Germany as a country and I couldn't do anything about the catastrophic consequences that I had seen coming for years, my obligation to the oath I had sworn to as a soldier was over. I had heard from snatches of conversations among my peers at the headquarters that the Stauffenberg conspirators had violated their oath of loyalty because they had not accepted its validity and constitutionality from the beginning (August 1934), but it was never discussed in public. Now I would have to account for myself like everybody else. The interrogator rose slowly, so I got up. He responded to my salute and I suddenly realized that for the first time since August 1944 I had instinctively saluted in the military way, not with Hitler's straight arm.

We were given one tin of corned beef and a bag of very hard biscuits and then we were shipped by open truck in a southeasterly direction. My lieutenants discovered to their surprise that the truck came through many towns, which were familiar to them during the fighting in the second half of 1944 such as Faenza, Montene, Cesena. The young men were very excited to rediscover this part of the country. Before we crossed the Rubicon (we couldn't help drawing analogies), we stopped and had some tea at Forli and ended up in a transfer camp on the Adriatic Sea near Rimini. In Ancona, we were unloaded again and put into another transit camp for the night. Again, I was singled out for a doctor's checkup looking into my eyes and ears and was pronounced fit for railway transport. I was glad because I would have hated to lose the company of my friends. Dinner again was corned beef and hard biscuits. None of us remembered having been fed this well in years, even if we did have to use our fingers to scrape the meat out of the tin.

After roll call, next morning, we were driven to a soccer field surrounded by barbed wire where hundreds of German prisoners had been assembled, many of them from our Battalion. Zoschke suddenly stood in front of me. "What have they done to your face, Captain?"

"Well, I must have run into a street lamp or something. How are you, Herr Zoschke?"

"Fine, Herr Panny. I'm glad you made it. Anything you need?"

We shook hands and he patted me on the shoulder. "Would you believe I need a spoon, Herr Zoschke?"

He pulled his spoon-fork army combination out of his pocket.

"No, that's yours. If you could just see if there is a spare one somewhere that would be helpful."

He tipped his cap and started his inquiries.

I saw the Tommies entering the field with rifles and their gear on their shoulders. At the same time, a freight train was slowly sidling up along the stadium. I looked around for Zoschke, since I couldn't be sure we would be allowed to travel together, and as usual there he was out of nowhere and on time with a folding mess tool and my safety razor and two blades, which he habitually carried for me on his person. "You need a shave, Captain."

"Thank you very much, Herr Zoschke. I'm so deeply obliged to you that I may have to join your Party too."

He acknowledged my teasing. "You'll see, Herr Panny, you'll see."

I don't recall the route or the stops from Ancona where the harbor crews were busy unloading tanks and ammunition. We crossed the country, stopped on the outskirts of Rome very early the next morning, or was it a day later; I still was a bit woozy. But I'm sure that then we were moved back to the Adriatic side through Bari, Brindisi to Taranto.

We were heading toward Taranto when our train was stopping next to a train load of these Hiwis going the other direction. Their train was guarded by British soldiers and some Russian personnel. It was a warm day and fortunately our guards allowed the opening of the cattle car doors and so we were facing the former German Hiwis a few feet away. (These Hiwis were Russian POW volunteers who preferred wearing German uniforms to dying of hunger or typhus in those open-air prison camps. They were an important part of each German unit.)

"Where are you going?" one of my men asked.

"Back to Mother Russia," was the answer.

Orje wondered aloud, "Do you want to?"

There was a pause. The Hiwis furtively looked around and then two or three of them shook their heads no. One of our boys asked, "What are these *Politrucks* for?" (political commissars)

Again a pause. One prisoner of war made an unmistakable gesture, his hand cutting across his throat. We all watched a British and a Russian soldier walking by. When they were gone finally, a gray-haired Hiwi answered. "We are prisoners again and there will be hell to pay. Only day before yesterday, some in the next car killed themselves rather than enter the train."

I asked, "The British handed you over?"

"They said they had no choice," was the answer.

One by one the cattle car doors were closed and locked. I will never forget the solemn faces, the passiveness of these unfortunate muzhiks. I explained to my men that to Stalin a prisoner of war had lost his honor, and all those millions of Russian prisoners in German hands were classified traitors.

How many days it took us I can't recall. We were given water, tea and food at appropriate times. Of course, we had to stay inside this ex-German freight car. There was a note on the door in German stating x-number of horses or x-number of men. Luckily someone discovered a rotten plank in the floor and we found part of a steel brace from one of the sliding doors, which came off easily after some "persuasion." We took turns in scraping a hole in the floor large enough for the intended purpose. I christened it "OKW." *Offizierskackwunder* (officers' defecation miracle) in honor of our friend Mügge, who had designed a collapsible folding tripod under the same name and had carried this contraption with him all through the war. It gave me great satisfaction to use this abbreviation known the world over as the OKW, the Supreme Commander of the Armed Forces of Germany under Keitel. Even the Nazis among us in this group accepted this, Keitel we all despised.

Our crisscrossing Italy appeared to be a bit mindless, but it kept us on our toes. The Tommies looked after us with tea and food. We did not lack for any necessity. We were taken off the train at Taranto and were driven to the harbor where we soon embarked on a converted tramp steamer. The ship doctor checked my eyes and my ears and pronounced me fit for sea voyage.

The change from the blinding sunshine to the dark passageways made seeing difficult for a while. We stumbled down various ladders into the deep cargo hold where, in a dimly lit room, a couple of tables, wooden benches and hammocks were waiting for us.

Heymann suggested that he, Dietrich, Peichel and I should stay close. None of us had much English in school, we had taken French instead. I was hoping they would all be agreeable that we try to stay together and I was pleased that my rudimentary skills in English somehow became useful.

The following morning, after some tea and porridge, we were allowed to come up from our cargo hold, again having difficulty with the change of light. It was a gorgeous day, a fresh breeze and the shipmate made good progress in a southerly direction. A wooden barrier was separating us from some British soldiers who were not at liberty to fraternize with us, but we had a lively conversation with them anyway. They were just bursting with all the latest news from the various war theaters, the most important being Hitler's death in Berlin. Peichel refused to believe it since the Tommies could not come up with any details as to how Hitler had died. We let that pass. Since Peichel did not ask me to express his doubts as to the veracity of the story, I didn't see why I should take it on myself to ask further questions. The Tommies could see that only Peichel among us refused to believe this.

There was a lot of talk about negotiations for an armistice, but again the Tommies had no details. When we thought about this, the details didn't really matter. We had often talked about the demise of Germany being close at hand and we had only begun to come to grips with what that meant for us. The Allies wanted to break up the country into various zones of occupation, which meant that there would be no authority to look after our interest as prisoners of war. If there is no country, would we lose our citizenship?

The uncertainty about the fates of friends and relatives was constantly on our minds and in our conversation. Where were they shipping us? Wild speculations were rampant. From the worst scenario - Yalta and the Russian POW camp - to the most agreeable, South Africa, Canada, New Zealand, Australia.

The Tommies, to whom we were talking, didn't know what would happen to them either. All they knew was that they would disembark somewhere in Egypt for duty in the Suez Canal district. That was a new term for me. I thought Egypt was a sovereign country. They explained that they were "Pioneers," The Royal Pioneer Corps, and when I expressed respect because the German "pioneer" was a sapper, an engineer and a member of an elite force, they found that rather amusing and said that the Royal Pioneer Corps had only administrative and support functions and certainly was not by any means an elite anything. They became even more loquacious since this seemed to have broken the ice, disregarding their non-fraternization orders.

I found understanding spoken English relatively easy. Speaking, however, was quite another matter. With my limited vocabulary, I often had to use hands and body to demonstrate, or even go into some pantomime to make myself understood. They found that entertaining too. In these early hours of my existence as a prisoner of war, I sent a few grateful thoughts to my English teachers in Hamburg. My English, such as it was, would give me some kind of status among my peers, even with those fellow officers who disliked my frank admission that I, with all due regret about the war and its consequences, was actually quite glad it was over and that, so far, I could only say I felt lucky to have survived it to be in this situation. I refused to pull rank or to think in military terms, addressed everyone as Herr, even staff officers, making friends and/or enemies, depending on their viewpoint.

The Tommies tried to set up a military discipline inside the POW group, but my three friends and I refused to have anything to do with it. I was willing to interpret whenever there was a need, sickness or emergency, but I was not going to stand in front of the assembled prisoners passing on British orders and making sure they were carried out.

None of us while on board ship learned much English because the soldiers seemed to have a limited vocabulary. The "f" word dominated their conversation from morning to night. I was curious whether this was an expression of their basic attitude towards the British Army, a negative one if true, or whether they used this four-letter word because it was the thing everybody did.

The voyage was uneventful. Some of the POWs were anxious to get back to *terra firma*. Peichel, for instance, was sure that we would run over a mine and kept asking for swim vests. If it wouldn't be a mine then he was equally sure that there was some German submarine commander still down there somewhere who hadn't heard the news about the impending armistice and had one torpedo left.

At Alexandria, the Tommies were not the only ones to disembark. We had to come up from our bottom hold and we were put on a train, which headed due east. We crossed the fertile Nile Delta and its numerous canals. Whenever the train slowed down, we had a chance to experience what we guessed was 100 degrees in the shade. The glimpses we had of the population varied from totally veiled women to scantily dressed housewives frolicking on the back patios of their homes, all of them observing us with curiosity and some friendly waving. I don't recall many details of this journey except two stops, one at Taint and one at Zigezaz, or Zagiziz, I could never remember, apparently, district capitals of some kind. We were in a relatively good mood expecting to be kept in this country.

CHAPTER VII

AT DUSK, WE WERE ALL DETRAINED NEAR TEL-EL-KEBIR
and transferred to open lorries. We arrived soon at a huge army camp
- rows and rows of tents as far as the eye could see. With dusk came a
sudden drop in temperature, which had us shivering. Then the column
of hundreds of POWs was marched to the center of a passageway separating the two rows of compounds filled with Italian POWs. They
were just being locked up for the night and welcomed us, gesticulat-
ing, waving and shouting. It all appeared to be friendly, but none of us
understood a word, so who knows.

Our marching column raised a huge cloud of dust, which together
with strategically positioned military outhouses didn't make for plea-
surable breathing. About 200 of us were herded into one of the empty
compounds at the very end of this tract. We were given tea, another tin
of Bully Beef and a bone-hard biscuit. This time we were told to keep
the mug and the spoon.

I was called out first into a big tent to face another interrogation. The
officer was another ex-patriot, this time from Austria, who surprised

me by assuming I was an Austrian too. He said that the name Panny took at least one column of one page in the Vienna telephone book.

"You have a choice," he said. "Would you prefer to go to a democratic camp or stay here?"

"Democratic?" I wondered.

"Yes. Anti-Nazi, deserters some of them."

I was confused for a moment. "Sir, I am lucky to have three of my men with me. I'd prefer to stay with them. Could I go and find out what their choice would be?"

"No. Each one of you has to decide for himself. There can't be exceptions."

"Oh. They were soldiers who did their duty, no matter how they felt about political matters."

I could not see Lt. Heymann suddenly declaring himself a democrat, whatever that was. He and I shared a number of hate sessions with plenty of red wine where we ran down the German leadership starting with General Hoppe all the way up to our OKW, but to associate with deserters? No.

The officer gave me some minutes to make up my mind. I was glad to have been asked these questions in German. I would not have been able to express myself in English. I had barely finished saying that I would like to go where my men were, when the interrogator was called away.

Now I was facing an English Captain who, seeing my quandary, broke the silence by saying in German, "It's your choice, you know. I guess we're doing it to avoid violence, which would upset the camp discipline."

I tried to ask what he meant by democratic.

"You have the option to be with people who are not Nazis."

"Well, one of my Lieutenants was a party member, but he was as critical of Hitler and the German leadership as we all were, but we were soldiers. What was this violence you mentioned?"

He frowned. "Well, sometimes these radical Nazis have been known to lynch somebody they considered a traitor or defeatist. They were from the 'Afrika-Korps' under Rommel and most of them have been shipped to Canada, but the possibility still exists for trouble."

"I'll stay here. I'm sure that is the right decision." I was led into an empty compound and one by one the others joined me, Heymann, Peichel and Dietrich. Heymann said, "Fancy meeting you here." It turned out that they all made this choice, rather than be lumped together with "deserters" and/or people who suddenly "discovered" they always had been democrats, whatever that was. By this time, it was past midnight.

We were told the palliasses would be in our tent. This caused a lengthy discussion among the few out of around 200 of us who knew some English. Nobody had heard that word. Finally, we had to ask the sergeant what he meant by that and he found the word "mattress." It was then that we realized a little more what our change in status meant. If such a chore as dragging heavy bedding was required from now on there would be no one but ourselves to do it. That kind of chore heretofore had been carried out by each officer's "batman." In this case, we were relieved we wouldn't have to do it.

As it turned out, we had to carry quite a bit anyway. The army blanket had to be spread out in the sand and into it went all the mess gear, towels, wash rags, two bed sheets, two pillow cases, and our POW uniforms consisting of a gray blouse with a big black diamond on the back, and gray cotton pants with a big black stripe on the outside. The soap was army issue and somebody remarked that it smelled of dead dogs. The towels were so thin that they were more like kitchen towels. The blanket served as carrying device flung over our shoulders like a sack. At dawn, we finally fell asleep in tent No. 50, Cage (sometimes called Pen) #12, still shaking with cold. My last thought was that I must get another blanket and then I passed out.

We woke up mid-morning drenched in perspiration. Peichel was sitting in the entrance hugging his bed roll. He said, "That Viennese Jew told me the Austrians will be classified 'victims of Adolf Hitler's aggression' soon. Can you believe it?" Our young Hitler Youth fanatic clearly had become wide awake to the possibility of preferential treatment.

We looked around for the first time and were pleased to see our tent in the middle of the row bordering Cage 13 occupied by German officers who had come long before us. Some of them came to the fence eager to get news from the Front or from home. They dismissed the story of Hitler's death as propaganda and if we believed it we should go to hell they said.

The ridge tent held up by two strong bamboo poles covered about sixteen-by-sixteen feet. You could stand up only in the center, the highest point of the inner ceiling. A fly sheet above the top allowed for air circulation provided the guy line and all the other lines on the sides were under proper tension. A small table and four stools were in the center. We had all we needed.

As we became aware of our home away from home, the first shock was the smelly orange looking traces the bed bugs left when we smashed them with our finger nails. Our palliasses were hopping with them. The sun was powerful, although it wasn't even noon yet. Heymann had improvised the classic sundial in the sand with one of the tent pegs. None of us had arrived in Egypt with our watches.

One man per tent was called to the kitchen only to hear that they should have brought the big pot that was in their tent to receive tea. It took a while, but finally we had our breakfast of tea and biscuits.

Afterwards, we were herded onto the soccer field at the entrance of the camp to go through our first roll call. 200 bleary-eyed men were called by name. Our Sgt. checked and rechecked the numbers and then pointed to a demonstration package, which had been placed in front of him. We were told through an interpreter of an unknown nationality that there would be an inspection this evening at 6:00 p.m. Would we be kind enough to arrange our belongings in the prescribed military fashion outside of our tent exactly as shown in this exhibit - the palliasse folded up to one third of its size, the blanket folded on top. Sheets and pillow cases likewise on top of the pillow, the artifice to be crowned by the washbowl, the mess gear and the toiletries. This detailed instruction was translated by a corporal in a halting German that was a lot worse than my English. "The colonel expects to go through the narrow passage between tent rows and find the ground free of litter, the inside of the tent spotless. Special attention is to be given to the lineup of each member's display as if for a parade."

This order, in turn, woke us up, infuriated and then amused us to no end. We controlled ourselves for a short time and then gave the man a "standing" ovation. The whole thing was hilarious - the dead earnestness of this incompetent interpreter and the officiousness of the sergeant reading the order out loud. I was grateful to see that our British sergeant took the applause with good humor. Much later, he told us he had expected the cage to riot.

Surely, there was some bitterness in some of the remarks I heard afterwards, but generally we spent the whole day setting up these monuments to British military drill. One tent row even managed to line up the display for the whole row, eight tents times four officers for each tent.

The camp commandant came at 6:00 p.m. The colonel was a heavy-set man with a reddish face and the obligatory mustache, his left hand holding a swagger stick under his arm. And swagger he did. He was followed by his adjutant, a major, the master sergeant and another interpreter. He actually went from row to row checking all the sixty-four tents, stopped to express criticism or ask questions. Our cage sergeant hopped around him like a bull dog, ready to bite any POW who had fallen short in one way or another.

Our tent was picked on for a total absence of toiletries and our bearded faces. The camp commandant must have complained to the German lieutenant colonel in charge of Cage 13 because the next morning this gentleman still in full German uniform passed on the criticism and had someone throw a package with Red Cross toiletries over the separating barbed wire. It was all used and discarded stuff, so we gave it back with thanks. In the heated argument that followed, the lieutenant colonel let it slip out that he was passing on the instructions of the camp commandant.

This was a bad start for my relations with this man whom the British considered to be ranking POW and thus in charge of all the German POWs. I let him know that the three officers from my battalion and I addressed each other as Herr and expressed the hope that he would soon adapt to the new situation. That didn't help either. I was disturbed by this conversation. It set the tone for the next three or four weeks.

The German POW cooks had a lumpy porridge swimming in powdered milk for our breakfast next morning and tea which was considerably weaker than the tea we had enjoyed so far.

Somehow I managed to maintain a certain stoicism amid the general irritation that accompanied the long hot days. It could have been something in the experiences of the *Jungenschaft* that helped.

Number one on the list was the water situation. Next to the kitchen was a fifty-by-fifty concrete slab with some drainage, concrete wash stands with two thirty-foot water pipes and a number of faucets where low pressure water trickled out. To wash the tin used for breakfast, everybody trooped to this one source of water. That meant long lines. We made an ad hoc agreement that in the future this function would be taken over by only one man per tent who on a rotation basis would do these chores.

Personal hygiene was a cumbersome time wasting procedure. During the day the sensation of water on our sweaty over-heated skin would have been a pleasure. Of course, thousands of Italians and thousands of other Germans had the same idea at the same time, competing for what little there was. As a result, there was only a trickle of water to be had. At night, when there was more water for our sponge baths the air was unpleasantly cold. From our wash stand I could overlook most of this huge military encampment. Next to it was the kitchen, a shed covered with corrugated iron where the cooks had two or three vats sitting on oil burners.

After the roll call on this second morning, we watched three Fellahin carrying supplies. The stronger one had half a side of "beef" flung over his shoulder. It was in reality the carcass of an African water buffalo, or so we were told. This slow procession was accompanied by innumerable flies. I lost my appetite for lunch right there.

From our border to Cage 13 we saw a structure where six mess tents were put together to form one big room. Our neighbors told us that sometimes they had meetings in that tent when the weather was inclement during the winter. From the kitchen down to the entrance there were four rows of tents on either side of the central passageway, a wide-open lane towards the soccer field. Next to the soccer field along the frontal barbed wire were the officers' tent housing the cage sergeant and two identical latrines. Every morning the buckets of the latrine were collected by an Egyptian (Fellahin) contractor.

The gate was locked at all times. The outer perimeter was closed by eight-foot-high barbed wire fences with an eight-foot-wide no man's land between them, while the cages themselves were separated by single barbed wire fences. All along the outer fences of the cage, there were six-inch steel pipes driven into the ground topped by a three-by-two sheet of corrugated iron, which sported a thick coat of black disinfectant smelling of creosote. These were our urinals, out in the open. The urinal in the upper right corner of the cage was about thirty feet away from the black colonial rifleman on his watchtower who was guarding us.

* ◆ ◦ ◦ ◆ ◦ ◦ ◆ ◦

After two or three days the cage had settled down to certain routines. Within our tent at a given time in the morning "tent duty" or room service, as we called it, was handed over to the next inmate who would fetch tea and breakfast including the heavy food tureen, which served to carry the porridge and the tea canister. Lunch was mostly an indefinable stew of sorts again carried in that tureen. For the Sunday meal we had to come personally with our plates and bowls, lining up in long rows at high noon. Whenever there was food left, after twenty minutes many of the younger people went again.

There was nothing we could do about the way the side of our water buffalo was routinely trooped from the gate to our kitchen. The flies enjoyed it and we just learned to hope that it would be cooked well done. Flies were everywhere as long as the sun was above the horizon. When two prisoners talked to each other in the open, you could always see them both facing whatever breeze there happened to be while their backs were covered with flies. Some people even made a study out of slowly walking backwards just to keep their faces in the wind.

When the flies retired in the evening, the bedbugs came out. Each palliasse had a goodly number of bedbug families, I was convinced. They sucked your blood and when you killed them, the orange spot appeared. I began to doubt my blood was still red. I went to the sergeant who had a wonderful piece of advice. "Take your palliasse out in the sun and leave it there to fry, turning it over every two hours. They will desperately try to get out of the heat by crawling off the mattress into the sand and die there."

Morale was low. Men blew up at each other over the slightest irritation, yelling, shouting and then in the course of the argument collapsed laughing, realizing the absurdity of it all. Our tent was relatively quiet because Heymann, the "old man," more or less set the tone and kept Peichel, our Austrian Hitler Youth, in check with his biting sarcasm. I was concerned about Peichel, he was so sure that he would be released any minute. He kept telling us how he and his wife would start up again, how he would lie down on the kitchen table and she would bathe him like a baby from head to toe, etc.

We agreed that we could not go on living at ground level as it were. There was no room to stand up except in the center of the tent. We were on our knees if we wanted to move around. In the neighbor cage they had dug into the ground three or four feet, which gave the tent almost the appearance of a room making the heat less oppressive. This meant we all would need to chip in and, I dare say, we kept that oral contract. Since we didn't have shovels we had to use our tin plates, an exhausting procedure. We took turns two hours digging, two hours sleeping. The tent was dismantled each night, we excavated as much as we could and put the tent back up in the morning. Most of the day we slept, just making sure we wouldn't miss out on mess calls.

As the digging proceeded, we found that the walls needed no bracing. A friendly neighbor told us across the barbed wire that one could mix the sand and the clay with water and dry it in the sun to make pretty solid building bricks. We first wanted to get down into the ground. The finer points of masonry could wait.

I don't know how many weeks it took us, it was very slow without shovels. The British were still afraid we might tunnel out of the camp and escape. A couple of times the blisters on our hands became infected, but we persevered and we discovered that most of our neighbors were doing the same thing with slight variations. I think it is fair to say that this herculean undertaking did a lot to improve the general morale within the cage.

Suddenly, new prisoners arrived. All work stopped. We gathered on the soccer field and were amazed to see a sizable column of German officers in full uniform, suitcases, backpacks and musical instruments. That was an unbelievable sight.

We soon learned these were the German Occupation Forces who had been "defending" the Islands of Crete and Rhodes before they finally had capitulated, having been "starved" by a British blockade. The Cages 12 and 13 were now filled to capacity and Cage 16 and 17 across the big divide were opened up as well. Not only did these new arrivals bring their luggage, they still had cameras, watches and military decorations as well. It was a shock to us living in this squalor to come up against this sight in June 1945. We could see they were German soldiers, untouched by hostile action. The British were happy to simply blockade the two islands until they were starved to surrender.

Many of these newcomers landed in Cage 13 next to us. As I looked at their uniforms, the like of which I hadn't seen for quite a while, I was reminded of the numbers of officers and noncoms who had initially been killed or wounded because they presented such an inviting target for snipers, particularly in Russia. These officers wore shiny aluminum shoulder epaulets, aluminum lined collar patches and even the noncoms wore aluminum laces all around their collar. In addition, of course, they all wore their decorations proudly on their tunic. I could see the German "Cross in Gold," a three-inch mirror with a swastika in the center worn on the front of the uniform. It was so shiny it could be used as a shaving mirror. Interrogations of Russian prisoners at the headquarter yielded some snipers' commentary that, "To us your officers looked like moving German Christmas trees glistening in the sun." After weeks of horrendous losses, the army at last issued an order requiring officers and noncoms to wear the rifleman's uniform.

To watch them come up for the Sunday morning roll call, one might have expected preparations for a parade of some kind. Some Air Force officers were in their white dinner jackets with their silver braided peacetime caps. I turned around and looked at our motley crowd with their mixture of prison uniform or whatever they had left.

The adjutant of the Camp Commander, Major Hunt, was the only one in the Colonel's entourage who came close to my former Gary Cooper-Franchot Tone "Bengal Lancer" ideal. One day at the cage gate he started a conversation with me as I walked by him. I then asked him tongue in cheek, "Any more inspections, sir?"

He grinned and explained that the excessive pedantry of the colonel on that day had been caused by an impending visit of Red Cross representatives, who allegedly were touring the Middle East. "We were supposed to make sure that every last prisoner was in possession of certain utensils, etc. By the way, as the ranking officer in Cage 12, why don't you make me a list of desiderata, would you? I can't guarantee that I'll be able to meet all your needs, but I'll see what I can do for you."

This phrase became one of our standing jokes. Heymann would come into the tent hysterically shouting: "Sir, could I get a bucket of water, the tent is on fire!" and that would be my cue to answer gravely, "I'll see what I can do for you."

My wish list included:

#1. When are we getting our first Red Cross postcard to notify our families in Germany that we are alive and here?

#2. What status do the POWs have, now that Germany has ceased to exist? Is the Geneva Convention regarding this still in force? If there is no German government who is looking after our interest?

#3. Is there a possibility to activate those loudspeakers, which are hanging along the barbed wire fences? We would like to get the BBC news.

#4. Are we supposed to get mosquito nets?

#5. Is there a possibility to get papers, magazines or books in the English language?

#6. Is there a possibility to have fresh fruit more often?

#7. Our friends in Cage 13 are receiving a nominal amount of credit as "canteen fund," which allows for them to buy toiletries, tea, cigarettes, etc. Is this possible for us also?

A few days later I was pleased to receive his answers.

#1. Postcards were on their way.

#2. #Sorry, I have no idea.

#3. The speakers are scheduled to be fixed. Some Italian POWs will come around to activate them.

#4. Mosquito nets are on back-order. Should be here soon.

#5. I passed your request on, meanwhile I'll let you have this copy of *Laburnum Grove* by Priestly, which I have on loan from the British Council. No time limit. Do you need a dictionary?

#6. I passed your request on.

#7. The canteen money is administered through the camp commandant. It gets every POW a certain amount of credit regardless of rank. By the end of

June, you should receive a catalogue from which
to order.

I thought this was absolutely wonderful. This man had exceeded my
fondest expectations. With the appearance of these "chocolate soldiers
from Crete," I had a dictionary. In fact, we had everything including
German dictionaries and cameras. We felt rich.

The cage sergeant was impressed with my connections, although I'm
not sure he liked his role as a mailman having to go back and forth for
me. He gladly passed on my primitive thank you note in which I asked
the major for paper and pencil, now that I had the book. Two days later
the sergeant brought army stationary and pencils and I began to translate the British play merely to expand my command of the language.

Towards the end of June, the mosquito nets came and what a difference that made. From now on, we could at least spend the daytime
hours protected from the flies and keep the mosquitoes out at night. All
four of us spent most of the day under our cubicle within the tent. It was
privacy of sorts, yet we could communicate freely if we wanted to. The
bedbugs were enthusiastic about the nets too. I always suspected they
had a death wish because now when they had their fill, they crawled
all the way up to the top of the mosquito net where they were easy to
see and kill.

Close to dusk most of us would come out of our net and out of our
tent to "promenade" up and down the soccer field eager to converse with
one another. It was there we could best enjoy the change from daylight
to darkness, which took place in a matter of minutes, a phenomenon
we were unaccustomed to. In this short time, the fading light turned
the dull gray sand of the day into sparkling ever-changing muted tones
of blue, violet and brown. Only then, we could see the minute crystals
in the sand reflecting any of the remaining angled light.

All around us, along the various barbed wire fences, powerful flood-lights brightened the sudden night, oddly pleasing to our eyes after a day with the harsh sunlight of North Africa. Usually a fresh breeze started up, inviting physical exercise. The first few times we were not dressed warmly enough for the sudden drop in temperature, somewhat chilling to us after having perspired heavily all day. We soon found out why our cage sergeant always came in an army pullover at gate closing time.

With the canteen order, came primitive heaters, teapots, even rum, which was something close to methylated spirits in taste (an awful booze) and kerosene lamps which, although smelly, made a kind of "indoor social life" possible at night. With the playing cards brought by our island warriors, most of us played Skat, a rather harmless German game. However, it wasn't long before Poker became popular, which wasn't so harmless. The "upper crust" island warriors even played Bridge. Needless to say, I found better things to do with my time.

In spite of all their "wealth," the people from Rhodes and Crete had difficulty with the challenges in adjusting to our hardships. How spoiled they had been? Their descriptions of those two very beautiful islands I found depressing - especially their insensitivity towards the hapless peasants and fishermen. Strict rationing among the populace and soldiers was enforced, while some of the officers were living high, handing each other decorations for bravery at afternoon coffee klatches complete with real Mocha and Hennessey cognac.

Our tent was now an acceptable living room-bedroom combination, if you will. The four palliasses were in the rear half, arranged parallel to the guy line of the tent. I had one of the outer ones. The table was close to the entrance on the right side, where the entrance flap was permanently closed. The left side of the opening allowed entrance and a view of the left wall where we had three wooden crates, which held our mess gear, etc. Two steps led down from the desert floor but, of course, not being reinforced, they deteriorated quickly. In the end, leaving and coming became a physical challenge.

Since the island warriors had to wait one month for their canteen money, they sold us spare underwear and socks, even shoes and coats. I, for one, was much in need of the basics. The Egyptian cigarettes we could buy, I found distasteful, besides they were irritating my throat so I traded them. Come to think of it, black market was sprouting out all over the camp. The kitchen personnel were mostly from the former Afrika Korps, who had free access to the camp. They became our wheelers and dealers. For fifty Egyptian cigarettes, I could get one package of decent British Woodbine cigarettes or other English brands. I looked for Indian tea, British army clothing and especially a pullover for the chilly night temperatures; it became my prized possession. Twice or three times a day, a cup of tea became a treat. I dropped my European prejudice against hot drinks in this kind of heat. We copied the British habit of using condensed milk and sugar. After a cup like that we worked up a healthy perspiration and then during whatever activity to follow, the slightest breath of air felt refreshing. Could this be the secret that kept the British Empire going?

The used tea leaves became an item for collectors. We had a number of people who hoarded them saying they would start mixing them with the desert sand to grow flowers and even vegetables. None of us believed that, but the Italians confirmed that this was the way they grew their lovely little flower patches. The Egyptian contractor was approached. Would he sell us any seeds? "I'll see what I can do for you," was his reply.

Soccer in the late afternoon became an organized competition. Each tent row was scheduled to play each of the other tent rows in a cleverly worked out round robin. Major Hunt sent word that he had two soccer balls per cage for me, so my long-suffering cage sergeant had to make another trip down to the office with me. He allowed me to stop at some of the Italian cages to inquire where they had gotten their seeds. I found enough German speaking Italians from the South Tyrolean Alps to communicate with and they were very helpful.

Two days later a mystery parcel came flying over the wire fence. It had originated in the Italian Cage No. 9 and had been passed on over the fences all the way to us in No. 12. We were very grateful and asked how we could show our appreciation.

The more we saw and heard of the Italians, the more we were impressed. Some were hard-core fascists, who had been in this camp since 1940 or 1941. They had a tremendous sense of allegiance to the group without any officer being around. They marched as if on parade to the weekly shower, a demonstration, if you will, of military discipline. We admired those sun-tanned Italians marching and singing and yet we couldn't help compare this display with the feeble efforts of their government and their officers during the war. We watched them doing P.E. calisthenics outside their tents on a little piece of rag. They had competitions in floor gymnastics. Whatever they did, they did enthusiastically, shouting joyfully at mail call or very angrily when something had gone wrong, as in an escape attempt or when their team had lost in a soccer game.

Since the soccer fields consisted of hard desert floor, the Italians played the most gentlemanly soccer you ever saw. The arms pointed strictly downward and using the elbow was prohibited. We immediately adopted their rules. Our neighbors told us that hundreds of thousands of these Italians had worked in British installations in Egypt and North Africa for years. A doctor from Bozen said that there was a rumor, allegedly based on a reliable leak from the British House of Commons, that the Italians would soon be replaced by the Germans here; so, they could finally go home.

The Italians shared their newspapers with us, which they bundled up and threw over the wire fence. These papers were full of bad news about Central Europe: most countries were still on food rationing.

There was still malnutrition in Germany, rape and looting in the East German enclave. They told of massacres in Poland where thousands of Germans were killed. For the first time, there were stories about massed killings and the suffering of millions of concentration camp victims. The mood in Cage 12 sank to another low.

June 30, 9:00 a.m., we heard our first newscast from the British Forces Services Network originating at BBC. It came over the loud-speakers audible in every tent. To make sure we heard everything, those of us who understood spoken English had to move close to the speaker to take notes.

"A certain William Joyce, who had been broadcasting for the German propaganda in the English language – 'Lord Haw Haw' as the British called him - was tried and convicted for treason and will be executed."

"The Philippines are nearly liberated," MacArthur announced.

"Okinawa is taken."

"The United Nations Charter was signed by fifty countries."

"Since June 29 Japanese people in big cities are notified by leaflets from the air that they will be bombed." When I translated that, some of my fellow inmates bit their lips.

◦◈◦◦◈◦◦◈◦

June 30, 1945 was a hot day even at 9:30 a.m.. We stood perspiring in the merciless sun, a motley crowd slouching, smoking. I noticed the military spectacle in Cage 13. Our island heroes had taken over the front-line of the fall-in. Some of their Air Force officers appeared in their white dinner jackets, silver piping on caps and on shoulders, Iron Crosses, German Crosses and any other kind of decoration.

"Morning, gentlemen," the lieutenant colonel yelled.

"*Morgen, Herr Oberstleutnant*," they yelled back.

It was as if nothing had changed, they still clung to their military way of life in the face of our present reality. I could understand German soldiers trying to escape from a given POW camp. I could identify with people who thought it was their duty to risk punishment or their lives in an attempt to escape while a war was still going on, but now this display looked like a pretty empty bit of charade to me.

Ever since childhood, I had mostly unpleasant memories for this calendar day, my birthday. Probably this superstition was most strongly reinforced this day in 1934 when the alleged "*Röhm-Putsch*" took place - later revealed to have been a massacre by Hitler and the SS. (In English, it is called 'The Night of the Long Knives'). This particular day, I had no foreboding until we received the order to go to the west gate of the encampment for the showing of a documentary film. By order of the camp commander everyone would attend, the only exception being the two cooks staying in the cage to guard supplies.

Rumors and speculations all day. Apprehension. Some people suggested this would be the beginning of political re-education. So at the appointed time we marched down the central avenue, our *Via Dolorosa*, and were allotted an open space among a huge audience of German POWs seated in the sand on a slight rise in the terrain. In front of us was a big screen visible to all.

As darkness fell and the movie began, we became aware that there were no news reels as we had hoped. This movie was an attempt to make a documentary as quickly as possible of the conditions in the first concentration camp the British had encountered. There was a nervous apprehension among us. I heard voices around me.

"Bergen Belsen?"

"No idea where that is."

"Near Hanover," Heymann said.

"No, we hiked through there. It's about eighty kilometers south of Hamburg and there was no concentration camp there in 1934 as far as I can remember," I said with my throat beginning to dry up.

It didn't matter where it was. That night this camp stood for all those institutions for "political re-education" or "forced labor camps for incorrigible misfits" that sprang up since 1933. We had heard about those in the abstract, but nobody had firsthand knowledge or had seen any photos except for those of the entrances with the logos *Arbeit macht frei* (Work liberates you). Some people had been released, like the man I had overheard next to Pastor Remé's office years before.

The camera went right into groups of freshly liberated inmates who still were able to move and show any emotion, but from there it was nothing but fields covered with corpses of those for whom April 24, 1945, had come too late. A voice, "Man, that was eight days after we were captured."

For the next twenty minutes, nobody said a word. The images on the screen were overwhelming. In the faces of the captured SS guards, male and female, we saw sullen defiance or resignation as they recognized their situation. These thirty or forty odd uniformed well-fed SS guards were surrounded by either irate inmates cursing them or by joyous youngsters relishing their freedom who still had the strength to laugh at their former tormentors. The British soldiers made sure that nobody laid a hand on the SS.

From there the camera switched to the remains of those unfortunate inmates strewn all over the open fields surrounding the barracks. It was as if a giant vise was gripping my chest and I had trouble breathing. Corpse after corpse lay there, the blank stare of the eyes, the various stages of starvation, image after image heaping horror upon unimaginable horror. I kept wishing this was only a nightmare, since it couldn't possibly have any basis in fact. Not here, not in my country, not ever.

There was no chance to run away from these sights. My worst forebodings of Germany's regression into barbarism had been exceeded.

How many times had we broached the subject in conversation with friends, particularly in the headquarters, but nobody had ever dared to face up to it, mostly for lack of firsthand information or any other kind of proof. We certainly had felt uneasy about the activities of the SS administration in the occupied countries, but I suppose we always changed the subject and I was paying for that on this June 30, 1945. With both hands I was holding my head, straining my eyes, which had never seen a human being about to die or dead of starvation.

The captured guards were made to load these corpses on trucks, heaving them over the tailgate like sacks of vegetables. They drove them a few hundred yards off to a hastily dug pit, unloaded and shouldered them across the loose white sand, finally dropping them into the mass grave. This must have gone on for a long time. Finally, the guards were so exhausted they just dragged each corpse through the sand by a hand or foot leaving a trail. It was agony to watch this slow process over and over, one corpse after another. Each corpse became an individual person having a life, hopes for a future, now finished.

Three German officials, one of them the mayor of Bergen, were made to watch hats in hand. A chaplain said a few words. The guards were made to stand at attention, while an interpreter addressed them and reminded them that they would be held responsible for this horrible crime against human beings. There were no German church representatives to be seen. A Tommy started a bulldozer and began covering one layer of destroyed human lives.

By this time, I was shaking with cold or was it the shock of what I was seeing. I heard a voice of protest behind me. So did Heymann, apparently. He tore into our Austrian Hitler Youth snarling, "Peichel, shut up, you imbecile." Having been through this experience most of us were extremely irritable, cursing our fate, Hitler and the people who had caused all this killing. Some of us were mad at the British for showing it to us.

On the way back to our cage the timeless adage occurred to me, "There for the grace of God go I." How easily could I have been in a situation like the ones shown. What if I had by chance witnessed a situation like this one. What would I have done? Would I have done the right thing? What would have been the right thing, grab a platoon, take the guards prisoners and end World War II? What about those guards? Were they enlisted men who happened to have been placed in the SS, whether they liked it or not, or were they SS volunteers, Hitler's true elite? They certainly did not look like that. They did look like volunteers from somewhere in Eastern Europe.

One of them was singled out to speak up in the movie ("I am Dr. Fritz Klein. I am the Camp Doctor. I am a German from Romania.") He looked forbidding, I thought. A camp doctor, watching thousands of people die from starvation. Whether these guards were volunteers or not, what did they think when they put professional criminals (*Kapos*) or corrupt prisoners who had ingratiated themselves to the SS, in charge of the working details and in charge of the barracks and in charge of the distribution of food. They must have known these people would abuse their privileges, steal the scarce food and aggravate the suffering tremendously.

The health data shown in the movie made it clear that these inmates were intended to die a slow painful death. Because of the starvation and the indescribable sanitary conditions, there was typhus, dysentery, tuberculosis and typhoid fever. In March alone allegedly 18,000 people died. And the film ended with a note that 50,000 corpses were buried under British supervision.

Heymann interrupted me. "Peichel, this was reality and if you can't recognize reality, our German reality, you are beyond help. I joined the party in '32, full of idealism and this is what I got. For these scoundrels, I risked my butt for six years and told my soldiers to do the same - adding that they were to defend their home and Christian Western culture. You can think what you like, but don't mouth this kind of bullshit again in my presence!"

I couldn't have said it better myself. It could be millions of human beings had been sacrificed senselessly all through this war. This was the end of twelve years of national insanity. It was not even a death camp, this was not like Auschwitz, which was in the news almost daily now. There, we were still hoping that it wasn't all true - after all, the information had come from the Russians. This camp at Bergen Belsen was supposed to be merely a labor camp. No matter, I knew immediately that this would be our burden, everyone's burden, be they Germans or Austrians or whatever foreign volunteers who had participated in the German war effort. The comforting illusions my friends and I had nourished that as soldiers were just doing our duty, I could see was only valid to a certain degree. It would be so easy to say, "You see, this was all done by the SS. They were the bad guys." And even there, we would distinguish between the SS Fighting Forces from those who wielded power inside the Reich and those in charge of the Concentration Camp System.

I couldn't help pondering the many discussions I had been part of in '43 and '44 especially after the Stauffenberg disaster. What we were afraid to formulate then, had now come to us. It didn't help that we said then and I would have liked to say now that we were not "decision makers," but were being ordered. How many times had I questioned the moral foundation for fighting this war? For the rest of my life, I would carry the shame of having played a part in this horror.

Fifty years later, I am just as incapable of describing my emotions as I was at the time of that showing. Periodically, in the previous ten years I had misgivings about the direction the nation was taking and about my role as part of it as a career officer, but, since most of these doubts were based on tales related by the sons and nephews of German generals with whom I was serving, I often dismissed their information as mere hearsay. What made me skeptical about the veracity of these allegations was what amounts to the German phrase *sich interessant machen* which means to try and make oneself look more interesting by passing on privileged information.

We returned in small groups, loosely bunched like tourists - some of us silent and some of us noisily decrying the affront done to us by our captors. Why did they have to expose us to such a propaganda film? We went past the Italians again. Cage after cage they were displaying their nightly activities, singing, drinking, fooling around. There was a Punch and Judy show in one cage and we saw rhythmic exercises on one soccer field.

Before coming to our cage we stopped to watch what was left of a raunchy slapstick farce put on by some Italian prisoners. The female impersonators struck us as overly made up looking more like caricatures, but at the same time I couldn't help but notice what little effort seemed to be required to produce a play even on a very small stage under primitive conditions. Foremost in my mind, however, was to retire under my mosquito net and to be by myself, as it were. I had no illusion that sleep would come easily. I don't know how long I lay there. Real thought, a disciplined analysis, was impossible. I caught myself again and again finding new justifications for my tendency to accept only firsthand or physical proof of any wrongdoing on our side.

Like myself, the others came and went to bed without undressing. Peichel was still swearing under his breath about the "brazen propagandistic brain washing" showing this movie to us. I finally took my blanket, paper and pencil and cautiously made my way past Heymann, just in case he was able to sleep. I could not face another of our slumber time discussions where our talk of the past went around and around leading nowhere.

I sat down on some wooden steps lining the soccer field. The black soldier on the watchtower was humming again some of his monotonous melodies, waving his hand each time the rotating searchlight hit him, as if to say, "You see, I'm not sleeping." I tried to catalogue all those instances that I now called personal defeats, there may have been twenty in all. Twenty opportunities to show some gumption, to stand up for something, were wasted. I found a logical explanation for each of these failures listed on the paper in front of me. Past and present was becoming intertwined. My past choices or my attempts to repress opportunities to make choices seemed to bode ill for my future. As I sat there, my scribblings became barely legible in the dim light. I gave up and went back to the tent and to bed. Tomorrow it was my turn to have tent duty, which was what I needed - to keep busy.

The next morning at roll call, we were told about an escape attempt that had failed. Our sergeant warned that once out in the open a runaway POW would be fair game. He warned, "There are Fellahin so poor they would kill for a good pair of shoes. The small arms fire you heard the other day was a foiled attempt of an armed break-in to Barkley's Bank only three miles from here. Gangs of roving robbers are all over the district."

We weren't much interested. We just stood there, a grim looking bunch, still absorbed with our mental hangover from last night. I noticed our neighbors in Cage 13 looked exactly as dumbfounded as we were. For once they were not making a sound. No "Good morning, gentlemen" and no choral answer. There were no fancy uniforms and they looked as unkempt and as pitiful as we did.

We heard some rumors of suicides. We just nodded. Nobody took the trouble to ask for confirmation or specificity. Years later, I found confirmation of sorts, again without specificity, in a book about prisoners of war, but the interesting thing was that the rate of suicide in the

Middle East was relatively higher than the one in Russia, where conditions were much worse.

I always came back to my family as if some salvation could be found in my upbringing, education, or lack of it. January 1933, I was a schoolboy of fourteen, and by the time of my capture by the New Zealanders on April 16, 1945, I was twenty-six and a captain in charge of a battalion. Between those two dates, I had seen a dozen years of Hitler's regime ending up in the grimmest barbarism since the darkest middle ages. From a relatively civilized society, with undeniable cultural life, my country had regressed into unimaginable disgrace. I wrote and rewrote sentences like the one above, sitting on the edge of that soccer field, tearing up page after page of that precious paper I had been given to translate Priestley's play, stuffing the crumbled rejects into my pocket. I did not get anywhere that night. I always ended up concluding I was a coward as well as my father and most other people, because in certain situations I knew something was wrong, yet I didn't have the civil courage to speak up. Without cowards dictatorships could not exist, I ruminated, and with us German cowards the special slant was that we were brave soldiers, but too weak to find a way to see through what was going on and then to speak up.

Since our generals did not stand up to Hitler either, the rifleman in the front-line had to be even braver. I ended up thinking about all those promising young men I had known, now dead for nothing, having inflicted untold harm all over the world. I wasn't trying to look for excuses when I, at moments like this one, looked back on my own family. My father couldn't see it and he could not answer my questions. My mother was too overworked, too sickly, who did not understand politics at all. But when Hitler came and appeared to be able to create some kind of order, she embraced him with a religious fervor and she even dropped her fundamentalist community. By the time she found out that all was not well, and we did have another war after all, she had another breakdown and blamed all the underlings, absolving Hitler, who in her mind had nothing to do with it. I said and thought this so often, I just gave up and went to bed. Heymann was right, so was Letschert. There will be a 1,000 year Reich. Not in 1,000 years will people forget what happened in these twelve.

◆ ◆ ◆ ◆

The next day, I was grateful I was on tent duty. I tried to not think about much at all. Having done the dishes, I lined up the four deep bowls on the dish box, the four spoons and the empty cigarette carton, which had at one time been filled with a hundred Egyptian cigarettes. Only a few days ago, we had renewed our pledge to utmost fastidiousness because of a fuss over the dish cloth having been used for personal hygiene, so I felt watched.

There was, all of a sudden, a commotion at the gate. Half a dozen Tommies and half a dozen civilians had entered the cage and through the loudspeaker we were called to fall in for a medical examination. The roll call lasted longer than usual, the counting and recounting took at least fifteen minutes, during which time we had to stand in the afternoon heat. All around us the desert was now in bloom, as we called it. Everything up to about three feet above ground seemed to swim before our eyes. The air was filled with a waving haze - Fata Morgana time, we called this phenomenon.

"Strip to the waist." Jim, our Sgt., motioned us to move apart so that the inspection team could move between the lines of the POWs. We were dumbfounded as to the purpose of all this. Nobody had been sick that we knew of. We were not amused to have to stand around in that heat with our upper body exposed to the sun. What was the point of this?

We soon had the answer. They were taking some known SS men and one policeman out of the line. I suddenly recalled the 1943 discussion I had among like-minded friends at the German headquarters concerning the pampering of the SS. We mentioned how they, as Hitler's elite, continually had been equipped with the latest weapons, tanks, and guns, not to leave out their underarm blood group tattoos. What irony, I thought. The blood group tattoo meant to save their precious lives, now marks them. I passed on my observations as to what I was seeing and word went through the line quickly. We then submitted to the examination of our armpits somewhat relieved. Personally, I was glad everything was clear and in the open considering the tension created from last night's film. We were all reeling from trying to cope with the new facts and the reality of the death camps. The vociferous rejection by our "Nazis," along with our general irritation, could have led to some ugly repercussions. There was no love lost between the rabid Nazis and the regular soldiers. This lineup became a fitting rejoinder to the horror film of the previous night.

In the evening, our BBC news discussion group met to discuss the position of the SS in general. According to the BBC, Heinrich Himmler, the SS leader, had committed suicide following his arrest. He had been caught in the uniform of a German rifleman, as he was attempting to slip through the British lines. Much later, we learned that Himmler had been actively engaged behind Hitler's back in trying to secure a truce with the Western Allies through the help of Swedish Count Bernadotte.

Some of the youngsters were quite cheerful that evening. They were already sounding the soon-all-too-familiar note: "You see, it was the SS who committed all the atrocities. We in the army just did our duty."

Monday came another shock. Sgt. Jim came with a list and announced, "We are now in three groups: the white group is the democratic; the rest of the camp, except for a few party members, is now categorized as 'gray'; the Nazi Party members and the SS belong to the 'black' group and will be moved to Cage 18 in the Satellite part of the camp."

Heymann and I looked at each other. Since February, he and I had been running down authority, army leadership and the Nazi party in particular. And yet here he was, labeled a Nazi because of his party membership since 1932. He had joined as a German patriot and idealist in his law school days when the conditions in the country were close to chaos. He, along with many other people, had thought that Hitler was the only political leader who seemed convincing in his promises for affecting change.

I looked at him and I said, "This is it." He just nodded. At noon a truck came to take Heymann and a number of other prisoners categorized as "black" to an outlying part of the camp called the Satellite. That was the bad part of Monday, July 2, 1945. But another truck came and Peichel and all the other Austrians were taken out too. That was the good part of Monday. On the one hand, most of these Austrians were fiercely loyal Hitler Youth who, on the other hand, constantly reminded us that they, after all, were victims of Hitler. They had been getting on our nerves.

This meant that young Dietrich and I had two empty palliasses complete with mosquito nets in our tent. And that meant we each had two beds, one to sleep in by night and another to sweat in by day.

* ◆ * * ◆ * * ◆ *

I asked Sgt. Jim for permission to see Major Hunt. I accompanied him on the long walk to the office of the camp commandant. The major was again very friendly. He was glad I was working on the translation of *Laburnum Grove*. In my mind, I gave myself some credit for avoiding the typical German custom of coming directly to the point. I was practicing my newly discovered Anglo Saxon niceties, and carefully inquired:

   a. How was his state of health?

   b. What did he think of the weather?

   c. I hesitated for the proper amount of time to give him the opportunity to lead our conversation to the point.

Appropriately, he asked, "What is on your mind?"

"Well, sir, the indiscriminate lumping of the Nazis in one camp concerns me - in this specific case, Lt. Heymann, who was in charge of a company in my battalion. I met him at least every second day and got to know him personally. If there was a more articulate critic of the Nazi hierarchy and the German Army leadership, I'd like to meet him." I proceeded to explain Heymann's party membership and then added, "The 1935 disenfranchising of the Jews made him understand that his choice had been a bad one. He did his duty as a soldier, but was deeply troubled about the developments that led to World War II. Must he be in the camp with people who are still unconvinced and continue to keep their loyalty oath to Hitler?"

On and off Hunt helped me with my halting English and then he said, "Panny, this is out of my hands. All the party members in the 'black' cage in the Satellite will be regularly interviewed and re-evaluated. This time I cannot say, 'I'll see what I can do for you.'"

The various tent groups worked feverishly improving their accommodations, but that kind of focused activity wasn't enough to stave off depression for some. Dietrich, for one, took to brooding. Whether he was sitting or lying, his eyes were wide open staring into space. The few times he did talk, it was about his home, family or his past regardless of the context of our conversation. We didn't know how to handle the obvious signs of his depression.

I could understand his distaste for the chatter that went on most of the day, the same stories repeated again and again with the urgency of competition for attention. Moreover, it didn't seem to matter if anyone wanted to listen or not. Even Heymann at times had kept spinning yarns disregarding the interest and the attention of his audience.

As a way of keeping an audience, some of the POWs resorted to becoming rumor factories. Early on one of these pranksters could have claimed some success with his "hint from an impeccable source" that in light of the mushrooming black market the Brits would subject all of us to a thorough shakedown. Some of us took this seriously and hastily buried our treasured possessions in the sand, being careful to record where to find them later. Cameras and pullovers were buried with other ill-gotten gains. Some tried to hide cash, drugs or cigarettes and documents referring to their career under Hitler.

Among the storytellers I objected to most were those chaps who had to re-fight all the battles they had been in during the war stressing how heroically they had acquitted themselves. Exaggeration became the norm. Our Austrian Hitler Youth, Peichel, was the biggest liar in our tent, but Heymann had always managed to put him into his place.

It was difficult to find a substitute for Heymann - someone to talk to. I continued to brood over my "twenty failures" list. I was not getting anywhere. Ruminating on any one of these items made me fear for the future. At the same time, the daily routine of translating the play and translating BBC newscasts for a number of the youngsters helped me regain confidence and to enjoy myself in the desert.

There was a general tendency to get busy doing something. I noticed with great pleasure our neighbors at last were using the tea leaves we all had collected for them to raise a few flowers. They had them growing in tight little patches either in front or alongside of their tents, sneaking out at night to collect water for them which was strictly forbidden.

I became aware of bird life. Every morning, we heard traveling scratching noises up and down the sun-sail above us. After a few days of this, one of us caught sight of the birds going after insects up there.

They were Wagtails, we were told, and one of them became trusting enough not to fly away whenever we came out of the tent. When our biology expert protested that Wagtails had no business being in the arid desert, they needed water, we were pleased to hear Sgt. Jim point out that there was a canal about a mile away from the camp. By now, we had been here three months and nobody had ever mentioned a canal.

The crows obviously had had years of camp experience and had lived off the former inhabitants of these tents, the Australians, the New Zealanders, the Indians, the South Africans, the Poles, the Italian POWs, the British and now us. With a heavy tea tureen in one hand and a flat platter with bread, margarine, cold cuts, cheese in the other, the poor prisoner who was on tent duty had to run a gauntlet with these creatures. They came down on the platter like a dive bomber and without fail grabbed the most appetizing morsels. It wasn't long before we decided to wash one specific towel for the purpose of covering up the food platter. Those of us who had lost part of our dinner were mad about it, yet we admired the chutzpah of these crows. Some sat outside our tent at a respectful distance to watch us eat. There was one character, obviously young, who we were sure could eventually be turned into a pet.

* ◆ ◆ ◆ ◆ ◆ ◆ ◆

End of July, we had the gates opened from 10:00 a.m. to 10:00 p.m.. "You are all 'gray,'" Sgt. Jim said, "You are considered harmless." Now, we could visit the people across the big divide in Cage 14 and Cage 15, where we found a number of former 278 Division lieutenants. I could not do much with them, not having shared their long fighting withdrawal along the Adriatic Coast during 1944.

Towards the end of the month, on a Sunday afternoon (god knows why we were still conscious of calendar and time), a familiar voice outside our tent asked, "Is a certain Herr Panny by any chance living here?" Here was Zoschke looking sun-tanned and fit. He had gained weight too, all dressed up like the proverbial retired British colonel on a fishing trip, but his POW moccasins gave him away. The soles were made from tent rope sewn together like a rag rug. He had fashionable sunglasses, a short-sleeve golf shirt, officers' shorts and white athletic socks. We had a wonderful reunion.

Even Lt. Dietrich, who had been pretty morose lately, came out of his mood and joined us. He had recently become a member of some kind of religious discussion group and had stopped smoking and abhorred drinking. But when Zoschke took a little flask out of his back pocket, he was easily persuaded to join us. The right-hand man of the British Army Bakery Foreman was his job description. He was well-paid and had freedom of movement until a certain curfew time. His boss did not notice whenever he, Zoschke, was wheeling and dealing in the thriving black market, or if he knew he didn't care. All the German POWs working for the Administration of the Canal District lived in nice clean tents, had plenty of food and surrounded their domiciles with neat retaining walls around their imaginative landscaping.

As a touch of home Zoschke had put a poster into the ground, *Betreten Verboten* (Don't tread on my grass). The Tommies living around them, knowing of the German fussiness about their lawns and gardens, found this amusing, Zoschke said. He was full of confidence that he would be accepted in the Communist Party in Berlin and might even get an early release.

He made list of all the things we needed such as underwear, clothing and those POW moccasins. He gave me a letter for Heymann whom he could not visit in the "black" compound. He said he would be back. His visit was by far the most exhilarating experience since we had arrived. Two weeks later there he was again laden with goodies. I had to ask him how come the Tommies allowed him to carry this kind of merchandise. He showed me his work pass, so apparently he could afford to carry things that were not issued to a POW. Then he grabbed into his shirt and out came a sleepy puppy, all fluff and no coordination. "This is Woton," Zoschke said. For three hours, we had a heart-warming visit and playtime, which was dominated by this little mutt.

● ◆ ● ● ◆ ● ● ◆ ●

We remained concerned about Heymann who had gone to the Satellite. I inquired after him and received an affirmative response. We could visit the "black" sheep on Sundays. So it wasn't long after Zoschke's visit that Dietrich and I made the long walk to the "black" compound. Heymann was very touched, particularly when I brought out Zoschke's letter and told him about Zoschke's posh situation.

Heymann was frustrated because he just could not stand the level of conversation among his fellow prisoners. If they weren't self-righteous and trying to juxtapose one nation's war crimes with another nation's civilian casualties – they were going on and on in a frenzy of self-pity. But otherwise, he said, he had no complaints about his treatment and they were all living in very well-constructed tents. They even had raised the bunks within the tent excavation so it really looked like a two-room flat. He showed us the wooden forms they used to contain the sand, loam and water to form bricks, which then were placed in the sun to bake. He allowed me to borrow one of the forms to import to the "gray" compound.

We came back from our visit to the "black" cage of the Satellite pleased with our new tools. Looking around us at all the other tent cages, we noticed we were not the only ones who had profited by the new freedom of movement. So much for our dreams of free enterprise and monopoly. Our Cage 12 soon was flooded with brick layer tools most ingeniously fashioned from British food cans, some more practical than the ones Zoschke had consigned to us. Cutting a piece of metal was easy, but to fashion some kind of handle, that was the crux of the matter. A construction boom was the consequence. Sgt. Jim was so impressed, he must have told the major about it, so the cage received three spades to speed up the digging.

As for our tent, as planned, we left a sixteen-inch ledge around on the back and the two sides as a handy shelf to store belongings, books and utensils. From the level of the shelves we dug two more feet into the ground and began filling the fresh dirt into those brick forms having added a mixture of loam and water. We baked enough bricks to wall up the excavation all around and to form a six-inch-high outside wall to protect us from wind and rain. At that time, we had no idea what winter would be like, rumors of flash floods and sand storms had been passed on to us by the Italians. The bricks were then covered with a plaster mix. We used our top secret foolproof mix of loam, sand and water, which Zoschke had passed on to us; however, each tent swore by its own formula.

Zoschke and two of his friends helped tremendously and we in turn promised to keep their tools clean and rent them to other tents for brick laying purposes. The going price, we were told, was ten cigarettes per tool per hour. One was a wooden float to smooth plaster, one was a triangular shaped trowel and the third a rectangular laying-on trowel. Capitalism reigned!

We were very pleased with the results. During the day, we still kept taking the tent down so everything could cure and dry properly in the hot sun. Some of our more exciting events centered around catching two scorpions and one *Vogelspinne*, a hairy allegedly poisonous spider the size of a golf ball with over inch long legs. Dietrich developed a phobia about these creatures.

Zoschke came now every two or three weeks to collect the tool rent and to bring new surprises: Increasingly, skilled German workers were called on to replace the Italian POWs; so, as a result more and more the black market became a profitable activity. The personal attitude of a prisoner became: "You take the quality time of our lives away from us and we will steal anything that can be moved." As a consequence, everything from platinum spark plugs down to army socks was fair game.

The camp commandant through Major Hunt was pleased to hear that our "island heroes" had brought all those musical instruments, so a band was started. They had twelve or fifteen amateur musicians and the colonel expressed the hope that sooner or later the whole installation could enjoy occasional concerts.

By now it was August and I was very taken with the activity in the night sky above us. I had never seen that many shooting stars before. A young assistant from Munich University started a volunteer group that went around gazing into the night sky every second or third evening. He explained that the North African sky is recognized for showing much more of this activity than the northern hemisphere. Once the shooting star had disappeared, we had the impression of a kind of jet trail or haze where the star had been. I was so impressed. I asked the man whether it would be possible to make an inventory of all the professional people in the camp, reserve officers from university or technical schools. He very energetically took this matter in hand, visiting all the cages to find other academicians. The ground work for some kind of schooling took many weeks and I lost track of it because Mr. Wahl, a radio producer from Radio Cologne in Cage 15 passed the word around that he wanted to direct the Easter walk scenes from Goethe's *Faust* to be produced as readers' theater plus a few actual scenes to be staged, Easter 1946.

Sgt. Jim and I had to walk all the way down to Major Hunt again, and he was agreeable to have all the theater people concentrated in Cage 13, which of course, featured that big tent which would lend itself for staging a show. I was very pleased to meet Mr. Wahl to bring the good news and he said he would be very glad if I were to accept the role of Faust *famulus* (Faust's graduate assistant). I said I would be flattered.

"Who did he have in mind for Faust?" And of course, as I expected, his answer was, "Well, of course, I'm the only one over age fifty here, I'd better do that myself."

I asked him how much time he thought he would need to assemble the cast and how many scenes he would have in mind. He was quite sure that if we started during the winter, sometime in November or December, then by Easter we should have some results. He figured it would be difficult to find an adequate number of German lieutenants willing to appear made-up and dressed as women.

I thought he would do very well for the part of Dr. Faust, if conceived in the classical way. Very ponderous and theatrical.

July 1945. Sgt. Jim must have bragged about our construction frenzy because it wasn't long before the camp commandant offered his help to build our theater. He must have seen the possibilities of it as a showcase for his administration. Would we supply the manpower if he took care of the expenses? He said he would ask for architectural proposals and then he would decide what kind of theater and concert tent would be feasible. He offered cement and the necessary tools to build the classical Greek type flanking supports of the proscenium opening, which would hold up the rod for the draw curtain.

About fifty POWs volunteered to help with the building, mostly musicians and theater people. Although we had several experts plus the cement mixer, wheelbarrows and shovels, it was still a monstrous undertaking. When the two so-called pillars were standing, we took a break to celebrate - prematurely, it turned out. The left one collapsed during the first night of its existence, a wet and windy night in October. A religious kook predicted it would end up like the Tower of Babble and we would be punished for this amateurish, arrogant, unsafe dabbling in desert masonry. During morning roll call two days later, the same pillar collapsed again. Some had been inclined to suspect sabotage; however, the timing of the destruction was such that it eliminated that possibility.

This disaster was a big frustrating annoyance to everyone involved and the colonel had to supply much more cement than he had budgeted. Nevertheless, he paid, sent a note of encouragement and announced the arrival of some more musical instruments for our mini pop band.

We were lucky the third time. Both pillars served until 1947, when our camp was transferred. So the band got ready for a Christmas concert. Mr. Wahl rehearsed his crowd scene for the Easter performance of *Faust*. The colonel mailed out his invitations to the brigadier and entourage for December 25.

Wahl approached me, inconsolable over the loss of a very good looking, but somewhat awkward, young man who apparently had second thoughts about impersonating a young peasant girl in the crowd scene. Would I have a suggestion for a replacement? Inspired, I thought about Eger, my most ardent student of English. Apart from his good looks, he had an ideal voice for the purpose. Of course, nothing could be done about his dialect - Saxon, what else. After some soul searching, he agreed to offer himself for the part, provided I went with him to Mr. Wahl and did the talking.

The interview went well. Wahl was happy again. I was a bit concerned, though. Eger, the tough First Paratroops Division Lt., had never even been in a theater before, let alone act in a play. Thus, the stress of the rehearsals, memorizing those songs and those few lines of dialogue while picturing himself as a young woman at the same time could be too much for him. It turned out quite the opposite. He insisted on reading the whole play and, as a matter of fact, he was the first one to comment on the possible relevance of Faust's ethical dilemma and Wagner's defense to the present concerns of German soldiers. Here it was, the same topic that my friends and I had begun to discuss at the headquarter in 1944.

The theater tent was ready about the time in late November, when the Nuremberg War Crime Trials began. For the first time in history, generals of the losing side had been accused and indicted for their actions in the course of a war.

● ◆ ● ● ◆ ● ● ◆ ●

Winter introduced itself by two big rain storms, torrents of water that disappeared into the desert sand within minutes. The sand storms, which occurred later, on the other hand, were much more violent than expected and more physically painful than the Russian snowstorms, but unlike the latter, they didn't kill anyone. When we tried to move against the wind during that first sandstorm we found ourselves groping in a black, gray haze. We soon gave up and went to bed until it was over. It took hours afterwards to clear out the tent, shake out all our belongings and get the stuff out of our nose and ears.

The second sand-storm came under abnormally high temperatures reminding me of the *Föhn* wind in the Alps. It created an ugly state of nervous agitation. Tempers flared as we sat in the tent waiting for it to blow itself out. Days later again we heard rumors of suicide, but, as before, I could not get specific information.

Most of the time the sun made it possible to have a sponge bath around noon, the temperature held around fifty-eight degrees as a daily high. Christmas was more or less indistinguishable from any other day. We were concerned about the general news from Germany and frustrated in our attempts to understand what the Nuremberg Trials were all about.

It turned out that the concert given by our band was the highlight of the brigadier's visit. The colonel wished us happy Christmas, praised us for our construction effort and in turn denounced the godless Communists in Moscow. Zille tersely commented, "Nice to hear that, but a bit too late, isn't it?" This was the first time, outside of the BBC news, that antagonism among the victorious anti-German coalition

Allies had manifested itself to us. There was no New Year's celebration either. Everybody had his own thoughts and went to bed early.

At first, I had to take what was available in Cage 13. After a few days living with a very sedate group of "island warriors," I was lucky to be able to find a place with members of our new theater group. So, I joined. Among them was Curt Boch from Saxony, a comic talent of the first order. He was hoping to become a lawyer if they wouldn't accept him in the theater because of his lack of height. He was bubbling over with excitement when he saw me working on *Laburnum Grove*. Next to him slept Volkman, a Frisian from the Danish border. He was only interested in stage management and lighting. The fourth was Oswald, a military policeman from Crete born and reared in Danzig. He was ready to impersonate females from time to time and was rather proud of his legs.

The next tent below us, the last in our row, had the most humorous talents of all of them. Dr. K., the chemist turned Air Force weather man was not interested in theater. Lt. Schäfer, from Silesia, an athlete, passionate brick layer, not interested in theater either. "Zille," as he was known, was the embodiment of all that was good, and everything that is outrageous about Berlin. He claimed to have worked in construction as a *Bretterträger*, which is an unskilled laborer who, with a bundle of two-by-fours, climbs up ladder after ladder when a house is being constructed. None of us believed that this was really his job. He was a managing genius, a first-rate guitar player, a stand-up comedian, interested in acting middle-aged females, a man who could turn a wake into a hilarious bit of slapstick. Last, not least, Harald Quandt, step-son of Josef Goebbels, student of architecture, Air Force lieutenant. He too played an excellent jazz guitar and was interested in acting. Since our tent was only five feet away from this collection of clowns we spent at least half the day watching and enjoying their antics. Their sense of humor was an inspiration and nothing was sacred for them.

Quandt, who found out about his mother's death through the BBC, was very disgusted at hearing about the way his little brothers and sisters had been killed before Goebbels and Quandt's mother had taken their poison in Hitler's bunker. From time to time Quandt was taken to the infamous prison near Cairo called Mahdi for further interrogation. Each time he came back, he was depressed and stayed away from the tent for hours just sitting in a corner of the soccer field playing his guitar. When we asked Zille if we had been too hard on him, he said, "No, don't worry, Harald was born with a key to a BMW in his little fist. He will be all right when he gets home."

One row off there was another theater tent, all paratroopers: Eger and Mäurer - both willing to play female parts, and Landgraf - interested in set building and stagecraft. Next to them lived Eggers who had passed the actors entrance exam, and Goroncy, interested in acting, and Peters, a Navy lieutenant who was another actor. The only POW with a record as a professional actor was Köstering, who had been a successful member of various small boulevard theaters, and he decided to stay in Cage 14. There were two soldiers assigned to us. One was a sail maker from Berlin who went under the name Bolle. He had considerable experience with POW theater and had very good connections with the black market. His friend was a navy ensign who likewise promised to be a great help, and he specialized in middle-aged female character roles and male crooks.

During January and February, it did get colder. The first mail call brought good news for some, even reasons to celebrate and very bad news for others - loss of loved ones, loss of homes, of jobs. Some found out that their families were refugees living in camps. The news that created the most violent reaction came for some husbands and/or boyfriends when they heard about the rape of their women, mostly in Eastern Germany.

There actually was a series of local elections in occupied Germany on January 24. Christian Democrats and Social Democrats were declared winners. Since November of '45 the Nuremberg Trials provided the biggest source of the daily news of the BBC. Palestine increasingly was under tension through the immigration of Jewish families from all over the world and concentration camp survivors. The Zionists and the British Administration were at loggerheads.

Meanwhile, as if we had nothing to worry about, our rehearsals went on and became quite interesting. Eggers' Mephisto was very much worth watching even in these early rehearsals. Wahl looked a bit weak next to him. The use of hurricane lamps as the only source of lighting was unique. I marveled at the inventiveness of the people dealing with them.

Easter, 1946 was the big day, the one and only performance of *Scenes from Faust*. For the majority of the inmates this was an entirely new experience. They enjoyed light operas maybe or Hollywood films, but this was quite a different story.

Wahl had made rather clever cuts in the text, but the dialogue between Faust and Wagner was left intact. In the performance while I, as Wagner, was trying to console him, as Faust, by saying, "What else can a good man do but to perform his duty to the best of his knowledge and according to the standards of excellence of his times?" There was a ripple in the audience.

Wahl approached me afterwards. "Did you notice the applause?"

"Yes, I felt like the Marquis in *Don Carlos*. There was a pause and then I looked at him and said, "Oh, you sneaky devil, you were waiting for that."

"Yes," he said. "It is the second time I am on the losing side in a world war, and in both cases I did my duty and I have nothing to fault myself with. While we are talking in Nuremberg two brave German generals share the dock with those Nazi criminals."

I quickly changed the subject. It would not be wise for me to get involved in another dispute between our nationalistic or militaristic faction (Christian Democrats) and those in the camp who were looking forward to creating a new Germany without an army and without superpower ambitions. I thought if this theater is going to last, we have to keep politics out of it. The hatred within the camp between those factions had increased commensurate with the amount of bad news from home where people were still starving.

My *Laburnum Grove* was not finished, but they all liked the novel *The Poor Millionaire* by Kästner. I finally gave in and undertook the Sisyphean job to turn a novel into a play utilizing the dialogues and trying to eliminate any scenes that did not advance the plot. We ended up with a two-and-a-half-hour marathon show of Wagnerian proportions with over twenty characters and a clear lesson that prose fiction does not necessarily lend itself to dramatization. Nevertheless, it brought the group together more than one way and we discovered a number of talents otherwise unnoticed. We had three performances and collected thousands of cheap Egyptian cigarettes at the box office, a small fortune for us. As luck would have it, one of our "island warriors" had a copy of one-act plays by Curt Goetz. It was a trilogy, *The Fairy Tale*, *The Murderer*, and *The Dead Aunt*. Goetz was a well-renowned playwright and actor-director staging tours all over Europe during the twenties and thirties. He did not kowtow to Minister Goebbels, the Kultur Czar, but the Nazis tolerated his very popular shows.[7] After our monster show a one act play was considered welcome and Eggers was happy to direct it: the Lord, Köstering; the attorney, Bock; the butler, me; the gypsy girl, Eger.

---

7. One of them was filmed in Hollywood starring Cary Grant and the name of the movie, *People Will Talk*.

For Eger's wig, Bolle came up with a solution. He directed the officers to start haggling with the Arab who came each morning to collect the refuse. This crafty Fellah was known to be interested in any black market activity. Four or five of us approached him to barter a Royal Pioneer Corps bed sheet, in demand for their kaftas, and cash was used as bait. The Arab enjoyed the haggling and while he implored Allah to verify that he could not give more than five piastres - two of our boys patted and talked to his tiny horse, which had a tail much too long for the purpose of chasing flies. One of the men shortened the tail hair considerably and while we produced more contraband they sneaked away with their prize. This was Eger's first real part and he stole the show all through rehearsals and on the performance night, horse hair wig, Saxon dialect and all.

Unfortunately, no photos of the play and the actors were taken of those first three shows, but I have photographic copies of the stage designs. If nothing else, the sheer inventiveness of our technical staff would have merited documentation. The colorful costumes consisted primarily of stolen tent material. How these things were obtained, I was never allowed to witness. Our managing genius and Bolle the sail maker and tailor told me to stay out of this so that if there ever were problems I would be able to honestly claim innocence. At this time my fortunes with Major Hunt and the colonel were such that the group profited handsomely and they would hate to lose that advantage.

Much later, someone explained to me how these sheets of colored cloth were taken out of the tent material. It meant undoing the rough stitching, cutting out large sheets and then sewing everything back together again. Since the sun-sail or the top-sail on the tent was not involved and stayed on to cover the operation, they were never caught.

Word got around about our fairy tale performance. Our public wanted more; so, we decided to do our first full length "legitimate" play.

I presented *Laburnum Grove* as our next possibility. It was accepted to be staged in two successive weekends. Eger wanted to sit this one out, so Mäurer, another paratrooper, agreed to play the young daughter. Köstering played the father; Boch played Köstering's wife; Bolle played the brother-in-law; Zille, his wife; Quandt, the young lover and Maart, the villain; and I played the detective.

Since some escapes had been tried in an Egyptian POW camp, using civilian garb, Major Hunt sent a memorandum, "All stage costumes and civilian clothes wearable outside the camp that were donated by prisoners have to be registered." The group had to set up a costume tent with Bolle as costume director and from then on, we were to keep all our material in clearly marked boxes which periodically could be checked against our inventory. Of course, Bolle marked his boxes in German, which led to interesting episodes from time to time with the British guards. At the first check-up, the very officious sergeant wanted to know what he would find in the box on his list marked, *Titten und Kleinkram* on his list (Teats and Miscellaneous). When he was shown the padded breasts, he turned puce in the face and just nodded. We were allowed to use civilian clothing as long as they were treated as a controlled item. By virtue of the fact that the island warriors could provide quite a selection of civvies, which they offered on loan, we were in good shape.

The script was typed on a portable typewriter courtesy of Major von L., who was from Rhodes or Crete. He donated it and even two spare ribbons, provided that we would try a play by Shakespeare - and let him direct the show. If that wasn't a mouthful already, he decided on *The Taming of the Shrew*. He was quite insistent on it, he would cast Bolle as Petruccio, of all people - Berlin dialect and all. I had a pretty good hunch that Bolle had a hand in the choice of this play because he had told me more than once how wonderfully well they had staged *The Taming of the Shrew* in an open-air POW theater, while the Afrika Corps soldiers were still in Egypt.

The next question was who would want to tackle the female counterpart. A deal is a deal. We had tryouts. Major Hunt duplicated the text for us in the camp office, but we still didn't find a German lieutenant courageous enough for the part. At last Waldemar, the proud owner of the best pair of presentable legs, agreed to subject himself to the chore.

Fate interfered. After a few rehearsals, the major took ill and disappeared. We were sorry to see him go, but had a collective deep sigh of relief at the same time. The costumes alone for that show would have killed us. We had to pacify Bolle and we gladly did because his contribution in many technical ways was really outstanding, ever since the inception of the theater group. We found a stark rustic farce where he could play the villain as well as the hero and Waldemar could play his daughter. I was an unfortunate DA again. Everyone used the play as a free for all. The show was such a success that Major Hunt allowed us to pack our sets in a truck and present the show to the Satellite cage of Nazis.

● ◆ ● ● ◆ ● ● ◆ ●

After that, the political situation back home in Europe, as related in many of the letters to us, the British papers and the BBC news, contributed to a deterioration of life in the camp. October, '46 the top war criminals had been hanged in Nuremberg, only Göring had escaped by taking poison. Two weeks later, Americans decreed a political amnesty and Mr. Byrnes suggested a more lenient treatment of the Germans and a re-unification of the divided country. There still was hunger and the dismantling of various industrial installations went on uninterrupted.

Political discussions in our four cages produced no reasonable point of view. The right-wing people encouraged by the American amnesty raised questions about war crimes committed against German civilians. Their motto was: "The Americans need us. Let's use them."

And the other more left-wing oriented people responded, "Yes, the Americans need us - as cannon fodder in the looming cold war with Russia." I heard people criticize the British for going back on their word and stopping the Jewish immigration to Palestine. July 22, 1946, when Jewish extremists blew up the King David Hotel in Jerusalem killing ninety-one people, I heard nasty cracks about the Jews outrageously continuing to use World War II terrorism.

The lack of fresh vegetables caused a number of prisoners to volunteer for garden work outside the camp where the Italians had been growing vegetables. There was a relatively small plot where a great deal of dedication, a constant supply of horse manure and the rather questionable liquid that came flowing down from the camp had produced some tangible results. This liquid was the water from the various wash areas, allegedly containing merely residue of soap, but we made a strict compact that those who worked down there should not nibble without washing the vegetable in clean water. I helped for a few days in order to get an idea of what was going on and it was amazing to see what could be grown out of desert sand. We had radishes, cauliflower, various kinds of lettuce. The gardeners came home every night at six with a load of fresh vegetables. There was, of course, never enough for everybody.

At this point Major Hunt approached me, would I help him find a dog trainer to make sure that the colonel's Boxer could be put under quarantine conditions safe from the nervous distemper, which apparently was killing dogs all over Egypt. I showed him the photo of Ivan, which I always had in my pocket, and he was glad he didn't have to look any further. He showed me an officer's tent outside the camp in a secluded corner. I would get food from the sergeants' mess, and look after the colonel's dog, keeping it away from all other dogs.

I was introduced to the colonel and found out that my charge would not be only one male dog as I had at first been told, there was a female and a puppy involved as well. I immediately questioned whether one man would be enough to handle all three and they allowed me to look for some suitable companion who might enjoy this kind of work. My first thought was Eger who would appreciate the possibility of getting away from teasing remarks. He was very interested. Every afternoon, Eger and I paraded our dogs up and down the *Via Dolorosa*, so our participation in theater activities did not suffer. The daily morning walk with the dogs was hard work in the beginning because that Palestinian male was pulling even worse than Ivan used to, but eventually we came to terms and explored the surrounding countryside - the desert.

We had a big surprise on our walk the second morning when all of a sudden water came flowing all around us in tiny little irrigation canals, and we found ourselves standing in the middle of a watermelon field. The Fellahin, after friendly greetings, rushed off to get the boss and he brought a young student, the son of the owner of that land, a very hospitable friendly chap. He insisted that we each had to carry a huge watermelon home and agreed to our having another meeting the following day. Watermelon was a daily occurrence from then on. After a while he said how impressed he was with the Germans since they had "almost" liberated them from the British - and surely, we would have some weapons hidden away and couldn't we sell them to him - and if need be British weapons would do. We said we'd see what we could do for him.

We found him almost impatient when he asked for the weapons the second time. Of course, there was not the slightest chance anyone could smuggle any weapons out of the camp in broad daylight, let alone steal them from the British.

We always ate one watermelon ourselves and carried the other one back to the cage, the load was not easy in that temperature. I had to take all the dogs and Eger carried the melon like a heavy baby.

Major Hunt didn't really explain why we suddenly had to give up the colonel's dogs and our plush situation, but our Sgt. Jim let on to me that the colonel had been breeding the female whenever she was inclined and had sold the puppies. Allegedly, he made himself a nice trip to Cairo every once in a while where he enjoyed wine, women and song. Someone in his family got on to him, probably his wife, so his little money making operation had to stop.

I had enjoyed this bit of freedom and missed it, but Eger was heartbroken. During our time together, I had learned that he was actually a mechanic apprentice, a commissioned lieutenant from his bravery in the Battle of Cassino, 1944. Eger and I at least got a trip to El Firdan where there was a military police dog station. It was a sad journey, Eger and I sitting with our backs against the driver's cabin and the dogs excitedly looking around. We came through the town of Ismalya and turned north along the Suez Canal. The driver was nice enough to stop at a place very close to the water where we could watch the ships go by. It was all in a southerly direction and mostly French Navy ships heading in a southerly direction. We asked the driver what they were up to and he said, "Well, there is trouble in Indo-China, you know, Vietnam."

Leaving the dogs was not too difficult. The military policeman loaded us up with food and beer and a special package for the driver, not to be opened until we got back to camp because it too contained beer. Although, we did not shed tears about losing the dogs, the trip home was not a very cheerful affair. Eger hated the political emotionalism in the cage, it really depressed him. It poisoned the atmosphere in the camp and was beginning to infiltrate the theater group. On this trip, we developed the idea to write a political cabaret, satirizing the various positions and the immature way in which people approached political thinking and political responsibility. That somewhat distracted us from the loss of our freedom and we immediately began our search for concrete ideas to use.

When we arrived back, there were rumors that the camp was about to be transferred to some other part of Egypt, probably close to the Suez Canal. Our Sgt. Jim did neither deny nor confirm that this was in the wind and it created some kind of psychosis. Almost every week now, some people made an attempt to escape. I had no direct knowledge, but we just heard that so and so wasn't in camp anymore because he had been caught trying to escape and was now in military prison because he was caught.

One of our black market connections, a friend of Zoschke, came to our tent and said he had a contact outside of the camp and if anyone wanted to sell bed sheets or whatever, he would take them out. Eger and I told him of our watermelon connection and he thought that was a great idea. He told us we could even watch how he would go about it. So Eger and I and two other friends who wanted to sell something actually watched him. The minute the little troop carrier that was going around the camp passed, he crawled through both fences, carefully avoiding both barbed wire fences, looked around, and then ran for about fifty yards to hide behind a deserted piece of wall about two yards long and about three yards high. Behind that he waited for the little carrier to come around again and then he just walked straight into the night. We didn't wait for him to return because we had not agreed on any specific time. He was back the next morning and handed some money to whoever had given him the merchandise.

The escape psychosis continued. Zoschke came and introduced another friend who claimed that he went out of the camp whenever he needed to with impunity, and asked me whether I could introduce him to the watermelon connection. In the past I had talked to the son of the owner that I would look for the weapons he wanted, but I had very little hope to find any. I asked him whether he would in turn look for theatrical lipstick, some wigs and the odd female negligee. We both had assured each other to see what we could do, but I was sure that he hadn't done anything about it either.

Eger said that if I wanted to risk it, I should go with our new black market friend and see whether his merchandise hits the spot with our Egyptian connection. I am hard put to admit with all my struggling maturity, what made me go with him a few days later. People were looking up to me and I had a lot to lose if caught. However, like an idiot, I crawled under the barbed wire following Zoschke's friend who had trouble this time with the barbed wire, because he had two bed sheets and one blanket wrapped around his body. When I had offered to take some of the load he declined disdainfully and said, "You better make sure you get through as you are."

We did get out all right, but when we came to the watermelon field dogs were barking all over the valley. It was shortly after 1:00 a.m. when a very threatening large Fellah with a vintage rifle threatened us. I asked for Halif, son of the owner, but he said, "*Nix Halif, nix Halif.*" We had to raise our hands and were taken prisoner all over again and directed to approach the village. There were Fellahin standing around in a half circle facing us. Some of them meekly greeted us, acknowledging that we had met before in the watermelon field. The night watchman ordered some of them to tie our hands and then told my companion to disrobe. So there we stood there under the threat of an irritable armed guard who was not at all impressed when I repeatedly assured him that Halif, the son of the owner repeatedly had invited me to come back, that I was not an intruder. Some of the Fellahin nodded, they remembered me. The guard yelled something that I understood to mean that he didn't care a fig about Halif, and that if any more German prisoners disturbed him at night, he would shoot them. Then he participated in the general discussion over the two sheets and the blanket and nobody paid any attention to us anymore.

I found myself watching them realizing that I very foolishly had stumbled into one of the most humiliating messes I could have imagined. I was a prisoner taken prisoner outside the prison camp. Physical harm was a possibility. It was possible they would hand us over to the British in the morning when I would have to face Major Hunt who had trusted me and would be very put out and might even lose interest in our theater group. To be sure I would disappear in the calaboose (the British prison) for several weeks.

Fritz, my companion, started to undo the rope around his wrists. When the night watchman detected that he became really furious. He said in broken English that all these German prisoners that are coming out every night were a hell of a lot of trouble. Then Fritz said, "Give me five piastres and we'll go." But the night watchman said that if he was spending any more time with us, he might lose out as far as the loot was concerned.

And so one Fellah had to untie us and he yelled, "No come back," and then waded into the group of Fellahin, pushing them out of his way to get to the blanket. Fritz and I beat a hasty retreat, expecting to be shot in the back at any minute. We were lucky to reach that little ruin, the little wall fragment. We waited for the armed personnel carrier to go by and crawled in great haste under the barbed wire again. I ruined my best shirt in the process.

We woke Eger and he said, "Those dogs are still barking. You're lucky to have made it."

I could have kicked myself for taking these risks on the vague hope for some kind of business success. Eger took it philosophically the next morning and said, "Vincenz, after this I am not sure I'd like to trust you with 1,500 Egyptian cigarettes. You're bound to lose them."

I said, "I wouldn't blame you. It wasn't one of my more heroic episodes."

Some people were totally unreasonable. Our tent neighbor to the left reported that his friend came to rudely shake him awake at 1:00 a.m. saying, "I'm going to escape. Are you coming with me?" Of course, our neighbor refused, but that was typical for the psychological insecurity rampant at that time. What motivated these people to try to escape? I imagine that, for one, they didn't want to give up the university, their nicely organized tent, the theater and the music, but generally they distrusted the British who had just painted themselves into a corner in Palestine. And besides, they had heard in letters from home that German prisoners of war returning from United States or Canada were suddenly diverted to France, many of them losing all their savings and food, and then they were forced to do hard labor in coal mines or in French Army detachments who were trying to find the land mines that were still in the ground all over their country. I suppose this insecurity was part of the explanation for this behavior. The facts weighed heavily that we were not any longer being treated as prisoners of war under the Geneva Convention, the rationale being that after all there was no such country called Germany anymore.

As the rumors of an impending relocation gained more credibility, the executive committee decided that we should prepare for any possibility that the camp would be broken up and we should become separated, that the four of us should each take responsibility of one quarter of our theater proceeds, which meant about 1500 cigarettes each.

We wrote a manuscript for a political satire for our contribution to defuse the tension, a contradiction in terms considering we were in a camp of irate, frustrated German officer-prisoners. The sketches and songs were rather funny. Zille and Quandt as a guitar duo were the hit of the evening. We had a parody of all the entertainment the Third

Reich had to offer in its last year, and Zille and Quandt sang about the Swedish singing and film star Sarah Leander.

There was one attempt to teach tolerance by introducing the word "self-criticism" into the German language. The main thrust was, "Let's take stock of whatever it was we were doing in the Third Reich under the motto, 'Did you ever see a yellow star?'" We had applause, lots of belly laughs and some hecklers. I lost my voice in the process. It was a good experience for me, inasmuch as I discovered I had a lot to learn about "making friends and influencing people."

My voice was not recovering well, so the British sent me to the hospital in Quassassin where a Polish doctor rammed some kind of instrument down my throat and warned me that my vocal cords were not separating properly. He said that his assumption was that this would happen each time I'd be under emotional stress and breathe wrongly.

It wasn't long after that I had another occasion to seek the help of doctors. I don't remember what my first symptoms were except for a very high temperature. The camp medic just shook his head when he saw me, did some tests and said, "I could have told you right away, you've got malaria." I packed up my small bundle of personal items, including the blasted 1,500 cigarettes, the only things of value in my possession, and reported to the infirmary.

❖ •• ❖ •• ❖ •

The medic gave me two aspirins followed by two cups of strong coffee - the first decent coffee I had in years. Then he bundled me up in three or four blankets. All one could see of me was my face. I thought that this was a bit of medieval quackery, but I was so weak from the fever I let everything happen. After a few minutes I knew that this was an effective home remedy used by the British army. I practically melted under those covers. He kept me perspiring for a long time and when I finally was through with this, he unwrapped me and gave me a vigorous rub with a huge towel and he had me change to a nice fresh clean bed where I immediately fell asleep.

The following morning, the doctor had me shipped to the hospital at Quassassin. After four or five days, the same doctor came to say goodbye and said that he had appreciated my pointing out from the beginning that I had hepatitis before. He told me that I could not go back to my former camp, which had been transported close to the Suez Canal and for the time they would put me into the 278 Working Company and he wished me a speedy recovery.

I arrived at 278 shortly after lunch, a German maintenance man took me to a tent on the outer row of the cage. It was the most fabulous tent I had ever seen, apparently built by two intelligent prisoners who insisted on as much privacy as could be had under the circumstances. So I had one bedroom now and in the front part of the tent I had a lovely working table and room enough possibly to have a daybed there. I was still a bit weak so I went to bed right away, still not sure this would remain my tent but ready to enjoy at least this night.

I woke up after a wonderful sleep. Very close to me somebody was practicing on a bass viol. I was sure I was dreaming, but got more or less dressed and went to check it out. I looked into this big above-ground officers' tent next to mine. It was almost as big as the camp theater I had been used to and there was a surprising sight. A huge man in POW uniform, yet with khaki shorts, with long unwashed black hair almost shoulder length and a bushy neglected mustache was standing over three double bass players.

Three double bass players in a British POW camp in Egypt? Should I go back to the hospital and tell the doctor I was hallucinating? The music stopped and I could not control my curiosity. I said, "Hello." The conductor turned around and we introduced ourselves to each other and then he said, "You're new here?" I nodded and he continued, "What are we smoking?" I happened to have a box of woodbine cigarettes on me. Dr. Hörner's face lit up. "You can come anytime. What's the story?"

I explained that I had been separated from my camp through my getting malaria and was supposed to live here for a while. I live right in the tent next to this.

He grinned, "Next to our rehearsal tent, eh?"

"Yes."

He was still grinning. "Let's see how long you can stand it. This afternoon we have five cellos for you, and so it goes."

I asked, "What are you rehearsing?"

"Dvořák, the New World Symphony. We're going to perform it in a few weeks in 'Music for All' in Cairo. We're traveling all over the canal district, but Cairo is the big concert."

"What do you mean, 'Music for All?'"

"All ranks and civilians - a public concert."

I excused myself, knowing that he didn't want to spend all morning educating me, but I knew I would want to hear more from this man. I went back to my tent in utter disbelief to the accompaniment of the viol's disconnected grumblings. What a morning that was! I was in a cage with a symphony orchestra! Hörner had told me that the orchestra was too small for the Dvořák's piece, but he said, "We will do. We had the same problem in Belgrade and in Athens, but a very good time was had by all - musicians and audience." This last remark in itself was highly perplexing. What the hell was he doing in Belgrade and Athens? I was sure I would soon find out.

After some tea and porridge, I looked around in the camp. Every third or fourth tent housed musicians of some kind, practicing in the morning by themselves. Next to the cage was an eight-foot-high brick wall. I went around it and found myself at the entrance of an open-air theater at least forty yards wide, with four or five levels descending down to the orchestra pit. The proscenium was raised six feet with a wide and very deep stage and some prisoners were busy building furniture and constructing a set. I walked to the edge of the proscenium and discovered they had electric lighting. Now, I really thought I was hallucinating.

I returned to my tent and was unpacking my luggage when I heard someone at the tent opening.

A tall chap asked, "*Gestatten Sie?*"

"Yes, come in."

"My name is Kurt, I just saw you in our theater. You're new here, aren't you?"

"Yes, I just had malaria and have to stay here for a while. Were you one of them, working on the stage?"

He said he had just arrived when I had left. I had to know who built that fantastic theater.

"We all did, of course."

"You must have had a bulldozer."

"No, it was all shovels and wheelbarrows. Are you interested?"

"Am I interested! I've been working my ass off translating, acting and coordinating in our 'little' theater in Camp 305. I can't believe my luck here. Who is running this show?"

He explained that after the 278 POW camp had been disbanded, all the various entertainment groups, the symphony, chamber music, the theater, the ballet…."

"The what?" I interrupted.

He laughed. "Yes, there is a ballet, named after the director Meissner - and there are the dance bands and the acrobats - all these groups were put under the direction of the British Army Welfare with a German lawyer, Dr. Hartlieb, as the coordinator. I'll take you to him if you like."

On the way, he explained he was a corporal from Silesia in this camp for two years, that he had no idea what had happened to his family and that he was hoping to become professional in one way or another in show business. Would I be interested to see the last performance of *Turandot*?

I said, of course I would. By that time we were at Hartlieb's tent. There before us was Hartleib and his blonde secretary. The lawyer greeted me with some distance when he heard that I had been in the officers' camp 305. But when we came to discussing my interest in translating plays into German, he immediately warmed up because his own English was atrocious; his "secretary," however, spoke the most authentic Oxford dialect I had ever heard in my life. Hartlieb explained the setup to me. The director of the Army Welfare Service, he said, was a certain John Mason, a very kind British gentleman who had volunteered to work in wartime troop welfare. He commented that even had Mason tried to enlist, no army in the world would have accepted him - he had a frail constitution and a stammer in his speech. However, he had a big heart for German prisoners of war - particularly those who worked day and night to entertain their fellow prisoners and while they were at it, provide tremendous entertainment for the British army personnel. Hartlieb was a suave, good-looking red head and I could see that he was the right man to coordinate the various activities of this bunch, but he too, like the Mr. Mason he had been talking about, shied away from exposing himself.

I felt we had a good rapport, but not as good as the one I felt I had with Dr. Hörner. This was my first day in "Never-never Land." Kurt promised to come back next morning and take me to meet the other members of the theater group.

I borrowed a kerosene lamp and went back to my dream tent and tried to concentrate on my next translation job, *Charlie's Aunt*. I was so fired up that by 1:00 a.m. I had used up the last of Major Hunt's typing paper. Since I remembered the German movie, *Charlie's Aunt* from showing it two or three times at the German headquarter in 1944, I had no trouble with this translation at all - even without the dictionary. I had to return it to the "island warrior" I had borrowed it from in the other camp.

The next morning brought the meeting with the acting group. There was Kurt, of course, and Hans, who had just directed *Turandot* - the play with the ballet and costumes that no one would believe - and Wolf who was about to direct *Jugend*, by the German playwright Halbe. In the corner of the tent was "Dolly" smoking a British cigarette. Kurt explained that Dolly had been impersonating females on the Troop Entertainment in Italy already.

Then Dolly pointed to Erich who had been a plumber apprentice from Bremen and had permission to wear his hair shoulder length because he always played young women's parts. Next to him sat a six-foot-five giant called Lulatsch, an anemic looking comic from Berlin. There were two or three more actors whose names I have forgotten. There was Fritz who had been directing the last operetta. There were two acrobats and Mr. Meissner and his five *balletratten* as they are called in German.

I had to give them a short rundown of our activities in 305. Whenever they had questions they used the polite German form of addressing me, but we gained an immediate rapport, particularly when I agreed to try out for the fanatic young Catholic priest in *Jugend*.

In the evening, I sat down in the nicely filled audience not knowing what to expect from *Turandot*. They had a hand-bill with a short synopsis and the name of the author, some Italian named Gozzi. I was sure that Mr. Gozzi had had no intention to write a musical, but here we were with an overture of some kind played by an orchestra of about fifteen musicians. Then the foot lights came on - electric lighting, colored bulbs - and the curtain opened into the big hall at the emperor's palace.

At least twenty-six or so colorfully garbed actors and dancers were on the stage. When the visiting Prince Calif had been seated, the Meissner Ballet danced some kind of Oriental belly dance. I had no idea where this show would end up, but this certainly was a delightful spectacle, extremely well-choreographed, and at the same time obviously kitsch - I couldn't help being critical.

◆ ◆ ◆ ◆ ◆ ◆

Dr. Hartlieb came by and asked me, "Now that you've seen it and know what we can do, when is your translation of *Charlie's Aunt* finished?"

I said, "Very soon. It's a pushover - I have seen the German movie version so many times I don't even need a dictionary."

"No problem, I have a German-English, English-German one here for you. They tell me you have the part of the young priest in *Jugend*. Welcome aboard."

It was a very exciting evening, full of promise, and I felt fortunate to have a chance to work in this wonderful open-air theater.

The next morning was first full orchestra run-through of the "New World." Of course there were many interruptions and many passages were repeated over and over, but the sound was deeply moving to me as I lay there in my bed. Without ever having heard or read any commentary on the "New World," I immediately assumed that Dvořák must have had something to do with the United States which, considering my limited opportunity to listen to American folk music, I thought was remarkable when my assumption was later acknowledged to be true. I'll never forget it - the haunting lines of the spiritual, as it was later explained to me. To be able to hear this music any time day or night in this camp was unbelievably wonderful. As much as I missed my buddies in 305, I was beginning to think that the malaria had done me a service.

After the rehearsal was over, I went to tell Herr Hörner how impressed I was.

"Ehhh. There is a lot of work to be done," he replied. "I am sorry you have to go through this step by step with us."

"I assure you so far it has been a pleasure."

He touched the pocket of his POW shirt and said, "What are we smoking?" I made up my mind that I would always have some Woodbine with me. He invited me in his Bavarian dialect to come and see his tent. It was in the opposite corner of the cage along the barbed wire fence opening. I was impressed that his tent opened up into a commanding view of the desert. It struck me that all the other POWs had their tents open to the center of the cage and facing each other.

His table was covered with sheets of music, two or three kinds of ink-pots, old fashioned wooden ink pens, two or three ashtrays made from food tins full of cigarette butts. Everything was covered with dust or actual sand.

If he had anything different from his daily costume to wear I didn't see where it was, except for a bogus tuxedo put together by a POW tailor, two or three pairs of POW sandals, and maybe two or three German or French books on music. There was one instrument - I think it was a viola.

"You live like a hermit," I said.

He replied, "That is a good way to describe it - except that there is a corporal bringing something to eat three times a day. I have that much. And they allow me to grow my hair long and sport a goatee." I watched him look at himself in probably the dirtiest mirror I've ever seen and then he said, "Oh shit, I have to shave." He then turned back to me, "We won't have time now, but I'd like to hear about your impressions. The symphony isn't hundred percent satisfied with Dr. Hartlieb. Have you talked to him?"

"Yes. I'm a member of the group, would you believe? Tomorrow we start rehearsing *Jugend*. I heard that they take pride in rehearsing only three or four weeks and then travel extensively with the show - a courageous schedule."

We wished each other a delicious bean stew for lunch and I returned to my empty, orderly tent.

In the afternoon, Hartlieb gave me a run-down on the administrative side of the groups and a bit of the behind the scenes problems and he described his difficulties with Mr. Mason, the British director, who for some reason didn't seem to warm up to Hartlieb's interpreter, who was sitting right next to him with a somewhat petulant expression. This young man was a German boy straight out of high school who had worked for a while with the British quartermaster and knew all the ins and outs of the black market. One of the dancers during our first theater group meeting had made a rather catty remark that he wasn't called merely "secretary," he was called the "abdominal secretary" - the pleasure boy - of Mr. Hartlieb.

In being with the two of them at this point I could see why someone would make a remark like that because Hartlieb was rather possessive in his attitude towards the young man, almost displaying the intimacy between them as some kind of achievement - not good form, I thought, under these circumstances especially.

The next morning, John Mason, the director, came. He was a tall fifty-year-old gentleman in a pseudo military uniform. We shook hands and if there is such a thing as friendship at first sight, this was it. He had a few things to discuss with Hartlieb and then he wanted to know all about my life and how I got there. Frequently, he had trouble speaking and started stammering and I looked him straight in the eye and in some cases had the good fortune to be able to finish whatever sentence he was having trouble with. He said that my English was excellent.

He excused himself, he had to go back to Quassassin, but if I needed any books or materials from the British Council he would be happy to provide them. I asked for *Journey's End* by Sherriff, the play we had done as boys in Hamburg. It was a wonderful beginning. I felt I would not be just wasting my life here.

During the rehearsals for *Jugend*, I could see that this was a group of the more gifted actors. The single female impersonator took his part seriously and was wonderfully convincing. We did each scene separately so that whoever is not involved doesn't have to attend rehearsal. After three-and-a-half weeks, we had our first night in the open-air theater in front of this relatively educated audience who had by now had a number of theater experiences. Still, the hostility towards this young priest, the part I was playing, was palpable. It got much worse when we started traveling with the show. Simple, uneducated people who never in their lives would have gone to see a live drama were reacting almost as children might react to a Punch and Judy show - jeering at the perceived villain, remarking about the stage action as it was going on. We made five trips to various working companies. All the theaters were in the same style tents as we had in 305; the four performances in the open-air theater, I found the most memorable.

Mason came the next morning after the first night and said that he wanted someone to give him a hand with the management of the symphony - there had been some complaints. It would have to be someone who would travel ahead and arrange with the local authorities for food, lodging and all the technical details so that the artists would not feel like entertainers of little value. Even though the orchestra was performing in their striped POW uniforms, they should be treated like valued artists. I told him I would be interested in his offer. We shook hands and he said he would come on the weekend and discuss details.

To forestall political trouble I went straight to Dr. Hartlieb, who as I had expected, was looking at me with some caution. I quickly tried to give him a rundown on what Mason had proposed. Then I asked him, didn't he always go with the symphony orchestra as some kind of manager and I didn't want to step on any toes. That probably was what made us overcome this distance I had been sensing.

He said the camp commandant was quite happy to rely on his judgment as far as the theater was concerned, but for some reason had a different attitude regarding the symphony. He assured me that he was very pleased that the British enabled all these groups to work because of the entertainment value for their troops in Egypt who, having been far removed from the actual war, did not feel very useful anymore and had some trouble with morale. He thought it was fair and businesslike that the British undertook to make the best use of the symphony for their troop entertainment, and if I felt my English was good enough he personally would be very glad to get out of it because he did not enjoy haggling with local authorities through an interpreter. I'm not sure he was totally sincere, but I think we had reached a *modus vivendi.*

All in all this first week had my head swimming. There was Mason, the symphony, an ongoing production *Charlie's Aunt* in process and the personal interest in Dr. Hörner who became more and more someone I felt protective about. He was a genius, I was quite sure. He told me he had played Athens with a mixed German-Greek symphony and Belgrade under even worse conditions. On the other hand, he was so impractical I had to go into a huddle with the corporal who was looking after him that we could get him to look more or less presentable. Hörner took our nagging in good humor. He even accepted a second pair of khaki shorts; but first or second pair, they always looked the same crumpled, dirty mess. His philosophy was "I have nothing to worry about. I don't have to pay taxes. I don't have to stand in line for food stamps. All my needs are taken care of. I never had so much time in my life to do exactly what I love to do. So, what's the fuss?"

We started to talk politics and he expressed interest in the deplorable conditions in Palestine, but ended each talk with a shrug, "What can we do?"

I said after one or two weeks, "Would it help if the orchestra would not wear these atrocious POW uniforms? I just thought that if we had the British battle dress and we dyed it some acceptable color that the group would have the feeling of distinction and something apart from being a POW."

He thought it was a good idea. John Mason agreed the next morning and added, "Get yourself some kind of civilian garb from the theater group. We're going to Cairo and in the meantime, I get some offers from dry cleaners that can dye the woolen uniforms and then we decide on the spot which ones we want."

By this time, the *New World* symphony was almost ready, so that would mean that this month, January 1947, I would go to Cairo twice. There is a photo from that trip. I look like a German civil servant in my cheap suit. Mason and I did go in a jeep, had a room each in a hotel and then went all over town to three different businesses who had made an offer. The third dry cleaners was in the part of Cairo close to the university and our arrival in an army jeep and Mason, being in uniform of sorts, didn't sit very well with the students who were loitering around that corner. I felt somewhat self-conscious about my cheap gray suit. Somehow, I resented Mason putting me in this awkward situation. The students did not heckle us, but crowded around us.

It was a tense moment until finally a fat little guy said, pointing to me, "That's a German." That started off a lively discussion in Arabic, which Mason and I were happy to get away from. I must say I was a bit mad, but then I said to myself that Mason could not have anticipated this. It did give me a general impression of anti-British feeling concerning the conditions in Palestine.

We ordered a dark brown dye with a slightly bluish tinge for the suits and the uniforms arrived in time for the great first performance of the *New World* ever in the city of Cairo. This was just a concert, I had no obligations, so I just sat there in the concert hall and enjoyed it immensely. Afterwards, there were tea and crumpets for refreshments for everybody - British officers, noncommissioned officers, other ranks, Egyptian officers, and Egyptian civilians. It was an unforgettable experience.

Dr. Hörner never talked about his past either in Germany or during the war. Once he mentioned that there was a Mrs. Hörner in Frankonia.

"Frankonia?" I said with some surprise.

"Yes. You must have gathered that, judging from my round head and penetrating black eyes."

"Your glasses are covering your eyes, Doctor. And by the way, can't the British get you better glasses?"

"I have a pair in the breast pocket of my formal coat to be used for performances only."

"Does the Royal Pioneer Corps appreciate what they have in you?"

"I have no complaints," he said. From a wonderful little quartet they helped him with instruments for a chamber orchestra. In those days they were doing Sunday forenoon concerts in hospitals and clubs. From there to the symphony orchestra was somewhat of an arduous climb, which took enormous patience and tenacity. Finding musicians among the 90,000 German prisoners was not without its difficulties. Most prisoners still had no news from their families in Europe and were under great stress because of it. To detect real talent and skill without creating expectations, which in turn might lead to prima donna attitudes later, was the problem.

The bureaucrats in uniform and Dr. Hartleib's often gauche and inflexible way of negotiating frequently created more obstacles for Hörner's work. He had no complaints about the heat or about the players he had now and felt very pleased with his work. I felt humble and encouraged in his presence. In my opinion, he must have been a pioneer among his peers in the world of music, since he had done this twice before - once in Belgrade, 1941-1942, and later in Athens.

I went to the first open-air concert. The *New World* was on the program. Yes, the glasses were very good looking and in one piece, which was more than could be said for the ones he used daily. Those were brittle and kept together with pieces of adhesive. He looked splendid as he worked his way through his orchestra, slender and attractive, charismatic we say nowadays, but he still wore his POW sandals and gray socks.

"*Oben hui, unten pfui!*" he said grinning when I talked to him how good he looked after the concert. ("Outside great looking, inside a bit pitiful.")

I sat down in the back of the open-air theater and when the first chords of Beethoven's *Leonore*, No. 3, reached me I was not ashamed of my emotions. I'm afraid I did cry. I was very glad I was sitting by myself in one of the back rows. That sky. The stars overhead. It was so incredibly beautiful. I knew I was stuck here for god knows how long, but with this music I recognized that I had so much to be thankful for.

The Dvořák symphony went off without a hitch and I enjoyed it even more this first night than during the concert three weeks later in Cairo when the presence of civilians - whole families, high ranking military personalities distracted me somewhat. I did feel immensely pleased to know that none of this music had ever been played in this area in history and we had brought something positive.

The assignments for the symphony became more varied. The first time I was the traveling manager, we played in Ismailiya and returned the same night. At 2:00 a.m. we came close to our camp, but the convoy ran into the crossfire between military police and some gang of Fellahin robbers. We all left our seats and tried to lie down as much as space would allow, hearing the ghastly shriek of the ricocheting ammunitions go past our truck. My thought was that I didn't think it funny to have survived World War II and now get into this kind of situation. At the camp, we found out that nobody got hurt, but at noon the following day the oboe player reported that he would need a new instrument - and soon.

◆ ◆ ◆ ◆ ◆

The rumors of difficulties back home became reality. Apparently the "Cold War" was getting hotter. Overnight we received the news that the British would recognize the Geneva Convention after all, which meant improvement of living conditions of prisoners and the officers would be paid according to the internationally accepted standards.

I didn't believe it. I went to the office and they had to read it to me twice. Obviously, by now a considerable amount of money in terms of back pay had accrued. That first month when I saw the figures in British money, it was suddenly like I had become a millionaire. First, I set up a certain amount for foodstuffs to take home - whenever that would happen. At last, I could buy myself some decent things to wear. I was not throwing it around at all, but I was able to provide some conviviality for close friends in the orchestra as well as contribute heavily to two or three very nice parties with the theater group. This was at the same time we were rehearsing *Charlie's Aunt*.

It turned out to be a big success, judging by the need to add two more performances to the local working company. Mason and Dr. Hartlieb took me to the center of the cage and opened one of the empty officers' tents. There was a couch, meaning the front seat of a truck. There was a table and a chair and on the table was a typewriter and behind the typewriter stood one member of the theater group now a designated typist. When I thanked them profusely, the typist pointed to the ceiling tarpaulin and there was dangling slowly in the wind an electric bulb. I must say I felt on top of the world. There was a bucket with sand and a fire extinguisher, Hartlieb explained, just in case I wanted to engage in any more conviviality - I could sleep in my own tent or here.

◦◆◦◦◆◦◦◆◦

It was by now winter 1947. Dr. Hörner started quite a number of rather ambitious projects, among them a concert of music written exclusively by British composers. John Mason gave me the script of T.S. Eliot, *Murder in the Cathedral*. I thanked him, expressing the hope that this was not an assignment. Reading T.S. Eliot was one thing, but translating and casting it with German POWs was quite another. I found out later that he was really hoping we would tackle it. In those days, T.S. Eliot was a big name. The next play was a comedy by Thoma, where I just helped with the production. In this play, Dolly at last had a chance to play a German prostitute and loved every minute of it. They traveled around with *The Morality*, and then, over my protest, they insisted on doing *The Cock*. Not only did they override my misgivings, they didn't have anyone in mind to play the middle-aged shrewish wife. At this point in the discussion I was not really listening because I had thought I had done my duty to try to talk them out of it. Suddenly, there was a pause and when I looked up Kurt said, "They're all looking at you."

"What for?"

"The way you described your experience with this play, you certainly would be the best choice for Mrs. ..."

"You can't make me do that."

"No, but we all have to cooperate."

I thought it over. It was the cool season and I supposed I could let go of my beard for two or three weeks. So that's what we did. Peukemann made me a lovely dirty grayish wig and he said, "This is the first wig I made for a *non-Tunt*." This is the German derogatory word for describing the behavior of an effeminate gay man - so in a way, he was teasing me for not being gay.

After three hilarious performances in our own camp, we were scheduled to travel to Faid for the first outside engagement. When the trucks were ready to load up the company and the set, a number of British soldiers and officers appeared and handed Dr. Hartlieb a list of actors they wanted to interview. I didn't think anything of it. For some reason, I just didn't happen to be on that list. As their names were called they were told to go to a nearby tent. As they disappeared one by one we noticed that the people who were on the list were all the dancers, and acrobats and female impersonators. For some reason, I was not on the list, although in this play I was playing a female role. Those not called stood waiting for this nuisance to be over with for quite a while. The first one to come out of the tent was the young man who had played the young female lead in *Jugend*. He was highly agitated, red in the face and used rather graphic language to say that there would be no more girl's parts for him. The same thing happened each time some-one came out of that tent. We began to piece together the story of what was going on in the tent. There were two doctors there who gave every one of them a rectal examination. After a very short interview without giving any explanation or apology, two doctors were giving them all a rectal examination.

The mood of the whole theater group was becoming ugly. Almost all of them had in one way or another worked very hard to entertain not only their fellow prisoners but the British troops and their hospitals as well. They felt insulted. It was a tremendous affront to their human dignity. I tried to get Mr. Mason, but he wasn't available. Hartleib was ashen in the face and showed no willingness to immediately do anything about this embarrassing situation. The group sat down in the sand and had it out. Many of them wanted never to perform for these ungrateful bastards again. After twenty minutes or so, cooler heads won out. We voted not to strike and would honor our commitment to play at Faid. When it came to it, our performance certainly suffered. Nobody had their heart in it, nobody seemed motivated to do what normally was an uplifting experience - no matter how dumb the show.

Mason came to the meeting in my tent at 11:00 a.m. the following day. He was livid and it was very difficult for him because under this emotional strain his stammer became almost uncontrollable. I had to translate to the group what he had attempted to stammer out.

He was not fully informed who had ordered this tactless and cruel behavior, but this much he had found out: Some church person had been in some officers' mess when Dolly along with the acrobats and the dancers were invited for an after-performance drink, before taking off costume and makeup. That's all Mason could say at this moment, but he apologized on behalf of the decent people in the Canal District who had heard about this and were just as upset. He closed his remarks by saying that this incident would have consequences, but he realized that for the people involved it was too late.

I think it took us a whole week to get over this experience, particularly the young man who played the farmer's daughter in our play, who happened to be straight. He certainly promised that this was the last show he would do in a female role. He would never again subject himself to this kind of hazard.

Unfortunately, there were other effects too. As a result of this insult some people in the group intentionally overacted in a provocative manner to purposely shock and upset the sensibilities of any conservative element in the audience. It got so raunchy and so graphic that in the end we had a falling out among ourselves, and I for one did voice my displeasure. Thank god Mr. Mason had invited my former theater group, now in Faid, to bring the two one act plays *The Fairy Tale* and *The Murderer* to perform for our company. That sort of distracted us. We had never posted another theater group before and there were many things to be done in preparation.

Mr. Mason apologized once more before my former 305 cast. The Faid theater group arrived to do their one night stand with the Goetz plays. Mason provided a lovely dinner for the guests and for us after the

305 cast's hysterically funny performance. There our boys had a chance to talk to the ex-officers' theater group and to compare notes, as it were.

Mason came back the next morning and had breakfast with our Camp 278 guests. On his way out of the cage, he suddenly stopped and said, "How did it feel to watch your friends do such a polished job? Apart from the short synopsis you gave me I had no idea what the German dialogue was all about, but I think it was a close to professional performance. I was with Tim, who does understand German and he expressed interest in writing about this experience in 'Sphinx', the local paper for the Cairo Garrison.[8] You know I wouldn't want to lose contact with you, but wouldn't you be much happier with your original gang? I even have thought of T.S. Eliot. You could make a real contribution if you translated *Murder in the Cathedral* and produced it with these chaps. I don't see our group having the scope of education it would take to do this. I don't understand German, but there is a difference in style here."

I didn't have to think. "Look John, we talked about this before. T.S. Eliot is something else again. I'm just finishing the translation of *Journey's End* and even that is possibly too ambitious, as much as I would love to expose every German POW to the ideas expressed in that

---

8. "Throughout the centuries, art has had a continual struggle to be fully recognized and during the last ten years it has slowly come into its own. However, the struggle still continues in the Middle East where difficulties of all descriptions present themselves. The men and women in the desert outposts during the war managed to overcome their difficulties by sheer determination to carry on, and small and large productions continued to be presented to the troops. A few days ago, I went along to see the German prisoners of war present the theater to men of their own kin, and they deserve the highest credit for their performance. We went back into the Shakespearian era when the female characters were played by men and the performances given here were of a very high standard (high enough to convince the audience that the parts were being played by real women). Costumes had been made out of anything they could lay their hands on, and also the sets."

World War I drama." We shook hands and he left me thinking about the feasibility of rejoining Cage 13 theater group.

Weeks went by when I was not directly involved in a play production, but I did a lot of work with the German play *Moral*, a turn of the century satire on German bourgeois politics and went with the symphony all through the Canal Zone.

The next weeks were spent translating *Journey's End*, working on *Blithe Spirit* by Noah Coward and reading Priestley's *Duet in Floodlight*. When I wasn't translating, I was traveling with the current production, which was *Moral* and later *Ingeborg* by the German playwright Curt Goetz.

Dr. Hörner became quite despondent for personal reasons. Mason put him into the hospital for "rest and recreation." John and I took turns in visiting him until we found out that he really would rather be left alone for a while. He told us that he had been under this kind of depression two or three times before and there was nothing to worry about. He loved the attention and the good food at the hospital and would be back in ten days.

◆ ◆ ● ● ◆ ● ● ◆ ●

I don't know exactly when I was transferred to the officers' cage in Faid near the Suez Canal. I must have established deep roots in Tumilab because John Mason came by any time of day to have a request or to take me with him to whatever concert of the symphony. He still wanted me to continue reading those short blurbs from the program to the concert audience. I asked him, "Is this really necessary? They all do have a program."

"No. I still want a German to read it to the audience," he said.

In Faid things had changed tremendously. They were now, all of them, living in white tents heretofore reserved only for the British soldiers. We were now living only two per tent. The cage was wide open. A number of German soldiers had moved in with us and represented in their various talents high levels of professionalism, quite an improvement. (I found some of these theater people still acting in the theater in Germany in 1984.) We still did not have electric lighting when I came to rejoin them.

The next play after *Charlie's Aunt,* which was a smashing success, was played with a boyish exuberance that delighted the audiences. Most of them had seen the German movie version of it. Eger directed this German mystery, which somehow had been mailed to one of our members called *Park Street 13.* One of the grenadiers joined Mäurer for the two female parts. They both looked striking. They had me playing a detective again.

After this play, Bock and Elser insisted on doing a German tragedy, *Agnes Bernauer* by Hebbel. I wrote a short paper dissenting, trying to convince them that this kind of play at this point in time was not a constructive choice. It showed the cruel murder of the young daughter of the village barber-doctor who had the misfortune of getting involved with the Crown Prince of Bavaria. The marriage was declared null and void. When the prince refused to acknowledge the government's demands, the poor woman was drowned for "reasons of state" because that meant none of their children would ever be eligible to inherit the crown, and civil war would result from their marriage. On top of it, it was written with an excess of nineteenth century bombast. My last sentence was: "I don't think that the role of this young woman could possibly be played by a man."

I assured them I would cooperate in any way, even prompt, but I would not want to have a hand in the actual staging. As I predicted, there was unwanted laughter at times, but everybody was full of praise for the set design and the fabulous costumes that our newly won decorator, Hans Geyer, had created. We had one tailor and one makeup man at Tumelab, here Geyer did everything. He designed and sewed costumes, did the makeup and the hair, designed the set and arranged, together with Landgraf, the lighting. The girl was played by a soft-spoken wonderful chap who did manage occasionally to move the audience to tears.

I had a chance to see the movie *Blithe Spirit*. I told Mason about it at the time. He didn't think much of the movie and was still coming back to T.S. Eliot's *Murder in the Cathedral*, but he did produce one copy of the acting text of the Samuel French London Ltd. version of *Blithe Spirit*. I had translated it, so I knew there would be some problems. Four parts for women was one problem. Another was that I seemed to remember that German audiences don't enjoy ghosts appearing on the stage. I read the play to the group, one of my fastest and most imperfect translations, but they liked it and it turned out that Bock directed it. The big thing was that even Eger came back for one of the main parts as the ghost #1.

Right in the middle of the production, Bock was shipped home to Germany as a "hardship" case. Since Eger had a part and Bock had left, there was only Elser who had the background and confidence to direct a play. He, of course, picked another tragedy and it was Ibsen's, *Ghosts*. It was an experience unforgettable for anyone involved in it. Karl-Heinz who had been one of our most productive actors all the way through, a would-be professional actor, about seven feet tall, volunteered to play the mother, Mrs. Alving. I played her son. A Berlin businessman played the pastor. Fat little Wolff, still a professional actor in Hamburg (1995), played the carpenter, and of all people - as his crowning effort - Eger, played the maid. We were, I'm sure, the most devoted cast imaginable and we had some evenings when our audience walked out of the theater deep in thought without applauding, while we were standing behind the curtain hugging each other.

I had deep trouble explaining the synopsis of the play to John Mason, who still had tears in his eyes. He would not accept my remark that the central theme of the play, that character is inherited, of course, had become long since outdated. We were all pretty exhausted after this one, mostly performed in closed up tents in extreme temperatures.

● ◆ ● ● ◆ ● ● ◆ ●

After a short hiatus the group met to discuss what we would do next. Elser turned to me and opened a discussion of whether or not we should produce *Journey's End* by Sherriff. We had a short but frank talk about it and agreed to disagree. The gist of the problem was that they wanted to turn Captain Stanhope into a war hero and I wanted to leave the message of the play as it was written, saying that the worst thing about war is that it destroys the best people first. So, we dropped the matter.

After ten days we met again and agreed we should really make a statement of some kind about the world situation. The cold war was in full swing, the Russians were blockading Berlin and had overtaken all of Eastern Europe. There was a clandestine, but an extremely barbarous war between the British and the Jews on immigration policy. At one particular time two British sergeants were found hanging upside-down, badly mutilated. The anti-Semitism among the British soldiers was threatening some of the Jewish re-educators. So we, of all people, decided to make a statement and have some fun at the same time. I wrote a satire titled, *Napoleon Does Not Necessarily Have to Go To Nuremberg*. The second half we did a one act play by Bernard Shaw, *A Man of Destiny*, a delightful play about something that happened to Napoleon as a young general in Italy. The heart piece was fat little Wolff as Napoleon explaining to the Italian innkeeper the character, the strength and the weaknesses of the British people - with a monologue to the play by Bernard Shaw spoken by Elser, who in his makeup really looked like Bernard Shaw. The final line of the play was, "You see, the British can stand self-criticism."

For all we were able to find out, the British re-education team did not raise objections to the ideas expressed in our "political cabaret". They themselves were busy with their own problems at the time. Ever since the atrocities against those British sergeants had made headlines all over the world, they had been under a terrific pressure from openly anti-Semitic military personnel. We heard reports that the Jewish members of the Re-education Office were exposed to harassment and one of their tents was collapsed by saboteurs one night.

● ◆ ● ● ◆ ● ● ◆ ●

Apart from the constant invitations from John Mason to still participate with the symphony orchestra, I had developed very strong ties to the musical group of former Cage 13. The pitiful little pop orchestra that played Christmas 1945 had now absorbed many talented musicians from the surrounding working companies. Thus, without the official sanction from the Army Welfare Service, one or two jazz combos went out at least every weekend to play at various clubs. The dance socials at some of the sergeants' messes paid handsomely.

Since I had worked in the Hamburg radio station, I was interested in anything that had to do with amplifiers, microphones and loudspeakers, and so that expertise was what I offered them. I sometimes ended up carrying all these implements and rolls and rolls of cable, setting it up, and then played master of ceremony. I had to introduce the band and its players whenever that was called for and to announce the dances. Of course, some of them danced everything the same way whether it was a waltz, a tango, a rumba or a fox-trot.

Through this experience as announcer, I was offered the job of technician at the camp radio station, which I gladly accepted.

The camp radio was in a very airy structure made of all sand bricks, but a neat wooden structure with a corrugated roof allowing lots of ventilation. Our schedule was simple. We had to relay the BBC news in the morning and in the evening, courtesy of the British Forces Radio. Every four hours, I would give local news and instructions from the Tommies. In between I filled the air with jazz from used records, some overused by various military installations. Most of them were in an acceptable shape. I just had to react quickly when the needle refused to leave a given groove. After our "political cabaret," I moved into the radio station full time and had to train a substitute in case the symphony or one of the dance bands needed my services.

There was one serious aspect to our duties: the British Forces Radio Station Kabrit gave a signal from time to time. Receiving this, we had to plug in our lines to Kabrit where we were given detailed instructions about shark movements from the Indian Ocean into the Suez Canal at the southern end as well as Lake Timsah. British personnel and German POWs were enjoying a swim at the beach. They had to be warned without delay by us through loudspeakers, which were covering the respective beaches.

I was always interested in jazz with my limited understanding of a music that had so long been forbidden in Germany. Now, I was inundated. Not only that, almost weekly the jazz musicians had an informal meeting, sat down in the shade and had a jam session, which was something entirely new to me. It was just as good as I had seen in those American movies. They were so good in the end that they played without looking at their scores and merely improvised. Soon they had a big following, which brought Zille to the idea of collecting the cigarette donations in a badly dented old British steel helmet.

* ◆ • • ◆ • • ◆ •

Mason was now under increased stress. I didn't want to come right out and ask him, but finally he let on. "Top secret: Dr. Hörner has a contract in Ankara. Vince, do you think it is conceivable that if a given somebody smuggles him out after a concert, that you could organize some kind of cover-up so that his absence will not be noticed?" I assured him that I would do my damnedest if we could sit down, really look at the problem and play through potential dangers, which might lead to consequences for Mason, Dr. Hörner or myself. We had a number of meetings, most often sitting on the bank of a canal outside Ismailia and we agreed on a set of code words for written communications. That was, as far as we went by, the middle of 1948. After the last big concert March 24, 1948, at Port Said, the Symphony, by and by, lost a number of musicians who had been declared "cases of hardship" and who were then scheduled for repatriation. In fact the whole camp at Fayed was shrinking under our very eyes for those of us who were left and functioning.

Harald Quandt, Goebbels' step-son, at last had to go too. We had an emotional last chat and he presented me with the large cardboard game called "Monopoly," which he, Zille and I had primitively designed once we had kerosene lamps in Camp 305 and could play games at night. Since nobody remembered all the English names for places on the board, we had made up a Teutonic Monopoly and the most expensive place was *Badewiese*, the resort featuring the epitome of comfort and luxury, one that I had never heard of. This was created out of Harald's one and only indiscretion about life among the chosen few in the Third Reich. He had told us at the time that extremely good-looking daughters of the rich and famous were selling their services in a cleverly arranged resort, which had a huge heated swimming pool in the center surrounded by two stories of tastefully furnished single room apartments. It was here, according to Quandt, that the party awarded, bribed, flattered anyone who had done something useful or had the potential of being useful to the party hierarchy.

I was never quite sure that I should believe this story, I still haven't heard any confirmation here in 1995. Anyway, we played this damn monopoly with the help of some Egyptian rum until 3 or 4:00 a.m., much to the disgust of the tent mates who had not joined us. The most interesting aspect of this game came to the fore each time two or more players went into negotiating with a united front against the leading player, who had the most profitable hotels, streets and god-knows-what. The next morning we were all good friends again, I might note. I had the impression that Quandt had adored his mother and was hard hit by the loss of her and his six step-siblings. He said he had never been impressed with the minister, his step-father, and had labeled him *Minus-cavalier*.

Dolly came by once in a while. He was in good shape, had gained weight, looked much healthier than he did at 278. He too had made quite a bit of money because they could never hear enough of his songs to the accompaniment of his guitarist and without fail he touched his audiences deeply when he sang "Lili Marlene". Sometimes he himself was closed to tears, but he said he wasn't sure whether he was sorry for himself or for these poor Tommies who were sitting here in the desert sands wasting away their lives and suffering from an ever increasing anxiety that the Middle East powder keg next door in Palestine would blow up any minute and they would be right in the crossfire between Jews and Arabs.

In July, Mason and I had a taste of that when we went with the variety show to a working company across the Suez Canal and were stopped twice on the way back, first by a bunch of Jewish insurgents with masked faces who unloaded some of the ammunition we were supposed to bring back across the canal, as all British installations tried to leave Palestine. Shortly afterwards, we were stopped again and again at the point of some Tommy guns, part of the ordinance including two whole trucks were captured by some Arabs. I've never been so afraid in my life. Mason and I were sitting next to the driver and constantly had a Tommy-gun in our faces.

CHAPTER VIII

Return to Germany

(((ⓒ ⑨)))

WE HAD TO LEAVE OUR UNCOMFORTABLE WOODEN
Austrian railway compartments and move with all our luggage into
the familiar cattle boxcars. At least there was straw in them so we
could stretch out and sleep. Most of us did just that. The next morning we arrived at Münsterlager, a former training site of the German
army where a number of British lorries were waiting for us. We found
ourselves in clean but evil smelling barracks and were told that our
release would take place the following morning. I didn't think I would
enjoy wasting twenty-four hours sitting in these ghastly surroundings.
My two buddies, being from southern Germany and stranded here in
the north, resigned themselves to staying put. However they convinced
me that I should make use of the time to hitchhike to Hamburg and
back, check out the situation with my family and they would look after
my luggage in the meantime. The sleepy guard at the entrance to the

camp wasn't even interested in the details of my explanation, he just let me go. I had the feeling he was glad that he had one German prisoner less to worry about.

So, with two packages of cigarettes in the pocket of my greatcoat, I easily found transportation with a delivery truck. A stocky graying middle-aged driver motioned me to get into the cabin with him. I made sure that he had a cigarette every half-hour. When I guessed his ethnic background as Romanian, we immediately began a nice conversation and I told him of my contact with the German settlements there. He said he was worried about the political situation and contemplated claiming the status of a displaced person to try and put some distance between himself and the Russian threat. He said he sometimes woke up in the night quite sure that the Allied Air Lift to Berlin had started the outbreak of World War III. I noticed how he carefully extinguished the leftover butts and put them into a special container, explaining that everybody was rolling cigarettes from leftovers.

I have no recollection of where he dropped me, but I know I had to walk across Lombardsbrücke, and found Gundel's house damaged but occupied and, since the lift was out of action, I slowly walked up four flights of stairs. When I reached the door, my heart was racing and I was bathed in perspiration. I had not been in a building, let alone on a staircase since Christmas 1944. I felt a growing anxiety each time I discovered another crack in the plaster on the walls. I kept counting the levels as I reached them, reading the names on each door. They all appeared to be unfamiliar. I had gone up this staircase many times before during the war when the damn elevator hadn't worked and my habit was two stairs at a time instead of one. Now, I felt utterly drained and weak and wondered if this would ever end. Of course, the doorbell didn't work, I started knocking. After two attempts, I heard some movement, the sliding of house slippers approaching the door and Teddy's slightly annoyed voice, "Yah, yah, yah."

Thank god it was Teddy. Gone was her matronly shape that had provided the reason why everybody in the first place came to call her "Teddy". What I was hugging was a skinny grandmother with sunken cheeks and a pale complexion. Her tears and my perspiration mingled on my face. I had never been that close to her before and I kept apologizing for springing this surprise on her. She said she wouldn't have anything of that because the main thing was that I was there and that we all had survived. We sat down and I offered her one of my Egyptian cigarettes. She accepted the cigarette, but could not take her eyes of the box that contained them. She stared at it as though transfixed, still looking at it when she lit a match. "I haven't seen that many cigarettes for years."

I placed the box in front of her and said, "Teddy, they're all yours."

"You can't do that!" she said.

"Never mind, I have a few more in Münsterlager." I replied. "Tell me about the family. Are you still forced to quibble over milligrams?"

"We're still on rationing, if that's what you mean, and I'm at the end of my rope. When things ever return to normal I'll go into a convent."

I was so relieved to see her with the same saucy sense of humor in spite of everything. She explained that everybody had gone to barter household goods for foodstuffs. She made me a cup of chamomile tea, the only thing she had, and offered me some whole grain crackers. After another half-hour of filling me in on family matters, I jokingly reminded her to hide the cigarettes well and I would be back in a few days. She wished me well and assured me that her home, such as it was, was waiting for me.

Feeling refreshed and looking forward to seeing them all in a day or two, I started the long trek down those stairs, crossed the river and found my parents' house practically untouched, except for a few cracks in the plaster. On the street from his doorway, the greengrocer waved me into his shop and told me how he and his family had come through, and how all of a sudden, he had produce to sell and could look forward to good times. While he was talking with tears in his eyes about friends and family members he had lost, I looked around in the shop and was overwhelmed by the opulence of his offerings. He insisted on filling a brown paper bag with all kinds of October apples, grapes and then bananas that I hadn't seen in years. He told me that my family too had left shortly before noon to visit farmers and barter food. I thanked him for saving me another four flights of stairs and would he please tell them that I had to go back to get my release and my luggage.

His son came in ready to load up another assignment of vegetables, so he gladly agreed to drive me across Hamburg back to the Autobahn. He too told me that my family was okay and that people were still gratefully remembering how my father and his crew had protected the building during the big attack.

I then sat in silence for the first five kilometers or so. Going in a southerly direction we crossed again the vast area that had been flattened and cordoned off after the big attack in 1943. It was still the same. In a few places, mixed work gangs of men and women were still digging up the rubble and carefully collecting all bricks that were still usable. This will take decades, I thought to myself.

I arrived back at Münsterlager before chow time where my buddies and I shared the fresh fruit from my sack. This was a mass feeding station where thousands of people arrived from those countries belonging to the British Commonwealth. There was a perfunctory medical examination, each received 42 German marks and a document confirming the length of time spent in the British POW camps and a statement that there were no physical or other handicaps related to war injuries.

Luckily my buddies had to go to Hamburg too, so we all three took the train ending up in the main railway station where we said goodbye. The station was under reconstruction. Sheets of corrugated iron had been installed to protect the public from rain or snow. I did find a taxi since I couldn't possibly drag my blasted wooden box, as much as I hated to spend this ridiculously low severance pay in this way.

The four flights of stairs with the duffel bag and the wooden box became a major endurance test. At each landing I sat down, smoked, rested. It took quite a while before I had everything assembled in front of Teddy's door, but I wasn't in any hurry anyway.

The first impression was claustrophobic and a bit too much to handle; three noisy little boys, Tutta and Gundel both joyfully and with relief cried in my arms, Teddy crying again, surveyed the spectacle, grandfather and JR paced up and down waiting for the moment when I would have a free hand to shake. I've never been asked so many different questions by so many different people all at the same time, with three little boys probing at my wooden box, impatient to see what was in there. When the din had subsided, I brought the first of those two kilogram tins of shortening. Teddy and Tutta produced a huge frying pan, which showed signs of not having been used for years. They sliced the newly acquired potatoes, scooped big globs of fat into the pan and began to fry. They all looked at each other as if it were the first Christmas in their lives. I kept warning them to go easy on the fat, but they wouldn't listen to me. To make the story short, it was a wonderful meal, but there were some complications afterwards which I'm not going to explain.

Everything was love and honey and well-being and patience for a few days. By the fourth day when Teddy had laid down laws about rationing the fat, there were the first signs of unrest and it was only a week later that JR complained behind my back about the thoughtless way I was smoking cigarettes, killing them in the ashtray in the face of people who were painfully used to smoking and re-smoking every carefully collected cigarette butt.

From the beginning, it was clear to me that Gundel's nerves were frazzled and she was exhausted by having to live in this family inferno. She resided in the so-called study together with her very lovable little boy. It was only when she was with him that she regained that sense of humor and that confidence that first attracted me to her.

She was badly paid by Lola Roggi whose dance studio was based on the Laban School theory. It was a more choreographed group movement than the very subtle and often too intellectual approach of Mary Wigman.

We were comfortable hugging and kissing in short moments of privacy. Neither one had any energy to discuss our situation and to express any thoughts about what we had expected from one another. In that flat, no intimacy was possible. We decided to rent a room in a one-day hotel near the Dammtor Station. These establishments were one step closer to respectability compared to the hourly rented rooms available in some of the seedier hotels. Still, we had to sign the guest-book as Mr. and Mrs. and the hotelier was required to account for our comings and goings, identification, passports, etc., to be reported to the police. You could not then and you still cannot today stay in a German community without going through this kind of registration.

I made the mistake to suggest that we should see a play --*Draussen vor der Tür* "Unwanted". This play had originally been for radio, had a big success in 1947 and my former classmate Roth had the leading role. I knew it would be heavy going since it had to do with returning POWs but it was much more than that. A very young invalid POW returns from Russia and finds no open doors, very little sympathy. Paul-Edwin played this young man who had survived and then attempted suicide since he could not find the answer to the question, "What use was it to have survived when all his friends had not." He jumps into the river Elbe, our river in Hamburg, and even the river spits him out and calls him a wimp. It was certainly more than I could take at that point in time. Gundel and I had a cup of tea in the barely functioning railway waiting room which smelled of disinfectant and urine. Then we quietly went home, our tooth brush in the pocket. I remember clinging to the toothbrush, glad to have something to hang on to. There was nothing to say, so we both went to bed, each to his own.

My would-be father-in-law, last occupation architect in Bromberg, was a World War I invalid veteran who had innumerable questions to ask me because as a member of the German Expedition Force he had been captured by the Arabs under Lawrence of Arabia. He too had lived for quite some time in the very same type of tent close to the Suez Canal and was delighted when I could tell him that sometimes we found pieces of Imperial German insignias and belt buckles, which had been rusting in the desert sand only to be dug up by the next generation of German prisoners. He confirmed that the British and the Arabs had treated them with great respect and there was never any breakdown of group loyalty among the prisoners.

Days later, Gundel and I did get together. In the middle of the night, she came into the living room finding me wide awake. We talked for a while whispering and found ourselves in each other's arms and I immediately noticed again what I had already felt every time we had hugged each other; she was literally nothing but skin and bones. Everything seemed to be sagging, even the skin under the upper arm had lost its beautiful hue. It was so shocking to me, that while we were furtively and hastily making love, always conscious of the possibility of someone interrupting us, I finally just had to ask, "What in the world happened to you and all you people?" We stopped and smoked a cigarette and then it came.

She said, "Even before the end of the war we were down to 800 to 900 calories a day and it didn't get much better that whole year - until the middle of '46. I can't describe it," she said, "but I certainly began to understand the behavior of Tutta and JR. I have only one child to look after. They have two. And that's what you do before you go to bed hungry, you do what else you can do to make sure that the child does get something more to eat. And after whatever sleep you do find, you get up with a pain, which I can barely describe - just animal hunger. I haven't seen much of the statistics, but I caught one. In 1946, the average weight of a grown man was fifty-one kilograms, 102 pounds. Even JR, who received a little bit more, looked like one of those victims in the concentration camps. In our town, 100,000 people showed hunger edema."

"By the way, have you seen yourself in the mirror lately? Your biceps and your pectoral muscles, where are they? You are a perfect example of muscular atrophy." I suddenly remembered that I did have one photo from Egypt where I was startled how my torso had changed.

The next evening, I went to see Alice Pollitz for the first time since Christmas '44. We had a tearful hug and she immediately said, "I thought they treated you decently, those Englishmen. My god, are you skinny!" She had a bottle of red wine and we talked until she had to throw me out because her little apartment was now taken by a former student sent in by the housing authority and by her sister.

Alice was very happy to have been put back in charge of her old high school for girls, a job she would have to leave again in a few months to become a school inspector. She would have her own office downtown at Dammtor. Her responsibility would be the teacher training and selection, a job she was eminently qualified for. She invited me to come to her school for a performance of *As You Like It*, here all the men's roles being played by young women.

She was most interested in my stories about the theater and orchestra and wanted to see all the photos. I told her how horrified I was to find out what my future family had gone through and she was full of sympathy and invited me to come visit her. She had many good things to eat. She told of a British man of letters, a Victor Golancz, who had started a food drive for the German people under the motto, "Save Europe Now". He had successfully persuaded politicians and statesmen to raise the daily calorie rate to 1500 around the end of 1946. "You see, it had to be a Jew to grasp the initiative," she said, which gave me a lot to think about. I went home by subway.

The second weekend the city of Hamburg scheduled a charitable series of events to collect funds for returning POWs in need, mainly those who could not return because their ethnic groups and families had been displaced and were now vegetating in some unknown refugee camp, if they were indeed still alive.

During the ensuing week on three different mornings almost at the same hour three ex-prisoners came visiting. The first one was Joachim Wolff, who had done the part of Napoleon in our last production. He sat down next to my couch while I was still in bed and began to wax enthusiastically about the Hamburg Acting School where he was enrolled.

Two days later, Dolly came by. He did not ooze optimism and described his efforts to find work. If he thought that I would be with influential people, my appearance on the couch must have been a disappointment.

On Friday, again around 9:00 a.m., Zille came. He had not changed at all. He complained loudly about people who live on the fourth floor with no elevator working. He too had not found promising employment, and my pessimism about that wouldn't faze him. He told me that his tent mate was working in a reconstruction job downtown as a bricklayer apprentice and was determined to make a career in the construction trade.

I finally found Jörgensen, the faithful follower of General Wenck. He found a nice job managing some apartment houses and offered me employment as supervisor for the Central Washer and Dryer Room, provided I could keep washers and dryers running. We both had a good laugh and I thanked him.

The continuation of industrial dismantling of harbor facilities created quite a stir among the otherwise docile population of Hamburg. The workers came down to the harbor just to watch from a distance how their former work sites were destroyed and their machinery crated for delivery to Russia. Years later the modern rebuilt facilities replacing these old ones would be a great advantage in European harbor competition, but now it was a tragedy for these workers.

My youngest sister sent me the invitation and the necessary railway pass to visit their home in Starnberg, Bavaria, near Munich. It was a relief to be out of the flat in Hamburg for a few days, although the train travel gave me the view of 800 kilometers of destruction, poverty and the shock of large numbers of invalids in the train as well as in the countryside.

The reception in Starnberg was overwhelming. I was very impressed by the energy that Fred showed in spite of his severe handicaps. He had lost his left arm and his right leg and the scars of shrapnel were visible all over his body. He stepped on a mine early on in Russia, and survived miraculously after a number of progressive amputations. It was encouraging to see how he had pulled himself out of hopelessness and suffering and had become a successful businessman, albeit on the black market, under his motto, "The world stole my body and the purpose of my life, so I'm going to get some of my own back one way or another." He was quite outspoken about that.

They overwhelmed me with a hospitality that seemed like a dream after all these years of want: gobs of American bacon in huge cans, peanut butter, whatever else the Americans had plenty of in their Post Exchange (PX). There was a whole gang of young people, ex-officers and soldiers, students who were mostly female, thirteen maybe in all, and there was a party every second night in Starnberg or Tutzing. It was exhausting. We never came home before 3 or 4 a.m., mostly for a sun-up supper.

My sister, Jutta, told me she had a confession to make. She said that she had forcibly broken open my trunk, which I had left with her in Starnberg before going to Italy because she had remembered my saying there were some weapons in there. When the Americans came in 1945 for the occupation, all guns or any kind of weapon had to be surrendered by a certain day. She had found among my various uniforms an Italian nine-millimeter Barretta and suddenly remembered that the due date had passed, so for the next forty-eight hours she did a lot of walking around with my gun under her coat hoping to find a chance to throw it into the millrace. Starnberg was hopping with American soldiers so she was never quite sure whether she was being observed or not. In the meantime, a friend had thoughtlessly put a pair of borrowed, worn, army wool socks she had received from another of her American friends into my hamper. Now knowing that I would be coming, she had opened the box again and saw that all my precious uniforms had been nibbled by a family of moths who did their work in the most conspicuous places. If I had any ambition to turn this stuff into civilian garb, I should forget it.

I was hoping my sister wouldn't be disappointed at my less than enthusiastic reception of Fred's remarks showing a resentment of anything and everything that the Occupation had brought to the country. He was still sounding like an unrepentant Nazi at the time and still allowed tones of racial superiority to creep into the conversation. He had seen the movie *The Best Years of Our Lives*, envied the Americans and resented them at the same time. I knew from the beginning we would never see eye to eye.

When I got back to Hamburg, Gundel had acquired the use of a trailer, outfitted like a small RV. She said it stood on a quiet street in front of a friend's property in one of the best parts of that suburb. The trailer could not be connected to any utilities; so, it was just a glorified meeting place for Gundel and myself to enjoy a few moments of peace and quiet, but it was certainly nothing one could live in.

That first evening, we went home to Teddy's flat and we had scrambled eggs. The shortening from Egypt was still a life-saver and I had brought with me one of those large tins of American bacon, thinly sliced and packaged in a very appetizing fashion.

The next day, I had a quiet moment with Teddy when Gundel had taken her son to a children's party in the neighborhood. Teddy cautiously asked whether or not it was possible if Gundel could be with child.

For quite some time I had been under the impression that the damage done in the winter of 1941 might have affected my ability to father a child, in fact I had been counting on it. If this now became reality, I felt twice as awful and tremendously stupid for being so irresponsible. In retrospect, I couldn't believe that Gundel and I had never discussed this issue. She had not become pregnant from our being together ever, nor had anybody else since Gundel, that is, after I had assumed Gundel and I were finished.

I didn't say anything that evening in the RV. We had a long talk about her professional plans and mine. She had written to Mary Wigman in Dresden, but if she received an offer she still was very much afraid to go into the Russian Occupation Zone. And as for my chances to become an actor or do anything in show business, it looked unlikely. Our future was just a big question mark.

Teddy had a heart to heart with Gundel that next morning and she learned Gundel's pregnancy was very much a possibility. Tutta had mentioned a doctor with whom she had dealings through Hank Franke, who had a gynecologist friend in Wandsbeck.

Hank and his wife Ruth received me with open arms. Franke was glad to see me because he wanted to talk to me about my mother who he had been treating for another one of her "nervous breakdowns". He was only too glad to give me a clear picture of my mother's problems after the end of the war. He assured me that there was nothing to be concerned about as long as people would keep stress around her to a minimum.

I immediately took to Franke's wife Ruth, who was the daughter of a former railway man. She had very red hair, lots of freckles, and a great sense of humor, which she said she needed to work in the publishing house of Paul Parey.

I came right to the point, mentioning that Teddy had given me Tutta's tip that he, Franke, might recommend someone who might be willing and who is reliable enough to be trusted with interrupting a pregnancy.

Hank looked up with a quizzical look, which at the time I couldn't interpret. He fished out a notebook and gave me the name and the address in the suburb of Wandsbeck. He asked that we keep this information between ourselves.

After a few more days, we were booked for an interview with this doctor and took the hour-long tram ride to this suburb. He was very understanding and agreed to do some testing. He wanted to know what the social indications were, wasn't there any way we could have this child. He ended our interview by saying, "Well then, this gives you another two days to think about it and then I'll call you."

The discussion during the tram ride home made it clear that transportation after the abortion would be a problem. Gundel was adamant that she would be able to handle that. The operation obviously would be expensive even though the man charged only the bare minimum. I had heard stories of much more expensive operations of this kind.

Soon after he telephoned to inform us in a discrete manner that Gundel was pregnant, and that we should come the next Tuesday at 2:00 p.m.. So, we spent the next days and nights discussing this step, finding no alternatives under our circumstances.

Later, I went home by myself to my parents' flat to get the confounded amplifier, which now became our only possession of value with which we could fund this thing and I was able to get 80 German marks for it.

There was nothing new with my family. Uncle Helmers, the one who had paid for most of my uniforms in 1938, invited me to come to Berlin. He talked about old times. I knew he was back in business, but I had to turn down the invitation mentioning personal problems as an excuse. I had no intention to present my ID to Russian or German communist border guards, in light of the fact that I had been connected with Gehlen at the German headquarters for a while.

There was another letter from Frederic, the half-Jewish Corporal who had helped me retrieve my dog Ivan in Poland in 1940. He expressed the hope that I was in a position to read his letter in good health and that he did get the study place at the medical faculty at our Munich University and that he would be very willing to "put in a good word for me" should there be a need for that. At first I was upset for him to think there might be a need for that, but then I remembered hearing all these stories around me of court procedures in the cause of the so-called denazification and I put away the letter with a nice feeling.

Whenever Gundel and I were together, the impending visit to the doctor's office loomed over us like a cloud. We were extremely caring about each other, talked the problem over as if anything could be gained by still fishing for alternatives. The receptionist in Wandsbeck was especially caring yet professional and put us in a waiting room separate from the general urological practice. After a long twenty minutes or so, the doctor came in and again inquired whether we had changed our mind. After a few more exchanges he took Gundel with him, leaving me with a number of well-read magazine titles I recognized from my new job at the publishing house, which I had found through Ruth Franke.

Finally the receptionist came in and beckoned me to follow her. They had put Gundel on a daybed, of sorts and we were told to wait for further instructions, because Gundel at this moment needed to rest. So, there we were together hand in hand. She looked pale and spent.

She acknowledged that according to her impression everything had turned out all right.

It wasn't until 5:30 p.m. or so that the doctor came in and gave her some medication, checked her pulse and blood pressure again. He was very kind and apologized for the long wait. We would receive his bill in due course and he wished us well.

Gundel was able to get up with some help, and we slowly moved out on the marketplace where we waited for the next tram. The tram ride was jarring and noting that Gundel was in agony, we got a taxi for the final stretch of the journey.

The ensuing weeks were spent in quiet discussions when I came home from work, mostly in Teddy's presence. There were no complications, thank god.

In the publishing house, the lunch meetings with Ruth continued to be most enjoyable; however, they got so chummy that she began talking about her family's problems. Hank's repeated stomach operations forced him to adhere to a strict diet. While he was working very hard in the psychiatric ward of his hospital, he had very little companionship to offer when he came home at night. She even let on how desperate she was to have a baby since there was a possibility that Hank's health might deteriorate even further. I was beginning to feel uneasy for being trusted with this intimate confidence.

As luck would have it, Gundel's uncle, a retired merchant seaman who was living with his widowed sister-in-law in the country had invited Gundel to visit for a period of convalescence. He had found out about her difficulties during a surprise visit he had paid Teddy. He didn't care what the health problem was, she just needed rest and good food and he had plenty of both. Her uncle was a very robust and noisy type, but we were able to convince Gundel that it would be good for her. We put Gundel on the train and then Teddy and I agreed on the way home that I too might enjoy a break from "closely knit family" living.

So, I changed from one closely knit family to another. I arrived at supper time. My parents and Carola spent dinner time almost uninterruptedly giving all kinds of admonitions to my sister's three-year-old son, Jochen, who couldn't do anything right. It went from posture, "Sit up straight," to eating habits, "Don't take such big bites," to his curiosity. Whenever he asked a question he was reminded that children at dinner table should be seen and not heard. I just had one sandwich and then excused myself saying I wasn't feeling too hot, it was so unbearable. I stretched out on my bed, but when I heard steps in the hall. I came out to offer my help with the dishes, which of course, encouraged my sister. "Vince wants to do the dishes. Go, Jochen, and help your uncle Vince."

The work at the publishing house was boring, but was going okay since there was a lot of pre-Christmas overtime. It was getting colder. There was some icy wind blowing in Hamburg.

Teddy passed the doctor's bill on to my new address. I made sure the letter would stay out of my sister's or parents' reach and took the long tram ride to Wandsbeck to pay. While I was waiting for the receipt I heard someone from the interior of the office say something to the effect, "But she paid the other bill only recently, didn't she?" which I just registered as having heard, but unimportant. It was the same voice that handed me the receipt a few seconds later and I went home.

Two nights later, I was again with Hank and Ruth and we had a number of toddies. Ruth made a remark that was again somehow linking Gundel to that same doctor prior to our recent experience. I forgot what she said, but I do remember Hank looking with contained annoyance and abruptly changed the subject and did not fully participate in our conversations after that.

It was only after the following weekend that Ruth came back to this incident. "I was pretty mad at Hank to make such a fuss about this."

"About what?" I asked.

"Well, you know. Obviously Gundel had told you about it."

"Gundel had told me about what?"

"Well, I'm sorry. It is probably too late now, but I was sure that this would be no surprise to you."

"I don't know what the hell is going on. You mean there was another?"

"Yes. And between you and me the doctor had told Hank that this was all he would be willing to do for this young lady."

I was too upset to realize what was really at stake. For one thing the fact that doctors were sharing matters of professional confidence with their wives was astounding if not outright unethical. Now Ruth, seeing my consternation, fell all over herself apologizing. "Oh, my god. You didn't know?"

I forgot what I answered, but I do remember that we changed to some trivial topic and I pretty soon excused myself saying that I needed time to think this one over.

So, I had to sort out that one. Ruth was not lying, I said to myself, otherwise Hank would not have reacted the way he did. What puzzled me was that neither Gundel nor Teddy had given me the slightest indication that anything was out of the ordinary and that an identical crisis of this kind had happened more or less recently. I kept talking to myself. What if something goes wrong, assuming that complications are still possible this long after the procedure. I would spend the rest of my life feeling miserable for not behaving more responsibly. I could never keep from blaming myself for my part in all this if Gundel should not heal properly or be traumatized in any way.

I wouldn't want to go back to Teddy's flat until such time this could be reasonably discussed in a grown-up fashion. Before she had left, Gundel and I were circling around each other, neither of us communicating about anything because we were both postponing a discussion of what had happened and how to avoid it in the future. We had been affectionate those few days after the operation. I had felt some heavy apprehension between us, which I explained by my anxiety about our future and I assumed that she had the same kind of thoughts.

Now, it was a different story. I had been purposely left out of knowing the truth of Gundel's situation. Until I knew from her exactly what had happened and the circumstances around it, I reasoned, I had no right to allow myself to feel hurt or deceived. I had no concrete knowledge of her circumstances, but I had a sense this relationship would not last.

At the same time I was trying to adjust to my own family across the river. Everything was changed. My parents now occupied the room next to the door. Carola and Jochen had moved to the room with the rear balcony. My brother was in the small room designed to house a maid and I was given the former so-called master bedroom. The living room in the rear was still occupied by a tailor and his wife.

For those few hours, I was at home in the evening everybody tried their best to palm off the little three-year-old nephew to his new uncle. The little tike was reacting by just calling me "my uncle Vinci". Strangely enough, there were all kinds of chores to be done where he and I had to go together. I did nothing to discourage him from helping me. We even had to go shopping together and it had to be done before 6:00 p.m. before all shops closed. I gained immediate acceptance by the shopkeepers when Jochen introduced me as his "Uncle Vinci from Egypt".

I appreciated being given a chance to become a foreign correspondent, but the work at the publishing house was way out of my reach. For one, my written language skills did not measure up and, on top of that, the first three or four letters that ended up on my desk, one from Canada and the rest from the UK, were written by gun crazy reactionaries who complained that Hitler was badly misunderstood. My disgust gave me a rationale to quit this job before my inadequate English skills would become obvious to my friends. And also after the New Year's dance, Ruth wanted to be too personal for my taste. She was desperate and so was I, but not in the same direction. She was the most helpful of all my friends in making things happen, instead of just being an interested bystander, but I was fed up with the lot of them, my family and Gundel and her family, the world in general, Germany in particular, and, although I didn't admit it at the time, quite a bit with myself.

I was unemployed again, but instead of claiming unemployment compensation I left for Munich where my sister and her husband immediately threw a big party for me again. Munich was not a good choice for a returned POW out of work because the state of Bavaria was the German collecting point for all the holocaust survivors and displaced persons in general. Tens of thousands of people were still living in big camps, some of them former concentration camps where they were housed and screened by the American authorities. Anyone who wanted to live in Munich had to show that he had a job and anyone looking for a job had to show a document that he had a permit to stay, and that was only given when he had a job. A vicious circle. At least I was away from Hamburg.

Fred Lauer had news. He thought he was on to a connection where I could get some personal documents and a work permit showing me as a displaced person about to leave the continent. It would cost about 110 or 120 marks, but there would be very little problem.

With the work permit in hand it wasn't too difficult to find a job where I could make use of my language skills such as they were. The United States High Commissioner used the almost untouched buildings that used to house the Nazi Party officials.

I had a German female boss in charge of translating articles and books from English into German. The Allies had decided to forego copyright regulations since there was very little printed material in the German language. Most articles had to do with all the changes in science, medicine and technology, which had been unavailable under the Nazis.

My boss was not a pleasant person, but as long as I did my job she more or less left me alone. I drew my first paycheck as a German employee working for the Occupation Administration. My first purchase was a little jar of deodorant, a triumph of modern hygiene. I had so far been able to survive without the use of such a product, provided I could wash myself five or six times a day, which of course, was not always possible. The whole continent, as far as I recall, was a pretty smelly affair. Railway and subway compartments sometimes reeked of stale sweat and the more south or east one went, there was the added and very pungent presence of garlic. I translated an article on scoliosis, which found my boss's approval. Months later I was pleased to see that my treatise on functional colors in hospitals had found some printer.

The American bosses came in two shapes - mostly slender clean looking civilians, many were former soldiers, or the GIs whose noisy boisterous presence around the buildings was interesting to watch, particularly when they were practicing baseball.

By chance I ran into a certain Mr. Pickeral who worked for the United States Food and Forestry Office of the Land Commissioner. He told me I was just what he was looking for to do a special project in the agricultural advising system. The next day I found myself facing Mr. Dankworth and was hired on the spot to help as an interpreter and as an assistant in the building of five exhibition trailers to be ready by September. They were to be displayed with the other exhibits at the Octoberfest and after that I was to take those five trailers all around the state of Bavaria from one county fair to the next. The itinerary, we would discuss later. Would I be able to run American movies and give a simultaneous commentary in German?

I was so happy I could have hugged the old man. He noticed my interest and said, "Take it easy. First we have to build the damn things and you will be traveling with Mr. Pickeral and put some fire under the

German contractor somewhere near Passau." I couldn't believe it. The next morning at 7:00 a.m. I reported to Mr. Pickeral.

I had to sit up next to the driver to interpret instructions if needed and Pickeral sat in the back enjoying the ride in the early fall and never stopped marveling at the way all these German drivers were communicating their irritation with each other. The so-called insulting "finger" had not been developed yet, but they used other gesticulations - the fist, or thumb down - along with verbal abuse. The traffic in Munich was uncontrollable.

The negotiations with the small factory became a real headache at times. I was able to find a technical dictionary and by hook or by crook five trailers moved out at the agreed upon date and were placed on the *Octoberfest Wiesn* (Octoberfest fairground). Right next to the trailers was a comfortable tent housing about 200 seats where all through the day the American movies were shown. I had a German projectionist who doubled as the electrician and mechanic for the train of trailers.

The audiences showed great interest in our movies as, for instance, "The praise of the success of the Tennessee Valley Authority's project," where they damned the river and rearranged the agriculture of the area. There were many types of short subjects and documentaries.

When I came home at 10 or 11 p.m., I was day-dreaming that this could be a position worth expanding and I felt pleased and, for the first time I must say I enjoyed life in post-war Germany.

The Octoberfest ended as a huge financial success, or so we were told by the newspapers, and now we had daily meetings at the office of the U.S. Commissioner how to get this train of five trailers with exhibits on its way through the various counties in the state of Bavaria. There was a solemn dedication of the vehicles, which were given to the state of Bavaria as a gift from the American taxpayers. We then were introduced to our new boss who worked as assistant secretary in the Ministry of Agriculture in Munich. The electrician and I had our first business session with him. He made no bones about the fact that it was all very nice for the Americans to be able to feel good about having given a helpful hand, but it was felt to be very arrogant for these foreigners to attempt to tell the Bavarians how to run their agriculture. "But," he said, "We'll have to grin and bear it and send you on your way six days from now to the County Fair at Neu-Ulm."

The appointed day arrived. We were duly entrained to begin the first leg of our journey. I had given up a room, which I had temporarily rented close to the Octoberfest and had said goodbye to my sister in Munich. The pay was good and since it included a daily expense account, I thought I was doing pretty well until we arrived in Neu-Ulm. It took a lot of effort to find the local representative of the Agricultural Advisory System there. Once we did find him, he barely took the time to show us where to place our trailers, namely in the worst spot in the county acreage, and then he excused himself leaving us to our own resources.

Robert, the electrician, and I worked all night to establish the necessary power lines. At noon, the next day during the solemn opening of the fair, we were still short of the German experts to explain the various features of our exhibits. Robert and I had to do the commenting ourselves to the peasants and their families. They came with curiosity mostly after a good lunch with gallons of beer.

Robert was from a family of cattle farmers so he took over the trailer that showed an efficient way of switching the herd from one part of the acreage to another. I had translated a movie on raising chickens in the Tennessee Valley, which qualified me to talk about the poultry exhibit, and I had taken great care in learning about *flurbereinigung* which, of course, was at the time a revolutionary concept. It called for dissolving all property ownership of a given community and redistributing it in such a fashion that:

a. Everyone in the communal acreage would get a fair share of the different soils and,

b. There would be a change from the inefficiency of the odd inherited portioning that made the use of modern machinery impossible. In the process of reapportioning the land obviously, any kind of water from the river down to a small brook would have to be redirected, which is the reason why I still feel guilty about having contributed to the propaganda for this.

Since dairy and cattle interest was high, Robert had both hands full with his exhibit. I had to switch to include the two kitchen exhibits. Of course, I knew all about the designing of functional and step-saving modern kitchens since I had translated the movie of *Step-Saving Kitchens*. It was one of my biggest successes.

Our second display location was in Swabia where we had the same experience. Nobody from the state system took any notice of the display. I phoned my boss in Munich and he asked me to go on to Marktheidenfeld where we would have two or three days before the county fair would open, and then take the train to Munich and report in person about what was going on.

A young woman named Wanda received us and offered help in whatever way we might need. She found a good place for us to store the trailers until I came back so I now was able to go to Munich to unburden myself.

From the information the American bosses had received so far they thought it would be a good idea to have a free-for-all confrontation with the Bavarian representatives. They pointed out to me that back home in Iowa under similar circumstances I would have to testify under oath, but they didn't want to carry it that far this time. During the confrontation, the Bavarian boss did not deny anything so there wasn't any argument. Everybody promised to be considerate and cooperative from now on; however, I left the meeting feeling that I would soon come back for the same reason.

I had learned only a few things about Wanda. She had been fortunate enough to have finished a degree in home economics and agriculture before the war so she now had a way to earn a living for herself, her daughter and her mother. She too was not sure that she could agree hundred percent with the five different projects we had to offer, but she thought that the commentaries that Robert and I were giving to the peasants under the circumstances were quite apropos. Wanda instructed Robert and myself as much as possible in the intricacies and in the pitfalls connected to our displays.

After one week in Marktheidenfeld, we went to Würzburg where I met the Representative of the U.S. Commissioner to tell him that at Marktheidenfeld we had received full cooperation from the local advisor, which pleased him no end.

The next stop was Aschaffenburg, quite a different story. Not only was there no field representative from the Bavarian government, there even was some hostility in the neighborhood because we had hired some personnel to clean the displays. They were all unemployed refugees and Protestants, at that. It was pointed out to us we should have observed some kind of quota. I phoned Wanda in Marktheidenfeld. She had a good laugh and said that she was surprised that this hadn't happened all the way through. The local people resented the refugees, no matter what religious affiliation they might have.

We did our job as well as we could. This was the northernmost point of our itinerary and was the last assignment. We loaded our trailers on open railway cars and returned to Munich. I received some flowery speeches about my achievement and a final lump sum of money and a letter of recommendation beginning with the phrase, "To whom it may concern."

◆ ◆ ◆ ◆ ◆

The long period after this successful job experience was marked by a string of disappointing dead-end jobs, new beginnings leading nowhere and illnesses with no solid future in sight. I moved four or five times, worked under the table, sold newspaper subscriptions, sold electronics, worked as a courier and as a stockroom manager in a textile factory, had two stints in the black market referred from Fred Lauer, and suffered two bouts of pneumonia.

On a trip to the unemployment office in late December 1951, I saw a notice on the wall. "The Australian Railway is looking for unskilled labor. Details at Desk # 5." There was just one flyer and I took it home with me. It appeared that the South Australian Railway was modernizing and expanding its facilities and service and wanted 30,000 unskilled European workers.

I phoned the Australian representative and he mailed me the information:

"A representative of the South Australian Railway is in Germany at this time in order to find young Germans aged between twenty-one-years and thirty-five-years who are willing to accept jobs for not less than two years. The contract envisages maintenance and repair work. The workers will be members of the AUW (The Australian Workers Union). Applicants who are accepted will pay for their trip themselves. The fare will be 150 £. The Commissioner of SAR will advance this money, which then must be repaid in installments of not less than 3 £ per payday every fortnight. Enclosed wage and benefit schedule show that the SAR offers an attractive and worthwhile contract.

Unskilled laborers are needed for widening the present line gauges from three-foot-six-inches to five-foot-three-inches, and for the building of new lines and for maintenance work on the present railway system. The basic wage at this time is 10 £ 13 shillings. In addition, there will be an extra 2 £ 6 shillings for workers who live in the railway hostels. In these hostels, the workers vote themselves a committee and the price of room and board will depend on the choices this committee agree upon."

At this point I stopped reading. I could just see myself in one of those hostels watching a committee consisting of workers of all nationalities trying to agree on an acceptable fare. I supposed the first warning shot was the fact that at this point the SAR had practically toy trains because a gauge of three-foot-six-inches is pretty small. I had always complained about the narrow gauge of German railways and was impressed with the broad gauge of the Russian lines. Still, I was intrigued with the whole tenor of this. All I would have to bring was two sets of bed linen and one blanket. Everything else I would find in my room. If I didn't have whatever I needed, I could buy it over there at discount prices.

There followed a list of illnesses that would disqualify an applicant, none of them applied in my case. After twelve months of work, I get two weeks paid vacation which together with the legal holidays came up to three weeks of paid furlough. I had five days of sickness full pay per year and after ten years, I'd get three months' vacation fully paid; after twenty years, six months; and after thirty years, nine months of a fully paid vacation. I have free rail travel within South Australia during any vacations. If I want to leave the state, I'd get rail tickets with a healthy discount and if I had to use the railway to get to my place of work, they would charge only half price. Most of these workers will work in the open country, only a few close to a big city. After one year, I could begin paying into a pension fund. If I had to dissolve the contract prematurely

I would have to repay the outstanding ship's fare in a lump sum. And the Commissioner hopes I find the above conditions acceptable.

I resolved not to tell anybody about this for the time except Alice Pollitz, perhaps. When I did show it to her she asked, "What would you like to do in Australia?"

I couldn't answer her with any kind of certainty because I didn't know what it would be like, but having been handled by the New Zealanders after the war and having read stories about the Australian Army, I felt the whole idea appealing. I would be getting a chance to explore a possible life away from Germany and I would be on my own without my personal history hanging around my neck. And this Pollitz could see immediately, herself having had contact with the various forms of Anglo Saxon culture. It seemed to me as far as I could judge, the Australians and New Zealanders had kept many of their British traditions and the way of life in the UK without the servility that unfortunately comes with Britain's class distinctions. But, and this Alice Pollitz applauded immediately, I surely would find time to come to grips with the loathsome conditions in post-war Germany and to study in detail what the last twenty years had produced by way of catastrophic developments. Difficulties still showed evidence of continuing in a looming Cold War combined with the unbridled greed that still reigned in central Europe.

Of one thing Alice Pollitz was sure: it was either learn a trade or skill from scratch or continue to swallow the humiliations and the hopeless conditions under which I had been operating. There was another alternative: The only thing I was trained to do was to be once again in the military, but on that I had definitely made up my mind in the negative and she didn't bring it up.

So I kept going through the various steps to prepare for Australia. I had to appear at the Public Health Office to get a clean bill of health by the resident doctor of the clinic. The other applicants with whom I had been standing in line were a pretty tough company. According to their boasting most of them were sons of Social Democrats or Communists whose fathers had insisted that they leave the country before the army could draft them in any rearmament against Russia. Even for this health check-up they had prepared themselves. Most of them were holding one of those huge German beer bottles in their hands and taking occasional sips. They were already rehearsing slogans for the train transportation towards the harbor for embarkment either Cuxhaven or Bremen and softly chanting, "Adenhauer. Adenhauer."

I was attempting to ignore my surroundings when the line rounded a corner and I recognized the doctor. Koehler, the fastest sprinter at my class, Johanneum 1934, was standing there with a white doctor's coat and the stethoscope around his neck. My first impulse was to turn and run. If I wanted to keep my Australian intentions a secret, I certainly could do without a class reunion and I wasn't too happy about the company I would be appearing with.

I tried to override my embarrassment by saying, "Hello, Booby," when my turn came.

He took half a step back and said, "Booby?"

"Yes, that's what we called you, our fastest sprinter."

His chin dropped and he said incredulously, "Panny? What the hell are you doing here? You're going to Australia?"

"Looks like it, doesn't it?"

"What will you be doing there?"

"Well, after a certain number of years and I have passed all the necessary exams, I will be the porter in the Overland Train from Sidney to West Australia."

He chuckled. "Is that so desirable?"

"No," I said. "I probably will take early retirement and write a little book about my adventures at the Johaneum."

While he was listening to my heartbeats and checked on my various other functions we kept a delightful banter and when it was over, we shook hands and he said, "I still don't believe it. I think this is one of your tricks."

When I got home, I found Fred Lauer sitting on the couch, looking pale and despondent. He reluctantly allowed me to wring out of him some information, essentially Jutta wanted out of their marriage. That was a tremendous shock because ever since I had come back it had been a foregone conclusion to assume that Jutta had made it her life's work to look after this hyperactive invalid. I couldn't believe what I was hearing.

Fred indicated that he would be in Hamburg for only three days on business, so he wouldn't be much bother. But I immediately realized that no matter what, I was going to have to do for my brother-in-law, anything and everything Jutta normally considered to be her business, from preparation of sandwiches to cooking a meal to help him dress and undress when needed. So for three days I had to listen to his side of the story trying to persuade me to do all in my power to bring Jutta around to reason.

I told him I was taking his side of the story, such as it was, and that I would find it unthinkable if they couldn't come to some kind of solution of this problem after all these years.

At times he became very agitated, even opening the door and looking down the four flights of stairs, threatening suicide. I think he considered this a wasted trip because his business project had not worked out either. All the while I took him seriously as someone in deep distress losing the person he was depending upon. But the repeated mentioning of suicide and his theatrical rushing to the stairwell began to seem manipulative.

I took him back to the railway station. We shook hands as good friends, but Fred's mind was elsewhere and so was mine. I was by now convinced that there was little difference between his personal problems with Jutta and whatever business frustration there was that brought him to Hamburg.

I was pleased to be able to announce to him that I had been accepted as an unskilled laborer by the SAR and that I did not see any prospects for my future here and that the only career for which I had any training was not in very much demand lately. However, I heard, like everybody else in Germany, that the army would start looking for soldiers again very soon and I wanted nothing to do with it.

My opinion at the end of the war in 1945 was that thinking and sensitive people believed that no German ever should wear a uniform again. I knew this idea was falling by the wayside as a result of the Cold War between the United States and Russia, which had been predictable and was now unavoidable.

My family was shocked. Sometimes I suspected them of not taking me seriously, my plan was so outlandish.

Pollitz nodded, "Start from scratch, huh? And then you will go into the bush and you will write a book."

"If that is where one goes to write a book, yes, that's what is going to happen."

She was not glad to be rid of me, she said, but felt that breaking the endless chain of convenient friendships, family, job, left hand of the boss, no future, was a good thing. And, she said, "At least I will not have to see you again wearing a uniform."

The last weeks Alice Pollitz was the only person I spent any time with. She said that I must be feeling strangely high for no reason whatsoever, but she had the same kind of feeling of excitement when after World War I she was the first German High School teacher to be sent to the United States in an exchange deal and had spent a most rewarding year at Whatcom County High School in Bellingham, Washington.

⚬ ◆ ⚬ ⚬ ◆ ⚬ ⚬ ◆ ⚬

Emigration Center - Lesum, Bremerhafen Boarding the ship 'Anna Salen'

Monday, February 18, 1952. Since 4:30 a.m. the "ship's company" was moving single file, luggage and all through the seemingly endless subterranean corridors of the emigration center. They shuffled from the customs officer to the purser, from there to a medical checkup performed by a Swedish Red Cross nurse with a spectacular purple hairdo. She must have just come right out from under the hands of a master coiffeur, or so it looked and smelled, yet she was very polite and extremely caring. To me the two or three minutes with her seemed like saying goodbye to civilization, metaphorically speaking.

Twenty yards further on I had to put down my suitcases again to declare under oath to some veterinarian with a thick Australian accent that I had not worked on a farm lately and had not touched any kind of manure. At the next stop there were two gentlemen from the South Australian Railway. I had to sign all kinds of papers and was informed that I now owed the company the equivalency of 1,500 German marks. I could not help thinking about all those millions of emigrants from Europe who must have gone through this kind of procedure before me. Suddenly, they became indentured slaves, as it were, in a faraway country without the slightest idea what they were getting into.

Being pushed through this subterranean rat race was one thing, but the sudden insight as to how deep one was in the red made this an even more claustrophobic experience. Nevertheless, there was no time for self-pity and I was too tired to continue this train of thought. With one suitcase in the backpack, the other one in my left hand and a stack of documents in my free hand, I shuffled around a bend into a sudden opening of the tunnel. There at last was daylight and fresh air. There were soft wet snowflakes and the sounds of a busy harbor. Well, it was

Bremerhafen - it was not too busy a harbor. Somebody hung a boarding pass on a cord around my neck. I felt like a school boy being packed off to summer camp. Out of breath, after a steep climb up the ladder, I took my first good look at the boat, "Anna Salen."

I was grabbed by a steward of sorts who took the boarding pass in his rather greasy hands and began studying it. The man looked and smelled awful, somebody one normally would not like to talk to, except maybe to say, "Must we be this close?" "Cabin D-2," I mumbled to get free from the steward who sulkily nodded and led me two ladders down a narrow passage. The man stopped at a rather vile smelling spot swearing to himself that it was the wrong way. He left me standing in the way of other stewards of the same indefinable South-Sea origin, guiding other victims presumably the wrong way too. Having waited for some time, I decided to get out of the way and attempt to trace my way back up to fresh air by myself. Of course, I lost my way and it took me about half-an-hour to get back on deck.

On deck I found more hapless victims of more confused and rude stewards yelling at each other. So, I decided to study the ship's layout on the bulletin board and find D-2 by myself. It took more than another half-hour, but my luggage got another good look at "Anna Salen's" interior. Ladders on tramp steamers like "Anna Salen" are not designed for passengers with more than one piece of luggage, I found out. The obstacle course left me short of breath and soaked with perspiration.

You could say what you liked about this ship, I was pleasantly disappointed to find it was beds not hammocks which I found in D-2. I was expecting the very worst since I had not discovered too many portholes on the picture postcard of the ship. I was sure this would be another tween-deck mass transportation with hundreds of hammocks hanging from the ceiling. Daily stew would be served in tin bowls and all food would smell and taste the same. No, there was a cabin on D-2, with thirty-five double tiered cots in long rows!

I was lucky to get an upper bunk, lucky, that is, as long as I didn't try to sit up straight. It wasn't the ceiling I banged my head against as I was trying to lie down to get a rest. It was pipes - drain pipes, insulated steam pipes and whatever kind of conduit one might imagine. A solid noisy row of pipes in various colors arranged parallel from bowsprit to poop deck. They were hanging a few feet above my nose whenever I was in the horizontal position.

It was time for meditation. How did I get into this mess? 1,500 German marks! Seventy warm bodies in the cabin! No matter. Surely it would be hell for weeks and weeks, but then at least there were beds and not hammocks. The noise of the ventilation drowned out all conversation around me and I fell asleep.

At sea, February 21, 1952:

Recovering consciousness in the morning, always was a period of mixed impressions. A good morning began mostly with the positive feeling - that I was at sea - several days and nights distancing myself from Germany, a country about to be re-militarized. What a relief to be able to face a new life in an entirely different culture. I was thinking about all this, while I was stretching in my bunk. We would be arriving somewhere in Australia on a nice warm dry day in autumn. I mused about this while listening to the gurgling pipes above my face. After four years in Egypt, the Hamburg winters were not exactly easy to take. Twice, I had had pneumonia. I was looking forward to the hot dry Australian bush. Of course, there would be adjustments. There would be all kinds of cultural differences, some of them would be difficult to adjust to. However, a load was lifted off my shoulders. There would be no more militaristic adventures. And if this odyssey turned sour, there was, at least for the moment, nothing I could possibly do about it. If only I could roll out of this bunk on this relatively cheerful note, it was going to be a good morning. A good morning indeed, no matter how bad "Anna Salen" rolled, creaked or smelled.

On the other hand, if I stayed in my semi-conscious stupor, half awake, roll over on the left side and possibly went back to sleep, that would be a sure way to ruin the morning. That's what happened yesterday. It never failed to happen back home in Hamburg whenever I didn't get right out of bed. I would hear noises joining themselves to nightmarish dreams recurring over and over. Yesterday, there was an earthquake I had experienced in Ferrara. I was in a cheap hotel. The wall opposite crumbled. Bits of plaster fell on the shabby threadbare bedside rug making a lot of noise and a cloud of dust. Then I was back in some battle in Russia, if the rounds of the Red artillery were not exploding around us, they came howling at us and disappeared with a thud in the frozen ground as if swallowed by the snow. Then there was a court martial. Somebody tried to establish some guilt or some innocence. I had no idea what it was all about, but felt distinctly guilty. Or I heard the tram coming around the corner in Cairo. Every time it negotiated this curve its wheels were squealing and it jumped the track. This time there was broken glass and women and children were screaming and everybody was abandoning the hapless conductor. Trying to get away from the tram, at this point, I banged my head and mercifully woke up. The images wouldn't leave me and I had a hell of a headache. That was twenty-four hours ago. Now, most of the cabin mates were long gone. The ship rolled and lurched. The coats and shirts on makeshift hangers were attached to almost every bed or to some pipe with bits of string. Those suspended freely from the pipes rigidly defied the ship's movements. Watching them made me feel sick. I held the new bump on my forehead and decided it really would not be a good morning.

EPILOGUE

VINCE SPENT 3 YEARS IN AUSTRALIA, INITIALLY WORKING for the railroad, and then as a farm hand and a primary school teacher. He continued to pursue amateur theater there. In 1955 he moved to the United States at the suggestion of his brother Rolf and Rolf's wife Carol. He studied at the University of Oregon in Eugene on a foreign student scholarship, where he received his Bachelors and Masters Degrees in Foreign Language. He accepted an Associate Professor position at Reed College in Portland Oregon. While at Reed, he also coached the soccer team and worked as director of the language lab. He married and had two daughters, Alice and Erin. His marriage, and a subsequent one were not long lived. During a sabbatical in 1977 Vince traveled back to Germany and began to do research with the goal of writing his memoir. In 1984 he retired from Reed College, and moved to Germany for several years to continue the research. Vince was active in amateur theater in various groups in Eugene, Portland and in Germany up until 1987 when he was a member of the Hamburg Players.